Dreamweaver MX:
Design and Technique

Dreamweaver® MX: Design and Technique™

ETHAN WATRALL

SAN FRANCISCO | LONDON

SYBEX®

Associate Publisher: DAN BRODNITZ
Acquisitions and Developmental Editor: MARIANN BARSOLO
Editor: SALLY ENGELFRIED
Production Editor: ELIZABETH CAMPBELL
Technical Editor: MARTIN REID
Production Manager: AMY CHANGAR
Cover, Interior, and Technical Illustration Designer: CARYL GORSKA
Icon Illustrator: TINA HEALEY ILLUSTRATIONS
Compositors: MAUREEN FORYS, KATE KAMINSKI, HAPPENSTANCE TYPE-O-RAMA
Proofreaders: EMILY HSUAN, DAVE NASH, NANCY RIDDIOUGH
Indexer: TED LAUX
CD Coordinator: DAN MUMMERT
CD Technician: KEVIN LY
Cover Designer: JOHN NEDWIDEK, EMDESIGN

LIBRARY OF CONGRESS CARD NUMBER: 2002101987

ISBN: 0-7821-4100-5

MANUFACTURED IN THE UNITED STATES OF AMERICA

10 9 8 7 6 5 4 3 2 1

About the Author

Born in Regina, Saskatchewan, Canada, Ethan Watrall completed his bachelor's degree with distinction at the University of Regina with a double major in anthropology and history. While an undergraduate, he was involved in many archaeological excavations in his native Saskatchewan, as well as Manitoba and Indiana.

After graduation, Ethan was accepted into the Ph.D. program in anthropology at the prestigious Indiana University. There, he has directed his academic energies toward two main subjects. The first, which represents a culmination of years of archaeological experience, is household craft production in Predynastic Egypt. He has worked at both Nabta Playa (an extremely large Neolithic habitation site in the Egyptian Western Desert) and Hierakonpolis (arguably the most important extant Predynastic site in all of Egypt), where he has excavated such cool things as prehistoric wells, clay mines, households, animal enclosures, pottery kilns, and cemeteries. His current research at the HK11 locality, a Late Predynastic village at Hierakonpolis, has consistently yielded information that challenges and greatly expands the current understanding of Predynastic Egyptian households.

The second subject on which Ethan has focused is the place of interactive media in archaeology. Whether from the standpoint of an educational tool, a method for scholarly publication, or simply an issue deserving academic discussion, Ethan has dedicated himself to expanding the dialogue surrounding interactive media and archaeology. Of particular interest to him is the role interactive entertainment plays in the public perception of archaeology—a topic on which he has published and delivered papers targeted toward both professional archaeologists and professional game designers. Not content to simply comment on the situation, Ethan preaches active involvement on the part of academics in the interactive entertainment industry.

Beyond academia, Ethan is also an active practitioner of interactive media. He is a faculty member at both Ivy Tech State University, Columbus (Indiana) and Ivy Tech State College, Bloomington (Indiana), where he teaches classes in interactive design and multimedia. As a Macromedia trainer for the Columbus Center for Visual Communication, Ethan has taught workshops on Dreamweaver, Flash, and Fireworks throughout the state of Indiana. Ethan's first book, titled *Dreamweaver 4/Fireworks 4 Visual JumpStart,* was published by Sybex, Inc. in February 2001 and has since been translated into Chinese and Greek. His second book, *Flash MX Savvy* (co-authored with Norbert Herber) was published by Sybex in the Spring of 2002.

Ethan's digital alter ego can be found hanging out at www.captainprimate.com.

Acknowledgments

Any book (large or small) is the product not only of the author, but also a host of other people working behind the scenes whose presence (either directly or indirectly) helps bring the project to fruition. This book is hardly any different.

At Sybex, many thanks to Elizabeth Campbell and Sally Engelfried for keeping things together and keeping me on track. Kudos to my technical editor Martin Reid for all his help and great suggestions. As always, I must express my profound thanks and gratitude to Mari-ann Barsolo, my acquisitions and development editor, who was phenomenally helpful throughout this project—as she has always been.

Many thanks to my agent David Fugate of Waterside Productions, Inc. I am forever in his debt for all the work, help, and wonderful advice he gave during this project. I certainly hope I'll have his wise counsel for years to come.

I must offer my gratitude to all the people who kindly let me use screenshots from their own digital creations for the "Inspiration: Design and Technique" sections and the color insert.

I need to thank my friend Norb Herber for all of his support and suggestions throughout the project. Thanks to my dad, who, besides lots of encouragement and thoughtful advice, never once asked what an archaeologist was doing writing a book about web design. Thanks also to my mom for her support during the project. My love and thanks to Taylor, who didn't complain too much when I kicked her off the computer because I needed to write. All of my love to Jenn, without whose unwavering support I wouldn't be able to manage sitting in front of a computer, day after day, pounding away at the keyboard.

Finally, my sincere apologies to anyone whom I managed to forget. Thanks, everybody!

ABOUT SYBEX

Sybex as been part of the personal computer revolution from the very beginning. We were founded in 1976 by Dr. Rodnay Zaks, an early innovator of the microprocessor era and the company's president to this day. Dr. Zaks was involved in the ARPAnet and developed the first published industrial application of a microcomputer system: an urban traffic control system.

While lecturing on a variety of technical topics in the mid-1970s, Dr. Zaks realized there wasn't much available in the way of accessible documentation for engineers, programmers, and businesses. Starting with books based on his own lectures, he launched Sybex simultaneously in his adopted home of Berkeley, California, and in his original home of Paris, France.

Over the years, Sybex has been an innovator in many fields of computer publishing, documenting the first word processors in the early 1980s and the rise of the Internet in the early 1990s. In the late 1980s, Sybex began publishing our first desktop publishing and graphics books. As early adopters ourselves, we began desktop publishing our books in-house at the same time.

Now, in our third decade, we publish dozens of books each year on topics related to graphics, web design, digital photography, and digital video. We also continue to explore new technologies and over the last few years have been among the first to publish on topics like Maya and Photoshop Elements.

With each book, our goal remains the same: to provide clear, readable, skill-building information, written by the best authors in the field—experts who know their topics as well as they know their audience.

CONTENTS AT A GLANCE

Contents

Spring Summer Autumn

Introduction

Back in 1989, Tim Berners-Lee of the European Particle Physics Laboratory (CERN) wrote an innocent little document titled *Information Management: A Proposal* that, among other things, outlined the development of Hypertext Markup Language (HTML). Little did he realize that the modest 18-page document would forever change the way in which we access, acquire, and share information.

HTML caught on like wildfire. By July 1993, there were hundreds of computers worldwide that could deliver HTML documents. The world had just gotten a whole lot bigger.

Fast-forward to 1997, when, much to the joy of the web-design community (and the average web user, for that matter), Macromedia Dreamweaver 1.0 was released. No more writing HTML by hand, no more puzzling over cryptic lines of code, and certainly no more head scratching for those who weren't trained programmers. Macromedia had unveiled the future, and the future looked good.

While Dreamweaver certainly wasn't the first WYSIWYG (What You See Is What You Get) web-design tool, it was arguably one of the best and brightest. Including such revolutionary features as an intuitive and flexible visual authoring environment, Roundtrip HTML, and support for Dynamic HTML, Dreamweaver was easily one of the most powerful web tools to come down the pipe.

Several years and several versions later, Dreamweaver is arguably the most popular visual web-authoring tool available. With over 700,000 users and a market share of more than 75 percent, Dreamweaver has made high-level web authoring accessible to both professional and amateur designers. In the summer of 2002, Macromedia announced the release of Dreamweaver MX, a phenomenal upgrade that not only pushes the boundaries of visual web design, but also helped to introduce Macromedia's new "MX" paradigm.

About This Book

The sheer popularity of the web has created a large group of people clambering to get their digital creations out there. It's only natural that many of these people would turn to Dreamweaver as their visual web design application of choice. It's at this point that this book comes in.

I've found that the vast majority of computer books are one of two types. They are either the bare-bones introduction to an application intended for those who have little or no experience, or they are the huge-tome-with-which-you-can-kill-a-rat variety of book that often leaves many readers scratching their head in confusion as to where exactly to start. I've written this book to fit somewhere in between these two extremes. While it is designed to provide a very fundamental introduction to creating websites with Dreamweaver MX, it also covers more intermediate topics. I've gone to great lengths to partition the content into manageable chunks whose chapter-by-chapter organization supports a smooth, progressive learning curve. As a result, one of the primary strengths of the volume rests on its step-by-step approach to the material, as well as the highly visual manner in which the information is presented.

Beyond the overriding technical, "how-to" purpose of the book, I've also attempted to weave in a strong web design theme—a topic that I firmly believe is neglected in many tool-based web design books. Not only will you find an entire chapter (Chapter 1) dedicated to an introduction to the art and science of web design, but you'll also find many design-oriented tidbits, called Design Reminders, scattered throughout the book. These Design Reminders are not only designed to refer back to many topics raised in Chapter 1, but also to call attention to many of the unspoken laws of web design that are usually gained through applied design experience.

As an instructor of new media, interactive design, and digital storytelling, I am proudest of the fact that this book is written for *students*. I'm not just taking about people involved in classroom-based studies, but anyone who finds instructor-led education fruitful. This doesn't mean that *Dreamweaver MX: Design and Technique* is only geared toward one learning style—quite the contrary! The point is that when I was writing this book I not only thought about the content itself, but also who the audience was and the way they'd approach and absorb the content.

Mac or PC: The Eternal Dilemma

A couple years back, when I wrote my very first computer book *Dreamweaver 4/Fireworks 4 Visual Jumpstart* (which is kind of the intellectual precursor to this book), I didn't give a whole heck of a lot of thought to the platform (Mac or PC) upon which the reader was working. One of the great joys of most Macromedia products (and Dreamweaver is hardly any different) is that they function almost identically from platform to platform. There are some superficial visual differences (which are a result of the different operating systems and not the programs themselves) and different hotkeys, but, generally speaking, you find very little difference whether you are using Dreamweaver on a Mac or a PC. On top of this, I teach on both Macs and PCs, and am a PC user at home and therefore don't have the same rabid Mac versus PC sentiments (it is *just* a tool you know) that many have. The bottom line is that, I didn't really tailor the book's content for one operating system or the other. While I did get some comments from readers complaining that the book was for PC users (primarily because I took all of the book's screenshots from a copy of Dreamweaver running on a PC), this strategy served me fairly well.

However, for a number of different reasons I had to put a little more thought into the eternal PC/ Mac dilemma when I wrote this book. To begin with, Dreamweaver MX features a cool new MDI (Multiple Document Interface) workspace. Not only does it feature the same streamlined integrated panel-based interface that is the hallmark of all Macromedia's next generation MX applications, but it also features a tabbed Document Window that allows you to easily switch back and forth between multiple documents during the design and development process. The kicker (and it's a big one) is that the new Dreamweaver MX workspace is only available on the Windows version of the program. This will come as a pretty heavy blow to those working on a Mac, who will have to make due with a Dreamweaver 4 version interface.

So, the big question, at least in terms of this book, became which workspace would be featured. Well—I cringe a little having to tell you this—I made the decision to focus primarily on the new Dreamweaver MX workspace. I must offer my most profound apologies to Mac users. My decision was motivated by the desire to look forward instead of back. (Besides, the book would be twice as long if I were to tailor each section so that it covered both workspaces.)

The second reason I had to put a little more thought into the Mac/PC dilemma while writing this book had to do with Dreamweaver MX's new dynamic database-driven application development tools. Generally speaking, for a whole bunch of reasons that are too lengthy to get into at this stage of the game, dynamic database-driven application development has traditionally taken place on PCs instead of Macs. This doesn't mean that Mac users can't create cool dynamic web applications with Dreamweaver MX—quite the contrary. However, PC users wanting to take advantage of Dreamweaver MX's cool new dynamic database-driven application development features will generally find themselves with more tools at their disposal. As a result, *Dreamweaver MX: Design and Technique* has a tendency, at least when it comes to this topic (which is covered in Part IV), to focus a little more on the PC side of things.

The bottom line is that the book is skewed a little more toward those working on a PC instead of a Mac. This doesn't mean that Mac users are totally alienated. When they crop up, I've gone to great lengths to point out important differences between Dreamweaver MX on a Mac and Dreamweaver MX on a PC (especially in Part IV).

Hotkeys will always be given for both Macintosh and Windows users, in that order. For example, Opt/Alt+F7 indicates that the Mac shortcut is Option+F7, while the Win shortcut is Alt+F7.

Who Needs This Book

You!

But seriously, folks, it's impossible to write a book that is all things to all people. This being said, I did my best to write a book that is many things to a lot of different people. I carefully selected the topics discussed and crafted the way I discussed them so that many different people, with varying levels of expertise and different goals, could pick the book up and find it useful. Granted, if worse comes to worst, the book is large enough to prop up the wobbly leg on your bed or serve as a pretty decent doorstop.

If you were to corner me in a dark alley, I would feel comfortable (*relatively* comfortable, that is, since I'm not used to being cornered in dark alleys by my readers) in saying that the people who will get the most out of this book will range from the savvy computer user who has never actually worked with the program or done any web design to someone who is experienced in the basics of Dreamweaver and wants to tackle more intermediate topics.

I strongly feel that this book is not that appropriate for people who already have advanced Dreamweaver skills. I certainly don't want to discourage any interested individual from using the book—it does cover a lot of stuff that even the more experienced user might not be famil-iar with. If everyone who looked at this volume in their local bookstore ended up buying it, I would definitely be a happy camper. However, I feel that those more-experienced Dreamweaver users might not find exactly what they are looking for in *Dreamweaver MX: Design and Technique* and would therefore be disappointed—something I definitely don't want.

Having said this, anyone eager to take part in the digital media revolution should read this book! Any student wanting to put their class project on the web, any new parents want-ing to put pictures of their newborn on the web, and certainly anyone who wants to stake their claim on their own parcel of the digital frontier. In short, this book is for anyone who is excited about the endless possibilities of the web but is a little befuddled about where they should start.

How the Book is Organized

I firmly believe that there is a natural progression of skills involved in working with Dream-weaver MX. The chapter-by-chapter structure of this book is designed to emulate this pro-gression. Although each chapter builds on the previous one to a certain extent, the book can, in fact, be used as a reference for those wishing to tackle specific problems.

I've been quite careful about pointing out which features are new to Dreamweaver MX—a handy feature if you've used Dreamweaver 4 or if you are completely new to DWMX. Be on the lookout for the handy-dandy "new to MX" icon!

This having been said, here is a quick look at what you can expect to explore in each chapter.

Part I ▪ A Taste of Design and Embarking on Technique

Part I sets the stage for all your future work in Dreamweaver MX. In **Chapter 1**, you'll start off by getting a nice (and very important) introduction to some of the fundamental principles of interactive design. In **Chapter 2**, you'll explore the cool new updates that Dreamweaver MX features, get a whirlwind tour of the program's interface, and learn how to customize your working environment. From there, in **Chapter 3**, you'll delve deeply into the earliest steps that need to be taken when creating your first web page/site. Topics such as opening and saving a document, setting page properties, and previewing your work in a browser are all covered. In **Chapter 4** you'll learn how to create and manipulate text using Dreamweaver MX. **Chapter 5** covers the addition and manipulation of images to your digital creation. From there, **Chapter 6** will look at the lifeblood of the web: hyperlinks. You'll learn, among other things, how to attach links to text and images, change link color, and create named anchors. Finally, **Chapter 7** will introduce you to the wonderful world of table creation and manipulation.

Part II ▪ Intermediate Dreamweaver Techniques

Part II is geared toward empowering you to take your first steps into a more intermediate set of skills (which wouldn't be possible if you hadn't mastered the more basic topics covered in Part I). In **Chapter 8**, you'll learn how to create and manipulate a frame-based web page. From there, **Chapter 9** will cover the tools (including Templates and Library Items) geared toward streamlining the production process. **Chapter 10** will teach you how to collect user data using forms. In **Chapter 11**, you'll learn how to add some serious "oomph" to your web site with all manner of different types of multimedia. Finally, in **Chapter 12**, you'll explore the tools that empower you to manage and manipulate an entire website (as opposed to just a web page).

Part III ▪ Working with Dynamic HTML

Part III is designed to teach you how you can create and manipulate Dynamic HTML (DHTML) using Dreamweaver MX. To start off with, **Chapter 13** will thoroughly explore how to use Cascading Style Sheets (CSS) to exert total and complete control over the way into which your page's content appears. From there, **Chapter 14** will cover how to employ layers to absolutely position elements in your web page. In **Chapter 15**, you'll learn how to add JavaScript-based interactivity using Dreamweaver MX's behaviors. Finally, **Chapter 16** will teach you how to work with the Timeline tool to add JavaScript based animations to your web page.

Part IV ▪ Making Dreamweaver Dynamic

Easily one of the coolest new features in Dreamweaver MX is a whole host of tools geared toward creating and manipulating dynamic database-driven applications. Part IV is designed to give you an exciting introduction to these tools. To start off with, **Chapter 17** will explore how to set the groundwork for your very own dynamic database driven application. From there, **Chapter 18** explores the basics of displaying information from a database in your web page. Finally, **Chapter 19** will take a far more tutorial-based approach than previous chapters and teach you how to develop some of the more common database-driven applications, such as a registration/login page combination or a simple search engine.

Inspiration: Design and Technique

Every creative endeavor—and a web page or website is no different—definitely benefits from a little inspiration now and then. Let's face it folks, even the most innovative person on the planet feels a little creatively constipated now and again.

In order to help, I've included an "Inspiration: Design and Technique" section at the end of every chapter. Designed to highlight some of the best digital creations on the web, it's important to note that the sites featured in the "Inspiration: Design and Technique" sections were not chosen because they were created with Dreamweaver. Instead, they were chosen, regardless of their medium, as stunning examples of design, execution, and technique. So, in some cases, a chapter's "Inspiration: Design and Technique" example will have been created using Flash, while others were created using Dreamweaver and straight HTML.

About the CD

As with many computer books, *Dreamweaver MX: Design and Technique* comes with a handy-dandy companion CD-ROM, which is compatible with both Macintosh and Windows platforms. Although the CD would probably make a pretty decent Frisbee, I've included some pretty useful stuff on it.

First, you'll find a whole bevy of demo and trial software from Macromedia (including Dreamweaver MX). Second, the CD contains all the necessary support and example files that are used in some of the chapters (especially Part IV)

 Any time I want to point you toward files on the CD, the text will appear next to a cool little CD icon like the one on the left. Feel free to use these files as starter files for your own unique Dreamweaver creations.

Getting in Touch

As an author, I love hearing from readers. I always get a serious jolt out of getting an e-mail from anyone who has bought any of my books and goes to the trouble of actually sending me some e-mail. While I love getting praise, I also value constructive criticism. Think the tone of the book was inappropriate? Confused by the way in which I covered a particular topic? Wish I would have covered some additional topics? Send me an e-mail! I not only respond to all the e-mail sent from readers, but I also take suggestions into account when writing the next edition (seriously).

So, drop me a digital line at `ethan@captainprimate.com`. I'd love to hear from you!

PART I

A Taste of Design and Embarking on Technique

The process *of designing a good website that fulfills your needs and all the needs of the user is a pretty complicated affair. However, as with any journey, you must begin with some first steps. Not only will you have to learn some of the basics about the tool you'll be using (in this case, Dreamweaver) to create your digital masterpiece, but you'll also need to become familiar with some fundamental principles of design.*

CHAPTER 1

Web Design: The Big Picture

For the most part, if you were to venture to your local bookstore, you would find the web design books split into two separate sections: tools/technology and design. Why is this? Aren't design issues important to those learning web design tools? Absolutely! Unfortunately, most tool-specific books on web design are just that: tool-specific. Someone buys them so they can learn about a specific program. Many people have difficulty seeing that the tool itself is just the beginning of web design. It's something you use to realize the creations that, if you've done your job right, have already been completed in your head and on paper.

This paper and brain production (sometimes referred to as predigital production) is the web design topic that appears in those *other* books in the *other* part of your local bookstore's computer section. So, what's the big deal about big picture web design issues anyway? Well, your website will sink or swim based on its *design* (a general term that covers many differ-ent issues that will be discussed in this chapter). As a result, even if you are focusing on a specific tool (as you will be with Dreamweaver in this book), it's a good idea to at least have a primer in the basics of web design. Now, this chapter is an *introduction* to the big picture of web design issues; there is no way that I could cover everything you need to know in one chapter. However, this chapter, which is part web history lesson and part web design starter, should give you a basic introduction to web design, along with an idea of what you might want to explore further on your own. At the very least, it will introduce you to some of the most important design issues so you don't inadvertently make a major blunder when you are building your HTML creation.

- **How the Web works**

- **Browser madness**

- **Fundamentals of interactive design**

How the Web Works

As early as the 1940s, computer scientists were moving away from the notion of building computers that mimicked the Newtonian universe. Rather, computers were seen to be instruments to manage and distribute huge amounts of information. Douglas Engelbart, upon reading Vannevar Bush's 1945 famous *Atlantic Monthly* article "As We May Think," noted that "If these machines [could] show you information on printouts, they could show you that information on a screen." Further, he saw a link between the TV-like interface and information processor as a medium for representing symbols. An individual could steer through different information spaces viewing data and graphics in different ways. Most importantly, however, was the fact that Engelbart easily saw the expansion of the medium into a theater-like environment in which one could sit with colleagues and exchange information simultaneously on many levels. The realization of these ideas, however, did not come to fruition for some 44 years.

Why should a humble Dreamweaver user care about the roots of the Web? Well, in order to better understand the medium in which you'll be working, it's helpful to at least have a cursory idea as to how it all came about. After all, most traditional artists (whether they are painters, printmakers, or sculptors) benefit from a solid understanding of the particular form in which they are working.

This section of the chapter will start off with a brief exploration of how the web got started. From there, we'll move on to how Hypertext Markup Language (HTML), the lifeblood of the Web, works.

> It's important to remember that this book doesn't even presume to teach you HTML—that's best learned elsewhere if you are interested. However, your introduction to the big picture web design issues wouldn't be complete without at least a passing look at HTML. And I would be neglecting my duties if I did not say that if you are serious about web design, you should really become familiar with HTML.

Finally, we'll finish off this section with a brief look at the Web, as it exists today. Remember, however, that this section, while important, is just introductory in nature. If you are interested in bypassing it so you can get right on to the real meat of the chapter (the taste of design), go right ahead.

Not So Humble Beginnings

Originally developed as an initiative of the Defense Agency Research Projects Administration (DARPA) in partnership with several prestigious universities and research institutions, the Internet, which at that time was called ARPAnet, was a prototype communications system designed to withstand the inevitable electromagnetic pulse generated by a thermonuclear attack. Yeah, that's right, *the* bomb. It wasn't long before ARPAnet spawned a sister network for the research community supported and funded by the National Science Foundation (NSF). Called the NSFnet, the network soon found its way into most universities in the United States, Canada, and abroad.

For all of its technological wonder, however, NSFnet was little more than an obscure scientific endeavor. NSFnet, which ultimately became known as the Internet, required adeptness at cryptic computer programs and obscure protocols. Even if one mastered the necessary skill to take advantage of the Internet, where to go and what to do was pretty puzzling, and it wasn't useful for much other than e-mailing.

At its height, NSFnet was a massive library of some of the most advanced information on the planet. The problem rested on the fact that it was extremely difficult to identify and locate a given source of information. It was akin to walking down each isle of an enormous library in the dark, and scanning each book to figure out what was available. Once you found something relevant to your needs, you had to "read" (that is, download) the entire book rather than browse just the parts that were of interest to you. Worse still, once found, a piece of information often referred to another valuable source without providing the means to locate it.

In 1989, tired of the perpetual hunt and peck of the Internet, a researcher named Tim Berners-Lee at the CERN atomic research center in Switzerland proposed software and protocols that would allow computers to browse the information contained on the NSFnet. This one event irrevocably changed the nature of how this global computer network was used.

CERN stands for Conseil Européen pour la Recherche Nucleaire.

Berners-Lee's software (dubbed a *browser*) and protocols created the ability to easily browse information and navigate not only different documents on the same computer, but documents on other computers. Key to the technology was the concept of *hyperlinks*, which were highlighted words or symbols the user could click and be transported to the next "page" in the sequence. Berners-Lee's Hypertext Markup Language (HTML) made hyperlinks possible.

Within months of the release of the early version of the web browser developed by Berners-Lee, web software spread throughout the research community like wildfire. By July 1993, more than 130 servers were web-enabled.

Shortly thereafter, a small group of students at the University of Illinois, among them Marc Andreessen (who later founded Netscape), took it upon themselves to rectify many of the shortcomings of the very primitive prototype web browser available to the public. Most significant among their accomplishments was the addition of a GUI (graphical user interface) to what had been a mostly text-based software and the adaptation of the browser allowing it to function on the Windows operating system. Following this, there was an incredible jump in the number of websites—a phenomenon that can be directly correlated with the release of the first version of the University of Illinois NCSA (National Center for Supercomputing Applications) Mosaic web browser (see Figure 1.1).

The rest, as they say, is history. NCSA Mosaic changed everything. Not only did the web become graphical, but it became accessible way beyond the academic community. Not long after Mosaic's introduction, Andreessen, along with five others, left the University of Illinois to found the Mosaic Communications Corporation, which later became the Netscape Communications Corporation, one of the first truly commercial web software ventures. Before you could say "holy alleged antitrust, Batman," Microsoft got in on the action, and thus begun the browser wars. However, before we discuss these and other browser-related design issues, there is some additional ground that needs to be covered in this section.

HTML: The Lifeblood of the Web

As mentioned earlier, Hypertext Markup Language (HTML) was one of the things that made the Web possible. In reality, HTML is not a computer language such as C++ or Pascal; it is a system for describing documents. A plain text document is "marked up" using a series of commands called *tags* (see Figure 1.2). A browser interprets the HTML document and displays it. The fact that an HTML document is plain text is significant for a couple of reasons. First, because plain text can be interpreted by any platform (IBM, Macintosh, and UNIX), HTML is truly cross platform and universal. Second, because HTML is plain text, it can be written using the simplest of programs (such as Windows' Notepad or Mac's SimpleText).

Figure 1.1

Mosaic is crude by today's standards, but compared to what was available when it came out, it was an earth-shattering piece of software.

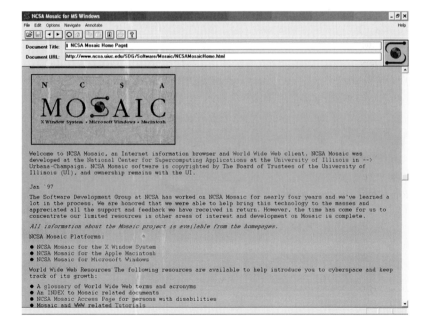

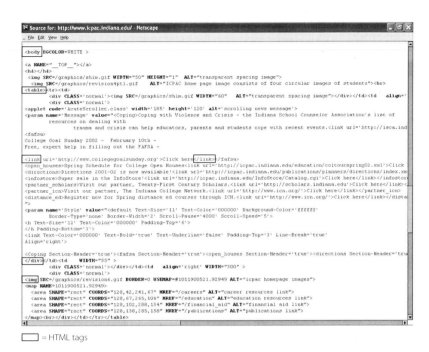

= HTML tags

The first incarnation of HTML (version 1) allowed very basic page layout including font size, hyperlinks, and embedding of graphics. It is important to remember that HTML 1 was only the standard insofar as the first popular browser, Mosaic, was designed to interpret it. It wasn't until more browsers appeared on the market that a standard version of HTML was defined. As various versions of HTML were proposed and adopted by the World Wide Web Consortium (W3C, an organization that develops web standards), the language became more powerful. The inclusion of new layout features, such as frames and tables, allowed greater options for the development of web pages. In addition, image maps and new graphics formats increased the integration of images and basic interactivity.

The most recent version of HTML (version 4.01), which has been dubbed Dynamic HTML (DHTML), has some very exciting features that give web designers a lot more freedom than they had previously experienced. While each successive version of HTML offered unparallel opportunities for publishing hypertext documents, the medium was not as malleable as many would have liked. HTML documents were far more difficult to lay out than traditional print documents. In HTML, text could only be arranged in a limited number of ways, making it hard to create a compelling visual experience. In addition, the way HTML treated graphics made it difficult to lay out a document. Finally, the interactivity in HTML documents was

On the way back, the router makes sure the requested document is sent to the client that originally made the request. The last leg happens when the client (the web browser) receives the requested document and displays it for the users' reading (or viewing) pleasure. That's the very basics of how the web works.

A little confused? Don't worry, even a description as stripped down as this can be a tad perplexing. This is where the whole restaurant analogy comes into the picture. Imagine if you were to walk into one of your favorite restaurants and were seated at your favorite table. You peruse the menu and decide upon a delectable soup to start your meal. You put down the menu and signal your waiter. When he comes to your table, you say, "Good evening my good man, I would like to start off with a bowl of gazpacho, please." He nods his head, quickly moves to the kitchen and hands the order to the head chef, who gives the order to one of his newest chefs (it *is* only a bowl of soup). After a while, the soup is made. From there, it is handed back to the head chef, who hands it to the waiter, who takes it to your table, where you sit back and enjoy the beginning of a lovely meal.

OK, let's recap: you tell the waiter what you want to eat: that is, you type a URL into a browser. From there, the browser/waiter sends your request to the head waiter, who fulfills a task not unlike a router, making sure the request gets to the proper place. After your request/order has been passed on to the appropriate chef/server, it is fulfilled, handed back to the router/head chef, who then hands it back to the waiter/browser, who finally gives it to you for consumption. Make a little more sense? Or are you craving some soup?

Browser Madness

We left off in our history of the World Wide Web somewhere in 1994. Netscape Communications Corporation had just released the first version of Netscape, affectionately nicknamed Mozilla. Not long after that, wanting to get in on the action, Microsoft released Internet Explorer, which quickly became Netscape's primary competitor. In addition, around the same time, Sun Microsystems developed a browser called HotJava, and America Online (AOL) developed one called the AOL browser.

> There are a lot more browser alternatives out there than Netscape or Internet Explorer. For a fully featured accounting, check out CNET's browser topic center at www.browsers.com.

It didn't take too long for things to get crazy—very crazy. The Web was becoming the hottest thing since sliced bread, and everyone wanted their piece. In an attempt to establish total market domination, the two primary browsers (Netscape and Internet Explorer) adopted a policy under which new versions were released at very regular intervals. Each time a new version was released, it often had a spate of new features (such as the ability to display new HTML content). It seemed like a pretty good situation—new browsers, new features, better looking and more fully featured web pages. There was one slight hitch: for the most part, the new elements were unique and exclusive to the browser in which they were featured. As a result, there was tons of content floating out on the Web that was only accessible with one browser or another. This constant attempt by Netscape and Microsoft to one-up each other is often referred to as the *browser wars* and was probably one of the most disastrous periods for web design.

> For a great look at the history of browser version releases and their associated features, check out Ann Navarro's *Effective Web Design* (Sybex, 2001)

Where does that leave us today? Well, a couple noteworthy things have happened. First, for all intents and purposes, Netscape lost (or, if you aren't keen on putting the last nail in the coffin just yet, is losing) the browser wars. While browser usage statistics are extremely hard to generate (and are often somewhat misleading) it looks like Internet Explorer (in its various versions and incarnations) commands between 58 percent and 65 percent of the market (perhaps even more depending on the source of the statistics), while Netscape has about 10 percent to 12 percent. The remaining slim percentage points are the domain of a myriad of different browser alternative that exist.

> For more information on browser usage statistics, check out either Browser Watch at browserwatch.internet.com or Browser News at www.upsdell.com/BrowserNews.

The second noteworthy thing is that the World Wide Web Consortium was founded. Established in 1994 by many of the individuals who "invented" the World Wide Web, the World Wide Web Consortium (W3C) was mandated to develop standards that promote the Web's evolution and ensure its interoperability.

In theory, the best way to prevent the sort of madness that resulted from Netscape and Microsoft's constant attempts to outdo one another and to ensure that web pages would display consistently and legibly in *any* browser would be to develop standards to which everyone could stick. The primary problem is (and was at the time when the W3C started its Herculean undertaking) that no one owns the Web. Instead, the Web is made up of thousands of individual networks and organizations, each of which is run and financed on its own. As a result, despite the fact that the W3C is a fairly powerful entity, it has no real way to enforce the Web standards that it proposes. Ultimately, it's up to those companies that make the browsers to adopt the standards themselves. The good thing is that, even before the browser wars were winding down, both Netscape and Microsoft were adopting many of the W3C proposed standards as baselines for their browsers. As a result, one could design with the most up to date W3C standard version of HTML and be relatively certain that it would work predictably on different browsers.

The W3C is an interesting entity. Not only does it develop standards for HTML, but it is also constantly developing other cutting-edge technologies for the Web in an effort to prevent any future browser arms races. For more information about the W3C, go to www.w3c.org.

However, even today, you'll find that many features (especially those associated with Dynamic HTML (DHTML) display inconsistently from browser to browser. Also, despite the fact that the W3C is the king of web standards, there are companies that integrate unique features into their browsers.

Designing for Today's Web Browser (and Yesterday's, While You're at It)

What's the moral of this story? Well, despite the fact that Microsoft's Internet Explorer seems to be reigning supreme (at least for now), lots of people are using lots of different browsers to surf the Web. If you want to ensure that the maximum amount of people can enjoy your website, you need to stick to the W3C's standards. One of the coolest thing about Dreamweaver is that it was built to design web pages that conform to these standards. Still, it's important that you constantly and consistently test your HTML creation in all of the browsers you foresee it being viewed with.

For more information on how you can use Dreamweaver to preview web pages in different browsers, see the "Previewing Your Work in a Browser" section of Chapter 3, "Setting Up and Managing Your Page."

Fundamentals of Interactive Design

Strictly speaking, the kinds of fundamental issues that you need to address when you're designing your website are relatively universal (at least when it comes to interactive design). Whether you are creating a CD-ROM, a DVD-ROM, a website, an interactive kiosk, or any information-driven application, you need to create something that fulfills the needs of your audience. From the designer's perspective, it would be great if everything created was intended solely for the consumption of the individual who created it—an audience of one so to speak. However, this is far from the case. Even the most insignificant of interactive creations is usually intended for a wider audience than just the designer. Because of this, you need to create something that, in the best case, is all things to all people. As such, there are some *extremely* important issues you should consider during the creative process. This section explores some of these issues.

It's important to remember that what is presented here is only an introduction to the fundamentals of interactive design. However, the discussion will provide you with the necessary foundations upon which to further your own exploration of the topic.

Information Design and Architecture

Information architecture has absolutely nothing to do with traditional architecture. In this section of the chapter, you won't learn how to tell the difference between an Ionic and a Doric column. (This was a big disappointment to one of my Web Design students who thought she could indulge her passion for Renaissance architecture in my class!) Instead, you are going to get an introduction to the art and science of information design and architecture for the Web.

Essentially, information architecture is the process by which a website's content is organized into easily accessible components that support a wide variety of user access techniques (casual browsing, direct searching, and so on). As one would expect, information architecture is intimately related to the navigational system of a site. As a result, you'd have a difficult time designing one without the other.

> This section of the chapter is designed to be a simple introduction to information architecture. Extra resources are a must. You might want to seek out Louis Rosenfeld and Peter Morville's *Information Architecture for the World Wide Web* (O'Reilly, 1998). If you are interested in extending your search to the Web, check out the Argus Center for Information Architecture at www.argus-acia.com.

At its most basic, the process by which you develop a site's information architecture is usually a two-step affair. The first step involves organizing your site's information into a variety of categories. You'll need to decide how many sections, subsections, and categories you need; how your site's content will fit into those categories; and how the units of information (individual web pages) will relate to units of information within the same category and to units in other categories. This is arguably one of the most difficult things about designing a site. The way we human beings organize information is largely determined by our cultural context. As a result, what constitutes well-organized information is *extremely* subjective. One must contend with all manner of problems such as linguistic ambiguity (a word or term may mean different things to different people) or different perspectives of how information should be organized.

As with many other issues in web design, the way you organize information will depend largely on your audience. You must put yourself in their shoes and predict the best way to develop an information architecture so that your users' needs are met. Developing a way to organize your content can often be a fairly painful process, but it is absolutely necessary in developing a functional and usable information architecture.

Once you've decided how to organize your information, you need to formalize that structure with something called an information architecture diagram (IA diagram). Designed to provide a visual representation of the information architecture of your site, an IA diagram can take many different forms (see Figure 1.4). Ultimately, the specific style is up to you.

Figure 1.4

There are many different ways to create an information architecture diagram. The example on the left is a reverse branching tree model; the example on the right is the spherical model.

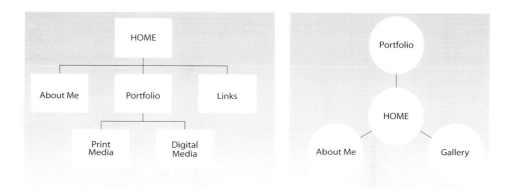

An IA diagram isn't supposed to show the links between various pages within your site. Instead, it represents the hierarchical relationship between sections/subsections, and individual pages.

> An IA diagram is also very useful for developing the structure of your site on the server (folders, subfolders, and so on).

Developing a Visual Metaphor

A visual metaphor is often a pretty slippery concept to put into words, but it can be easy to unconsciously interpret when it's used properly. Essentially, a visual metaphor, which is universally applied to an entire website, leverages familiar visual elements (such as images, interface elements, icons, colors, or fonts) to unconsciously reinforce the site's subject matter. The visual metaphor for a major Hollywood movie's promotional website will be completely different from that of an interactive design firm or an online merchant.

For example, in the screenshots depicted in Figure 1.5, the goal was to create a website for the Glenn A. Black Laboratory of Archaeology, a highly prestigious independent research unit at Indiana University, Bloomington. Because of the archaeological theme, the website used an earthy palette of colors consisting of shades of brown, gray, rust, dark green, and tan, combined with archaeologically oriented design elements to visually reinforce its content.

Creating an effective visual metaphor requires some serious brainstorming and inspired free association. You'll need to sit down and think about what kinds of colors, fonts, images, icons, and interface/layout elements unconsciously reinforce the site's content.

> Before you even begin brainstorming for your visual metaphor, you need to be rock-solid sure of your audience. You can't effectively design a visual metaphor if you aren't exactly sure of the demographic of those who'll be using the site.

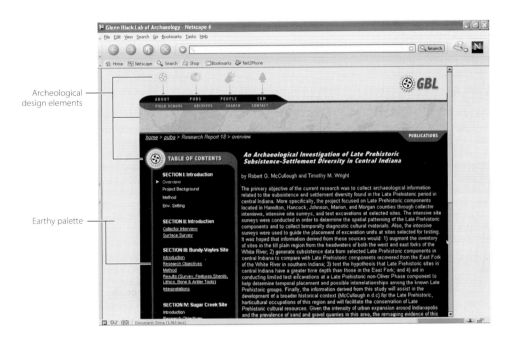

Archeological design elements

Earthy palette

Figure 1.5

The Glenn Black Lab of Archaeology's website employs earth tone colors and archaeologically oriented imagery to create a solid visual metaphor.

Say, for example, you are creating a children's online community site geared towards ages 7 to 10. You might think about using bold primary colors with cartoony interface elements and fonts. On the other hand, the website for a movie would draw its visual metaphor from the film's look and feel (check out the Planet of the Apes website at `www.planetoftheapes.com` for a great example).

There are no hard and fast rules for creating a visual metaphor. The only real guideline is that they should be used wisely: be subtle and don't overdo it. Always have your ideas vetted by individuals not associated with the project; they will often have suggestions or comments you never thought of. Don't get too attached to a visual metaphor because it's quite possible that, given an outside opinion (perhaps one of a prospective user), you'll decide that it doesn't work for your site.

Creating Storyboards and Concept Art

One of the most important steps in the paper and brain predigital production process is creating storyboards or concept art, an idea swiped from the film industry. Generally one of the last steps before you go digital with your grand creation, storyboards are used to visualize your design as a complete entity. With them, you get a chance, among other things, to see how colors interact with one another, how interface elements play off one another, how your navigational system is realized, how your visual metaphor plays out, and whether content is represented in the best way possible. Storyboards provide you with a painless way of catching any potential design problems before you get to the stage where you build your design in HTML and they become major obstacles. Storyboards are also a great way to play with design ideas and visually brainstorm.

As illustrated in Figure 1.6, there is no hard or fast rule as to how they should look. If you are brainstorming ideas, the back of a cocktail napkin is a good a medium as any. However, if you are preparing a pitch to a potential client, it's a good idea to come up with something more polished and formal. The bottom line is that storyboards, in whatever form they appear, should efficiently communicate your design ideas without too much ambiguity.

Figure 1.6

Storyboards can range from "quick and dirty" (left) to quite formal and polished (right). Whatever their level of quality, they should effectively communicate your design ideas.

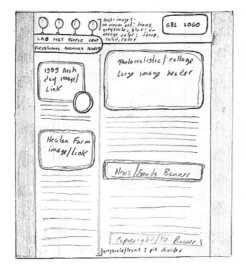

You may even want to create your storyboards in a photocopy of an empty browser window. This is a great way to give your client the necessary context.

Several browser templates for the purpose of storyboarding have been included in the Storyboard Templates folder of this book's accompanying CD.

Getting From Here to There: Developing Intuitive Navigation

One could easily argue that designing an intuitive and usable system of navigation is one of—if not *the*—most important goals when it comes to web design. User experience on the web is all about moving in space from one location to another in search of *something*. Whether or not the user knows what they are looking for is moot. It's up to you to crawl inside the heads of the users, figure out what they want from your site, and then figure out the easiest way for them to get it. If you don't provide a system for them to get from where they are to where they need to be, they'll go elsewhere, and this is the last thing you want.

Don't be fooled into thinking that a navigation scheme is simply buttons and hyperlinks. The best-designed navigation is a highly artful mix of many different things: a pinch of interface design, a dash of information architecture, and a generous dollop of psychology.

As I've mentioned, there is no way that I could effectively condense all that you need to know about designing intuitive navigation into one section of one chapter of one book. However, there are certain general, basic concepts that are both fundamentally important and self-contained enough that they can be discussed.

Keeping Things Consistent

One of the ways human beings define the world around them, and the way which they interact with it, is based on the consistency and predictability of events. When a navigational system works properly, people come to unconsciously rely upon it. For this to happen, the navigational system must be consistent. This means (as shown in Figure 1.7) that the menu must remain in the same location, it must retain the same appearance and contents, and the interface where the navigational elements reside must not change to any significant degree.

Consistent logo placement   Subpage navigation elements   Consistent logo placement   Subpage navigation elements

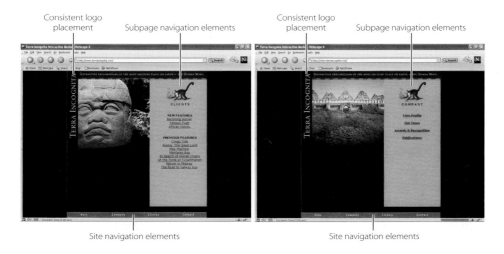

Site navigation elements   Site navigation elements

Figure 1.7

These two screenshots are of two different pages within the same site. Note that the navigational elements remain exactly the same.

One of the obstacles to designing a consistent and predictable navigation system revolves around the interplay between navigational elements and interface design at deep levels within the website. Often, as one gets deeper and deeper into a site, a certain point is reached at which the navigation scheme breaks down due to a lack of foresight. Designers tend to put most of their effort into developing a navigation scheme that will work best in the more consistently accessed areas of a site. As they move deeper and deeper into their site and the amount of information in any given screen increases, they spend less and less time ensuring that the navigation scheme they developed will function properly.

> The best-designed websites have a pyramid-shaped information distribution. The top levels of the site contain information that doesn't take up a great amount of screen real estate. As you move deeper into the site and into more specialized information, a larger amount of screen real estate is consumed by the website's content.

It's at this point that chaos often sets in and the all important consistency and predictability goes out the window. To cope with the additional information, designers will toss in additional navigational elements (menus, buttons, and so on) or even alter the existing navigational scheme that worked just fine in the upper levels of the site.

Instead of succumbing to bedlam and anarchy, make sure that when you create the navigational scheme, you think deep into your site's structure. It may seem time-consuming, but it could save you valuable time later. Because your user will probably spend more time in the deeper sections of your site, ask yourself whether what you've laboriously designed will work just as well with the content in the upper sections of your site as with the content in the deeper sections of your site. If you can't answer with a resounding "yes," start again.

> Remember, the Web is a nonlinear medium. Users don't always enter your site through the front door: they can just as easily enter through a side or back door into a section deep within your site's hierarchy. Because of this, you should make sure that your entire site maintains a consistent scheme of navigation.

Help Users Quickly Learn Your Navigation Scheme

When you create a website of any kind, you are providing something to your user. Whether it's a mega online bookstore like Amazon.com, a major educational institution like the University of Toronto, or your own personal corner of cyberspace, content is king. You don't want users to have to spend a huge amount of time learning how to locate what they desire. In other words, you don't want an overly complex navigational system to stand in the way of the user and what they want.

The key to easily learned navigational systems lies in several different issues. First, as I just mentioned, your navigational system should be consistent. If you switch the way you require your user to move about the site, they'll have to start from scratch and relearn your navigational scheme: not good. Second, as will be covered shortly, make sure the way your user identifies navigational elements (labels, visual imagery, and so on) is straight to the point and not overly complex or confusing. There is nothing worse than a series of buttons whose labels make no sense. The general rule of thumb (and this is pretty general as rules go) is to create navigational schemes that are not counter-intuitive and thereby difficult to learn.

Providing Clear and Obvious Visual Cues

Because the web is a visual medium, effective navigational schemes should provide clear visual messages. I'm not just talking about the buttons here. Integrating clear visual cues into a navigational scheme requires some very broad (and often subtle) thinking.

COLOR

One of the best ways to provide your users with a quick and easy (and often unconscious) method of identifying exactly where they are located in your site is to use color. You may have noticed that many large sites use a consistent navigational system whose color changes slightly depending on the section or subsection where the user currently resides. This is a very effective technique that, when used properly, creates "signposts" for the user that are easily learned and recognized. When using color to increase the usability of your navigational system, you've definitely got some options. Changing the background color of individual pages is one way, but you can also use color for subtle emphasis—highlighting certain navigational or interface elements like buttons, banners, or header graphics.

There are, however, some caveats to using color in this way. First, to avoid overwhelming the user with a new color for each subsection, pick a very limited palette and apply those colors to the top level sections of your site. For example, say you're designing your own personal website and you use a nice light rust color for the "About Me" section. To avoid overwhelming the user, you'd also use that color for the "My Favorite Movies," "My Family," and "My Favorite Music" sections, all of which are subsections of the "About Me" page. You should also carefully choose a palette of colors that fits with your visual metaphor.

BRANDING

Consistent and clear branding is also a good way to provide your audience with visual cues. Given the nature of the Web, people have a tendency to quickly jump from site to site with mouse clicks. When your audience is cavorting about your site, you want them to know *exactly* where they are. This is best accomplished with clearly and consistently placed logos, as shown in Figure 1.8.

Figure 1.8

Notice that in both websites, a logo is always prominently displayed to remind the audience exactly where they are.

BREADCRUMB TRAIL

One of the biggest problems in particularly large, content-heavy websites is that people can easily get lost and end up with no clue where they are located, and no idea how to get back to where they were several clicks ago. One of the easiest and most elegant ways (and most cost effective in terms of effort and screen real estate consumed) to work around this problem is to create a simple navigational tool called a breadcrumb trail (Figure 1.9). Essentially, a breadcrumb trail (sometimes referred to as a link buildout) is a horizontal line of hyperlinked words indicating the location of the current page within the site's overall information architecture. An example of a breadcrumb trail would be something like Home → About Me → Favorite Movies. Each item in the trail would be a hyperlink to that specific section or subsection.

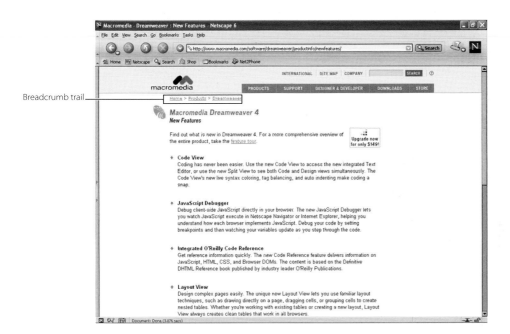

Breadcrumb trail

Figure 1.9

A breadcrumb trail provides a clear indication of the position of the current page within the site's overall structure; it also provides an easy way of moving back up that particular section or subsection's hierarchy.

LABELS

One of the most often overlooked methods to provide clear and concise visual cues to your audience is to use effective labels. We're not just talking about ordinary labels here, we're talking about concepts that have been boiled down to their basic understandable components. For example, suppose a section of your site had images of all the photographs you've taken, all the paintings you've painted, and all the sculpture you've sculpted. Instead of having a link or a button that said "Everything I've ever created on film, with canvas, or with clay," you could simply use the word "Portfolio" or "Gallery."

> It's important to remember that many of the conventional web labels used are culturally based. While your average web user in North America wouldn't have any difficulty understanding your intentions, if you used the word "Home" in your navigational scheme, someone from Egypt, the Czech Republic, or Malaysia may have absolutely no clue to what you are referring.

When creating clear labels, you must avoid using what I call *geek speak*, or terminology familiar only to those individuals within a specific field. For example, as an archaeologist, I've created websites where the term "Gray Literature" is used. If you have no experience in the field of archaeology, you probably don't have a clue what gray literature is. However, there are individuals out there who, despite the fact that they aren't familiar with the strange terms we archaeologists use, would be interested in gray literature. (Gray literature refers to the excavation reports generated by federally mandated salvage archaeological excavations.) To avoid geek speak in this particular situation, I substituted "Gray Literature" with the term "Excavation Reports," which is a lot more understandable to the general public.

VISUAL VOCABULARY: NAVIGATIONAL ELEMENTS

Another good way to provide users with clear visual cues is by using consistent and universally understandable visual vocabulary. There are three general schools of thought when it comes to creating navigational elements (buttons, menus, and so on). The first one tends to emphasize the use of icons or imagery, while the second one emphasizes the use of purely textual-based navigation. The third, which I think is the most rational, encourages the appropriate and contextually suitable use of both text and images as navigational elements.

If you've decided to use a purely visually based navigation system, you are in for some serious obstacles. Using icons or images in navigation is fine, but you must realize that the Web itself has no real standardized conventions for visual vocabulary. So, for instance, if you've created a button on your main page that links to your "About Me" section, what icon do you use? The possibilities are literally endless. The problem especially pops up when you choose an icon that, while significant to you, has no significance for your audience. In this situation, your audience will be faced with a series of acontextual (at least for them) icons with which they are expected to navigate your site. The only true universal solution for this problem is to create navigational elements that incorporate both text and images. If you include text that answers the user's "what the heck is this button for" kinds of questions, you can use funky icons that fit into your visual metaphor.

Multiple Roads from Here to There

Lots of people do things in lots of different ways. People drive differently, have different tastes in movies and music, talk differently, eat differently, and most important to this discussion, use different methods to move about the Web. Some like to wander aimlessly until they stumble across something interesting, while others want to locate specific information as quickly and efficiently as possible. Some people use the newest browser on a fast machine with a fast Internet connection, while others have an older browser on a slower machine with a slow Internet connection. Some people use text browsers or screen readers. Get the point? It's up to you to try to accommodate all of these "profiles" so that you don't alienate possible visitors.

CHAPTER 2

Starting Up Dreamweaver

After double-clicking the Dreamweaver program icon, you may be faced with a myriad of windows, palettes, and inspectors. The possibilities are endless. Don't get confused, though: every tool in Dreamweaver has its place and, by the end of this book, you'll know how to use all of them.

In this chapter, I'll introduce you to the Dreamweaver environment and the many ways it can be molded to suit your preferences. Then we'll look at how to set up a local site on your own hard drive—probably one of the most important first steps to take in Dreamweaver.

- ▓ **What's new in Dreamweaver MX**

- ▓ **A tour of the Dreamweaver interface**

- ▓ **Customizing the Dreamweaver environment**

- ▓ **Setting up a local site**

What's New in Dreamweaver MX?

It's official: Dreamweaver MX has some truly cool features. Never a company to follow others, Macromedia is leading the pack of interactive design software developers with its latest version of Dreamweaver. By introducing a horde of new and exciting features, Macromedia has once again managed to push the boundaries of cutting-edge interactive design tools. Don't take my word for it: check out the following laundry list, which highlights some of the program's latest and greatest additions.

Workspace and Workflow Enhancements

Macromedia knows that great software is easy to use and easy to customize. The following features in the new MX version of Dreamweaver increase its usability and streamline your workflow:

New user interface Dreamweaver MX's new MDI (multiple document interface) features fully dockable and collapsible/expandable panels and a tabbed Document Window that maximizes workflow so that you can focus on what is most important: creativity. Unfortunately, the new Dreamweaver MX workspace is only available on the Windows version of the program.

New Document dialog box With the New Document dialog box, creating a new page is easy. You can set the type of document with which you wish to work from the get-go, and you can take advantage of the wealth of preset page layouts.

Site Definition Wizard The new Site Definition Wizard lets you set up both local and remote sites quickly and easily.

Answers panel The Answers panel, which is common throughout all the MX generation of applications from Macromedia, is designed to give you direct access to online resources from the Macromedia Resource Center.

Site panel File Explorer With the new File Explorer in the Site panel, you can easily browse your hard drive without ever leaving the Dreamweaver MX workspace.

JavaScript drop-down menu creation Now you can create JavaScript drop-down menus directly from within Dreamweaver MX, a feature that was previously available only in Macromedia Fireworks.

Dreamweaver Template enhancements Dreamweaver MX now allows you to exert a far greater degree of control over how Templates are created, distributed, and managed.

Launch and Edit feature Macromedia's MX generation of applications are now more closely linked than ever. Dreamweaver MX's new Launch and Edit feature lets you work on Fireworks MX and Flash MX content directly from within Dreamweaver MX.

Enhanced Cascading Style Sheet support Dreamweaver MX's enhanced CSS support includes integration of many CSS2-compliant features as well as the ability to create design-time style sheets for easier document manipulation.

Enhanced Coding Tools

While Dreamweaver has always allowed designers and developers to work directly on their page's code, Dreamweaver MX now features some phenomenally powerful tools for creating and manipulating not only HTML code, but also XHTML, XML, and other emergent server technologies.

Syntax coloring You can now configure and customize the way different elements of your code are colored when you work from within Code View.

Snippets panel With the Snippets panel, you can now store blocks of useful code for later reuse.

Code Hints If you are working within Code View, Code Hints provide you with a dynamic customized menu of HTML elements appropriate to your immediate needs.

Tag Inspector The Tag Inspector, which functions from within Code View, is a quick and easy way to edit and manipulate the properties of a given tag within the structure of your HTML.

Support for XHTML With Dreamweaver MX's new full-featured XHTML support, you can now generate fully compliant XHTML code. You can also convert older HTML files to XHTML with the integrated XHTML converter.

XML support Dreamweaver MX now gives developers the ability to create and validate XML.

Support for Dynamic Database Driven Technologies

Arguably one of the greatest enhancements that Macromedia has made to Dreamweaver MX is the ability to create, manipulate, and deploy dynamic database-driven sites. Macromedia has combined UltraDev (its dynamic database-driven site authoring tool) with Dreamweaver to create an incredibly usable application geared both toward those just starting out in dynamic database-driven sites and those who are seasoned dynamic application developers. While the new information outlined in this section may seem a little on the light side, it's important to remember that everything related to dynamic database-driven application development in Dreamweaver MX is totally new. Rather than listing everything or saying, "It's *all* new, baby," I've opted to highlight some of the new features. See Part IV, "Making Dreamweaver Dynamic," to start learning how to create dynamic database-driven applications with Dreamweaver MX.

Support for a wide range of technologies Dreamweaver MX includes full-featured support for the most powerful dynamic database driven technologies available to developers: ASP, ASP.NET, PHP, ColdFusion MX, and JSP.

Live Data View Live Data View is vital to rapid dynamic application development because it allows you to preview dynamic content directly from within the Dreamweaver Document Window.

Integrated Database Explorer Now you can view the structure of the database with which you are working directly from within the Databases panel.

> The new dynamic database application authoring tools in Dreamweaver MX pretty much sound the death knell for Macromedia UltraDev. But, just as UltraDev replaced the aging Macromedia Drumbeat, Dreamweaver MX is a giant leap forward for those interested in developing dynamic database-driven applications.

A Quick Tour of the Dreamweaver Interface

One of the great joys of Dreamweaver is its interface. The program boasts an incredible set of tools, some of which need to be right at your fingertips at a moment's notice. The interface, which is designed to accommodate a wide range of expertise and working styles, allows you to maximize what's really important: creativity. The interface itself is broken up into a series of windows, panels, and inspectors. In this section, you'll be introduced to the most common of these tools.

Understanding the New Dreamweaver MX Workspace Options

One the biggest changes in Dreamweaver MX, at least from the perspective of the interface, is the new MDI workspace (see Figure 2.1). Not only does it feature the same streamlined, integrated, panel-based interface that is the hallmark of all Macromedia's next-generation MX applications, but it also features a tabbed Document Window that allows you to easily switch back and forth between multiple documents during the design and development process.

The kicker (and it's a big one) is that the new Dreamweaver MX workspace is only available on the Windows version of the program. This will come as a pretty heavy blow to those working on a Mac, who will have to make due with a Dreamweaver 4 version interface (see Figure 2.2).

If you are working on a Windows machine, you'll be able to switch back and forth between the two interfaces on a dime:

1. Open the Edit Preferences dialog box (Edit → Preferences).

2. Select the General option from the Category list box on the left.

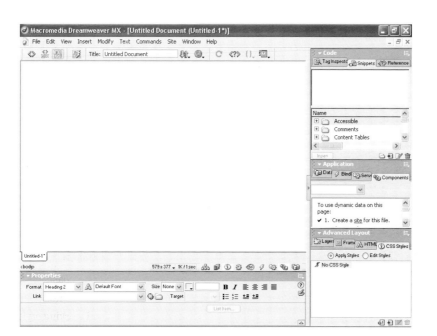

Figure 2.1

The new Dreamweaver MX workspace features a bevy of cool labor- and time- saving devices.

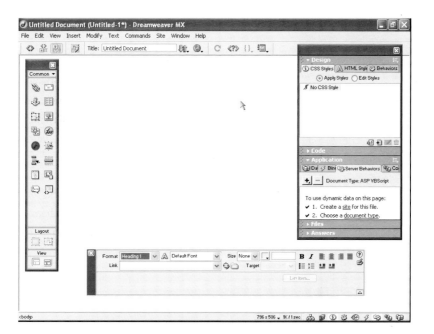

Figure 2.2

While Windows users will have access to both the new MX style work-space as well as the Dreamweaver 4 style interface, Mac users will have to make do with only the Dreamweaver 4 style interface.

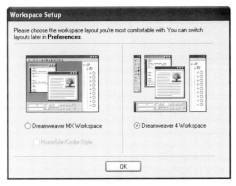

Figure 2.3

The Workspace Setup dialog box lets Windows users decide which Dreamweaver interface they want to work with.

3. Click the Change Workspace button (on the left-hand side of the Edit Preferences dialog box).

4. When the Workspace Setup dialog box appears (see Figure 2.3), click the radio button that corresponds with the workspace in which you'd like to work, and click OK.

The big question in terms of this book is which workspace will be featured in the coming chapters. Well, I decided to focus primarily on the new Dreamweaver MX workspace. I offer profound apologies to Mac users. Please understand that my decision is not motivated by the tired Mac vs. PC debates seen in many design circles. Nor is it because I'm not a traditional Mac user (in fact, I regularly teach on a Mac). Instead, it is motivated by the desire to look forward instead of looking back—and the fact that the book would be twice as long if I tailored each section so that it covered both workspaces! Despite this, Mac users will still find this book useful. While the screenshots in the book will be of the new MX workspace, the various step-by-step processes described will be almost exactly the same on a Mac as they are on a Windows machine.

The Document Window

All of your creations will take shape in the Document Window. Think of it as a canvas upon which you paint your web pages. Don't be fooled by its initial emptiness, however. The Document Window is far more than just a vacant space into which you mold your creations. There is also an abundance of information and tools built right into it. The following subsections explore the most important of these tools.

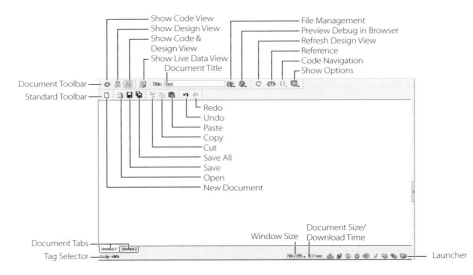

The Tag Selector

The Tag Selector is a nifty selection tool that displays the HTML tags that are associated with any given element you select. Click the particular tag of an element, and that element—be it an image, a table, or text—is automatically selected.

> If you right-click (or control-click on a Mac) a given tag in the tag selector, a pop-up menu will appear. From there, you can select Edit Tag, and then make any changes to the tag (as well as its associated content) in a neat little pop-up window.

Window Size

The Window Size serves two primary functions. First, it provides an indicator as to the current size (in pixels) of the Document Window you're currently working in. Second, if you resize your window, the Window Size changes immediately to reflect the new value. By clicking the Window Size and opening the drop-down menu, you can easily choose from a preset list of window sizes.

> One of the great things about the Window Size indicator drop-down menu is that you can create your own presets from which to choose. For more information on how to do this, see "Adding Window Size Presets" later in this chapter.

Document Size/Download Time

The Document Size/Download Time indicator is one of the unsung heroes of the Dreamweaver environment. Basically, it tells you the current size of your page (in kilobytes) and the amount of time (in seconds) it will take to download it over a 28.8KBps modem connection.

As you add objects to your page, both numbers will increase. For those who spend a lot of time thinking about bandwidth (which should be most people), this is definitely a tool to keep your eye on. Now, you're probably thinking to yourself "Hmmm…great tool, but what if I want to know how long my page will take to download over a 56Kbps modem, or even a cable modem?" A little later in this chapter ("Changing the Document Size/Download Time Defaults"), you'll learn how to change the reading to reflect the download time at different speeds.

> While the Document Size/Download Time indicator provides a nice indication as to the speed at which your page will download over a given connection, it's quite important to realize that it's just a rough indicator. There are more factors than the size of the page and the speed of the user's connection that affect the speed at which your page downloads, such as the speed of the user's computer processor or network traffic.

The Launcher

With a click of the mouse, the Launcher allows you to launch the Site panel, the Assets panel, the Cascading Style Sheet panel, the Behaviors panel, the History panel, the Bindings panel, the Server Behaviors panel, the Components panel, and the Databases panel.

> If your Launcher isn't visible, go to Edit → Preferences. When the Edit Preferences dialog box appears, select the Panels option from the Category list box. From there, select the Show Icons in Panels and Launcher option.

One of the great things about the Launcher is that you can customize which tools are visible. To add (or remove) tools from the Launcher:

1. Open the Preferences dialog box (Edit → Preferences).

2. Select Panels from the Category list box seen in the image on top.

3. If you want to add a tool to the Launcher, click the plus (+) button next to Show in Launcher and make your choice from the drop-down menu (shown in the image on bottom).

4. To remove a tool from the launcher, select it from the list next to Show in Launcher and click the minus (–) button.

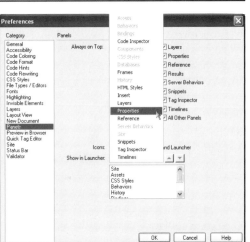

The Document Toolbar

The Toolbar, which can be toggled on and off by going to View → Toolbars → Document, contains a series of very handy tools, all of which are discussed next.

SHOW CODE VIEW BUTTON

As you work within Dreamweaver, the program automatically creates all the necessary underlying source HTML. By clicking the Show Code View button, you can display (and manually edit) the HTML.

SHOW CODE AND DESIGN VIEW BUTTON

The Show Code and Design View button splits the document window, displaying the HTML source code on the top and the visual representation of your web page on the bottom. When you make changes in either of the views, the other automatically updates.

SHOW DESIGN VIEW BUTTON

The core of Dreamweaver's WYSIWYG (what you see is what you get) authoring system, the Show Design View button displays your creation visually (opposed to the underlying HTML source code). When Dreamweaver is first launched, the Show Design View button is automatically toggled.

DOCUMENT TITLE Title:

You can give your document a title by entering a name into the Document Title field.

FILE MANAGEMENT BUTTON

By clicking the File Status button, you activate a drop-down menu that grants you access to a series of site-specific commands. For specific information on each of these commands, see Chapter 12, "Managing and Publishing Your Site with Dreamweaver."

PREVIEW/DEBUG IN BROWSER BUTTON

By clicking the Preview/Debug in Browser button, you can preview your page in any of the target browsers, debug your page, or edit the list of current target browsers.

REFRESH DESIGN VIEW BUTTON

The Refresh Design View button allows you to synchronize Design and Code view (while still in Code view) without switching back into Design view.

REFERENCE BUTTON

The Reference button automatically opens the Reference panel. The Reference panel will be covered later in this chapter.

CODE NAVIGATION BUTTON

The Code Navigation drop-down menu allows you to select and locate (in Code View only) any given JavaScript or VB Script functions in your page.

VIEW OPTIONS BUTTON

The View Options drop-down menu lets you access a series of options specific to either Code or Design view. In Code view, the options include Word Wrap, Line Numbers, Highlight Invalid, Syntax Coloring, and Auto Indent. In Design view, the options include Hide All Visual Aids, Visual Aids (which lets you turn specific visual aids on and off), Head Content, Rulers, Grid, and Tracing Image.

The Standard Toolbar

The Standard Toolbar, which by default isn't visible, can be accessed by going to View → Toolbars → Standard. With it, you can access some of Dreamweaver MX's generic program functions such as New, Open, Save, Save All, Cut, Copy, Paste, Undo, and Redo.

The Property Inspector

The Property Inspector is probably the most frequently used tool in Dreamweaver. Essentially, it serves as a doorway to the properties of any given object, be it a table, an image, or a string of text.

Its power lies in the fact that it is a dynamic tool, meaning that the options displayed change depending on the object you select. For example, if you select a string of text, you'll be able to change font, color, and size. But when you click a table, the Property Inspector changes to permit you to work with table properties such as number of rows and columns, relative dimensions, border thickness and color, and cell content alignment. So, you see, it's a pretty powerful and useful tool. To access the Property Inspector, go to Windows → Properties.

To access less common attributes of a given object with the Property Inspector, click the expander arrow (the down-pointing arrow in the bottom right-hand corner of the Property Inspector).

The Insert Bar

Aside from the Property Inspector, the Insert bar (Window → Insert), formerly known as the Object Palette, is probably one of the most widely used tools in Dreamweaver MX. Clicking one of the icons, all of which are organized under specific category-based tabs, provides a quick and easy way to insert almost any object into your document.

Panels

The majority of task-specific tools in Dreamweaver reside in a series of handy panels, all of which are accessible through the program's Window drop-down menu. In the following section, you'll be introduced to each panel. You'll find a far more detailed exploration of how each works in future chapters.

Before continuing, however, there are some things that should be noted about panels. While each panel has a different function, they all have some common characteristics. First, all panels

can be docked, a process you'll explore in the "Customizing Panels" section later in this chapter. Second, most panels have a drop-down options menu that is accessible by clicking the small icon in a given panel's top right-hand corner. While you'll find that the options in each panel's options pop-up menu will be unique to that panel, there are several common options, including Help, Rename Panel Group, Maximize Panel Group, and Close Panel Group.

WORKING WITH THE NEW PANEL PARADIGM AND THE BOOK'S EXERCISES

Because of Dreamweaver MX's groovy new workspace, there are any number of different permutations and combinations for the configuration of the interface. As a result, the workspace configuration that you're using might be slightly different from the one I used when I wrote this book, and therefore, there are a few things you should keep in mind as you work your way through the book. First, in many of the step-by-step processes, you'll be first asked to open a given panel. If the given panel is docked into the underlying interface (something we'll discuss later in this chapter), it will be brought to the forefront of the Panel Group in which it is located. However, if you previously created a floating Panel Group in which the intended panel was located, it will appear (or pop up) "above" the interface. The bottom line is that, however your workspace is configured, opening a panel using the process outlined in this book gives you access to it.

The Assets Panel

As websites have grown in complexity, managing media assets has become an increasingly daunting task. Any website can have hundreds of images, audio files, and multimedia files. The Assets panel provides a convenient way to view all colors, external URLs, scripts, Flash files, Shockwave files, QuickTime files, Templates, and Library items in a central location.

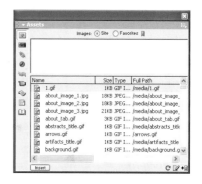

Each asset can be first viewed in the preview window of the Assets panel and then easily added to your web page by dragging it into the Document Window. To access the Assets panel, go to Window → Assets. It's important to note that the Asset panel will only work on a previously defined local site.

The Behavior Panel

For those who might be intimidated by the prospect of having to hand code non-HTML script directly into their document's HTML, there's the Behavior panel.

Definitely one of the most exciting features in Dreamweaver, the Behavior panel gives you the ability to seamlessly integrate JavaScript-based Dynamic HTML, called *Behaviors* in Dreamweaver, directly into your document. To access the Behavior panel, go to Window → Behaviors.

To find out more about Behaviors, the Behaviors panel, or advanced DHTML-based interactivity, see Chapter 15, "Adding Advanced Interactivity with Behaviors."

The Code Inspector

The Code Inspector, like Code View (accessible by clicking the Show Code View button in the Toolbar) is an additional way for you to get direct access to your document's underlying HTML source code.

To access the Code Inspector, go to Window → Others → Code Inspector.

The Code Inspector is an alternate version of the Code View—the only real difference is that it pops up in a panel rather than the Document Window itself. In addition, the Code Inspector shares a series of buttons (most of which access a drop-down menu) in common with the Toolbar: namely, File Management, Preview/Debug in Browser, Refresh, Reference, Code Navigation, and View Options.

The CSS Styles Panel

Cascading Style Sheets (CSS) are one of the many fine features of Dynamic HTML. Designed to let you exert total control over text in your HTML document, CSS are quite advantageous because they allow you to sidestep all the traditional limitations of regular HTML-based text formatting.

In Dreamweaver MX, Cascading Style Sheets are created, formatted, and manipulated using the CSS panel. To access the CSS Styles panel, go to Window → CSS Styles.

You will learn how to create, manipulate, and manage Cascading Style Sheets in Chapter 13, "Cascading Style Sheets."

The Frames Panel

Frames, one of the most widely used layout techniques, works by partitioning the user's browser window into a series of sections (or frames) in which different HTML documents are displayed. While you partition your HTML document into frames with either the Insert bar or the Modify menu, you manipulate and manage frames using the Frames panel.

To access the Frames panel, go to Window → Others → Frames panel.

Chapter 8, "Framing Your Page," will cover frames.

The History Panel

The History panel is a handy tool that keeps a record of all the actions you've performed in an active HTML document. While the History panel lets you undo any action or series of actions, its true power lies in its ability to record and replay any actions you've previously carried out within a page, thereby automating tasks that could otherwise provide to be lengthy and complicated. The history panel can also be used to backtrack if you've made an error.

To open the History panel, go to Window → Others → History.

The HTML Styles Panel

An HTML Style is a user-defined group of text-specific HTML tags that, in Dreamweaver MX, can be applied to any selected string of text in your document. By using Dreamweaver MX's HTML Styles panel, you can save text and paragraph formatting and then reapply it to any text in any document.

To access the HTML Styles panel, go to Window → HTML Styles.

The Layers Panel

One of the many drawbacks of traditional HTML layout and design is the inability to position elements exactly where you want them. One of the many great features of Dynamic HTML is the ability to exert pixel-precise control over your layout, positioning objects and elements with an incredible amount of control, thereby offering the kind of flexibility enjoyed by traditional print designers.

In Dreamweaver MX, this pixel-precise positioning is accomplished through the use of Layers, which are, in part, controlled and manipulated by the Layers panel.

To access the Layers panel, go to Window → Others → Layers.

For more information on using the Styles panel, turn to Chapter 4, "Adding and Manipulating Text." For more about layers, see Chapter 14, "Absolute Positioning with Layers."

The Library

As mentioned previously, Dreamweaver MX is as much a site design tool as an individual page design tool. As such, when you are working with an entire site (of any significant size), you'll find that you end up using the same elements (blocks of text, links, images, and so on).

This is where the Library comes in.

The Library serves as a central repository for any elements you'd like to reuse and update frequently. These library items can be drawn from the Library and placed in your document. When you do so, Dreamweaver MX inserts a copy of that item into the document and then adds a comment referencing the original item sitting in the Library. The reference makes it possible for you to change all the linked "children" library items used throughout your site by changing their "parent" in the Library.

To access the Library, go to Window → Assets and then click the Library button .

> The Library itself isn't really a discrete panel per se, it's a subsection of the Assets panel. For more information, go to Chapter 9, "Reusable Elements: Library Items and Templates."

The Reference Panel

The Reference panel is a built-in collection of documents designed to give you an available (and fully browsable) repository of knowledge pertaining to HTML tags, Cascading Style

Sheets, and JavaScript. One of the especially cool things about the Reference panel is that you can download new "libraries" covering such topics as ASP from Macromedia (`http://www.macromedia.com`).

To access the Reference panel, go to Window → Reference. Alternatively, you can click the Reference button in the Document Window's Toolbar.

The Site Panel

While Dreamweaver MX is a great tool for creating discrete web pages, it also includes some enormously useful tools designed to help you create, collaborate on, and manage web*sites*. Of these, you will probably find yourself using the Site panel the most.

To access the Site panel, go to Window → Site. Alternatively, you can go to Site → Site Files.

> By default, if you haven't already defined a local site (something that will be discussed later in the "Setting Up a Local Site" section), Dreamweaver MX will open the program's tutorial site.

If you've already defined a local site, you can open it by going to Site → Open Site → and then choosing from the list of local sites in the menu.

Designed to be a central location from which you can carry out standard file maintenance procedures such as creating new HTML documents, deleting and moving files, and creating folders, the Site panel is extremely handy when you want to exert total control over your HTML creations.

Even beyond this, however, the Site panel lets you structure groups of related files (HTML, images, and so on) into a local site that sits on your hard drive. You'll spend time later in this chapter exploring exactly how to set up a local site using the Site panel.

In addition to the benefits that come from working with a local site, the Site panel also contains an integrated FTP client that lets you move the files from the local site on your hard drive to a remote server without leaving the Dreamweaver MX environment. Once you've gone though the steps necessary to set up a remote site (something you'll look at later in Chapter 12), you can invoke a whole series of tools (such as the Check In/Check Out feature and Design Notes) that allow you to work collaboratively with a team of other designers.

The Templates Panel

Much like the Library panel, the Templates panel is designed to facilitate the creation of an entire site, as opposed to a single HTML document. A template is an HTML document upon which you can base multiple pages. Templates are best used in situations where you want to create a series of pages with an identical design. All you need to do is create a template, complete with all design elements (such as a navigation scheme, images, and so on), apply the template to a series of blank documents, and then add page specific content (like text) to each of the pages.

The Template panel, which is a subset of the Assets panel, is used to create, manage, and manipulate the templates associated with your local site.

To open the Templates panel, go to Window → Assets and click the Templates button .

If you want to learn more about Templates and the Template panel, see Chapter 9.

The Timeline

The Timeline is Dreamweaver MX's built-in tool for creating Dynamic HTML–based animations. The animations themselves are created by a frame-based system in concert with Layers and JavaScript.

To access the Timeline, go to Window → Others → Timeline.

For more about the Timeline, see Chapter 16, "Animating with the Timeline Tool."

The Sitespring Panel

Sitespring is Macromedia's new groupware tool. Designed as a tool that multiple design team members can use to track digital assets, communicate, maintain versioning, and create project schedules, Sitespring runs off a central server as opposed to the user's machine. The Sitespring panel, which is accessible by going to Window → Sitespring, lets you log in directly to a Sitespring server from within Dreamweaver MX.

The Components Panel

Accessible by going to Window → Components, the Components panel allows you to inspect, add, or modify code for JavaBeans, Macromedia ColdFusion components, or web services.

The Databases Panel

The Databases panel is a vital tool in creating and manipulating dynamic database-driven applications in Dreamweaver MX. With it, you can make a database connection and explore the structure of your database.

To access the Databases panel, go to Window → Databases. For more information about using the Databases panel, see Chapter 17, "Setting the Groundwork for Your Dynamic Database-Driven Application."

The Bindings Panel

The Bindings panel is an extremely important tool for creating dynamic database-driven sites. It allows you to create and manipulate sources of dynamic content. For more information on the Bindings panel, see Chapter 18, "Displaying and Manipulating Data from Your Database."

To access the Bindings panel, go to Window → Bindings.

The Server Behaviors panel

The Server Behaviors panel is the primary tool for adding discreet blocks of server side code to your pages. Accessed by going to Windows → Server Behaviors, the Server Behaviors panel is one of the most important tools for creating dynamic content in Dreamweaver MX.

If you are interested in learning more about server behaviors and how to use the Server Behaviors panel, see Chapter 18.

Customizing the Dreamweaver MX Environment

Dreamweaver offers you the opportunity to personalize its working environment. In this section, you'll explore some of the more popular ways in which you can go about customizing Dreamweaver's various preferences.

Editing Keyboard Shortcuts

Keyboard shortcuts are a quick and easy way to access a program's various functions. Until now, most programs only offered the user an immutable set of shortcuts. However, Dreamweaver MX offers a Keyboard Shortcuts editor that allows you to create your own shortcuts, edit existing shortcuts, or choose from the fixed list of shortcut sets. To access the Keyboard Shortcuts editor, select Edit → Keyboard Shortcuts.

To redefine a command's shortcut:

1. Go to Edit → Keyboard Shortcuts to open up the Keyboard Shortcuts editor.

2. If it isn't already selected, choose Dreamweaver MX from the Current Set drop-down menu (at the top of the Keyboard Shortcuts editor).

3. Click the Duplicate Set button ⊞ (to the right of the Current Set drop-down menu).

4. When the Duplicate Set dialog box appears, enter a name into the Name of Duplicate Set field and click OK. Notice that the name of the duplicate set you just created appears in the Current Set drop-down menu.

5. Choose the group of commands from the Commands drop-down menu with which you'd like to work.

6. If you choose Menu Commands or Site panel, click the plus sign to expand the command category (File, Edit, View, Insert, and so on) with which you want to work. If you choose any of the additional options in the Commands drop-down menu, go directly to step 7.

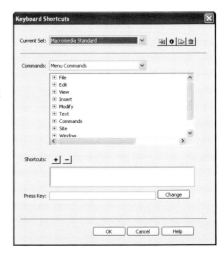

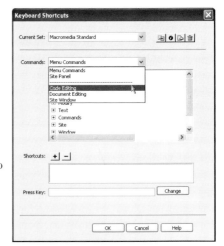

7. Select the specific command you want. Notice that the existing shortcuts attached to that command appear to the right of the command (the shortcut will also appear in the Shortcuts text box shown in the image on the left).

8. Select the command's existing shortcut in the Shortcuts text box.

9. Click the Remove Shortcut (–) button 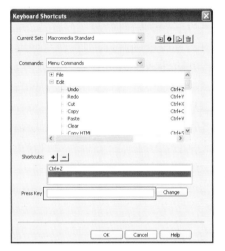 to strip the command's existing shortcut.

10. Press the Add Shortcut (+) button 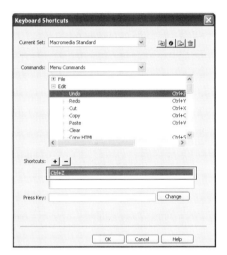; the Press Key field will automatically go live as in the image on the right.

11. Press the key combination you want to add; the key combination will appear in the Press Key field.

12. Click the Change button to assign the new shortcut to the command.

> If your key combination is already assigned to another command, Flash will alert you and let you either reassign the shortcut or cancel it.

13. When you finish, click OK, and the new keyboard shortcut will be assigned.

Defining an External Editor

One of the neat things about Dreamweaver MX is that it integrates well with external editors. Whether you're using an image-editing program (like Fireworks MX or Photoshop) or an HTML text-editing program (like BBEdit or HomeSite), Dreamweaver MX lets you define a series of editors. These editors allow you to open a given object (an image, for example), edit that object, exit the external editor, and immediately view the changes you've made. For our purposes, we're going to look at how to define an external media editor instead of a text editor. To define a media editor, follow these steps:

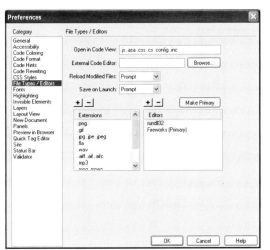

1. Go to Edit → Preferences.

2. Select File Types/Editors from the Category list box.

3. In the Extensions list, select the file type for which you want to define an external editor.

4. Click the plus (+) button above the Editors list.

5. When the Select External Editor dialog box appears, locate and select the file of the editor you want to associate to the file type.

6. Click OK.

To launch your external editor, either select the image and go to Edit → Edit with External Editor or click Edit in the Property Inspector. To make a program your primary editor, select it in the Editors list and click the Make Primary button.

Perhaps one of the most exciting things about Dreamweaver is how it works in concert with Macromedia Fireworks MX. You can easily place images and HTML produced in Fireworks straight into a Dreamweaver document. Fireworks can then be launched directly from within Dreamweaver to edit the source of the placed images or HTML.

Adding Window Size Presets

Earlier in the chapter, you were introduced to the Window Size indicator and how you can use the drop-down menu to choose from a list of preset Window Sizes. Now you'll learn how you can add your own Window Size presets to the drop-down menu. To do so, follow these steps:

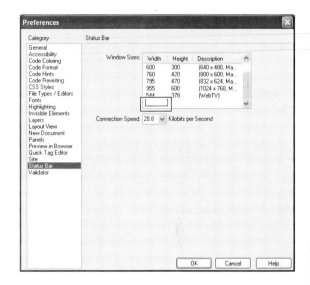

1. Go to Edit → Preferences.

2. Select Status Bar from the Category list box.

3. When you click your mouse below the list of preset Window Sizes, a blank edit box will appear. Enter the new width in the Width column.

4. Press Tab and enter the new height in the Height column.

5. Press Tab and enter a description of your custom settings.

6. Click OK.

Changing the Document Size/Download Time Defaults

In addition to being able to change the Window Size, you can also change the speed of the modem that determines the Download Time displayed in the Document Size/Download Time section of the Status Bar. To do this, follow these steps:

1. Open the Preferences dialog box (Edit → Preferences).

2. Select Status Bar from the Category list box.

3. Just below the Window Size Field, you'll see a drop-down menu labeled Connection Speed (Kilobytes per Second) from which you can choose the speed of modem you wish.

4. Click OK.

Customizing Panels

With the increasing complexity of the Dreamweaver MX, screen real estate has become increasingly precious. It's to Macromedia's great credit that the new Dreamweaver MX user interface's elements fit so seamlessly and efficiently together to create an extremely usable work environment.

One of the most obviously useful features of Dreamweaver MX's new-and-improved interface is its panels that, as mentioned before, can be combined into different Panel Groups and then collapsed/expanded as your needs require. There are 10 Panel Groups (Advanced Layout, Application, Answers, Code, Code Inspector, Design, History, Results, Timeline, and Welcome) into which you can group different panels. You can also easily create new custom Panel Groups.

In the following section, you'll learn how to make the most of the new panel paradigm by grouping panels, creating new Panel Groups, and expanding and collapsing panels.

Grouping Panels

When you group a panel, you physically combine it with another element of the interface. If you group two floating panels, you create a floating "mega" panel (see Figure 2.4).

Figure 2.4

The CSS Styles panel and Site panel have been combined to form a floating "mega" panel.

You can also group a panel with a Panel Group in the underlying interface to create an area where all of your commonly used panels reside, as illustrated in Figure 2.5. This process is often referred to as docking.

Ultimately, grouping panels makes it considerably easier for you to access tools and information while maximizing your workspace.

Figure 2.5

Dreamweaver MX interface with docked panels groups

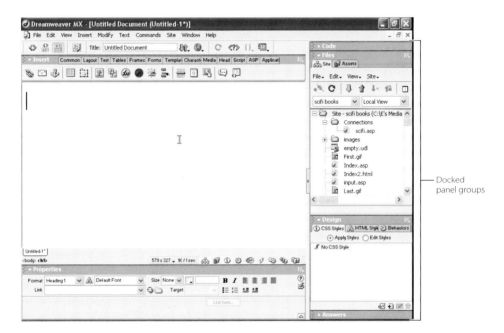

Docked panel groups

To group a panel with an existing Panel Group:

1. Open the panel you would like to group with an existing Panel Group.

2. Cmd/right-click on the panel's tab.

3. When the context menu appears, select Group *panel name* With and choose the Panel Group with which you'd like to combine the panel from the menu of available options.

You can easily rename an existing Panel Group by Cmd/right-clicking any of the panels within the Panel Group whose name you want to change. When the context menu appears, select Rename Panel Group. When the Rename Panel Group dialog box appears, enter a new name into the Panel Group Name field and click OK.

Collapsing and Expanding Panel Groups

As mentioned, the Dreamweaver MX interface has become a little crowded. As a result, Macromedia has provided users with the ability to expand and collapse panels (see Figure 2.6), thereby economizing on space while still keeping the necessary tools at their fingertips.

To expand a collapsed Panel Group (or collapse an expanded Panel Group), click the panel's name in the title bar. It's that easy.

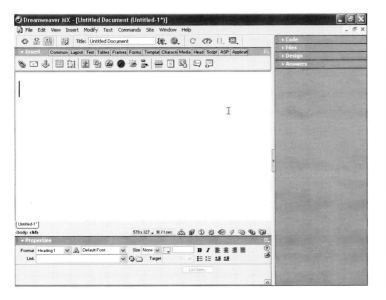

Figure 2.6

The left screen shows a series of panels that have been collapsed, and the right one shows the same panels expanded.

Setting Up a Local Site

As mentioned previously, Dreamweaver is as much a website creation and management tool as it is an individual web page creation tool. Here, website means a group of linked HTML pages with a shared topic and similar design. While you can certainly create a stand-alone page, Dreamweaver has a host of great tools, some of which have already been briefly covered earlier in this chapter, designed to help you create, manipulate, and manage whole sites. All of these tools revolve around the initial creation of a local site.

The local site (which will include all the files in your site) should reside in a separate folder on your hard drive, mainly because when you get to the point where you want to establish a remote site and upload your creation to a web server, you'll upload the entire site's folder. By doing this, you ensure that your local site won't be missing any components when you upload it to a remote web server. When you set up your local site, you'll also be able to track and maintain your links.

Its important to note that without having set up a local site, you'll be unable to set up a *remote* site, and therefore, won't be able to take advantage of Dreamweaver's integrated FTP client or invoke the series of tools (such as the Check In/Check Out feature and Design Notes) that allow you to work collaboratively with a team of other designers on a site residing on a remote web server. You will get ample time to explore the intricacies of creating and manipulating a remote site in Chapter 12.

> If you are inserting elements (images, multimedia files, and so on) that reside outside of the folder in which your local site sits, Dreamweaver will always prompt you to save them to your local site. If you want your site to be complete when you upload it to your remote server, be sure to take advantage of Dreamweaver's prompt, and move external files over to your local site.

In Dreamweaver MX, there are two ways of setting up a local site. The first, which is outlined in the following section, involves manually inputting the local site information into the Site Definition dialog box. The second, which is new to Dreamweaver MX, involves using the Site Definition Wizard, a handy-dandy little tool that walks you through the process of setting up a local site (and also walks you through setting up a remote site and a testing server, for that matter).

Defining Your Site

The first thing you must do when you set up a local site is tell Dreamweaver where on your hard drive you want your site to reside. You also need to input some additional information about the structure and properties of your local site.

Manually Setting Local Info

Setting Local Info entails telling Dreamweaver where your local site will be stored on your hard drive. To do this, follow these steps:

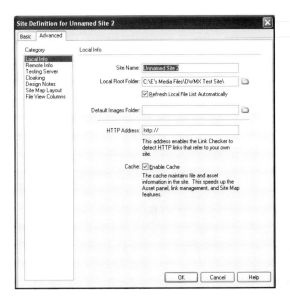

1. Open the Site Definition dialog box (Site → New Site).

2. If you haven't already, click the Advanced tab at the top of the Site Definition dialog box.

3. Make sure Local Info is selected in the Category list box.

4. In the Site Name field, enter the name you want to give to your site.

    The site name is not your filename or your page title; it's a name that is used when you're working with the Dreamweaver site tools. When you upload your site to a remote web server, the name won't appear anywhere on your pages. Giving each a unique name is very handy if you are working with more than one local site—it will help you avoid getting mixed up.

5. Click the Browse button (to the right of the Local Root Folder field). When the file navigation screen appears, locate and select the folder on your hard drive where you want your new local site to reside.

6. If you want the structure and content of the site to refresh automatically every time you copy a file into your local site, click the Refresh Local File List Automatically option.

> If you leave the Refresh Local File List Automatically option unchecked, Dreamweaver will copy over files to your local site more quickly.

7. If you are planning on storing all of the images in your site in single folder, click the Browse button (to the right of the Default Image Folder field). When the Choose Local Images Folder dialog box appears, navigate to where the folder is located and click Select.

> For a default image folder to work properly, you need to make sure it's within the local root folder of your local site—otherwise, when you upload your site to a web server, the images won't go with it, and you'll have nothing but broken images.

8. If you know what the URL, or *domain name*, of your site will ultimately be after you've uploaded it to a remote web server, enter it in the HTTP Address field.

> If you fill out the HTTP Address field, Dreamweaver can verify links within the site that use absolute URLs. We'll talk more about absolute and relative URLs in Chapter 5, "Linking Documents with Hyperlinks."

9. Click OK.

After you finish entering all the local site information, the Site Window will open automatically. On the right side of the window, you'll see your local site. If the section is blank, you need not worry: your local site doesn't have any files in it yet.

Setting up a Local Site with the Site Definition Wizard

Instead of manually setting up your local site, you can take advantage of the Site Definition Wizard, a new feature in Dreamweaver MX. If you're new to Dreamweaver, the Site Definition Wizard might be a good choice to start with. However, in the grand scheme of things, setting your site information manually gives you more control over the process.

1. Open the Site Definition dialog box (Site → New Site).

2. Click the Basic tab at the top of the Site Definition dialog box.

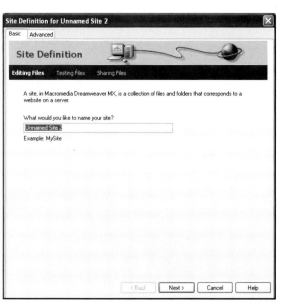

3. When the first screen of the Site Definition Wizard appears, enter the name of your site into the field and click Next.

4. Click the No Server Technology radio button. While you very well might be interested in creating a dynamic database-driven site (a topic covered in Part IV), I don't want to complicate things at this stage.

5. Click Next.

6. Click the Edit Local Copies on My Machine radio button. While you can set up a remote site on this screen, we won't cover that here (for more information on this topic, see Chapter 12) .

7. From here, you need to tell Dreamweaver MX where on your hard drive all of the files in your local site are going to be stored (this is called the Local Root folder). Click the Browse button (to the right of the Where on Your Computer field). When the file navigation screen appears, locate and select the folder on your hard drive where you want your new local site to reside.

8. Click Next.

9. Select the I'll Set This Up Later option from the drop-down menu.

10. Click Next.

11. From here, the Site Definition Wizard will give you a rundown of the parameters of your local site. If you see something wrong, back up to the appropriate point in the process by clicking the Back button. If you are happy with the results, click the Done button.

Setting Site Map Layout

The Site Map is a handy feature that produces a visual representation (a reverse branching tree) of the structure of your website (see Figure 2.7). Located in the left side of your local Site panel (after you click the Site panel's Expand/Collapse button), the Site Map not only lets you get a comprehensive structural representation of your entire site, but also lets you add new files or add, modify, or delete links between files in your site.

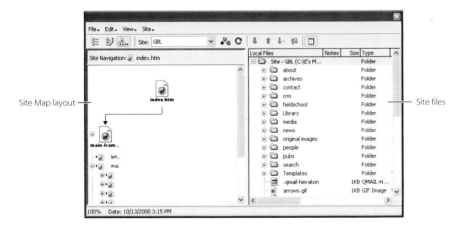

Figure 2.7

The Site Map layout displays the structure of your site as a reverse branching tree issuing forth from a single page—your home page.

In the following section, you are going to learn how to define and view your site map, manipulate the Site Map layout, work with files in the Site Map layout, and save the Site Map as an image.

A Site Map will only function when you're working with a local site, not a remote site.

DEFINING AND VIEWING YOUR SITE MAP LAYOUT

Before you can actually work with, or even view, your Site Map layout, you first need to define a home page (the front door for your website, so to speak) from which the reverse branching tree-like structure issues forth. The following steps assume you have already defined a local site using the procedure described earlier in this chapter. You certainly don't have to start with an already defined site. However, given the fact that newly defined local sites rarely have anything in them, they really don't have anything to visualize in a site map.

1. Open the Define Sites dialog box (Site → Define Sites).

2. Select the site you want to work with, and click Edit.

3. When the Site Definition dialog box opens, click the Advanced tab and select Site Map Layout from the Category list.

4. Click the Browse button (to the right of the Home Page field).

5. When the Choose Home Page dialog box pops up, navigate to the file which will serve as the home page in your site map layout, and click Open.

> Another neat thing about Dreamweaver is that, even if you haven't set a home page, it still tries to create a site map. In this event, it looks for an index.html or index.htm file on which to base your site map.

Now that you've established a home page, you can view your Site Map layout. To do this, follow these steps:

1. Make sure you are currently working in the local site for which you set the home page. Open the Site panel (Window → Site Files).

2. Click the Site panel's Expand/Collapse button 　．

3. Click the Site Map button 　 (to the left of the Site Name drop-down menu). This will cause the Site Map to appear in the left-hand portion of the Site Window.

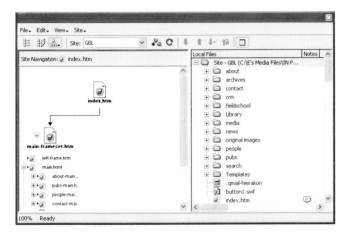

Instead of choosing Site Files from the Site drop-down menu, you can also choose Site Map. This automatically opens the Site Window with the Site Map already visible, thereby saving you the step of having to hit the Site Map button in the Site Window.

MANIPULATING THE SITE MAP LAYOUT

You certainly aren't stuck with the default look of the Site Map. There are a number of operations you can perform to alter the appearance of the site map so it's easier for you to work with and interpret. To manipulate the Site Map Layout:

1. Open the Define Sites dialog box (Site → Define Sites) and select the site whose Site Map you want to manipulate, and click Edit.

2. Click the Site Definition dialog box's Advanced tab. From the Category menu, select Site Map Layout.

3. From here, you can manipulate the Site Map's various options in order to alter its appearance:

- By entering a value into the Number of Columns field, you can set the number of pages that are displayed in a single horizontal row in the Site Window. The higher the number, the fewer rows in the Site Window, and the more your Site Map will look like a reverse branching tree.

- By entering a number into the Column Width, you set the width (in pixels) of each vertical column in the Site Window. A higher number results in more of any given filename or title being displayed. If you enter a lower number, filenames/titles will be truncated.

The maximum column width is 1000, while the minimum is 70; you can have a maximum of 9999 columns and a minimum of 1.

- By selecting the File Names option, each of the files in the Site Window will be identified by their actual filename. Conversely, if you select the Page Titles option, the files in the Site Window will be identified by their page title.

- By selecting the Display Files Marked as Hidden option, you can display files that have been hidden by the user (with the View menu). If this option is selected, hidden files are displayed in italics.

- The Display Dependent Files option displays all of the files (all non-HTML content) associated with any given HTML file in your local site.

WORKING WITH FILES IN THE SITE MAP LAYOUT

The Site Map is not just a simple tool for visualizing the structure of your site; it can also be used to carry out some limited editing tasks on the files in your local site.

To add a new file to the site (and automatically link it to an existing file in the hierarchy):

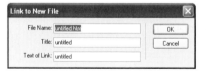

1. With the Site Map open, select the file to which you want to link the new file.

2. Go to Site → Link to New File.

3. When the Link to New File dialog box opens, enter the filename of the new file into the New File field.

Remember to include the proper file extension, either .html or .htm. If you don't, Dreamweaver will be unable to open the newly created file.

4. Enter a title for the page into the Title field. This sets the page's title just as if you were doing it in the Modify Page Properties dialog box (something you'll explore next chapter).

5. Enter some text into the Text of Link field. This text will serve as the hyperlink to the newly created site, which is inserted into the body of the selected file.

6. When you finish, click OK.

In addition to linking a newly created file to an existing file, you can also edit the page titles of the files in your Site Window. To do this, follow these steps:

> You won't be able to modify the page title in your Site Window if you haven't selected the Page Titles option in the Site Map layout section of the Site Definition dialog box.

1. With the Site Window open and the site map visible, select the file whose title you want to modify.

2. From here, there are a couple of things you can do:

   - Go to File → Rename (Windows) or Site → Rename (Mac). After doing this, you'll notice that the selected file's title becomes editable. Type in a new title and click your cursor anywhere off the file when you've finished.

   - After having selected the file, click the filename, type in a new title when it becomes editable, and click anywhere off the file with your cursor when you're finished.

3. From here, the Update Files dialog box will appear. Click the Update button, and all the files that reference the file whose name you changed will automatically update so you won't have any broken links.

SAVING THE SITE MAP AS AN IMAGE

The Site Map is quite a handy little tool for visualizing the structure of your site. However, there is a distinct possibility that somewhere along the line you are going to want to be able to view the Site Map *outside* of Dreamweaver, say, to share it with a colleague or a team member. This is pretty easy, as Dreamweaver lets you save your Site Map as an image. To view the Site Map outside of Dreamweaver:

1. With the Site panel open, go to File → Save Site Map.

2. When the Save Site Map dialog box opens, enter a name in the File Name field, select either .bmp or .png from File Type drop-down menu, navigate to the location on your hard drive to which you want to save the file, and click Save.

If you are using a Mac, the steps are a little different:

1. Go to Site → Site Map View → Save Site Map → Save Site Map as PICT. Alternatively, go to Site → Site Map View → Save Site Map → Save Site Map as JPEG.

2. From here, navigate to the location on your hard drive to which you want to image to be saved, enter a filename into the File Name field, and click Save.

Editing an Existing Site

If you've already defined your site but you want to go back and change some of its information, follow these steps:

1. Open the Edit Sites dialog box (Site → Edit Sites).

2. Choose from the list the site you want to access and click Edit.

3. This will open the Site Definition dialog box from which you can make any changes you want.

4. Click OK.

Deleting an Existing Site

After you've established a local site (or a series of local sites), you may decide to delete it. If so, follow these steps:

1. Open the Edit Sites dialog box (Site → Edit Sites).

2. Choose from the list the site you want to delete, and click Remove.

3. When you do this, a dialog box pops up, asking whether you indeed want to delete the selected site. If you wish to continue, click OK. If you don't want to delete the site, just click Cancel.

If you delete a local site, you cannot undo your action.

Inspiration: Design and Technique

Through the use of inspirational digital content and innovative design, **digital**organism (see Figure 2.8), a full-service multimedia and design studio based in Baltimore, strives to merge cutting-edge aesthetics and functionality to advance corporate identity and branding. **digital**organism's Flash-based interface, the center of which is a stunning 3D DNA menu system, is remarkably stylish and sleek. Exploration is made easy and entertaining by the site's integrated navigation system.

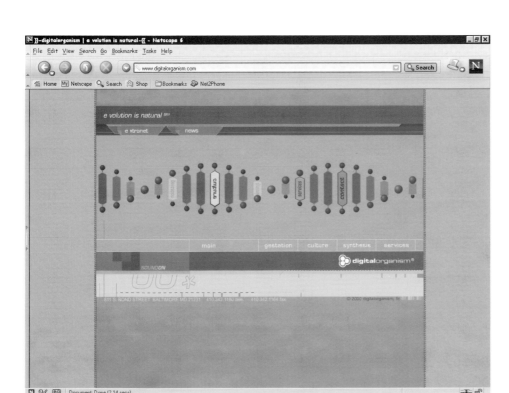

Figure 2.8

digitalorganism

Summary

This chapter explored Dreamweaver's interface. Further, it introduced you to some ways to customize your working environment. Finally, you learned one of the most important aspects of Dreamweaver: setting up a local site. Next up, in Chapter 3, you'll start laying the foundations for a web-designed site by leaning, among other things, how to manipulate overall page properties.

Setting Up and Managing Your Page

Now that you're familiar with Dreamweaver's environment, including how to make it work the way you want it to and setting up and customizing your local site, there are some skills you need to learn before you jump into adding content to your wondrous digital creation. In Chapter 2, "Starting Up Dreamweaver," you learned how to adjust settings for the entire site. In this chapter, you'll learn how to manage individual HTML documents by setting and altering the parameters for an entire page. You'll also learn how to open and save documents, as well as set a target browser and preview your creation—a must for anyone serious about cross-browser compatibility.

- Opening and saving documents

- Naming your page

- Changing background color and adding a background image

- Setting text and hyperlink color

- Setting a target browser and previewing your work

Opening a New Document

By default, Dreamweaver opens a new document when it's launched. However, at some point while working in Dreamweaver, you'll probably need to open an additional new document. To open a new document:

1. Open the New Document dialog box (File → New).

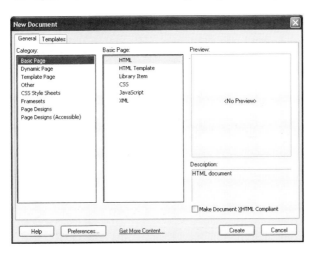

2. Make sure the General tab is selected.

3. In the Category list box, select the category of document you would like to create.

> If you want to use an existing predesigned page layout, select either Page Designs or Page Designs (Accessible).

4. Select the specific type of document from the Basic Page list box (to the right of the Category list box). If applicable, you'll see a preview of the document in the Preview section of the New Document dialog box.

5. Click Create.

You can also create a new document in the Site panel:

1. Go to Site → Edit Sites, choose from the list of sites, and click Done.

2. After the Site panel opens, Cmd/right-click the folder in which you want to create a new file. Choose New File from the menu that opens (seen in the figure on the left).

3. Type in the name you want for the new file (see the figure on the right).

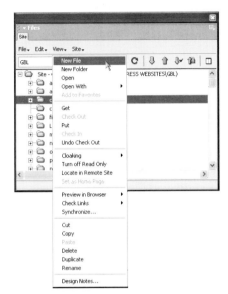

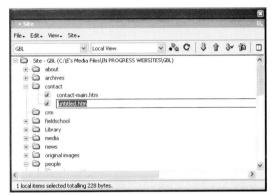

When you type in the new name, make sure it has a file extension of HTML or HTM. If it doesn't, Dreamweaver won't recognize it as an HTML document.

Opening an Existing Document

After you've worked with Dreamweaver for a while, you'll accumulate files that you work with on a regular basis. There are two simple ways to reopen existing documents:

1. Open the File Navigation screen (File → Open).

2. Navigate to the area where your file is and select it.

   To open an existing file with the Site Window:

1. Go to Site → Open Site and choose from the list of sites.

2. Navigate through the folders and double-click the file you want to open.

> While you will be able to open a file through the File menu, you won't be able to open an existing document through the Site Window itself if the file you want to open isn't in a defined local site.

Saving a Document

Don't forget to save your documents. To do so, choose File → Save. If you have multiple documents open and you want to save one, make sure you select the appropriate document before saving. If you have multiple documents open at the same time and want to save them all in one fell swoop, choose Save All instead of Save from the File menu.

Setting Your Page Properties

Before you add content in the Document Window, you need to set the page's properties in the Page Properties dialog box. When you set the properties of a given element (text color, for example) with the Page Properties dialog box, you affect all those elements on that page. To open the Page Properties dialog box:

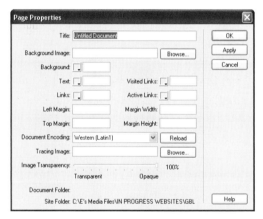

Select Modify → Page Properties.

From this point on, you are going to explore how to set the individual page properties with the Page Properties dialog box.

> An alternative way to open the Page Properties dialog is to Cmd/right-click anywhere within the Document Window and choose Page Properties from the pop-up menu.

Naming Your Page

Even though it may seem obvious, it's remarkably easy to forget to name your page. Naming your page is not the same as naming your file. The name of your page is displayed in the title bar of the browser. Leaving your page untitled will result in an unseemly "Untitled Document" in the title bar of a browser—something that should be avoided at all costs.

To title your page:

1. Open the Page Properties dialog (Modify → Page Properties).

2. Enter the title of your page in the Title field.

3. Click Apply.

4. Click OK.

You can also title your page by typing in a name in the Page Title field in the toolbar.

Setting a Background Image

You can spice up a web page by adding a background image. A background image can consist of either one large image or a smaller one that the browser tiles in a continuous pattern. If someone enlarges the browser window, the number of tiles will increase to fill all the available space.

You'll learn more about web graphics in Chapter 5, "Inserting and Controlling Images," but it's important to know that background images are no different from any other kind of web graphic. The only graphic files that can be displayed by a web browser are GIFs, JPEGs, and PNGs.

To add a background image to your page:

1. Open the Page Properties dialog box (Modify → Page Properties).

2. Click the Browse button (to the right of the Background Image field) to open the Select Image Source dialog box.

3. Navigate to the location on yo[...] your file is, click it once to se[...] Notice that a small thumbna[...] image appears in the Image P[...] you select an image.

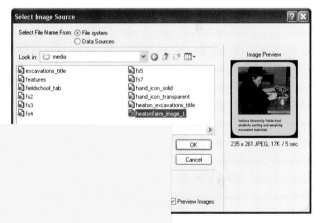

If you select an image that reside[...] will prompt you to resave it to th[...] this, see the "Setting Up a Local S[...]

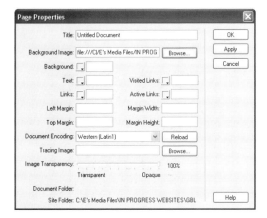

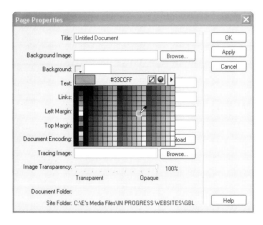

4. When you are returned to the Page Properties dialog box, notice the document's path appears in the Background Image field of the Page Properties dialog box. Click Apply and then OK.

Changing Background Color

When you start a new document, the Document Window has a white background. By default, this is the color that Dreamweaver sets as the background color for all new documents. Like background images, you can easily choose the background color you want. You do this by using the Color Palette or the Color dialog box, both of which are accessible through the Page Properties dialog box.

Using the Color Palette to Set Background Color

To change the background color of your page with the Color Palette:

1. Open the Page Properties dialog box (Modify → Page Properties).

2. Open the Color Palette by clicking the color swatch (which has the down-pointing arrow in its lower-right corner) next to the Background field.

3. Move your mouse over a color you like and click it. Notice that the color swatch in the Page Properties dialog box has changed to the color you've chosen.

4. Click Apply and then OK.

■ ■ ■ ■

DESIGN REMINDER: Web-Safe Colors

Even though most monitors out there can display at least 256 colors (most can display millions), there are really only 216 colors that all computers display exactly the same. These colors are part of what is called the web-safe color palette and make up the colors you'll find in the Dreamweaver Color Palette. If you use a color outside the web-safe color palette, the browser will convert it to the closest color it can find in your audience's computer's system palette. This means you run the risk of having your colors look slightly different from machine to machine if you stray from the web-safe color palette.

Using the Color Dialog Box to Set Background Color

If you aren't satisfied with the colors offered in the Color Palette, you can always use the
Color dialog box to mix an alternate color:

1. Open the Page Properties dialog box (Modify → Page
   Properties).

2. Open the Color Palette by clicking the color swatch
   next to the Background field.

3. Move your mouse over the open Color dialog box icon
   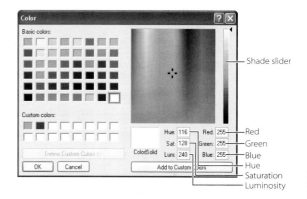 (in the top-right corner of the Color Palette) and
   click it to open the Color dialog box.

4. From here, you can choose the color you want by
   entering its corresponding numerical RGB (Red/
   Green/Blue) code. Alternatively, you can enter a
   numerical HSM (Hue/Saturation/Luminosity) or adjust
   the shade slider.

Any color you use will automatically be added to the Colors section of the Assets panel
(Window → Assets). This way, you don't run the risk of finding the perfect color only to lose it
because you didn't write down its numerical code.

Changing Text Color

Changing the color of your page's text is similar to changing your
page's background color:

1. Open the Page Properties dialog box (Modify → Page
   Properties).

2. Click the color swatch next to the Text field.

3. The Color Palette will open, allowing you to immediately
   choose the color you wish or to open and select from the
   Color dialog box.

4. Click Apply and then OK.

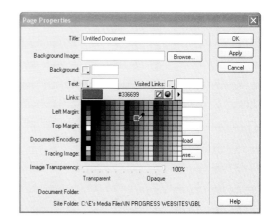

LINK, VISITED LINK, AND ACTIVE COLOR

Link color refers to the color of a hyperlink before the user interacts with it. *Visited* link color refers to the color of a hyperlink after it has been clicked by the user. The *active* link color, which is probably the least important of the various hyperlink color "states," refers to the color that the link turns between the time the user presses their mouse button down and when they release the mouse button (the click).

Changing Link Color

While changing your text color involves only one color, changing your hyperlink color involves manipulating three different colors: link color, visited link color, and active link color.

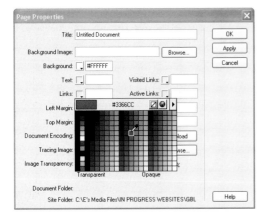

The process is the same if you're changing the regular link color, the active link color, or the visited link color:

1. Open the Page Properties dialog box (Modify → Page).

2. Click the color swatch next to the Links field (or the Active Links/Visited Links field).

3. This will open the Color Palette and allow you to choose the color you wish or to open and select from the Color dialog box.

4. Click Apply and then OK.

Working with a Tracing Image

Tracing Images is a really nifty feature in Dreamweaver. Remember back when you were a kid and you were really keen on drawing but weren't that confident about your skills? You'd sit down with a picture from a book and a piece of tracing paper and proceed to draw something that was just right. This approach to drawing by the young comes not so much from lack of skill, but from a desire to produce something that is *perfect*. Well, with tracing images, Macromedia has brought all of this back.

DESIGN REMINDER: Choosing Link Color

For the most part, the classic blue (which is the default color) underlined text is universally recognized as a link. If you change your link color to something else, there is the possibility that people might not even recognize it as a link. So, unless there is some pressing design need to change the link color (or you detest the color blue) stick with the default.

Despite all the electronic tools available, most interactive design (whether it is HTML based or rooted in another technology such as Macromedia Flash) is still conceived and fleshed out on paper before it goes anywhere near a computer screen.

The problem with this is that things on paper don't always translate to digital form exactly as the designer conceived. This is where Tracing Images come in. Essentially, you scan a pen and paper design and stick it in the background of your web page. You can then line up elements on the page exactly (or as close as they can get) to the scanned image.

A Tracing Image isn't the same thing as a background image. When you go live with your page (or preview it in a browser), the Tracing Image isn't seen. The only time it's ever visible is when you are working on your creation in the Document Window.

Follow these steps to try it:

1. Open the Page Properties dialog box (Modify → Page Properties).

2. Click the Browse button (to the right of the Tracing Image field).

3. Navigate to the appropriate file and select it. Notice that a small thumbnail preview of the image appears in the Image Preview area of the file navigation screen.

4. Click Apply.

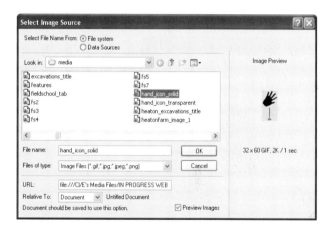

DESIGN REMINDER: Storyboards

You use storyboards to visualize your design as a complete entity on paper before you go anywhere near a computer. With them, you get a chance to see how colors interact with one another, how interface elements play off one another, how your navigational system is realized, how your visual metaphor plays out, and whether content is represented in the best way possible. Storyboards provide you with a great way to brainstorm visual ideas as well as catch any potential design problems before they become serious.

5. When you are returned to the Page Properties dialog box, you can adjust the transparency of the tracing image by using the slider.

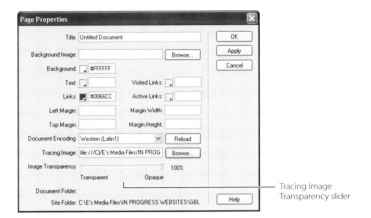

Tracing Image Transparency slider

Previewing Your Work in a Browser

After Mosaic was released, the size of the World Wide Web increased exponentially. Many software companies realized that the browser was the key to the whole shebang and quickly responded. The most notable were Microsoft and Netscape. Despite the fact that both companies are now the giants of the scene, many smaller companies still offer their own take on the browser.

You can never be absolutely sure what kind of browser is being used to view your page, and most browsers display HTML a little differently.

DESIGN REMINDER: Browser Power

As you already learned in the "Browser Madness" section of Chapter 1, "Web Design: The Big Picture," all browsers (especially Netscape and Internet Explorer) are hardly created equal. Not only do you have to contend with the same generation of browser (at this point 6 for both Netscape and IE) that do not support the same features, but you also have to deal with older browsers. This is why it's extremely important to either get to know your audience and design specifically for the browser they most commonly use, or design your page for the lowest common browser denominator. Want to know which browsers support which specific features? Check out CNET's Browser topic center at www.browsers.com.

This is where Dreamweaver's Preview in Browser function comes in. You can set it so that a simple stroke of a hotkey will load your page in a browser of your choice.

You can preview work only in a browser that you have installed on your computer.

Adding a Target Browser

Before you can preview your work in a browser, you first need to tell Dreamweaver which browsers you've loaded on your computer and which hotkeys you want to associate with them. To set a target browser, follow these steps:

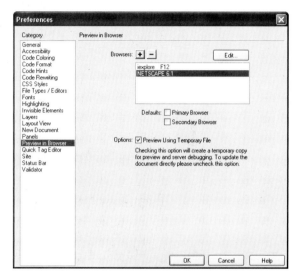

1. Open the Preferences dialog box (Edit → Preferences).

2. Select Preview in Browser from the Category list box seen in the image on top.

3. Click the plus (+) symbol to open the Add Browser dialog box shown on the bottom.

4. In the Name field, type in the browser name as you want it to appear in the browser list.

5. Click Browse to open the file navigation screen. Navigate to the browser program file and select it.

6. If you want Dreamweaver to preview a temporary copy of your document (as opposed to the document itself), click the Preview Using Temporary File check box.

7. Click OK.

Editing Your Browser List

Because there are many different browsers on the market, and new browser versions come out at a regular pace, you may find it necessary to edit your browser list so that new browsers can be added and old browsers removed:

1. Open the Preferences dialog box (Edit → Preferences).

2. Select Preview in Browser from the Category list box.

Depending on your preference, you can designate one browser as primary and another as secondary. The primary browser will be designated the default.

3. Select the browser you wish to edit and click the Edit button to open the Edit Browser dialog box.

4. Make your changes and click OK.

Launching Your Target Browser

Once you've defined your target browser and its associated hotkeys, there are two ways to preview your creation:

- Hit the hotkey you defined for the target browser. In most cases, the default for your primary browser is F12 while the default for your secondary browser is Cmd/Ctrl+F12.

- Click the Preview in Browser button in the Toolbar to open a drop-down list of target browsers to choose from.

If you've only defined one target browser in the Preferences dialog box, clicking the toolbar's Preview in Browser button will automatically launch that browser.

Inspiration: Design and Technique

Founded by Doug Chiang, the design director for the *Star Wars* prequels, Doug Chiang Studio (`www.dchiang.com`) is currently working on a film/book project called *Robota: Reign of Machines*. The website is intended to cater to those fascinated by the incredible work of Chiang, as well as to publicize and explore the studio's current project.

Robota: Reign of Machines is a 160-page "film-format" illustrated book to be published in 2002 that explores the relationship between technology and nature against the backdrop of a futuristic society.

The website (see Figure 3.1) was designed by Red Industries (`www.redindustries.com`) using a combination of Dreamweaver, Fireworks, and Flash, and it combines Chiang's compelling style of illustration with a highly intuitive navigation scheme to create an exceptionally immersive experience. The site's design masterfully combines incredibly beautiful bitmap art and audio with consistently predictable and repeating interface elements, making it easily worthy to be this chapter's inspirational design model. Prepare to be inspired!

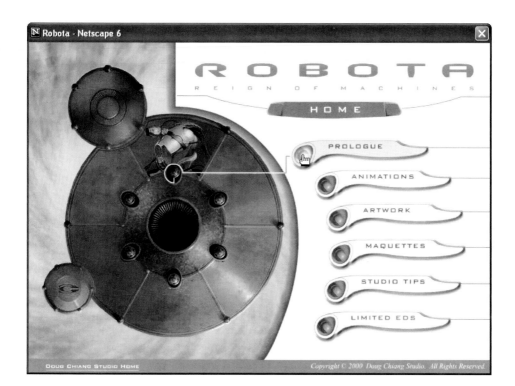

Figure 3.1

Doug Chiang Studio

Summary

This chapter covered opening and saving documents and setting page properties such as background color, page title, and text color. Most importantly, this chapter emphasized previewing your work in a browser, which is a key to any successful web design project. In the next chapter, you are going to learn how to work with the web's most basic content: text.

CHAPTER 4

Adding and Manipulating Text

When Edward Bulwer-Lytton penned the phrase, "Beneath the rule of men entirely great / The pen is mightier than the sword," in his famous early 1800s play *Richelieu*, he couldn't have foreseen the digital age. Yet his words still ring true in the day of the Web. Despite the fact that the Web is becoming an increasingly more visual medium by the second, the vast majority of the information is still textual.

In this chapter, you're going to explore how Dreamweaver MX lets you add and edit text to get your desired message across. You'll explore the following topics:

- **Creating and placing text**

- **Changing text size**

- **Changing text font and color**

- **Aligning, indenting, and outdenting text**

- **Adding Horizontal Rules**

- **Creating text lists**

- **Adding special characters**

- **Using HTML styles to format text**

- **Managing your page's textual content**

- **Creating Flash Text**

Creating and Placing Text

There really is no mystery to creating and placing text in Dreamweaver MX. Just click in the Document Window and type. It's that easy! In fact, adding text in Dreamweaver MX's visual authoring environment (as opposed to its coding environment) is just like working in a word processor. The real fun comes when you get to change the text from its default size, font, and color (which is Times New Roman/Times, black, and size 3) into something that will fit with the design of your page.

> You can also copy text from another application, switch to Dreamweaver MX, click the cursor at your chosen insertion point in the Document Window, and choose Edit → Paste as Text. Dreamweaver MX won't preserve text formatting from the other application, but it will preserve line breaks.

Manipulating Text

Manipulating text you've created in Dreamweaver MX is relatively straightforward and, for the most part, happens with either the Property Inspector or the Text menu. Changing the text size, font, color, and style are the most common changes—processes you will learn in the following sections.

Sizing Text

Web text size is not represented in the same way that digital text usually is. Instead of being measured by point size, the size of web-based text is represented using a sizing scale from 1 to 7, with 1 being the smallest size and 7 the largest. Dreamweaver MX offers two sizing systems: absolute and relative. I'll discuss them in detail in the following sections, but both systems are based on the 1–7 sizing system, which can be pretty limiting.

DESIGN REMINDER: Text, Typeface, and Fonts

When you work with text, you'll find that the words *text*, *font*, and *typeface* are often used interchangeably. Don't be fooled, however; there is a big difference between them. Text refers generally to any characters that combine to make up a written document of some sort (whether a word, a sentence, or this book). A font, on the other hand, is a complete set of characters in a particular size and style. This includes the letters, the numbers, and all of the special character you get by pressing the Shift, Option, or Cmd (Mac) or Ctrl (Win) keys. Finally, a typeface contains a series of fonts. For example, the typeface Arial contains the fonts Arial, Arial Bold, Arial Italic, and Arial Bold Italic.

Setting Absolute Text Size

There are 7 sizes in the absolute sizing system—size 1 is the smallest, and size 7 is the largest. Each size is fixed and is one increment larger than the previous.

To change the absolute size of text:

1. Select the text whose size you want to change.

2. Open the Property Inspector (Window → Properties).

3. Click the Size drop-down menu in the Property Inspector. There are three sets of numbers: –1 to –7, +1 to +7, and 1 to 7.

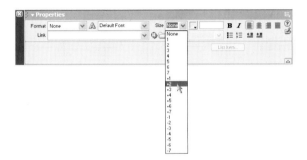

Text Size 1

Text Size 2

Text Size 3

Text Size 4

Text Size 5

Text Size 6

Text Size 7

4. Choose a size from the 1 to 7 list (these are the absolute sizes). The text will automatically change to reflect your choices.

DESIGN REMINDER: Working Around HTML Text Limitations

There are ways around the limitations of HTML text sizing. The most popular is to create an image of text. If you do this, you can make the text in your image any size and insert it into your document. Dreamweaver MX sees it as an image, not text. Additionally, you can create nonstandard text (nonstandard in the terms of size and font) using Flash Text, a topic that I'll explore later in this chapter. Finally, if you want to exert total and complete control over your text and bypass the problems traditionally posed by standard HTML-based text (including size and font limitations), you can go the full-fledged Dynamic HTML route and dive into Cascading Style Sheets, which is covered in Chapter 13, "Cascading Style Sheets."

As you work your way through this book, you'll find that there are often two ways to do the same procedure. For the most part, the first involves using the Property Inspector, while the other involves using one of Dreamweaver MX's menus. To help you make a choice that is best for you, both will be discussed.

You can also change the absolute size of text using the Text menu:

1. Select the text whose size you want to change.

2. Go to Text → Size and choose the size you want.

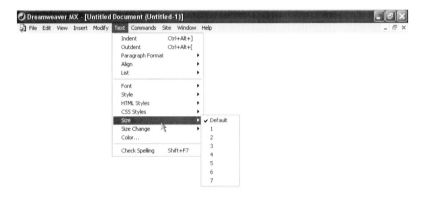

Setting Relative Text Size

Unlike the absolute sizing system, relative sizing doesn't really have a fixed size. When you choose a relative size, you increase or decrease the current text size by a number of fixed increments. To set relative text size:

1. Select the text whose size you want to change.

2. Open the Property Inspector (Window → Properties) and click the Size drop-down menu. Choose a size from either the +1 to +7 list or the –1 to –7 list (these are the relative sizes).

   If you choose from the minus (–) sizes, you will decrease the absolute size of the text by the increment you've chosen (for example, if you choose –3, the absolute size of the text will be decreased 3 increments). The same applies for the plus (+) sizes, except that they increase the absolute size of the text.

You can't use the relative sizes to increase text size more than 7 or decrease text size lower than 1.

You can also change the relative size of text using the Text menu. Select the text whose size you want to change, go to Text → Size Change, and make your size choice.

Changing Fonts

One of the great things about type is that because there are so many choices out there, you can always find one to suit your needs. When working with HTML-based text, the good news is that you aren't limited to one font. The bad news is that, for all intents and purposes, you are limited to three. How will you ever survive with only three fonts? Don't worry, there is actually quite a bit you can do with them.

You might wonder how this happened. Well, as with web colors, it comes down to the configuration of the computer that's opening the web page. Web browsers can only display fonts that are installed on the user's system. If a font is used on a web page that isn't installed on the user's computer, the browser substitutes a font that *is* installed. Now, as you can well imagine, this causes no end of trouble. The web designer (you) went to a lot of trouble to design something that used a specific font and looked good using that font. Then, along comes the web browser, and it displays the page using a totally different font. However, this sort of bothersome situation can be easily avoided.

Every computer in the English-speaking parts of the world that was built since 1994 (and was loaded with a Graphic User Interface operating system) was shipped with what are called system fonts. These fonts consist of Times New Roman, Courier New, and Ariel (on the PC), and Times, Courier, and Helvetica (on the Mac). If you design with these fonts, you don't have to worry about having them substituted, because everyone has them.

> Through the efforts of Microsoft and Apple, the fonts Verdana and Georgia are shipped with most desktop computers these days. As a result, you can add both of them to the list of fonts you can design with.

To change fonts in Dreamweaver MX:

1. Select the text whose font you want to change.
2. Open the Property Inspector (Window → Properties) and choose the new font from the Font drop-down menu.

You can also change text fonts using the Text menu. Just select the text whose font you want to change, select Text → Font, and make your choice.

You've probably noticed the Edit Font List option in both the Text → Font menu and the font list drop-down menu in the Property Inspector. By clicking this, you can add or subtract fonts to the list that is displayed. However, because of the browser limitation issues I just mentioned, unless you've got some solid design reasons, I strongly suggest that you leave the Edit Font List alone.

Changing Font Color

When it comes to font color, you've got to take into consideration the color issues we discussed in the last chapter. Beyond those limitations, you've got a really nice palette of colors that you can apply to text. In Dreamweaver MX, changing font color is pretty easy:

In Chapter 3, "Setting Up and Managing Your Page," we discussed using the Page Properties dialog box to change the font color for all the text on a page; the following process changes the font color only of specifically selected text.

1. Select the text whose color you want to change.

2. Open the Property Inspector (Window → Properties) and click the swatch to open the Color Palette.

3. Move your mouse over a color you like and click it. The color of your text automatically changes. If you want to choose a color that isn't contained in the Color Palette, follow the procedure described in the "Using the Color Dialog Box to Set Background Color" section in Chapter 3.

To change text color with the Text menu, select the text whose color you want to change, go to Text → Color to open the Color dialog box, and make your choice.

Changing Text Styles

One of the other handy things you can do with text is change its style. By style, I mean **bold**, *italic*, <u>underline</u>, and other such creative things you can do with text. As with many of Dreamweaver MX's features, there are two ways to change text style. The first way, which limits the amount of styles you can actually apply to text, uses the Property Inspector:

1. Select the text whose style you want to change.

2. If it isn't already, open the Property Inspector (Window → Properties) and click either the Bold **B** or the Italic *I* button, (in the top-right corner).

I've added bold and italic to the following text.

This is an example of text that has been both bolded and italicized.

To get a much wider range of possible text styles, you can use the Text menu. Just select the text and choose a style from the Text → Style drop-down menu. It's a good idea to play around with all available styles so that you can get a general idea of how each looks with different text sizes and fonts.

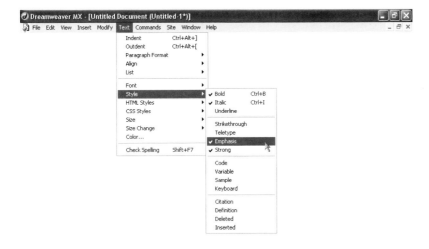

DESIGN REMINDER: Choosing Font Color

Unless there is a really strong design reason, try to avoid using "hyperlink blue" for your fonts. Because that color has become so synonymous with a link, users might mistake your text for a link and get frustrated when they click it and there's no result.

Organizing and Laying Out Text

Unfortunately, HTML isn't a design medium, so the control you have over how your text is laid out in your page is somewhat limited. You can only lay out your text by aligning it to the page, aligning it to other elements (like images), or integrating some block separation and arrangement techniques. All of these techniques will be discussed in this section of the chapter. Despite these limitations, once you've had a little practice with the available options, you'll be able to come up with some good designs.

Aligning Text

The most basic way you can lay out text is with the Alignment tool, with which you can justify text to the left, to the center, and to the right. Like most features in Dreamweaver MX, there are two ways to align text: the Property Inspector or the Text menu. To use the Property Inspector:

1. Place the cursor anywhere in the line of text you want to justify.

2. Open the Property Inspector (Window → Properties) and click one of the four Align buttons ▤ ▤ ▤ ▤ (in the top right-hand corner).

You can also align text using the Text menu. Just place the cursor anywhere in the line of text you want to justify and make your alignment selection from the Text → Align drop-down menu.

DESIGN REMINDER: The Power of Simplicity

Even though straight HTML prevents you from wielding total and complete control over your creative vision, you might find that its drawbacks are less painful than those of DHTML, which lets you exert a far greater degree of control over your document with Cascading Style Sheets. Ultimately, the question you have to ask yourself is whether it's better to make do with straight HTML-based text and layout or to open the Pandora's Box that is the cross-browser incompatibility of Dynamic HTML.

Inserting a Horizontal Rule

Up until now, all the things we've discussed have involved making an alteration to existing text. A Horizontal Rule, which is a great tool for breaking up blocks of text, is an object that needs to be inserted into a document. Essentially, a Horizontal Rule is a straight line that extends across the Document Window.

To insert a Horizontal Rule:

1. Place the cursor where you'd like to insert the Horizontal Rule.

2. If it isn't already, open the Insert bar (Window → Insert), select the Common tab, and click the Insert Horizontal Rule button ▦ .

Changing Horizontal Rule Dimensions

After you've inserted a Horizontal Rule, there are a few changes you can make to its appearance. First, you can change its dimensions:

1. Select the Horizontal Rule.

2. Open the Property Inspector (Window → Properties) and type a value into the Width or Height field. If you want the Horizontal Rule to always occupy a certain width of the page (regardless of how large or small the Document Window is), choose the percent sign (%) from the drop-down menu (to the right of the Width [W] field). If you want its width to remain fixed, choose pixels.

Changing Horizontal Rule Alignment

To change the alignment of the Horizontal Rule:

1. Select the Horizontal Rule you want to edit.

■ ■ ■ ■

DESIGN REMINDER: Scroll-o-Matic

Despite the fact that a Horizontal Rule can be used to break up text-heavy pages, people tend to dislike reading perpetually scrolling pages. Instead of putting all of your textual content on one page, try breaking it up so that it is spread over a bunch of different pages. This way, your audience will still be able to read all the text they want, but it will be partitioned into more manageable chunks that won't require a huge amount of scrolling.

2. Open the Property Inspector (Window → Properties) and choose Left, Center, or Right from the Align drop-down menu.

If the width of your Horizontal Rule occupies 100 percent of your document, changing its alignment will have no effect.

Shading the Horizontal Rule

You can also decide whether you want your Horizontal Rule to be shaded or not. When it's shaded, it has a three-dimensional look. If it isn't shaded, the Horizontal Rule looks like a simple solid bar.

Unshaded Horizontal Rule

Shaded Horizontal Rule

To change the shading of a Horizontal Rule:

1. Select the Horizontal Rule you want to edit.

2. Open the Property Inspector (Window → Properties) and either select or deselect the Shading check box (depending on whether you want your Horizontal Rule shaded or unshaded, respectively).

Indenting and Outdenting Text

As with word processing, you might find the need to indent portions of your text. When you indent text in Dreamweaver MX, the line automatically wraps to accommodate the changes. As a result, the section of text that you indent will occupy more vertical space. To indent blocks of text with the Property Inspector:

1. Select the text that you want to indent, or place your cursor somewhere on the line you are indenting.

2. Open the Property Inspector (Window → Properties) and click the Text Indent button ⁜ to indent one increment.

You can also indent with the Text menu: select the text you want to indent and go to Text →
Indent.

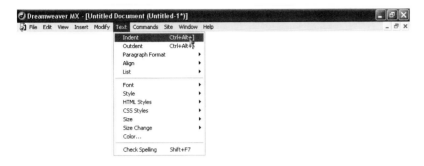

The opposite of indenting is outdenting. If you want to outdent text, you can either click the
Text Outdent button in the Property Inspector or go to Text → Outdent. But if text is already
flush with the left edge of the Document Window, using the Outdent feature won't change
anything.

Formatting Text with Lists

In Dreamweaver MX, you can format text into groups called lists. Essentially, lists are a good
way to organize information that would be best presented in a sequential fashion.
Dreamweaver MX provides two primary list types: ordered and unordered. Another list type,
called a definition list, is not as widely used as the other list types, but it is useful in some
situations.

You can at least marginally control the way lists (either ordered or unordered) look by using
Cascading Style Sheets. While the subject is a little advanced, if you are particularly interested
in learning about CSS, turn to Chapter 13.

Creating an Ordered (Numbered) List from Scratch

An *ordered list*, also referred to as a numbered list, presents information in a sequential,
structured manner. To create an ordered list from scratch:

1. Place the cursor where you want the ordered list to begin.

2. Open the Property Inspector (Window → Properties) and click the Ordered List
   button ⫶≡ . The number "1" automatically appears.

1. The first item in an ordered list

3. Type the first item in your list.

1. The first item in an ordered list
2. The second item in an ordered list

4. Press Enter. The next number in the list automatically appears on the next line.

5. Repeat steps 3 and 4 until you've completed the list.

6. To terminate the list, press Return (Mac)/ Enter (Win) twice.

Inserting an ordered list with the Text menu is just as easy. All you need to do is place the cursor where you want the ordered list to begin and go to Text → List → Ordered List. Then follow steps 3 through 6 as just described.

Creating an Ordered (Numbered) List from Existing Text

The previous process describes how you would go about creating an ordered list from scratch. However, I guarantee that you'll encounter a situation where you'll need to take a block of existing text and turn it into an ordered list. To do so:

1. Select a series of lines or paragraphs that you want to turn into a list.

For each item (line or paragraph) you select to be converted into a discrete list item, they need to be separated by a paragraph break.

2. Open the Property Inspector (Window → Properties) and click the Ordered List button.

Creating an Unordered (Bulleted) List

Unlike an ordered list, where the items are organized in a systematic manner, an unordered list, which is often referred to as a bulleted list, is designed to present information that doesn't need to be in any specific sequence. To create an ordered list:

1. Place the cursor where you want the unordered list to begin.

• The first item in an unordered list

2. Open the Property Inspector (Window → Properties) and click the Unordered List button ▤ . A bullet automatically appears.

• The first item in an unordered list
• The second item in an unordered list

3. Type the first item in your list.

4. Press Enter. Another bullet automatically appears on the next line.

5. Repeat steps 3 and 4 until you complete the list.

6. To terminate the list, press Return (Mac)/ Enter (Win) twice.

You can also insert an unordered list by using the Text menu. Place the cursor where you want the unordered list to begin and select Text → List → Unordered List. Then follow steps 3 to 6 as just described.

> You can create an unordered list from already existing text by selecting the items of text and then clicking the Unordered List button. Each item must be separated by a paragraph break to be an individual item.

Creating a Definition List

While not very widely used (primarily because they aren't included as an option in the Property Inspector), the definition list still deserves a place in this discussion. A definition list is used to create a dictionary-like structure.

Say, for instance, you wanted to create a definition list in which the word "Menshevik" was defined. In the first line, the word itself would appear. In the second line, which would be indented slightly, the definition of Menshevik ("A member of the moderate minority faction of the Russian Social Democratic Party which split (1903) from the Bolsheviks and was absorbed or liquidated after 1918 by the Russian Communist party.") would appear.

Menshevik
   A member of the moderate minority faction of the Russian Social Democratic Party which split (1903) from the Bolsheviks and was absorbed or liquidated after 1918 by the Russian Communist party.

To create a definition list:

1. Place the cursor in the Document Window where you want the definition list to begin.

2. Go to Text → List → Definition List.

3. Type the term that will occupy the first line (the word to be defined) and press Return (Mac)/ Enter (Win).

4. Type the text that will occupy the second line (the definition of the word that appears in the first line).

5. To continue adding terms (and their associated definitions), just press Return (Mac)/ Enter (Win) to move to the next line and repeat steps 2 and 3.

6. To terminate the list when you finish adding all the terms and their associated definitions, press Return (Mac)/ Enter (Win) twice.

Manipulating Ordered and Unordered List Properties

For the most part, the way Dreamweaver MX creates lists (whether ordered, unordered, or definition) is somewhat creatively confining. Despite this, you do have some degree of control over the way ordered and unordered lists look and behave. Through the List Properties dialog box, you can change the type of an already created list, alter list style, change the number at which an ordered list begins counting, and fiddle with the properties of individual list members. Unfortunately, you can't alter the properties of a definition list.

To access the List Property dialog box for an ordered or unordered list:

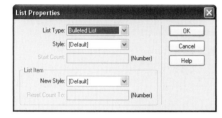

1. Select any individual member of either an ordered or unordered list

2. Open and expand the Property Inspector (Window → Properties).

3. Click the List Item button (located in the expanded portion of the Property Inspector). This will open the List Properties dialog box.

   After the List Properties dialog box opens, you can alter the various properties of your list:

List Type Lets you switch from your current type of list to another available type (bulleted, numbered, menu, or directory). In reality, both the menu and directory list types are nothing more than different names for an unordered (or bulleted) list.

Figure 4.1

The Style drop-down menu lets you change the style of either your list's bullets or numbers.

Style Accessible only if you are working with a bulleted or numbered list type, this option lets you change the style of your list's bullets or numbers. Figure 4.1 shows the range of possible styles for both ordered and unordered lists. This drop-down is dynamic—it will display the appropriate options depending on whether you've got bulleted or numbered selected from the List Type drop-down menu.

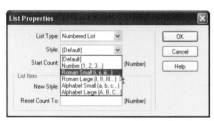

Start Count Accessible only when you have a numbered list type, this option lets you choose where your numbered list will begin. For example, if you have an ordered list with five items and you set the Start Count to 3, the items in the list will be numbered 3, 4, 5, 6, and 7 respectively.

List Item New Style Lets you specify the style of an individual item within the list (as opposed to the entire list). To use this option, you must select the item whose style you want to change and select an option from the List Item New Style drop-down menu. This menu is a dynamic tool, displaying only those options applicable to the list's current type (ordered or unordered). If you place your cursor next to an individual list item (instead of directly selecting it) and choose a style from the List Item New Style drop-down menu, you'll change the style of that list item as well as all those that follow—but not those above.

List Item Reset Count To Lets you input a value to which the selected item's number will be reset. Note that changing the List Item Reset Count To value not only affects the currently selected list item, but also all those that follow. For example, if you had a list of five items numbered from 1 to 5 and you reset the third item's List Item Reset Count To value 28, your list's numbering would be numbered 1, 2, 28, 29, 30.

> Once you finish manipulating the options in the List Properties dialog box, just click OK and the changes will be automatically applied to your list.

Inserting Special Characters

What happens if you need to insert a character that doesn't appear on your keyboard? You might come across a situation where you need to insert a pound sterling symbol (£), a copyright symbol (©), the euro symbol (€), or a trademark symbol (™), for example. You can add many special characters with the simple click of the mouse:

1. Place the cursor where you want to insert the special character.

2. Open the Insert bar (Window → Insert) and select the Characters tab.

> If you want to insert a character that isn't in the Insert bar's Characters tab or on the Insert menu, click the Other Character button (the button the furthest to the right) in the Characters tab. This lets you choose from a larger set of special characters.

3. Click the button corresponding to the character you wish to insert into your document.

Inserting the Date

In the process of creating a website, you'll find that you'll probably need to insert the current date at some point. Whether for use in a copyright statement or a list of updates, it can get a little tedious having to constantly check the current date and then type it into your document. Dreamweaver MX helps you on this front with a handy labor saving device that allows you to insert the current date into your document with a click of a button:

1. Place your cursor in the location where you want to place the current date.

Dreamweaver MX pulls the current date/time information from your computer. This means if your computer's date/time is wrong, the date inserted in Dreamweaver MX will be too.

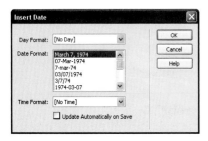

2. Go to Insert → Date. This will cause the Insert Date dialog box to open.

3. From here, choose the format you want the day displayed by selecting one of the options in the Day Format drop-down menu.

4. Select the way you want the entire date displayed by choosing one of the options in the Date Format list.

5. Select the way the time is displayed by choosing one of the options in the Time Format drop-down menu

It's extremely important to note that while most (if not all) U.S. institutions and individuals display the date as Month/Day/Year, most other countries display the date as Day/Month/Year. With this in mind, you might want to choose the appropriate format for websites that will be viewed by non-Americans. An alternative solution is to just spell out the date: for example, May 25, 2004.

6. If you want the date to automatically update whenever you save the document, check the Update Automatically on Save check box.

7. When you finish setting the date's properties, click OK.

The date inserted into your web page is not dynamic—once it's uploaded to the server, it will not dynamically change to display the current date. To insert a dynamic date into your page, you'll have to use a custom behavior which, unfortunately, doesn't ship with Dreamweaver MX but can be downloaded from the Macromedia Exchange. For more information on behaviors, see Chapter 15, "Adding Advanced Interactivity with Behaviors."

Using HTML Styles to Format Text

Until this point, you've been exploring how to manually set various HTML-based text properties in Dreamweaver MX. The problem with these processes is that, unless you are applying only one change to a string of text (such as size, font, or color), it can take some time to manually make all of the changes you want. Further, if you need to change all the text in your creation to something quite different from the default, you might find yourself carrying out the same series of steps over and over again. Say, for instance, you were using text that employed the Ariel font, 4-point, italicized, and red. If you were to manually edit the text so that it conformed to your needs, you'd have to carry out four separate procedures, which could get rather tiresome. This is where the HTML styles come in.

An HTML style is a user-defined group of text-specific HTML tags (such as those relating to font, size, color, and so on) that, in Dreamweaver MX, can be applied to any selected string of text in your document. In Dreamweaver MX, HTML styles are accessible through the HTML Styles panel. From here, you can create your own styles and apply them repeatedly to any selected text, thereby streamlining your work process and saving you a great deal of time and effort.

To open the HTML Styles Panel:

Go to Window → HTML Styles.

In the next section, you'll explore how create a new style (from both existing text and from scratch), edit an existing style, delete an existing style, apply styles to text, and clear styles from text.

Creating a New HTML Style

There are two ways to create your own custom styles: from scratch and from existing text. To create an HTML Style from scratch:

1. Open the HTML Styles panel (Window → HTML Styles).

2. Click the New Style button 🗗 (in the bottom right-hand corner) to open the Define HTML Style dialog box. Alternatively, you can choose New from the HTML Styles panel's Options menu or go to Text → HTML Styles → New Style.

3. Enter the name for your new style into the Name field. This is the name that will appear in the styles window in the HTML Styles panel.

4. Select one of the Apply To options. The Selection option will guarantee that the style will only be applied to selected text, while the Paragraph option sets the style so that it will be applied to the entire paragraph in which your selected text sits.

5. Select one of the When Applying options. The Add to Existing Style option will make sure that the attributes of your new style are added to any existing styles of the selected text or paragraph. The Clear Existing Style option will automatically remove any styles from the currently selected text or paragraph and then apply the new style.

6. Choose your style's font from the Font drop-down menu.

7. Select the size for your style from the Size drop-down menu. You have access to both the relative and absolute sizing systems.

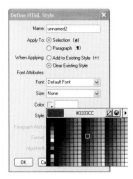

8. To set the color for your style, click the Color swatch and choose a color when the Color Picker opens (seen in the image on the top). If you want to mix your own custom color, click the color wheel (in the top right-hand corner) to open the Color Panel.

9. If you want to include any of the text styles such as bold or italic, click the appropriate button. If you want to include any additional text styles, click the Other button to access a drop-down menu of other choices (seen in the image on the bottom).

If you didn't select Paragraph in step 4, all of the next steps will be inaccessible.

10. Select one of the Paragraph Format options from the Format drop-down menu.

11. Click one of the Alignment buttons so that your paragraph style will align either to the left, the center, or the right.

12. Click OK.

13. The style (whose name you set in step 3) is now listed in the HTML Styles panel's main window.

The process for creating an HTML style from existing text is almost identical to that you just went through. There are, however, some minor differences that should be touched upon. To create an HTML Style from existing text:

1. Enter some text into the document window, and manipulate it (using the skills learned earlier in this chapter) so that its attributes are that of the new style you wish to create.

2. Select the text.

3. Open the HTML Styles panel (Window → HTML Styles) and click the New Style button. The Define HTML Style dialog box will open. Alternatively, you can choose New from the HTML Styles panel Options drop-down menu.

4. Enter the name for your new style into the Name field.

5. All of the text's attributes (font, color, size, and so on) will be transferred over to the Define HTML Styles dialog box. You can either leave the attributes as they are or manipulate them further.

6. Click OK.

Editing an Existing HTML Style

After creating an HTML Style (either from scratch or from some existing text), you aren't stuck with it as is—it's quite easy to go back and change any aspect of an existing HTML style:

1. Open the HTML Styles panel (Window → HTML Styles) and double-click the HTML style that you want to edit. Alternatively, you can choose Edit from the HTML Styles panel Options drop-down menu.

2. When the Define HTML Styles dialog box pops up, make any changes to you want.

3. When you're finished, click OK.

Any text in the HTML style you changed will not automatically update to reflect your changes—you'll need to reapply the HTML style to reflect the changes. If you want to work with styles that apply to an entire page (or an entire site, for that matter), you'll need to work with Cascading Style Sheets, a topic that will be thoroughly covered in Chapter 13.

Deleting a Style from the Styles Panel

As your sites get bigger, you'll invariably accumulate a fair number of HTML styles. Halfway through your design your priorities might change, making your currently used styles useless. Alternatively, during the course of the design process, you might have experimented with a number of different styles and decided to use only one of them. Given this, you are certainly bound to find that some of your HTML styles will be no longer usable and you'll need to delete them:

1. Open the HTML Styles panel (Window → HTML Styles) and select the HTML style that you want to delete.

2. Click the Delete Style button 🗑 . Alternatively, select Delete from the HTML Styles panel's Options drop-down menu.

3. When prompted, either click OK to delete the style, or cancel.

When you delete a style from the Style panel, text which previously had that style applied to it will remain "styled."

Applying an HTML Style to Text

Now that you've learned how to create and edit your own styles, it's important to learn how to apply styles to text:

1. Select the text to which you want to apply the HTML style.

2. Open the HTML Styles panel (Window → HTML Styles) and select the style that you want to apply to the selected text.

3. Click the Apply button, and *voila*! The HTML style is applied to the selected text.

If you want the HTML style to be automatically applied to the selected text (without having to click the Apply button), select the Auto Apply check box on the HTML Styles panel.

Clearing an HTML Style from Text

If you apply an HTML style to some text and decide later that you loathe it, it's quite easy to remove it:

1. Select the text to which an HTML style was previously applied.

> If you want to clear a Selection style, you need to select the entire string of text to which the HTML style was applied. If you want to clear a Paragraph style, just place your cursor anywhere in the paragraph to which the HTML style was applied.

2. Open the HTML Styles panel by going to Window → HTML Styles.
3. To clear a Paragraph style, click the Clear Paragraph Style option in the HTML Style panel's main window. If you want to clear a Selection Style, click the Clear Selection Style option instead.

Managing a Page's Textual Content

Even though text is the most basic kind of content on the Web, it can often provide some pretty serious (and incredibly frequently overlooked) problems.

The first is misspelling, plain and simple. There is nothing more unsightly than typos in your page. The second is outdated textual content, such as names or dates. Thankfully, Dreamweaver MX provides you a way to tackle both these problems with a minimum of muss and fuss.

Checking Your Spelling

Spelling errors are a surefire way to send people away from your site. Dreamweaver MX has made checking a document for spelling errors very easy by including a spell-check feature.

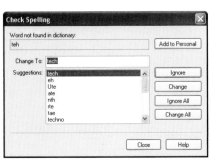

To use the spell-check feature, select Text → Check Spelling. Any errors will be picked up and you will get the option to make changes using the Check Spelling dialog box.

Using Find and Replace

The Find and Replace function is easily one of the most underutilized and incredibly useful tools in all of Dreamweaver MX. With it, you can search for either text elements within your document or specific tags within your HTML source code and easily replace them with any other string of text or tag that you desire. This can easily save you hours of time spent manually searching for (and changing) content within individual pages or an entire local site. To use Dreamweaver MX's Find and Replace tool:

1. Go to Edit → Find and Replace to open the Find and Replace dialog box.

The Find and Replace dialog box will change to display the options specific to the type of search selected (Text, Source Code, and so on). Because of this, fully labeled graphics for each search type are provided where those specific search types are discussed.

2. Choose the scope of your search by selecting one of the options from the Find In drop-down menu:

   Current Document Confines the scope of the search to the document that is currently open.

   Entire Local Site Expands the search scope so that the currently open local site is included.

   Selected Files in Site Limits the search solely to those files and folders that are currently selected in the Site window.

   Folder Lets you specify the folder in which you want the search to be confined. To specify the folder, click the Browse button that appears after you choose the Folder option. When the Choose Search Folder dialog box appears, navigate into the desired folder and click Select.

3. Select the specific search you'd like to perform from the Search For drop-down menu. Based on your choice, the Find and Replace dialog box will change to display the options for your specific search type.

   From here, you can explore the specifics of each type of search.

One of the drawbacks of the Find and Replace tool is that it doesn't include any text-based Library items when it's searching in the currently open document. However, when the scope is set to search the entire local site, it will include Library items. For more information on the Library and Library items, see Chapter 9, "Reusable Elements: Library Items and Templates."

Searching for Text

If you chose Text from the Search For drop-down menu, the Find and Replace dialog box will change to reflect a set of options specific to a text search.

To set the options for a text search:

1. Type the text for which you want to look into the Search field.

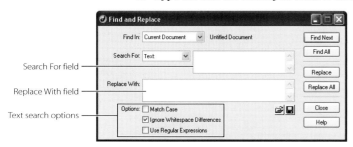

2. To replace the searched for text with some other text, enter it into the Replace With field.

3. If you want to limit the search to text whose case exactly matches that of the text you entered into the Search field, select the Match Case option.

4. If you want the search to ignore any differences in the number of spaces within the text that the search finds and the text upon which the search was based, select the Ignore Whitespace Differences option. For example, if you were searching for the words "my dog has fleas," and your document contained the words "my dog has fleas" (two spaces between each of the words instead of one), the search would ignore the extra spaces and locate the string of text regardless.

5. If you want certain characters and short strings of characters to be converted into expression operators, select the Use Regular Expressions option.

> Expression operators are characters (or short strings of characters) used as a sort of shorthand to describe character combinations in text. To find out more about expression operators, refer to Dreamweaver MX's help files (Help → Using Dreamweaver MX) and search for "regular expressions."

6. When you finish setting your search criteria, click one of the following buttons to initiate the search:

   Find Next Locates the next occurrence of the text, opens the appropriate file (if you've selected Entire Local Site or Folder as the search's scope), and selects it.

   Find All Generates a report (in the form of a list) of all the locations where it located the text.

> If your search scope goes beyond the currently open document, you can double-click any of the occurrences in the search result report to open the file in which the text was located.

Remove Attribute Removes a specified attribute from the searched-for tag.

Add Before Start Tag Lets you specify something (text or tag) that you want to be added before the searched-for tag's opening element.

Add After End Tag Lets you specify something (text or tag) that you want to be added after the searched-for tag's closing element.

Add After Start Tag Lets you specify something (text or tag) that you want added after the searched-for tag's opening element.

Add Before End Tag Lets you specify something (text or tag) that you want added before the searched-for tag's closing element.

5. Select one of the options (Match Case, Ignore Whitespace Differences, or Use Regular Expression). Refer to the previous section for a complete description of these options.

6. When you finish, click one of the buttons along the right side of the Find and Replace dialog box to initiate the search. Refer to the previous section for a complete description of what each of the buttons do.

7. When you finish, click Close.

Using Flash Text

One of the coolest technologies to come down the pipe in recent years is Flash, Macromedia's vector animation program. Since objects in Flash are vector graphics they look considerably smoother and crisper than graphics normally seen on the Web.

> If you are particularly interested in Macromedia Flash, check out *Flash MX Savvy* (Sybex, 2002) by Ethan Watrall and Norbert Herber. (Wink wink.)

In Dreamweaver MX, Macromedia gives you the ability to create editable vector text with the Flash Text feature. By using the Flash Text feature, you can avoid the font and size limitations that we discussed at the beginning of this chapter. In addition, if you use Flash vectors instead of an image for text, your graphics are scalable, smaller in file size, and look good when they're printed.

> It's important to note that users will still need to have the Flash plug-in installed on their computers to be able to view any Flash Text inserted into documents.

To use the Flash Text tool:

1. Place your cursor where you want to insert the Flash Text.

2. Open the Insert bar (Window → Insert) and click the Media Tab.

3. Click the Insert Flash Text button 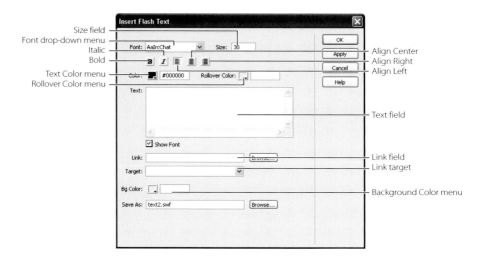 in the Media panel to open the Insert Flash Text dialog box.

If you haven't already, Dreamweaver MX will prompt you to save your page before you can add the Flash Text.

You can also access the Insert Flash Text dialog box by going to Insert → Interactive Images → Flash Text.

4. Choose a font from the Font drop-down menu. The menu will include all the fonts you presently have loaded on your system.

> Because Flash can display fonts that aren't loaded on a user's machine, you don't have to worry about using only the system fonts.

5. Enter the font size in the Size field. Unlike with normal web text, you can use points for Flash Text.

6. Click the color swatch to open the Color Palette. From here you can choose the color you want your Flash Text to be.

7. Type your text in the Text field.

8. Enter a filename in the Save As field. You can use the default filename (`text1.swf` and so on), but you must enter something in this field. The file is automatically saved to the same directory as the current document.

9. Click Apply and then OK. Here is an example of what your text might look like:

> By setting the other properties in the Flash Text dialog box (such as rollover color, link, and target), you can change your Flash Text into an interactive button that links to another portion of your site.

Inspiration: Design and Technique

There is little doubt that sound digital typography gives a well-designed site that extra creative punch. Let's face it, folks: type is power! No site illustrates this more than typogRaphic (`www.typographic.com`). Designed by Jimmy Chen, an astounding visual designer who lives in Los Angeles, typogRaphic takes web design beyond the realm of the commercial, the corporate, and the everyday into something far more potent (see Figure 4.2). Every square centimeter is packed with beautiful digital typographic design. The visual subtleties of typogRaphic are quite stunning and create a visual space that easily holds your attention for long periods of time.

Figure 4.2

typogRaphic

Summary

This chapter covered all things textual in Dreamweaver MX. It looked at how you add text to the Document Window and how to manipulate the text (resize, align, and so on). It also discussed why you should limit your designs to the system fonts. While the reasons for this may seem unimportant at this stage of the game, they will definitely come into play down the road. The chapter described ways you can arrange your text by using lists and the horizontal rule. It also explored how to insert special characters and the date. In closing, it focused on HTML styles, the Find and Replace tool, and Flash Text.

In the next chapter, you'll take another step along the content road with a thorough exploration of how you insert, manage, and manipulate images in Dreamweaver MX.

Dreamweaver MX Design and Technique Color Gallery

The following section is a gallery of websites (some of which have been featured throughout the book in the "Inspiration: Design and Technique" sections) that have been gathered together to illustrate the possibilities of web design. While some have been made with the help of Dreamweaver, others have been made with Macromedia Flash—the common thread is that all use their particular medium to its fullest extent to create compelling and interesting interactive experiences. The gallery includes examples from numerous entertainment sites, an edutainment site, a corporate communications company, and digital design firms.

The Matrix (www.matrixmag.com)

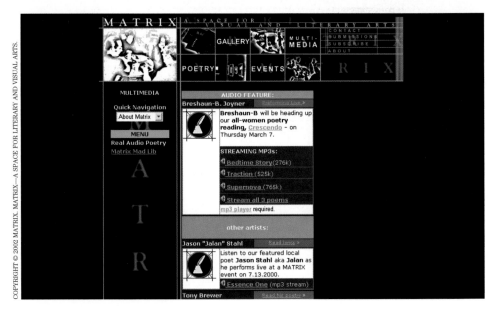

Matrixmag.com is the online home of MATRIX, a literary and visual arts organization in Bloomington, IN. Dedicated to providing consistent public forums for area literary and visual arts, matrixmag.com merges excellent visual design with RealAudio recordings to push the limits of the contemporary spoken-word art.

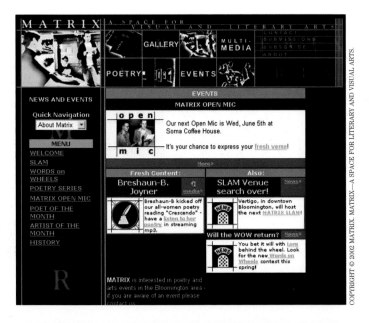

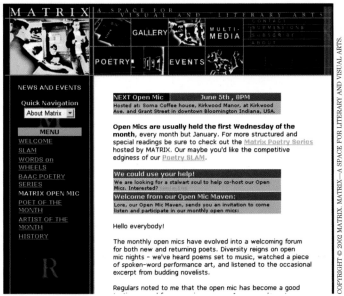

Designed by **Nathan Letsinger** entirely in Dreamweaver and Fireworks, matrixmag.com uses clean design and effective navigation that encourages exploration and accessibility. By creatively employing a very limited palette of colors and highly stylized graphics, matrix-mag.com effectively evokes a feeling of 1960s Beat poetry.

Doug Chiang Studios (www.dchiang.com)

Founded by **Doug Chiang**, head of the Art Department and Design Director for the *Star Wars* prequels, Doug Chiang Studios is currently working on a film/book project called *Robota: Reign of Machines*. The website is intended to cater to those fascinated by the incredible work of Doug Chiang, as well as to publicize and explore the studio's current project *Robota: Reign of Machine*.

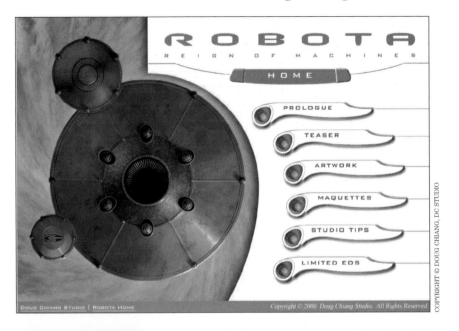

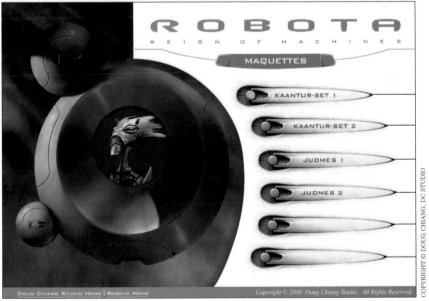

Designed using a combination of Dreamweaver and Fireworks (along with several other software packages), the website combines Doug Chiang's beautiful and compelling style of illustration with a highly intuitive navigation scheme to create an exceptionally immersive experience. *Robota: Reign of Machines* is a 160-page "film format" illustrated book due to be published in 2002 that explores the relationship between technology and nature against the backdrop of a futuristic society. The *Robota* section of the Doug Chiang Studios website combines incredible illustration and immersive navigation to allow the user to explore the world of *Robota*.

Becoming Human (www.becominghuman.org)

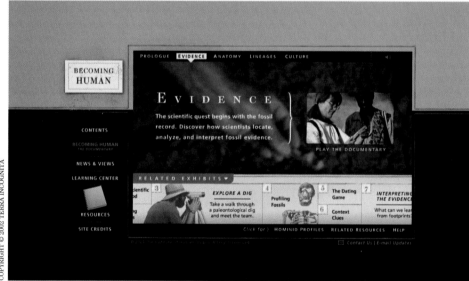

Developed jointly by **NeonSky Creative Media** (www.neonsky.com) and **Terra Incognita** (www.terraincognita.com) for the Arizona State Institute for Human Origins, Becoming Human is an original, interactive Flash documentary that explores human evolution from our earliest ancestors to the emergence of *Homo sapiens*. Becoming Human features a host of innovative and interactive tools (such as interactive exhibits) that allow you to go beyond the Flash documentary itself and pursue your personal exploration into the fascinating world of human evolution.

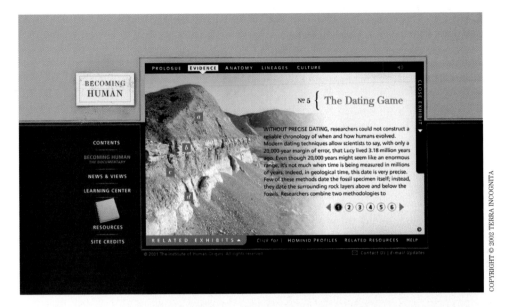

Becoming Human is partitioned into several sections that allow you to explore questions about culture, hominid anatomy, archaeological evidence, and lineage. Each section features not only a spectacular linear Flash documentary narrated by a prestigious paleoanthropologist but also topical discussions by many other prominent scholars in the field of human evolution. The combination of the linear documentary and the interactive exploratory tools (both of which were created totally in Flash) makes Becoming Human one of the most interesting, innovative, and cutting-edge interactive creations out there.

Titoonic (**www.titoonic.dk**)

Founded in August 2000, **Titoonic** (`www.titoonic.dk`) is a creative web production company located in Copenhagen, Denmark. Although the company specializes in all manner of web-based multimedia, it is best known for its 3D character animation and design. It has been responsible for the design and implementation of numerous 3D Flash characters whose implementation includes visual guides on websites, character-based Flash games, greeting cards, and "webisodes."

Founded by a group of highly creative individuals whose backgrounds include classical animation and graphical storytelling, Titoonic pushes the boundaries of the cutting-edge of 3D Flash development with their extremely stylish and compelling 3D character design.

Playdo Community (www.playdo.com)

Not to be mistaken for that weird doughy stuff you used to play with as a kid, **Playdo Community** (www.playdo.com) is an extremely entertaining and engaging virtual online community (with free membership) that lets you interact and communicate with other "citizens" in your choice of either a cool 2D or 3D environment.

At playdo.com, you can create a unique online character by choosing from over 40,000 different appearance combinations. Your character then plays a roll as a citizen in Playdo city, where they can gossip over a cup of coffee, send mail, get challenged in an online game, and meet (and interact with) fellow Playdo citizens.

Braincraft (**www.braincraft.com**)

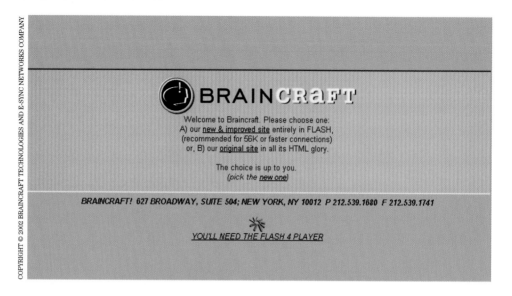

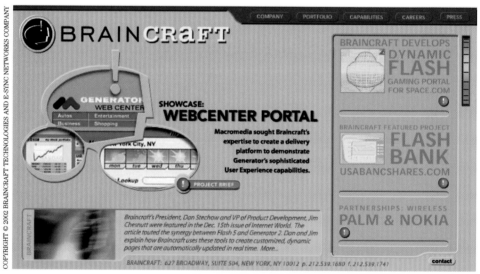

Founded in 1995 by President / CEO, **Dan Stechow** and Executive VP / COO, **Kevin Marth**, Braincraft combines cutting-edge programming techniques, advanced instructional design methodologies, out-of-the-box design, and proven project management methods to offer dependable solutions for business-to-business customers.

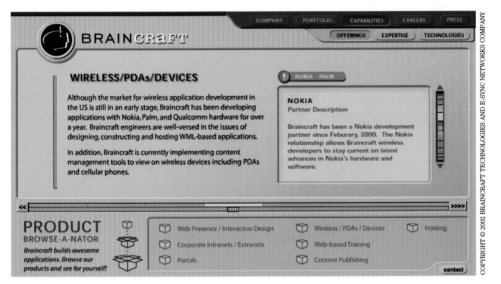

Braincraft.com is an excellent example of cutting edge and creative visual design. The beautiful and imminently usable interface, which was created using Macromedia Flash, is framed by a series of pop-up windows created and controlled by Dreamweaver HTML. During the creation of their self-promotional site, Braincraft used Fireworks to compress hundreds of clean, professional, and fast-loading bitmaps for quick delivery over the Web.

Rustboy (www.rustboy.com)

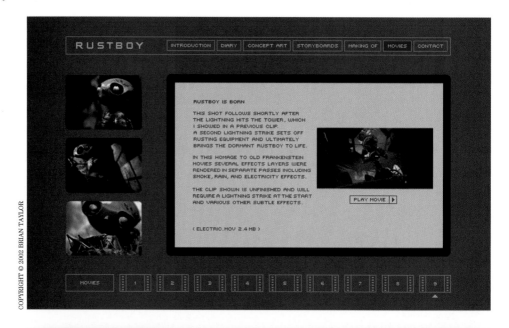

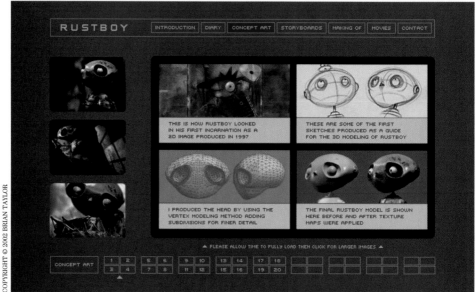

Created by **XL5 Design** (www.xl5design.com), Rustboy is a promotional site for a short film of the same name that is currently being created and will ultimately be distributed online by Brian Taylor. Rustboy (the primary character of the film) originally began life as a simple 2D creation but has since been thrust into the glorious world of 3D.

The site, which is a great example of simple but stylish design, features a constantly updated diary on the current Rustboy milestones, beautifully illustrated storyboards and concept art, short QuickTime teasers, and insights into the creation of the film. The site perfectly captures the slightly dark feeling of Rustboy (and the world in which he lives).

digitalorganism (www.digitalorganism.com)

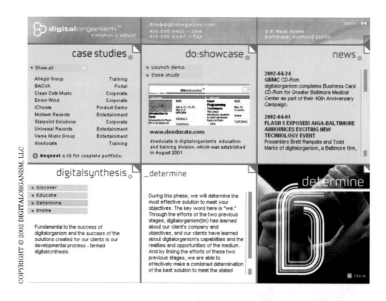

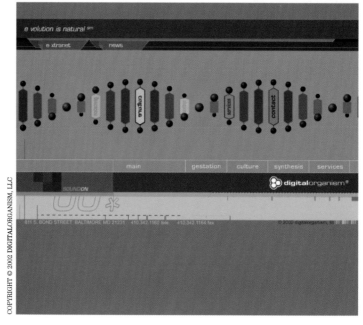

Through the use of inspirational digital content and innovative design, **digital**organism, a full-service multimedia and design studio based in Baltimore, MD strives to merge cutting-edge aesthetics and functionality to advance corporate identity and branding. **digital**organism's interface, the center of which is a stunning 3D DNA menu system, is remarkably stylish and sleek. Exploration is made easy and entertaining by the site's immersive and integrated navigation system.

CHAPTER 5

Working with Images

We use images in many interesting ways to represent all sorts of online information. As you would expect, Dreamweaver MX makes adding images to your web page a painless process.

However, as in the case of web-based text, there are some issues you need to be aware of when dealing with web images. This chapter will begin by looking at some of these issues and then go on to discuss inserting and manipulating images with Dreamweaver MX.

- **Understanding web image formats**
- **Placing images in a document**
- **Manipulating images**

A series of stock images of all types have been included in the Images folder on your CD for use during the exercises in this chapter.

Understanding Web Image Formats

One of the first and most important things about which you need to know is that, without the help of plug-ins, the web supports only three types of images: GIF, JPEG, and PNG. Before we dive into how Dreamweaver MX deals with images, it's a good idea to become familiar with the strengths and weaknesses of each of the three image formats so that you can decide which is best for your creative purposes.

GIF

Originally developed by CompuServe during the late '80s, *GIF*s (Graphics Interchange Format) are the workhorse images of the web. Because the format itself can display a maximum of only 256 colors (8 bits), GIFs are best used for relatively simple images with flat colors and are generally smaller in size (in terms of kilobytes) than other formats. One of the great things about GIFs is that they come in a few different forms: transparent GIFs, interlaced GIFs, and animated GIFs. Transparent GIFs allow the background upon which they are placed to be visible. When they are created, the user decides which color should be transparent in the image. Interlaced GIFs are structured in such a way that they come into focus slowly as the browser loads the image. Animated GIFs are simply a series of images saved in the same file. When a browser loads this file, all the images in the file are displayed in sequence, creating an animation much like a digital flip book.

JPEG

JPEG stands for Joint Photographic Experts Group. JPEGs came along sometime after GIFs, and were designed specifically to display photographic or continuous color images. Their main strength comes from the fact that they can display millions of colors. Because of this, JPEGs tend to have larger file sizes than GIFs—as the quality of the JPEG increases, so does its file size. Unfortunately, JPEGs come in only one "flavor": no transparency, no interlacing, and no animation.

PNG

PNG stands for Portable Network Graphic. Developed originally by Macromedia, PNGs are less straightforward than GIFs or JPEGs. They were designed to combine the best of both GIFs and JPEGs; they can therefore support indexed color (256 colors), grayscale, true-color images (millions of colors), and transparency. The problem with PNGs is that they have spotty browser support. Microsoft Internet Explorer (4.0 and later) and Netscape Navigator (4.04 and later) only partially support the display of PNG images. Because PNG is the native file type of Fireworks, Dreamweaver MX has some fairly sophisticated tools that are geared specifically toward PNG manipulation and management.

> For Dreamweaver MX to recognize a PNG, the file must have the .png extension.

Placing Images

Now that you know the basic web image types, you can insert an image into the Document Window. To do so:

1. Place the cursor where you want to insert the image.

2. Open the Insert bar (Window → Insert), select the Common tab, and click the Insert Image button 🖼️ .

3. When the Select Image Source dialog box appears, navigate to where your image is located, select it, and click OK.

To place an image using the Insert menu:

1. Place the cursor where you want to insert the image.

2. Go to Insert → Image.

3. When the Select Image Source dialog box appears, navigate to where your image is located, select it, and click OK.

New to Dreamweaver MX is the ability to insert an Image Placeholder, which serves as a generic graphic that can be used until final artwork is ready to be added to the page. To insert an Image Placeholder:

1. Place the cursor where you want to insert the Image Placeholder.

2. If it isn't already, open the Insert bar (Window → Insert), select the Common tab, and click the Image Placeholder button 🖼️ . This will open the Image Placeholder dialog box.

3. Enter the name for the placeholder into the Name field. The name simply acts as a label for the image placeholder.

4. Enter the dimensions of the placeholder into the Width and Height fields.

The whole point of an image placeholder is that it occupies the same amount of space in the design as the "real" image. Because of this, the dimensions of the two should be exactly the same.

5. To set the color of the placeholder, click the Color swatch and choose a color from the Color Palette.

6. Enter the placeholder's ALT text into the Alternate Text field.

To learn more about ALT text, see the "Using the ALT Tag" section later in this chapter.

7. Click OK.

Manipulating Images

It would do you no good if you could insert an image into a Dreamweaver MX document and then weren't able to manipulate it. In this section, you're going to cover some of the basics of how you can fiddle with your image so that it fits into the overall design of your page.

Something you must realize before you take one more step is that, because HTML isn't a design medium, you are going to be fairly limited in what you can do with images at this stage. However, given a firm grounding in what you *can* do, you'll be able to come up with some interesting creations.

Aligning an Image

One of the most basic things you can do with an image after it's been inserted into a Dreamweaver document is to Align (or justify) it to the page. Because an image can't be moved around a document as it can in an image-editing program like Fireworks or Photoshop, aligning it becomes an important part of your final design. Aligning an image is almost the same procedure as aligning text:

1. Place your cursor anywhere along the line that contains the image (do not select the image itself).

2. Open the Property Inspector (Window → Properties).

3. Click one of the three alignment buttons ≣ ≣ ≣ (Left, Center, or Right) in the top right-hand corner of the Property Inspector.

Aligning an Image with Text

Now that you can justify images to the page, let's explore how to align images with text. It's a fair bet that when you create a web page, you're going to have more than just text or just images. You will ultimately want to combine the two in a pleasing visual form.

If you've already experimented with images and text in the same document, you've probably noticed that they don't integrate very well. In fact, images have the tendency to break up the flow of text.

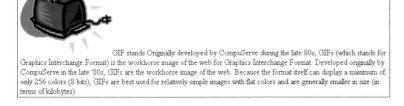

GIF stands Originally developed by CompuServe during the late 80s, GIFs (which stands for Graphics Interchange Format) is the workhorse image of the web.for Graphics Interchange Format. Developed originally by CompuServe in the late '80s, GIFs are the workhorse image of the web. Because the format itself can display a maximum of only 256 colors (8 bits), GIFs are best used for relatively simple images with flat colors and are generally smaller in size (in terms of kilobytes).

You can, however, exert some control over how the text on your page interacts with an image. To align an image to text:

1. Insert an image somewhere in a block of text.

2. Select the image you want to align by clicking it with your mouse.

3. Open the Property Inspector (Window → Properties).

4. Select Top from the Align drop-down menu.

You'll notice that only one line aligns itself with the top of the image. (We'll cover the other options next.)

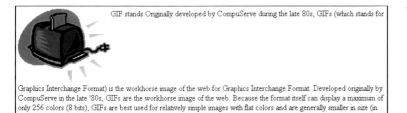

GIF stands Originally developed by CompuServe during the late 80s, GIFs (which stands for

Graphics Interchange Format) is the workhorse image of the web.for Graphics Interchange Format. Developed originally by CompuServe in the late '80s, GIFs are the workhorse image of the web. Because the format itself can display a maximum of only 256 colors (8 bits), GIFs are best used for relatively simple images with flat colors and are generally smaller in size (in terms of kilobytes).

Exploring Alignment Options

The Align drop-down menu has many more choices than just Top. Each aligns text to an image in a different way.

Text Top If you choose Text Top, the top line of the text aligns with the top of the image.

GIF stands Originally developed by CompuServe during the late 80s, GIFs (which stands for

Graphics Interchange Format) is the workhorse image of the web for Graphics Interchange Format. Developed originally by CompuServe in the late '80s, GIFs are the workhorse image of the web. Because the format itself can display a maximum of only 256 colors (8 bits), GIFs are best used for relatively simple images with flat colors and are generally smaller in size (in terms of kilobytes).

> While it may appear that Text Top is the same as Top, there are some differences. Top aligns text with the highest item on the line, and Text Top aligns the tallest character in the line with the top of the image.

Bottom and Baseline These choices align the baseline of the first line of text to the bottom of the image.

GIF stands Originally developed by CompuServe during the late 80s, GIFs (which stands for Graphics Interchange Format) is the workhorse image of the web for Graphics Interchange Format. Developed originally by CompuServe in the late '80s, GIFs are the workhorse image of the web. Because the format itself can display a maximum of only 256 colors (8 bits), GIFs are best used for relatively simple images with flat colors and are generally smaller in size (in terms of kilobytes).

Absolute Bottom This aligns the bottom of the image to the absolute bottom of the lowest characters (which includes descenders, as in the letters g or j).

GIF stands Originally developed by CompuServe during the late 80s, GIFs (which stands for Graphics Interchange Format) is the workhorse image of the web for Graphics Interchange Format. Developed originally by CompuServe in the late '80s, GIFs are the workhorse image of the web. Because the format itself can display a maximum of only 256 colors (8 bits), GIFs are best used for relatively simple images with flat colors and are generally smaller in size (in terms of kilobytes).

Middle This choice aligns the text baseline with the middle of the selected object.

GIF stands Originally developed by CompuServe during the late 80s, GIFs (which stands for Graphics Interchange Format) is the workhorse image of the web.for Graphics Interchange Format. Developed originally by CompuServe in the late '80s, GIFs are the workhorse image of the web. Because the format itself can display a maximum of only 256 colors (8 bits), GIFs are best used for relatively simple images with flat colors and are generally smaller in size (in terms of kilobytes).

Absolute Middle This choice aligns to the absolute middle of the current line.

GIF stands Originally developed by CompuServe during the late 80s, GIFs (which stands for Graphics Interchange Format) is the workhorse image of the web.for Graphics Interchange Format. Developed originally by CompuServe in the late '80s, GIFs are the workhorse image of the web. Because the format itself can display a maximum of only 256 colors (8 bits), GIFs are best used for relatively simple images with flat colors and are generally smaller in size (in terms of kilobytes).

Left This places the image on the left margin and wraps the text around it to the right. If left-aligned text comes before the image on the line, it forces left-aligned objects to wrap to a new line.

GIF stands Originally developed by CompuServe during the late 80s, GIFs (which stands for Graphics Interchange Format) is the workhorse image of the web.for Graphics Interchange Format. Developed originally by CompuServe in the late '80s, GIFs are the workhorse image of the web. Because the format itself can display a maximum of only 256 colors (8 bits), GIFs are best used for relatively simple images with flat colors and are generally smaller in size (in terms of kilobytes).

Right This places the image on the right margin and wraps the text around it to the left. If right-aligned text precedes the image on the line, it will force right-aligned objects to wrap to a new line.

GIF stands Originally developed by CompuServe during the late 80s, GIFs (which stands for Graphics Interchange Format) is the workhorse image of the web.for Graphics Interchange Format. Developed originally by CompuServe in the late '8Cs, GIFs are the workhorse image of the web. Because the format itself can display a maximum of only 256 colors (8 bits), GIFs are best used for relatively simple images with flat colors and are generally smaller in size (in terms of kilobytes).

While the differences between standard alignment and an absolute alignment are sometimes difficult to detect, they do exist. An absolute alignment will use the entire height of a line of text (which is determined by the very top of the highest character and the very bottom of the lowest character) for alignment purposes.

Browser default generally means a baseline alignment. However, the default may differ depending on the browser that is being used to view the page.

Resizing an Image

Resizing an image in Dreamweaver MX is really quite easy, but there are some important things you need to know before you start. Images in Dreamweaver MX are of very low quality: 72dpi (dots per inch), to be exact. If you increase their size, you'll see a marked loss in quality. The images will appear grainy and pixilated.

Making an image smaller in Dreamweaver MX won't cause the same problems as making it larger.

Think of it this way: if you draw a picture on a balloon, and then blow that balloon up, what do you get? Well, the image, which looked great before you blew up the balloon, has gotten all stretched out of shape. If you resize an image that you've already placed in a Dreamweaver MX document, you'll get an effect along the same lines. So, unless you have some pressing design need, avoid changing the size of an image in Dreamweaver MX. Instead, make sure the image is the exact size you want it to be *before you insert it into a Dreamweaver MX document.*

Resizing an Image with the Property Inspector

When you resize an image, you aren't resizing the original file, you're just changing the way it looks in your Document Window. To resize an image you've inserted into your Dreamweaver MX document:

1. Select the image you want to resize.

2. Open the Property Inspector (Window → Properties).

3. Enter a new width and height in the W and H boxes in the Property Inspector. Remember that all dimensions are in pixels, as opposed to another unit of measure like centimeters or millimeters.

4. The dimensions of the image will automatically update when you press Return/Enter or move the cursor out of either of the fields.

Resizing an Image with the Resize Handles

You can also resize an image by using the resize handles:

1. Click the image you want to resize.

2. Click and hold one of the resize handles.

3. Drag the resize handles until your image is the desired size and release your mouse button.

> If you hold down Shift while dragging the resize handles, your image will maintain the same proportions.

> If you have the Property Inspector open while you are using the resize handles, you'll notice that the values in the W and H boxes will change dynamically to reflect the increasing size of the image.

Reverting to the Original Image Size

If you've increased the size of an image and aren't happy with the result—and you've forgotten its original dimensions—there is an easy way to revert back to the original size of the document:

1. Select the image you've resized by clicking it with your mouse.

2. Open the Property Inspector (Window → Properties).

3. Click the Reset Size button [Reset Size] .

Using the ALT Tag

The ALT (alternative) tag is probably one of the most overlooked features you can use in creating an image. Essentially, the ALT tag is designed to provide extra information about an image when the image isn't visible. This handy feature provides information for text-only browsers (browsers that can't display images) or for browsers that are set to download images manually. One of the cool features about ALT tags is that they will display a pop-up (which is similar to a Tool Tip) when the user moves their mouse over an image.

To add an ALT tag to your image:

1. Select the image you want to add the ALT tag to.

2. Open the Property Inspector (Window → Properties).

3. Enter your text in the Alt field of the Property Inspector.

Setting a Low Source Image

A Low Source image is a helpful feature if you're designing a site that you know will be viewed by people with slower Internet connections. With this feature, you're essentially designating one image to load before the main image. Many designers use a small black-and-white version of the main image because it loads more quickly than the main image and gives visitors an idea of what they're waiting to see.

The Low Source image must have the same dimensions as the regular image it is associated with.

To add a Low Source image:

1. Click the main image for which you want to set the Low Source image.

2. Open the Property Inspector (Window → Properties).

3. Click the Browse button (to the right of the Low Src field).

DESIGN REMINDER: Designing for Accessibility

In recent years, there has been a growing desire to make web content accessible to everyone, including individuals with a variety of disabilities. One of the most pressing issues in designing accessible content is that images can't be interpreted by a screen reader, a type of software that "reads" the contents of a computer screen and then "speaks" it back to a visually impaired user. This problem derives from the fact that visual information, unlike text, involves a subjective interpretation. One person's description of an image will probably differ from another individual's description of the same image. Because of this, screen readers, which are simple pieces of software, are completely incapable of describing visual imagery, and visually impaired individuals are not only cut off from visual content, but they are often also cut off from navigation schemes—many of which depend heavily on graphical interface elements (buttons, menus, and so on). One of the best solutions to the problems is to use ALT tags for all of your images because they provide a textual alternative that can be "read" by the screen reader.

4. When the Select Image Source dialog box opens, locate the file you want to set as the Low Source image and select it.

Adding a Border to an Image

During the creative process, you may need to add a solid border around an image; for instance, you may want to set off an image from the surrounding material on the web page. However, remember to use image borders sparingly, as overuse can result in a very unattractive design. To add a border to an image in Dreamweaver MX:

1. Open the Property Inspector (Window → Properties).

2. Enter a value (width in pixels) in the Border field of the expanded Property Inspector.

Launching an External Image Editor

In Chapter 2, "Starting Up Dreamweaver," you learned how to define your external media editors. Now is the time to put all that work into practice:

1. Select the image you want to launch in the external editor.

2. Open the Property Inspector (Window → Properties).

3. Click the Edit button [Edit] (in the bottom right-hand corner) to launch the external editor associated with the particular image type.

> If Fireworks MX (or a previous version of Fireworks) has been set as an external image editor, the Edit button will feature the funky Fireworks logo.

4. Once you've made changes to the image in the external editor, save it and exit. The image in Dreamweaver MX will be automatically updated to reflect the changes. After saving the changes in the external image editor, Dreamweaver MX might prompt you to update the page. Click Yes if you want your image to be updated!

Inspiration: Design and Technique

Developed jointly by NeonSky Creative Media (`www.neonsky.com`) and Terra Incognita (`www.terraincognita.com`) for the Arizona State Institute for Human Origins, Becoming Human (see Figure 5.1) is an original interactive Flash documentary that explores human evolution from our earliest ancestors to the emergence of *Homo sapiens.*

Becoming Human features a host of innovative and interactive tools (such as interactive exhibits) that allow you to go beyond the Flash documentary itself and pursue your personal exploration into the fascinating world of human evolution.

Becoming Human is partitioned into several sections that allow you to explore questions about culture, hominid anatomy, archaeological evidence, and lineage. Each section features not only a spectacular linear Flash documentary narrated by the prestigious paleoanthropologist Donald Johanson, but also topical discussions by many other prominent scholars in the field of human evolution.

The combination of the linear documentary and the interactive exploratory tools makes Becoming Human one of the most interesting, innovative, and cutting-edge interactive web creations out there.

Figure 5.1

Becoming Human

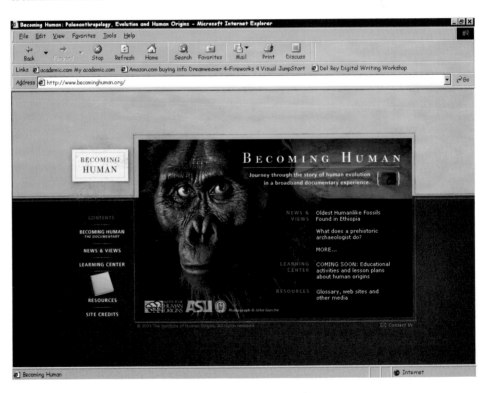

Summary

This chapter looked at how to insert images into your Dreamweaver MX documents and what you can do to them after they've been inserted. It covered such topics as aligning an image to the page, aligning an image to text, resizing an image, adding an ALT tag, adding image borders, and using an external image editor. Beyond the mechanics of adding and manipulating images in Dreamweaver MX, the chapter looked at the three web image formats: GIFs, JPEGs, and PNGs. If you're interested in learning more about the various web image formats, check out some of Webmonkey's informative articles (`http://hotwired.lycos.com/webmonkey/design/graphics/`).

In the next chapter, you'll learn how to create, manage, and manipulate the lifeblood of the web: hyperlinks.

CHAPTER 6

Working with Hyperlinks

After you've set up a local site on your hard drive, you're going to want to create links between documents and other types of media. This is where hyperlinks come into the picture. Hyperlinks are really the core of HTML. They allow the user to move effortlessly between documents, regardless of whether they're on the same server or another server entirely.

Dreamweaver MX allows you to create links between HTML documents, inline multimedia files, images, and downloadable files. In this chapter, you'll start off by learning how to add hyperlinks to both images and text. From there, you'll explore how to manage some of the finer points of link manipulation. This chapter includes the following topics:

- **Understanding hyperlinks**

- **Adding hyperlinks to text and images**

- **Changing link color**

- **Creating a named anchor**

- **Setting a link target**

- **Creating an Image Map**

- **Creating an e-mail link**

- **Building a Jump Menu**

Understanding Hyperlinks

It's no great exaggeration to say that hyperlinks (or links, as they are often referred to) are the heart and soul of the Web. When Tim Berners-Lee conceived of an Internet in which people could easily move between documents (something that hadn't been an option before), hyperlinks were the glue that held everything together. Without them, HTML documents would have existed in isolation, and the Web would never have become what it is today.

Before we start looking at how you add links in Dreamweaver MX, there are some general issues you need to know. In Dreamweaver MX, you'll be working with two types of links: relative and absolute. Technically, they aren't two different types of links but two different ways of representing the same thing.

Using Absolute Links

An absolute link—or path—provides a complete URL. For example, `http://www.macromedia.com/dreamweaver` is an absolute URL. It's important to include the `http://` protocol at the beginning of absolute URLs. If you don't, Dreamweaver MX will think that the document to which you are linking resides on your computer. The general rule is that absolute links are used to link to a document that sits on another server. You can certainly use absolute links for documents on the same server, but it's much easier if you use relative links instead.

Using Relative Links

Relative links are a little less straightforward than absolute links. Essentially, they are a cross between an instruction and shorthand. *Instruction* refers to the idea that the link itself contains information that uses the current folder on the server as a reference point for finding the document (HTML file, image, and so on) to which the URL refers. These instructions are called the path. *Shorthand* refers to the notion that a relative link doesn't need the same sort of strict use of structure and protocol (for example, `http://`) that an absolute link does. As a result, relative links can only be used to refer to documents that reside on the same server. For example, if you were linking to a document that was in the same folder, all you would have to do would be to enter the name of the file (`welcome.html`). Now, if the file was one folder above the current file, you would have to enter in the relative URL as `../welcome.html`. The `../` in the relative URL instructs the browser that the file can be found one folder above the current folder. If the file to which you were linking was two folders above the current one, you would need to enter the relative link as `../../welcome.html`.

If you are a little confused right now, don't worry too much. When you are using relative URLs, Dreamweaver MX does all the work for you. The real point of this section is to show the two types of links and give you an idea of where they should be used.

Adding Hyperlinks

In this section, you'll learn how to add links to both images and text. You'll also take a look at the handy Point to File utility that will make the creation of links a snap. In addition, you'll learn how to create a named anchor, a great feature that allows you to create a link to another point on the same page, and how to set up a link target.

> To change the color of links (including visited and active links), refer to Chapter 3, "Setting Up and Managing Your Page."

Adding a Relative Link to Text

Dreamweaver MX automatically takes care of the technical coding details necessary when creating a hyperlink, whether you are creating a relative or an absolute link.

To add a relative link to texts:

1. Select the text that you want to turn into a link.

2. Open the Property Inspector (Window → Properties).

3. Click the Browse icon  .

4. When the Select File dialog box appears, locate and select the file to which you want to link. You'll notice that the relative link, complete with the necessary path, has appeared in the Link field. If the file to which you are linking is not located in the Local Root Folder of your Local Site, Dreamweaver will ask you whether you want it copied to your local site.

The proper path to the file is automatically inserted in the Link field

5. To activate the link, press Return (Mac) or Enter (Win), or click off the Property Inspector anywhere in the Document Window.

In Dreamweaver MX, you can also insert a text hyperlink using the Hyperlink command:

1. Place the cursor in the location in the Document Window where you would like to insert the hyperlink.

2. If it isn't already, open the Insert bar (Window → Insert), select the Common tab, and click the Hyperlink button 🔗 . Alternatively, you can go to Insert → Hyperlink.

3. When the Hyperlink dialog box appears, enter the text for the link into the Text field.

4. Click the Browse button  to the right of the Link field. When the Select File dialog box appears, locate and select the file to which you want to link. You'll notice that the relative link, complete with the necessary path, has appeared in the Link field.

5. Choose the link target from the Target drop-down menu. A link's target determines where the document will load. For more information on this, see the "Setting a Link Target" section later in this chapter.

6. Enter a value into the Tab Index field. The Tab Index value determines the sequence in which links on your page will be highlighted when the user presses the Tab key.

7. Enter a title for the link into the Title field. The title itself has no bearing on how the link will look. Essentially, the name (which is not a requirement for creating a link using the Hyperlink command) is a unique identifier that you can use when you want to manipulate the hyperlink using Dynamic HTML.

8. Enter a value into the Access Key field. This value (which can only be a single key) will serve as a shortcut that your users can use to select the hyperlink in the browser.

9. When you're finished, click OK.

Adding an Absolute Link to Text

To add an absolute link:

> You can also use the Insert Hyperlink command to add an absolute text link by following the steps in the previous section. The only difference is that you'll need to manually enter the full URL into the Hyperlink dialog box's Link field.

1. Select the text that you want to turn into a link.

2. Open the Property Inspector (Window → Properties).

3. In the Link field, type in the full URL of the document you're linking to.

4. To activate the link, press Return (Mac) or Enter (Win) or click off the Property Inspector anywhere in the Document Window.

> If the full absolute URL is long and easily forgotten, you can open the file in a browser and then copy and paste the full URL into the Link field of the Property Inspector.

Using the Point to File Icon

The Point to File icon is a handy tool that works in tandem with the Site panel to provide a visual way to link to files within your site.

> Be forewarned, however, that despite its usefulness, using the Point to File icon can be a little frustrating.

1. Open the Site panel for the local site in which you are working by going either to Window → Site or Site → Site Files.

2. Select the text in the Document Window that you want to turn into a link.

> If the Site window disappears, use your toolbar to maximize the Site window (which brings it back into view). Alternatively, if you are working on a Mac, press Alt+Tab.

3. Open the Property Inspector (Window → Properties).

4. Click and drag the Point to File icon ⊕ to the file in the Site panel to which you want to make a link.

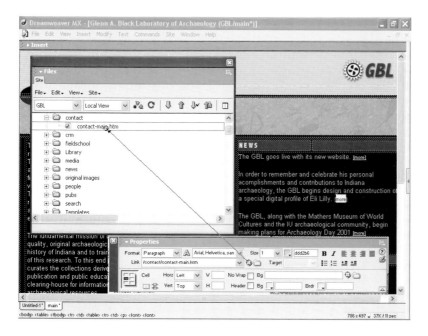

5. Release your mouse button over the desired file. The relative URL automatically appears in the Link field.

Creating a Named Anchor

Up until this point you've looked at how to create links to other files entirely. Now you're going to spend a little time exploring how you go about creating a link to a location in the same page.

At one time or another, you've probably visited an extremely long web page that uses links to transport you to specific locations in the text. This is done with something called *named anchors*. Essentially, named anchors (which are sometimes called jump links) create a defined point that you can link to from within a page. You can also use them to jump to a specific location in another page entirely.

Creating a jump link is actually a two-stage process: creating the named anchor itself and then linking to it. You'll start off by learning how to create the named anchor. Then, you'll go on to look at how you can create a link to that anchor.

To insert a named anchor:

1. Place the cursor where you want to insert the named anchor.

2. If it isn't already, open the Insert bar (Window → Insert), select the Common tab, and click the Named Anchor button ⚓ . Alternatively, you can go to Insert → Named Anchor.

3. When the Named Anchor dialog box opens, type a name in the Anchor Name field.

4. Click OK.

Unfortunately, Dreamweaver MX doesn't keep track of the names you give to the named anchor, so it's a good idea to keep the name simple and descriptive and to write it down so you don't forget it.

Because the named anchor isn't a visible element like an image or some text, it is represented in the Document Window by a small icon .

■ ■ ■ ■

DESIGN REMINDER: Scroll-o-Matic

Despite the fact that named anchors can be used to make long pages more usable, as I've mentioned before, people tend to dislike reading perpetually scrolling pages. Because of this, it's a good idea to break up your textual content so that it is spread over a bunch of different pages. This way, your audience will still be able to read all the text they want, but it will be partitioned into more manageable chunks that won't require a huge amount of scrolling.

Many other invisible elements like scripts, comments, embedded styles, line breaks, or server side markup tags are also represented by a small unique icon. While these icons only appear in the Document Window (and don't actually take up any real space) they can often become a little distracting, especially if you've got quite a few invisible elements in your document, each represented by its own unique icon. As a result, there are a couple ways to turn them on and off: you can go to View → Visual Aids and select Invisible Elements, or you can go to Edit → Preferences, select Invisible Elements in the Category list, and select the individual invisible elements that you want visible.

> If you've "turned off" a given invisible element in the Invisible Elements section of the Edit Preferences dialog box, it cannot be "turned back on" using the View menu. You'll need to go back and do it in the Edit Preferences dialog box.

Keeping Named Anchors Organized

As mentioned, Dreamweaver MX doesn't keep an easily accessible list of the various named anchors you created in the currently open document (or the currently open Local Site for that matter). As you add more named anchors, it's a very wise idea to write each down. Even if you do, however, it's quite easy to lose track of which named anchor has which name. Here is a trick for identifying each named anchor.

1. Select the icon for the named anchor you want to identify.

2. If your named anchors aren't visible, make them visible by following the process described in the previous section.

3. Open the Property Inspector (Window → Properties).

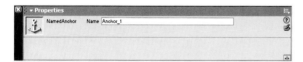

4. The Property Inspector displays the name of the currently selected anchor.

Linking to a Named Anchor on the Same Page

To create a link to the named anchor on the same page:

1. Select either the text or image you want to link to the named anchor.

2. Open the Property Inspector (Window → Properties).

3. In the Link field of the Property Inspector, type # followed by the name of the anchor you just created.

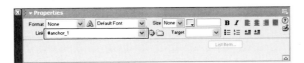

4. Press Return (Mac) or Enter (Win) or click off the Property Inspector anywhere in the Document Window. The text that you linked to the named anchor has now been activated.

> You can also click and drag the Point to File icon to the Named Anchor on the page to create the link.

Linking to a Named Anchor on a Different Page

You can take the process one step further and create a named anchor on another page to which you can link. The steps are almost the same as linking to a named anchor, but they take place over two different pages instead of one:

1. Place the cursor where you want to insert the named anchor.

2. If it isn't already, open the Insert bar (Window → Insert), select the Common tab, and click the Named Anchor button. Alternatively, you can go to Insert → Named Anchor.

3. Type a name in the Anchor Name field of the Named Anchor dialog box; for this exercise, enter **jumplink**.

4. Click OK.

5. Open (or create) a page into which you want to insert the link to the named anchor you created in the previous step (this means that you'll have two separate documents open at the same time—in one, you've just inserted the named anchor, and in the other you'll create the link).

6. Call the first page, the one in which you inserted the anchor, `anchor.html`. Call the second page, the one that has the actual link, `link.html`.

7. In `link.html`, select either the text or image you want to link to the named anchor.

8. Open the Property Inspector (Window → Properties).

9. Click the Browse icon 🗀 (located to the right of the Link field).

10. When the Select File dialog box appears, locate the file in which you placed the anchor (in our case, `anchor.html`) and select it.

    The correct filename and path appear in the Link field.

11. Directly after the path and filename, type # followed by the name of the anchor you inserted in the first document (in this case, **jumplink**).

12. To activate the link, press Return (Mac) or Enter (Win) or click anywhere in the Document Window off the Property Inspector.

For the named anchor to work properly, make sure that there aren't any spaces between the path/filename and the beginning of the # and anchor name.

Setting a Link Target

A *link target* acts as a command to the browser, telling it the specific window in which to load a link. For the most part, link targets are used in conjunction with frames (something you will fully explore in Chapter 8, "Framing Your Page"). However, there are two types of link targets that are easily used without the presence of frames. The first, a *blank target*, loads the link in a new browser window, maintaining the window in which the hyperlink was located just below the newly opened window.

The second type of link target that can be employed without the presence of frames is a *self target*. Essentially, a self target, which is the default type of link target in Dreamweaver MX, opens the link in the same browser window.

In the following step-by-step exercise, you'll learn how to set a link target for a relative link. (The process is exactly the same for absolute links.) You'll also explore how to create a blank link target (Dreamweaver MX will set a self link target by default if one isn't specified).

1. Select either the text or image that you want to turn into a link.

2. Open the Property Inspector (Window → Properties).

3. Click the Browse icon 📁 .

4. When the Select File dialog box appears, locate and select the file to which you want to link.

5. In the Property Inspector, open the Target drop-down menu and choose **_blank.**

6. To activate the link, press Return (Mac) or Enter (Win) or click off the Property Inspector anywhere in the Document Window.

You'll be spending ample time exploring the other types of link targets in Chapter 8.

Beyond the Hyperlink Basics

Up until this point, you've explored only the basics of creating and manipulating hyperlinks in Dreamweaver MX. There are, however, many other techniques that can be used to link different documents. In the following section, you'll learn how to create an e-mail link, an Image Map, and a Jump Menu.

Creating an E-mail Link

An e-mail link is a link that opens a blank message window in the e-mail program of the user's browser. When the blank message window appears, it contains the e-mail that was included in the link. To insert an e-mail link:

1. Click where you'd like to insert the e-mail link in the Document Window.

2. If it isn't already, open the Insert bar (Window → Insert), select the Common tab, and click the E-mail Link button   . Alternatively, you can go to Insert → E-mail Link.

3. When the Insert E-mail Link dialog box opens, enter the text for the link in the Text field.

4. In the E-mail field, enter the appropriate e-mail address.

5. Click OK.

You can also add an e-mail link manually by using the Property Inspector.

1. Select either the text or image that you want to turn into a link.

2. Open the Property Inspector (Window → Properties).

3. In the Link field of the Property Inspector, type **mailto:** followed by the appropriate e-mail address.

For the e-mail link to work properly, there cannot be any spaces in the text you manually enter in the Link field.

4. To activate the link, press Return (Mac) or Enter (Win) or click off the Property Inspector anywhere in the Document Window.

Nowadays, it's standard practice to show the actual e-mail address rather than random text that says something like "e-mail me." By doing this, your audience can copy and paste it into an alternate e-mail client or write it down for future use.

Creating an Image Map

An *Image Map* is a fusion of a link and an image. You've probably noticed that when you add a link to an image, the entire image becomes a link. With an Image Map, you can designate portions of an image (using hotspots) as links. You can even have multiple hotspots in the same image, each linking to a different page. Creating an Image Map involves two different processes: inserting the image and defining hotspots and links.

> Before you start inserting hotspots and defining links, you should decide which areas of your image you want to attach links.

Working with the Image

1. If you haven't already inserted the image you want to map, do so by following the procedure outlined in Chapter 5, "Inserting and Controlling Images."

2. Select the image to which you want to add an Image Map.

3. If it isn't already, open and expand the Property Inspector (Window → Properties). In the lower left-hand corner, you'll see the Image Map tools.

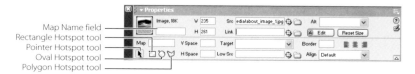

4. In the Map Name field, enter a unique name for your Image Map.

> If the name you choose is also used by another Image Map on the same page, neither will work. Also, try to not use spaces in the name

Now you must define your hotspots.

Defining Hotspots

Depending on the general shape of the area that you want to turn into a hotspot, you have three tools to choose from: Rectangular Hotspot, Circular Hotspot, and Polygon Hotspot. The Circular Hotspot and Rectangular Hotspot are self-explanatory. The Polygon Hotspot, on the other hand, is designed to create an irregular hotspot that is neither a circle nor a rectangle.

Depending on the shape of the hotspot you want to define, do one of the following:

- Click the Rectangular Hotspot button ☐ , move the crosshair (+) over the place in the image where you want the hotspot, and click and drag until you've covered the area you want. When you're finished, release the mouse button.

- Select the Circular Hotspot button ○ , move the crosshair over the place in the image where you want the hotspot, and click and drag until you've covered the area you want. Release the mouse button when you're finished.

- Select the Polygon Hotspot button ♡ , place the crosshair along any edge of the irregular area, and click once. A light blue point appears where you click as in the image on the bottom left.

- Move the crosshair to the next point along the edge of the irregular area and click again. A line appears between the two points as in the image on the bottom right.

- Continue clicking, adding points along the edge of the irregular area until it's fully outlined (and shaded) with the hotspot.

First point

Second point

First point

Once you successfully define a hotspot, the Hotspot view of the Property Inspector will appear:

Integrating the Link

Now you can integrate the actual hyperlink into your Image Map:

1. Select the hotspot to which you wish to attach the hyperlink.

2. Click the Browse icon 🗀 .

3. When the Select File dialog box appears, locate and select the file to which you want to link. Alternatively, you can manually enter an absolute URL into the Link field.

4. Choose a link target from the Target drop-down menu.

5. Enter any alt text that you want associated with the hotspot in the Alt field.

6. To activate the Image Map, click anywhere off the Property Inspector in the Document Window.

Once you create the Image Map, you can edit it by clicking the hotspot you want to edit (represented by the pale blue area on the image) and making any changes in the Property Inspector. To move a hotspot around, click and drag it with the Pointer Hotspot tool.

> If you create two overlapping hotspots, the area of overlap will be associated with the final hotspot created (as opposed to the first one created.)

Building a Jump Menu

A Jump Menu is a handy little widget that allows you to create a drop-down menu populated with a series of options, each of which serve as a hyperlink.

> A Jump Menu is really nothing more than a standard menu object (something you'll learn about in Chapter 10, "Obtaining User Information with Forms") to which the Jump Menu Go behavior has been attached. However, as Jump Menus are easily created without having to go anywhere near the Behavior panel (something you'll spend ample time investigating in Chapter 15, "Adding Advanced Interactivity with Behaviors"), this chapter is a far better place to discuss them.

To create a Jump Menu:

1. Place your cursor in the location where you want to insert the Jump Menu.

2. If it isn't already, open the Insert bar (Window → Insert), select the Forms tab, and click the Jump Menu button 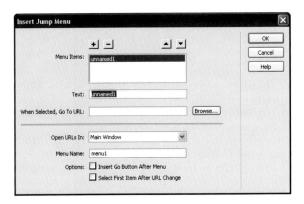 . Alternatively, you can go to Insert → Form Objects → Jump Menu. This will open the Insert Jump Menu dialog box.

3. In the Text field, enter the text you want for the first menu item.

4. In the When Selected Go To URL field, enter either the relative or absolute URL you wish to open when the user clicks the menu item. Alternatively, you can click the Browse button. When the Select File dialog box opens, locate the file you wish to open when the user clicks the menu item, and click Select.

5. Select the location where you want the URL to open from the Open URLs In drop-down menu. If the document in which the Jump Menu is located doesn't contain frames, the only option available in the Open URLs In drop-down menu will be Main Window. If, however, your document contains frames, the drop-down menu will contain their names.

> To learn about frames, see Chapter 8.

6. To add additional menu items, click the Add Menu button ➕ (at the top of the Insert Jump Menu dialog box) and repeat steps 3 to 5. When you finish adding all the menu items to the Jump Menu, go to the next step.

7. Enter a name into the Menu Name field.

8. To add a Go button , select the Insert Go Button After Menu option. If you do this, the user will have to click the Go button after selecting one of the options from the menu itself. If a Go button isn't added, the link will load automatically when the user selects it from the Jump Menu.

9. When you finish adding all of the menu items, click OK.

Jump Menus have a peculiar little bug of which you should be aware: once a user has selected a menu item, they cannot return to the page on which the Jump Menu is located and reselect the same menu item. To bypass this glitch, insert a Go button. The user will be able to use it to revisit any of the Jump Menu links by selecting it and clicking the Go button.

Editing a Jump Menu

Once you build a Jump Menu using the previous steps, you aren't stuck with what you've created. You can quite easily go back and make changes and modifications. The only hitch is that you can't make changes with the Insert Jump Menu dialog box (which fulfilled all your Jump Menu needs in the previous section); you must use a somewhat less streamlined tool accessible through the Property Inspector. To edit a Jump Menu:

1. Select the Jump Menu that you want to edit.

2. Open the Property Inspector (Window → Properties).

3. Click the Edit Initial List Values button `List Values...` to open the List Values dialog box.

4. When the List Values dialog box opens, you'll see all the menu items (whose names you set by entering text into the Insert Jump Menu dialog box's Text field) are in the Item Label column. Each menu item's associated URL is located in the Value column. From here you have two options:

- To change a menu item's text, select it in the Item Label column. The text will automatically change into a live field into which you can type some new text.

- To change a menu item's associated URL, select it in the Value column. When it turns into an editable field, just type in a new URL.

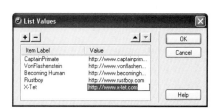

5. When you finish editing the Jump Menu items, click OK.

Inspiration: Design and Technique

Arguably one of the slickest and most talented visual designers around, Brian Taylor has worked in all sorts of different mediums: print, 3D, web; if you can think of it, he's probably done it. His talent and vision is nothing short of extraordinary—a fact that is reflected in his personal site XL5 Design (`www.xl5design.com`).

The site (see Figure 6.1) features an amazingly simple and well designed layout that highlights many of his previous creations, experiments, and ongoing projects, most notably the hotly anticipated short 3D animated film *Rustboy* (whose website is featured in the color section of this book).

Figure 6.1

Brian Taylor's XL5 Design

Summary

You spent this chapter fully exploring hyperlinks. We discussed the differences between absolute and relative links and covered the process by which you add links to both text and images. We also explored how you can add links to specific sections on the same page (or on another page) by using named anchors. The chapter closed with a look at link targets, e-mail links, Image Maps, and Jump Menus. In the next chapter, you are going to start exploring tables, a tool used both to present tabular data and lay out your page.

CHAPTER 7

Working with Tables

The placement of images, text, and other elements, and their relation to one another, contribute to the layout of your page. Until now, you haven't had a lot of control over where elements were placed in your page because you've been restricted by the inherent limitations of HTML. But that's going to change drastically with tables, one of the most powerful layout tools in Dreamweaver MX.

Dreamweaver MX offers two different creative environments in which you can create tables. The first is the Standard view, whose tools have been around since the first version of Dreamweaver. The second, Layout view, was a revolutionary new feature added in Dreamweaver 4 that allows you a great deal more control over the creation and manipulation of tables. Topics in this chapter include the following:

- **Understanding tables**
- **Creating tables in Standard view**
- **Manipulating Standard view tables**
- **Adding content to a cell**
- **Working with cells, rows, and columns**
- **Creating tables and cells in Layout view**
- **Manipulating tables and cells in Layout view**

Understanding Tables

As with tables in word processing or spreadsheet programs, web-based tables are composed of rows, columns, and cells.

Content, whether visual or textual, can be placed in any cell to create a vertical and horizontal structure. Dreamweaver MX provides two ways to create tables: Standard view and Layout view. In both cases, once you've created a table, there are many ways you can manipulate it to get the exact look you want.

Standard view is best suited for laying out tabular data or for simple organization of text and graphics. Layout view is better suited for laying out your entire page.

Creating Tables in Standard View

The tools in Standard view let you lay out tabular data and organize text and graphics in the Document Window. As with many features in Dreamweaver MX, there are two ways to insert tables in Standard view. The first uses the Insert bar:

1. Place your cursor at the location in the Document Window where you want to insert the table.

2. Open Insert bar (Windows → Insert) and select the Layout tab.

3. If it isn't already, make sure you have the Standard View button Standard View toggled.

4. Click the Insert Table button ⊞ . (Alternatively, you can click the Insert Table button located under the Insert bar's Tables tab.)

5. From here, you'll set the initial properties of your table using the Insert Table dialog box, a topic that will be thoroughly covered in the "Setting Initial Table Properties in Standard View" section.

To insert a table using the Insert menu:

1. In the Document Window, place your cursor where you want to insert the table.

2. Go to Insert → Table.

3. Once the Insert Table dialog box appears, enter in the values of your table. To set the initial properties of your table, go to the next section ("Setting Initial Table Properties in Standard View").

Setting Initial Table Properties in Standard View

The Insert Table dialog box appears after you use either the Insert bar or the Insert menu to add your table. This dialog box allows you to set the initial properties of your table. You can either accept the default values (which can easily be changed later) or type in some of your own.

Let's have a look at each of the values in the Table Properties dialog box and how you change them.

> Each of the following sections covers one table property, and each set of steps ends with the instruction to click OK. However, you can certainly set all of the properties at once; if you choose to do so, you should wait until you've set all of your properties before clicking OK.

Setting Rows and Columns

When you set the number of rows and columns, you are essentially setting the structure of your table. Each value is represented numerically and is set like this:

1. With the Insert Table dialog box open (which should have automatically opened when you used either the Object Palette or the Insert menu to add a table), click in the Rows field.

2. Type in the number of rows you want in your table (for our purposes here, enter 5).

3. Click in the Columns field and type in the number of columns you want in your table (for this example, enter 4).

4. Click OK.

Setting Table Width

Once you've set the number of rows and columns, you need to set the width of your table. There are two types of width values you can choose from: pixels and percent. As is the case with Horizontal Rules (see Chapter 4, "Adding and Manipulating Text"), if you choose pixels, the width of your table will be fixed, regardless of the size of the user's browser window. As a result, if the width of the table is larger than the browser window, the user will have to scroll to see the entire table. On the other hand, if you choose percent, your table will always resize dynamically. Be aware, however, that the minimum size is determined by objects contained within the table itself. For example, a table whose sizing is set to percent that contains an image measuring 200 pixels by 200 pixels will not be able to shrink any smaller than 200×200.

To set the width of your table:

1. With the Insert Table dialog box open, open the drop-down menu to the right of the Width field and select either pixels or percent. For this example, make sure Percent is selected.

2. Click in the Width field and enter a value for the width of your table (for this example, enter 75).

3. Click OK.

Setting Border Thickness

The next table property to set is the border thickness, or the solid edge that runs around the perimeter of the table.

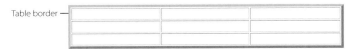

Table border —

The table's border, whose value is set in pixels, can be any color you choose; the default color is gray. Don't worry, you can change the border color after you've already set the initial table properties.

> If you want your table to be invisible, a common strategy for laying out your content is to set the border thickness to 0.

To set a table's border thickness:

1. With the Insert Table dialog box open, click in the Border field and type a value that you want for your border thickness (for this example, enter 1).

2. Click OK.

Setting Cell Padding and Cell Spacing

Cell Padding

Both cell padding and cell spacing can be tricky to get a handle on. Basically, cell padding refers to the number of pixels between the wall of the cell and the object within the cell.

■ ■ ■ ■

DESIGN REMINDER: Scroll-o-matic

One of the most heinous errors in web design is the unintentional creation of a page in which the user has to scroll to the right to see all the content. More often than not, this situation is caused by the use of tables whose sizing was fixed (as opposed to being set to percent), resulting in tables that are larger than some users' browsers and cannot be viewed without scrolling to the right.

Cell spacing is the number of pixels between each cell.

The values for both cell padding and cell spacing are in pixels. To set cell padding and cell spacing:

1. With the Insert Table dialog box open, click in the Cell Padding field and type in a value for your table's cell padding (for this example, enter 5).

2. Click in the Cell Spacing field and type in a value that you want for your table's cell spacing (for this example, enter 5).

3. Click OK.

Manipulating Tables in Standard View

With the Property Inspector, you can access and manipulate the properties of a table after you've created it. All of the initial table properties you set with the Table Properties dialog box are accessible, along with a host of additional properties such as table alignment and background color.

Setting Table Alignment

Like most elements in Dreamweaver MX (such as images and text), you can align a table to your page. However, as with any other alignment, you are limited to left, center, and right justification.

> If your table width is set at 100 percent, aligning it won't make any difference.

1. Select the table you want to align.

> To select the entire table, click its top-left corner, the right edge, or the bottom edge.

2. Open the Property Inspector (Window → Properties).

3. Open the Table Align drop-down menu (to the right of the Align field) and choose one of the Align options: Left, Right, Center.

Changing Background Color

Changing the background color of a table works pretty much the same as changing the background color of your page (see Chapter 3, "Setting Up and Managing Your Page"), except that the color is confined to the table itself. If you resize the table (a process you'll look at shortly), the background color will automatically increase to fill the entire table. To change the background color of your table:

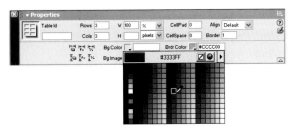

1. Select the table whose color you want to change.

2. Open the Property Inspector (Window → Properties).

3. Click the color swatch (to the right of the words Bg Color in the expanded Property Inspector) to open the Color Palette.

Remember, to expand the Property Inspector, click the down-pointing arrow in its lower right-hand corner.

4. Move your mouse over a color you like and click it. The background color of your table automatically changes.

If you want to choose a color that isn't contained in the Color Palette, you can follow the procedure described in Chapter 3 (see the section "Using the Color Dialog Box").

Setting Border Color

As mentioned earlier in the section "Setting Border Thickness," you can change the border color as well as the thickness:

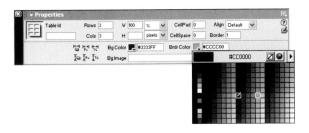

1. Select the table whose border color you want to change.

2. Open the Property Inspector (Window → Properties).

3. Click the color swatch, located to the right of the words Brdr Color, to open the Color Palette.

4. Move your mouse over a color you like and click it. The border color of your table automatically changes.

If your border thickness is set to 0, changing the border color won't have any visible effect. If you have your border thickness set to more than 0, you'll still be able to see the rows and columns after you've changed the table's background color. If you want your entire table to be one solid color, you can either set your table border thickness to 0 or set your border color to the same color as the background of the table.

Adding a Background Image

As in the case of your web page, you can add a background image to a table. The only differ-ence, obviously, is that the image is confined to the table itself. If you resize the table (as you'll learn how to do shortly), the background image will automatically fill its increased size. Note that when you add a background image to a table, the image tiles to fit the available space, just like when you add a background image to a web page.

1. Select the table to which you want to add a background image.

2. Open the Property Inspector (Window → Properties).

3. Click the Browse icon 📁 (to the right of the BgImage field).

4. When the Select Image Source dialog box appears, locate and select the file you want to use as a background image in your table.

> If you have both a background image and a background color set for your table, the back-ground image will always cover the background color.

Resizing a Table

You certainly aren't stuck with the initial table width you set. To resize your table:

1. Select the table you want to resize.

2. Open the Property Inspector (Window → Properties).

3. Open the drop-down menu to the right of the Width (W) field to choose either pixels or percent.

4. Enter a value into the Width (W) field for the width of your table.

5. Enter a value into the Height (H) field for the height of your table.

6. To apply your changes, press Enter or click anywhere off the Property Inspector in the Document Window.

> It isn't as important to set the Height value as it is to set the Width value because a table will constantly expand vertically to fit the content you add in its cells.

In addition to resizing your table numerically, you can also do it manually using the Resize handles that appear when a table is selected:

1. Select the table you want to resize. When it's selected, resize handles appear along the bottom of the table, the right side of the table, and in the bottom right-hand corner of the table.

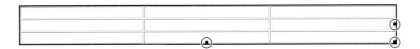

2. From here, you can click and drag any of the handles to manually resize the selected table:

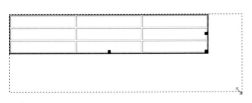

   - Clicking and dragging the handle on the bottom allows you to resize the table vertically.

   - Clicking and dragging the handle on the right side lets you resize the table horizontally.

   - Clicking and dragging the handle in the bottom right hand corner allows you to resize the table both horizontally and vertically at the same time.

3. When the table has reached the desired size, release the mouse button, and the table will automatically resize.

Adding Text to a Table

To add text to a table:

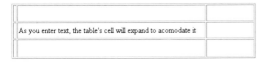

1. Click in the cell where you want to add text.

2. Type the text you want to add. The cell automatically expands to accommodate what you're typing.

> You'll find that as your text expands, the cell in which it resides will horizontally resize itself. This results in the adjacent cells resizing as well.

3. To move to the next cell, either click in the desired location or press Tab.

Adding an Image to a Table

To add an image to your table:

1. Click in the cell where you want to add an image.

2. Click the Insert Image button in the Insert bar, or go to Insert → Image.

3. When the Select Image Source dialog box appears, locate and select the image you want to insert.

4. The cell automatically expands to accommodate the image.

Working with Rows, Columns, and Cells

Now that you know how to apply changes to the table as a whole, it's time to learn how to work with individual rows, columns, and cells.

Selecting Individual Rows or Columns

Before you learn how to work with individual rows, columns, and cells, you need to know how to select them—as opposed to selecting the entire table. To select an individual table row:

1. Position your cursor just to the left (outside the table border) of the row you want to select. The cursor changes to a right-pointing arrow.

2. Click to select the entire row.

To select a column:

1. Position your cursor just above the column you want to select. The cursor changes to a down-pointing arrow.

2. Click to select the entire column.

Adding a Row or Column

A table certainly wouldn't be much use if you were allowed to work only with a fixed number of rows and columns. To add a row:

1. Select the table to which you want to add a row (or rows).

2. Open the Property Inspector (Window → Properties).

3. Enter a value into the Rows field for the total number of rows you want your table to have. For instance, if you have 3 rows and you want to add 3, enter 6.

4. To apply your changes, either press Enter or click off the Property Inspector anywhere in the Document Window.

Alternatively, you can add rows to a table by using the main program drop-down menu:

1. Place your cursor in the table to which you want to add a row (do not select the entire table as you did previously).

2. Go to Modify → Table → Insert Row. Alternatively, you can add an additional row by pressing Tab when you're in the bottom row of a table.

To add a column (or columns) to your table, the steps are almost the same:

1. Select the table to which you want to add a column (or columns).

2. Open the Property Inspector (Window → Properties).

3. Enter a value into the Cols field for the total number of rows you want your table to have. For instance, if you have 3 columns and you want to add 3, enter 6.

4. To apply your changes, either press Enter (Mac)/ Return (Win) or click off the Property Inspector anywhere in the Document Window.

As with adding rows, you can also add columns using the Modify menu:

1. Place your cursor in the table to which you want to add a column (do not select the entire table as you did previously).

2. Go to Modify → Table → Insert Column.

Deleting a Row or Column

You can also delete rows and columns. To delete a row:

1. Click in the cell of a row you want to delete (do not select the entire row).

2. Go to Modify → Table → Delete Row.

3. The row where you placed your cursor is automatically deleted.

To delete a column (or columns) from your table:

1. Click in the cell of a column you want to delete.

2. Go to Modify → Table → Delete Column.

3. The column where you placed your cursor is automatically deleted.

> You can also decrease the number of rows or columns in your table. Just follow the procedure you used to add rows or columns with the Property Inspector, but type in a smaller number instead of a larger one.

Aligning Content within a Cell

Because a cell is a unit unto itself, you have a few more alignment options than you normally would if you were aligning something to the page. While you can align content to the left, center, or right, you also can align content vertically to the top, middle, bottom, or baseline. This is handy when you want to exert a little more control over how the content in your table looks. Follow these steps to align content within a cell:

1. Click in the cell whose contents you want to align. Make sure that your cursor is visible in the cell before you continue.

> There is no need to select the object you want to align. You simply need to place your cursor in the cell you want to work with, and Dreamweaver MX will do the rest.

2. Open the Property Inspector (Window → Properties).

3. Click the down-pointing arrow to the right of the Horz field and choose Left, Right, or Center according to your page's needs.

4. The contents in the cell align automatically.

Horizontal Alignment drop-down menu

To align content vertically, the process is almost the same:

1. Click in the cell whose contents you want to align. Make sure that your cursor is visible in the cell before you continue.

2. If it isn't already, open the Property Inspector (Window → Properties).

3. Click the down-pointing arrow to the right of the Vert field and choose Top, Middle, Bottom, or Baseline according to your page's needs (for this example, choose Bottom).

Vertical Alignment drop-down menu

4. As in the case of the horizontal alignment, the contents of the cell align automatically.

> Once you set a cell's alignment (whether horizontal or vertical), all future content that you add to that particular cell will also be aligned this way.

Merging Cells

When you're working with tables in Standard view, you aren't stuck with the symmetrical layout of columns and rows that you initially created. It's quite easy to turn any number of contiguous cells into one "megacell," thereby allowing you to exert far more control over using a table to lay out content:

1. Place your cursor in the first cell you want to include in your multicell selection.

2. Hold down Shift and click in the next cell you want to include in your selection. A black selection box appears around both cells.

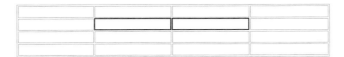

3. With Shift still held down, click any other cells you want to include in your selection.

4. If it isn't already, open the Property Inspector (Window → Properties).

5. Click the Merge Cells icon 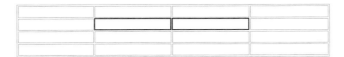 (in the bottom-left corner of the expanded Property Inspector).

6. Your selected cells will automatically combine into one cell.

Besides being contiguous, the cells you want to merge must also be in the shape of a rectangle. If they aren't, Dreamweaver MX will automatically expand the selection to make it a rectangle.

Creating Tables in Layout View

Layout view is probably one of the most progressive and useful features in Dreamweaver MX. With Layout view, you create tables with a much higher level of control than you have in Standard view. Layout view allows you to actually draw tables and cells (called layout tables and layout cells) and then manipulate them. The result is a page laid out with far more precision than is possible in Standard view. The cool thing (and this is the whole point of creating tables in Layout View) is that once you draw a layout table or cell in Layout view, Dreamweaver MX automatically takes care of the underlying table structure, thereby allowing you to focus on your creative endeavors instead of wrestling a table into the exact form you want.

Inserting a Layout Table

When you insert a layout table, you are essentially drawing the *external* structure of your table. A layout table, however, doesn't have any internal structure until you draw layout cells within it. Think of a layout table as a frame within which you create the internal structure (rows, columns, and cells) of your table. To insert a layout table:

1. Open the Insert bar (Windows → Insert), and select the Layout tab.

2. Click the Layout View button `Layout View` in the View panel.

> When you click the Layout View button, the Getting Started in Layout View dialog box will appear. Don't worry about this—it is designed purely to give you some quick information on Layout View and can be immediately closed down.

3. Click the Draw Layout Table icon 🖼 in the Layout panel.

4. Your cursor will automatically change into a plus (+) symbol when you move it off the Insert bar. Position the plus (+) cursor where you want to start your layout table.

5. Click and drag until the outline is the size that you want for your layout table.

6. When the outline is the size you want, release your mouse button. The layout table is automatically created.

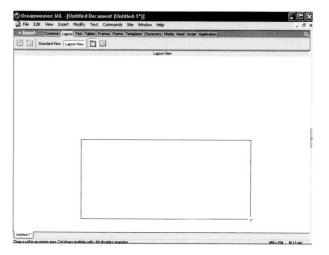

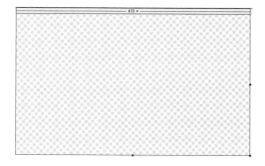

A layout table must be justified to the top right-hand corner of your Document Window. However, as you've probably noticed, Dreamweaver MX lets you draw a layout table anywhere on your page. If a layout table must be justified to the top right of the Document Window, how can you stick one anywhere you want? Well, essentially Dreamweaver MX cheats a little by placing the layout table that is not justified to the top right-hand corner of the Document Window inside a layout table (which it automatically generates) that is justified to the top right-hand corner of the Document Window.

Inserting a Layout Cell

Layout cells cannot exist without a table. If you want to insert a layout cell, you can first create a layout table, as just described, and then create a layout cell within it. Alternatively, you can draw a layout cell in Layout view, and Dreamweaver MX automatically creates a layout table as a container for the cell:

When you draw a layout cell, the layout table that is created by Dreamweaver MX automatically occupies the entire width of your Document Window.

1. Open the Insert bar Layout View (Windows → Insert), and select the Layout tab.

2. Click the Layout View button in the View panel.

3. Click the Draw Layout Cell button in the Layout panel.

4. Your cursor will automatically change into a plus (+) symbol when you move it off the Insert bar. Position the plus (+) cursor where you want to start your layout cell.

5. Click and drag until the outline is the size that you want for your layout cell (see the image on the left).

6. When the outline is the size you want, release your mouse button. Both the layout cell and its underlying layout table will be automatically created (see the image on the right).

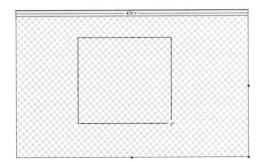
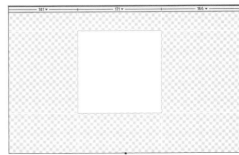

If you already have a layout table inserted (using the process described in the previous section), you can follow the steps just outlined to draw any number of layout cells within its confines.

> When you create a layout cell, faint lines are added to the layout table. This is the underlying structure (rows and columns) that Dreamweaver MX creates to accommodate your newly created layout cell.

Moving and Resizing Layout Tables and Cells

Both layout cells and tables can be resized.

> Any layout table that resides within another layout table can be moved around using the same process described in the upcoming "Moving Layout Cells" section.

The following section describes how to resize a layout table and then how to resize and move layout cells.

Resizing a Layout Table

To resize a layout table:

1. Select the layout table you want to resize by clicking either its edge or the Layout Table tab.
2. Resize handles will appear around the table's edge as seen in the image on the left.
3. Click one of the handles and drag the table to the desired size as in the image on the right.
4. Release your mouse button when the table has reached the desired size.

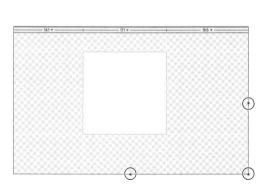
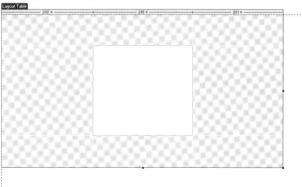

A layout table cannot be resized any smaller than the layout cells that it contains.

Resizing a Layout Cell

To resize a layout cell:

1. Select the layout cell you want to resize by clicking its edge. (The edge of this layout cell will change color from blue to red when you move your mouse over it.)

2. After clicking the cell's edge, the resize handles will appear (as shown in the image on the left).

3. Click one of the handles and drag the cell to the desired size (as shown in the image on the right).

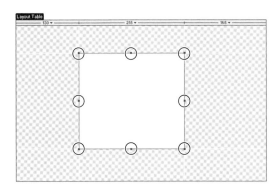 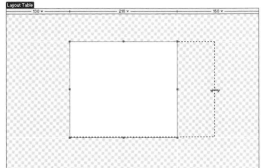

4. Release your mouse button when the cell has reached the desired size.

You can't increase the size of a layout cell beyond the edge of the layout table.

Moving a Layout Cell

You can easily move a layout cell around the layout table in which it resides. You can also move a layout table that resides within another layout table. Here's how to move a layout cell.

1. Select the layout cell you want to move by clicking its edge. (The edge of this layout cell will change color from blue to red when you move your mouse over it.)

You can't move the layout cell outside the confines of the layout table.

2. With your mouse still on the cell's edge, click and drag to where you want to move the cell.

3. When the layout cell is where you want it, release your mouse button.

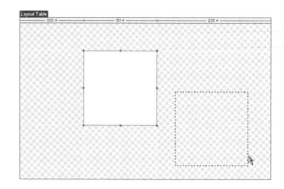

Manipulating a Layout Table with the Property Inspector

Once you create a layout table, you can access several of its properties using the Property Inspector. This section will show you how to change a layout table's width and height, as well as how to change its cell padding and cell spacing.

Setting Width and Height

Instead of resizing a table by dragging, the Property Inspector allows you to set the exact width and height of any layout table in pixels:

1. Select the layout table you want to resize by either clicking its edge or the Layout Table tab.

2. Open the Property Inspector (Window → Properties).

3. Make sure the Fixed radio button (to the left of the Width field) is checked.

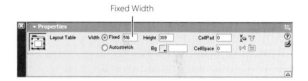

> In addition to the Fixed Width option, there is an option to make the Table Autostretch—a topic we'll explore later in the chapter.

4. Enter a value for the width of the layout table into the Width field. As soon as you enter it and move your cursor out of the field, your changes take effect.

5. Enter a value for the height of the layout table into the Height field. As soon as you enter it and move your cursor out of the field, your changes take effect.

> When you are in Layout view, the width of your columns (which are determined by the width of the various layout cells you've created) are displayed in the column header area at the top of each column.

Setting Cell Padding and Spacing

Here's how to set a table's cell padding and cell spacing in Layout view:

1. Select the layout table you are working with by either clicking its edge or the Layout Table tab.

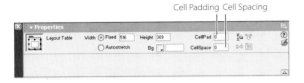

2. Open the Property Inspector (Window ➔ Properties).

3. Enter a value for your layout table's cell padding into the CellPad field.

4. Enter a value for your layout table's cell spacing into the CellSpace field.

5. To apply your changes, either press Enter or click anywhere off the Property Inspector in the Document Window.

If you don't have any layout cells in your layout table, your changes will not be visible until some are added.

Setting a Background Color

Much as was the case in Standard View, you can easily change the background color of your layout table:

1. Select the layout table you are working with by either clicking its edge or its Layout Table tab.

2. Open the Property Inspector (Window ➔ Properties).

3. Click the color swatch directly to the right of Bg to open the Color Palette.

4. Move your mouse over a color you like and click it. The background color of your layout table automatically changes.

If you want to choose a color that isn't contained in the Color Palette, you can follow the procedure described in Chapter 3 (see the section "Using the Color Dialog Box").

Manipulating a Layout Cell with the Properties Inspector

As with a layout table, changing the properties of a layout cell with the Property Inspector gives you far more control over its configuration than when it was initially created. In this section, you'll learn how to set the height and width of a layout cell and change its background color and internal alignment.

Setting Width and Height

When you create layout cells, you really don't have pixel-precise control over their size. If you use the Property Inspector, however, you can set the exact size of any layout cell:

1. Click the edge of the layout cell whose width and height you want to set. The edge will change color from blue to red when you move your mouse over it.

2. If it isn't already, open the Property Inspector (Window → Properties).

3. Make sure the Fixed radio button is selected.

Fixed Width

4. Enter a value for the width of the layout cell into the Width field. As soon as you enter it and move your cursor out of the field, your changes take effect.

5. Enter a value for the height of the layout cell into the Height field. As soon as you enter it and move your cursor out of the field, your changes take effect.

Setting a Background Color

You can get some genuinely interesting page layouts by changing the background color of your layout cells in Layout view:

1. Click the edge of the layout cell whose background color you want to change. The edge will change color from blue to red when you move your mouse over it.

2. If it isn't already, open the Property Inspector (Window → Properties).

3. Click the color swatch directly to the right of Bg to open the Color Palette.

4. Move your mouse over a color you like and click it. The background color of your layout cell automatically changes.

> If you want to choose a color that isn't contained in the Color Palette, you can follow the procedure described in Chapter 3 (see the section "Using the Color Dialog Box").

Setting Internal Alignment

You can align content within a layout cell in much the same way you align content within a cell in Standard view:

1. Click the edge of the layout cell whose content you want to align. The edge will change color from blue to red when you move your mouse over it.

As with cells in Standard view, you don't need to select the object you want to align—just place your cursor in the cell with which you want to work, and Dreamweaver MX will do the rest.

2. Open the Property Inspector (Window → Properties).

Horizontal Alignment drop-down menu

Vertical Alignment drop-down menu

3. Choose Left, Right, or Center, according to your layout cell's needs, from the Horizontal Alignment drop-down menu.

4. Select Left, Right, or Center, according to your layout cell's needs, from the Vertical Alignment drop-down menu.

5. The cell's contents align automatically.

Once you set a layout cell's alignment (whether horizontal or vertical), all added content will also be aligned this way.

Working with Autostretch Columns

Now that you've explored all the ways you can manipulate layout cells using the Property Inspector, it's time to get familiar with the Autostretch option. As opposed to the Fixed Width option, which gives you a cell (and therefore a column) with a specific numerical width that doesn't change, Autostretch allows you to create a column that will dynamically resize when the user changes the size of the browser window.

When you use Autostretch, the table will always take up the user's entire browser window.

You can create a table that has a mixture of fixed-width columns and one Autostretch column. This way, when the user resizes their browser window, the Autostretch column will expand or contract so that the table always occupies the entire width of window not taken up by the fixed-width column, while the fixed-width columns maintain their predetermined width.

You can only have one Autostretch column in any given table.

By default, all columns created in Layout view (including those columns created by Dreamweaver MX when you construct layout cells) are fixed width. To convert a column to Autostretch:

1. In Layout view, select a layout cell that resides in the column you wish to convert to Autostretch.

2. Open the Property Inspector (Window → Properties) and select the Autostretch option.

3. When the Choose Space Image dialog box appears, select one of the options and click OK.

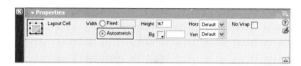

For more information on working with a Spacer Image, see the "Working with Space Images" section next.

After the column has been converted to Autostretch, the width value normally displayed in the header area at the top of each column is replaced by a squiggly line (illustrated in the image to the right). This indicates that the column is now Autostretch.

You can also convert a fixed-width column to Autostretch using the drop-down menu that's accessible in the header area at the top of each column:

1. Open the Column Header drop-down menu by clicking on the column's Width value.

2. Select Make Column Autostretch.

3. When the Choose Spacer Image dialog box appears, select one of the options and click OK. The spacer image options are discussed next.

Working with Spacer Images

One of the drawbacks of creating a table in which there is an Autostretch column is that any other columns (despite the fact that they are fixed width) have a tendency to collapse entirely and effectively disappear. The only way to avoid this is to add content to the non-Autostretch columns so that they are, in effect, "propped open." But what if you aren't keen on adding visible content just to avoid losing fixed-width columns when you add an Autostretch column? This is where a *spacer image* comes in.

A spacer image is a tiny transparent image that serves to maintain the width of any non-Autostretch columns—it acts as a digital shim that props open all non-Autostretch columns.

Adding a Spacer Image

To incorporate a spacer image into a table in which you've added an Autostretch column:

1. As mentioned in the last section, when you convert a fixed-width column to an Autostretch column, the Choose Spacer Image dialog box opens. You have several options:

   Create a Spacer Image File Opens the Save Spacer Image File As dialog box. From here, you'll need to navigate to the location on your hard drive where you want to save the spacer image (which by default is a GIF image).

   > Dreamweaver MX names the spacer image spacer.gif by default, but you can change the name. The image format, however, must remain a GIF so that it can be transparent.

   Use An Existing Spacer Image File Opens the Select Spacer Image File dialog box. From here, locate the spacer image you wish to use and click Select. For the most part, you'll choose this option if you've already created a spacer image and don't want to create an additional one.

   Don't Use Spacer Images For Autostretch Tables Prevents Dreamweaver MX from using a spacer image to prop open the non-Autostretch columns in your table.

   > As mentioned before, if you decide not to use a spacer image, any non-Autostretch columns in your table will probably collapse to such a degree that they will effectively disappear.

2. After making the appropriate choice in the Choose Spacer Image dialog box, the presence of a spacer image will be represented by a double bar in each of the non-Autostretch column's header areas.

In addition to automatically inserting a spacer image into all non-Autostretch columns when converting a fixed-width column to an Autostretch column, you can also manually insert a spacer image into any selected column:

1. In Layout view, select the layout cell to whose column you wish to add a spacer image.

2. Open the Column Header drop-down menu by clicking the column's Width value (or its Autostretch symbol, if you previously converted that column into Autostretch).

3. Select Add Spacer Image.

4. From here, a spacer image will be automatically inserted into the column of the selected cell.

Removing a Spacer Image

Manually removing a spacer image is just as easy as adding one:

1. In Layout view, select the layout cell to whose column you wish to add a spacer image.

2. Open the Column Header drop-down menu by clicking the column's Width value (or its Autostretch symbol if you previously converted that column into Autostretch).

3. Select Remove All Spacer Images.

4. From here, a spacer image will be automatically removed. The header area goes back from showing two bars (indicative of the presence of a spacer image) to showing a single bar (indicative of a standard fixed width column).

Inspiration: Design and Technique

Based in San Francisco, California, the Leakey Foundation was established in 1968 to support the pioneering work of renowned paleoanthropologist Dr. Richard Leakey. Within the first ten years of it being established, the Leakey Foundation provided grants to aid in the seminal studies of famous anthropologists Louis Leakey, Richard Leakey, Mary Leakey, Donald Johanson, Jane Goodall, Dian Fossey, and Birute Galdikas—all of whom were pivotal in our current understanding of early human prehistory and evolution.

Today, the Leakey Foundation annually awards more than $600,000 in field grants for vital new research in the exploration of human evolution. Currently, it is the only U.S. funding organization wholly committed to human origins research. Recent foci have included research into the environments; archaeology and human paleontology of the Miocene, Pliocene, and Pleistocene; the behavior, morphology, and ecology of the great apes and other primate species; and the behavioral ecology of contemporary hunter-gatherers.

Designed by Fluid (`www.fluid.com`), the Leakey Foundation's website (`www.leakeyfounda-tion.org`), which is illustrated in Figure 7.1, is intended not only to publicize the activities of the foundation, but also to make the study of human evolution and early prehistory far more accessible to the public—an endeavor in which it succeeds remarkably well.

Figure 7.1

The Leakey Foundation

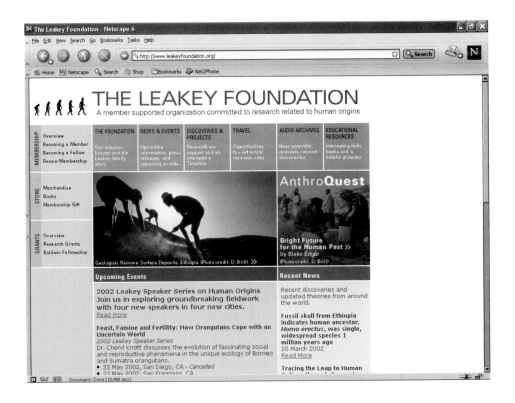

Figure 7.1

The Leakey Foundation

Summary

This chapter explored creating and working with tables, looking first at creating and manipulating them in Standard view. It then delved into creating and manipulating tables in Layout view, one of Dreamweaver MX's terribly cool features.

In the next chapter, you'll learn how to enhance the layout and design of your page by displaying multiple files in one document window with the help of frames.

PART II

Intermediate Dreamweaver Techniques

Until now, *you've spent the vast majority of your time learning the basics of working and creating with Dreamweaver: setting various document properties, working with text, creating hyperlinks, inserting and manipulating images, and building tables. If you've made it to this point and are still excited, you are sitting pretty. By mastering the fundamentals covered in the previous chapters, you've built a solid foundation upon which to base your exploration of more intermediate Dreamweaver techniques. In this section, you'll start off by learning how to create and manipulate frames. From there, you'll explore the wonderful world of digital recycling in Dreamweaver with a thorough look at Library Items and Templates. You'll also learn how to work with forms and insert and manipulate multimedia. Finally, you'll explore how to manage and publish your site with Dreamweaver.*

CHAPTER 8

Framing Your Page

As I've mentioned before and as you've probably experienced, HTML was not conceived as a medium with which to create intricate layout and design. I suspect that when Tim Berners-Lee envisioned HTML, he never imagined the explosion of sheer graphic design–oriented creativity that would happen on the web.

Whatever its original intent, the web blossomed into a medium to which traditional print designers have flocked to realize their creative vision. As a result, new methods have developed so the original design limitation of HTML can be bypassed. Tables, which you explored in Chapter 7, "Laying Out Your Document with Tables," provided digital designers the opportunity to lay out their content with an increased level of complexity. However, designers were hungry for new and innovative ways in which to mold their HTML creations. This was where frames entered the picture.

Introduced in about 1995 in Netscape 2, frames allow you to display multiple HTML documents in one browser window, thereby increasing the control over your page's interface and content. In this chapter, you will spend time thoroughly exploring the wonderful world of frames through the following topics:

- **Understanding frames**
- **Creating a frames page**
- **Manipulating frame properties**
- **Controlling frame border properties**
- **Adding content to frames**
- **Managing links in frames with targets**
- **Saving a frames page**
- **Creating NOFRAMES content**

Understanding Frames

When you create a frames page, you essentially combine a series of discrete HTML files into one entity that is displayed in a single browser window. Each HTML file is displayed in its own section of the browser window (called a frame) with its own discrete properties. One of the great benefits to using this technique is that different HTML documents can be dynamically loaded into one frame while maintaining the content of other frames within the document. As a result, generally speaking, frames are used to partition a document into several general areas such as content, navigational elements (like buttons), and static material (like banners and logos). You can think of a document which has been partitioned with frames as a television on which several channels are displayed using a split screen. While each channel contains different content, they are all being displayed in the same space (the television screen).

The way each frame looks and behaves is partially controlled by something called a *frameset file*, which is an HTML document that contains all the "guidelines" that set the location, size, and various other properties of each frame. If we were to extend the split-screen television analogy, the frameset file would be the television itself.

To view a frames page with a browser, you load the frameset file which, based on its guidelines, locates and displays the appropriate additional HTML files, which then populate the discrete frames.

When you create a frame page, you are dealing with multiple files. For instance, say you had a page which was broken up into four equal quarters using frames. Not only would you have four HTML files (each of which would be displayed in one of the frames), but you'd also have the frameset file—which is not visible, so you would actually be dealing with five discrete files (see Figure 8.1)

Figure 8.1

In any given page that employs frames, you are dealing with multiple files—the files that are displayed in the frames, as well as the frameset file.

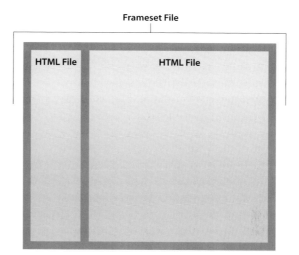

Creating a Frames Page

In Dreamweaver, there are two ways to partition a single document into several frames. The first, splitting, lets you manually set the number and position of frames in your document. The second method, using the Insert bar, lets you choose from a series of predetermined framesets, each with its own configuration.

The most important thing to remember as you read the following section is that whenever you partition your document into several frames, no matter which method you use, Dreamweaver automatically generates additional HTML files (each of which is loaded into one of the frames in your document). At some point, you'll need to save each of the files individually (a process we'll discuss later in the chapter). So, let's start with splitting your document into frames.

> In this chapter, the term *frameset file* and *frameset* will have slightly different connotations. A frameset file will refer to the HTML file that contains the rules for displaying the frames page. Frameset, on the other hand, will often be used to refer to a discrete group of frames with its own configuration and properties.

Creating Frames by Splitting

The first method of carving your page into a series of frames involves manually splitting it using Dreamweaver's Modify menu:

The following steps will discuss how to create frames in a document with no other existing frames. The process of creating additional frames in a page with an already existing frameset, a nested frameset, will be discussed later.

1. Make sure your cursor is placed in the document you want to split into frames.

2. Go to Modify → Frameset. From here, you have several options; each will carve up your existing document into different frames :

   Split Frame Left Creates two vertically parallel frames, shoving any existing content into the left-most frame as in the image below on the left.

   Split Frame Right Creates two vertically parallel frames, shoving any existing content into the right-most frame as in the image below on the right.

 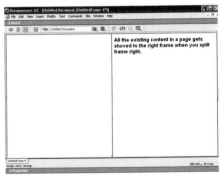

   Split Frame Up Creates two horizontally parallel frames, shoving any existing content into the top-most frame as in the image below on the left.

   Split Frame Down Creates two horizontally parallel frames, shoving any existing content into the bottom-most frame as in the image below on the right.

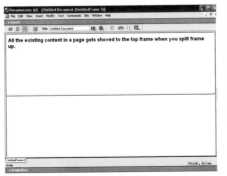 

3. At this point, you can save your frames page if you want. Later in the chapter, you'll be asked to begin with an already existing frames document, so it might as well be this one.

Saving a Frames page is slightly more complicated than saving a regular nonframes page. If you do decide to save the document you created in this section, see the "Saving a Frames Page" section later in this chapter.

Creating Frames with the Insert Bar

The second method of carving a page into frames is by choosing from a group of preset framesets, each of which has their own frame configuration, from the Insert bar:

1. If it isn't already, open the Insert bar (Window → Insert).

When you use the Insert bar to insert a frameset, you'll notice that the frames themselves look slightly differently than they did when you created them manually by splitting. This is primarily because when you use the Insert bar, the properties of the available options have also been preset, something you'll learn how to do manually later in the chapter.

2. Select the Insert bar's Frames tab. This will give you access to a series of preset framesets.

3. Select one of the framesets from the Insert bar:

Insert Left Frame ⬚⬚ Your page will be split into two vertical frames: a narrow one along the left, and a very wide one along the right. Any existing content will be shifted into the right-most frame seen in the image on the lower left.

Insert Right Frame ⬚⬚ Your page will be split into two vertically parallel frames: a narrow one along the right and a wide one along the left. Any existing content will be moved into the wide frame along the left seen in the image on the right side.

Insert Top Frame ▢ Your page will be split into two parallel horizontal frames: a narrow one running along the top and a wide one along the bottom. Any existing content will be shifted into the bottom frame seen in the image below on the left.

Insert Bottom Frame ▢ Your page will be split into two horizontally parallel frames: a narrow one running along the bottom and a wide one running around the top. Existing content will be shifted into the top frame seen in the image below on the right.

Insert Bottom and Nested Left Frame ▢ Your page will be split into three frames: one narrow frame that runs along the bottom from left to right and two others (one narrow and one wider) that vertically split the area left by the first frame. Any existing content will be shifted into the right-most of the two vertical frames.

Insert Bottom and Nested Right Frame ▢ Your page will be split into three frames: one narrow frame that runs along the bottom from left to right and two others (one narrow and one wider) that vertically split the area left by the first frame. Any existing content will be shifted into the left-most of the two vertical frames.

A nested frame results from a kind of frameset called a *nested frameset*. For more information on nesting frames and nested framesets, see the "Nesting Frames" section later in this chapter.

Insert Left and Nested Bottom Frame Your page will be split into three frames: one narrow frame that runs along the left from top to bottom and two others (one narrow and one wider) that horizontally split the area left by the first frame. Any existing content will be shifted into the top-most of the two horizontal frames.

Insert Right and Nested Bottom Frame Your page will be split into three frames: one narrow frame that runs along the right from top to bottom and two others (one narrow and one wider) that horizontally split the area left by the first frame. Any existing content will be shifted into the top-most of the two horizontal frames.

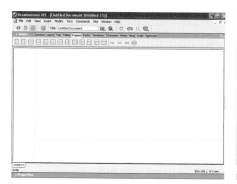

Insert Top and Bottom Frames You page will split into three horizontal frames: two narrow frames running along the top and bottom and one wider frame running through the middle. All of the page's existing content will be moved into the center frame.

Insert Left and Nested Top Frame Your page will be split into three frames: one narrow frame that runs from top to bottom along the left and two others (one narrow and one wider) that horizontally split the area left by the first frame. Any existing content will be shifted into the bottom-most of the two horizontal frames.

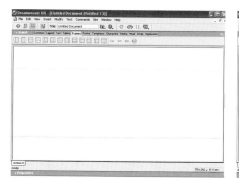

Insert Right and Nested Top Frame Your page will be split into three frames: one narrow frame that runs from top to bottom along the right and two others (one narrow and one wider) that horizontally split the area left by the first frame. Any existing content will be shifted into the bottom-most of the two horizontal frames seen in the image below on the left.

Insert Top and Nested Left Frame Your page will be split into three frames: one narrow frame running from left to right along the top, one narrow frame running from the bottom of the first frame to the bottom of the window along the left side, and a wider one running from the bottom of the first frame to the bottom of the window along the right side. Any existing content will be shifted in the right-most vertically running frame seen in the image below on the right.

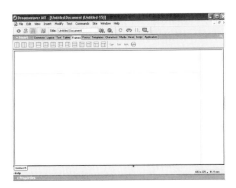 

Insert Top and Nested Right Frame

Your page will be split into three frames: one narrow frame running from left to right along the top, one narrow frame running from the bottom of the first frame to the bottom of the window along the right side, and a wider one running from the bottom of the first frame to the bottom of the window along the left side. Any existing content will be shifted in the left-most vertically running frame.

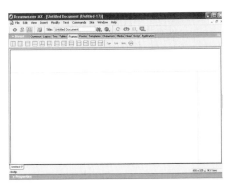

4. At this point, you can save your frames page if you want. You can use it later in the chapter.

> Saving a frames page is slightly more complicated than saving a regular nonframes page. If you do decide to save the document you created in this section, see the "Saving a Frames Page" section later in this chapter.

Nesting Frames

Now you know how to take a fresh page and carve it up into several frames by either splitting it with the Modify menu or using the Insert bar. What if you want to take one of those frames, and subdivide it further, creating a more complex frameset? This is where a *nested frameset* comes in. Essentially, a nested frameset is created when you take one of the HTML files occupying one of the previously created frames and convert it to a frameset file, complete with its own frames. This results in a frameset file nested within a frame of another frameset file.

To subdivide a frame into several additional frames (thereby creating a nested frameset):

1. Click in the frame you want to subdivide. Make sure your cursor is located in the frame before continuing.

2. Use either of the frame-splitting methods described previously to carve the frame into several additional frames.

You can continue to partition frames and create more nested framesets until your page is configured exactly as you want it to be.

Resizing Frames

> From this point on, all of the exercises in this chapter will assume that you have an existing frames page that you created using one of the methods just covered. Alternatively, you can use the page you created in the "Creating a Frames Page" section earlier in this chapter.

Frames wouldn't be that useful if you weren't able to resize them. To resize your existing frame:

1. Move your mouse over the border of the frame that you want to resize. Notice that your cursor will change to two arrows pointing in opposite directions. The directions the cursor arrows point depends on whether the border you've moused over runs horizontally or vertically.

> If you move your mouse over the spot where two borders intersect, your cursor will change to four small arrows pointing in the four cardinal directions. If you click and drag (as is described in the next few steps), you'll move both borders, as opposed to just one.

2. When the cursor changes, click and drag the border so that the frame either increases or decreases in size. Notice that you get a ghost-like preview of the position of the frame's border as it's dragged.

3. When the border is located where you want and the frame is the size you want, release the mouse button. *Voila!* Your frame has been resized.

Deleting Frames

Unfortunately, the process to remove individual frames from your document is somewhat counterintuitive. You'd think that you could select the frame in the Frame panel and simply press Delete—unfortunately, it doesn't work that way. When you need to delete a frame, you must drag it out of existence:

1. Move your cursor over the border of the frame that you want to delete.

2. Click and drag the frame border to the edge of the screen.

> If you are dealing with one frameset, you need to drag the border to the edge of the screen to delete the frame. However, if you are dealing with nested frames (one frameset embedded within another frameset), you just need to drag the border of the nested frame that you wish to delete to the edge of the parent frameset.

As you might have guessed, the direction you drag the border determines the frame that is removed. For example, if you had a page in which there were two horizontally running frames, and you clicked and dragged upwards, the top frame would be deleted. On the other hand, if you clicked and dragged downward, the bottom frame would be deleted.

Manipulating Frame Properties

Creating a frameset is only the first step in working with a frames page. As I previously mentioned, the slight difference in appearance between a frameset created with the Insert bar and one created by splitting is because framesets created with the Insert bar already have some of their frame properties changed from the default. Well, you certainly aren't stuck with the initial frame properties of a frameset, whether you create it by splitting or with the Insert bar. In the following section, you'll explore how to use the Property Inspector to manipulate the various frame properties, such as frame name, frame source, margin dimensions, border properties, scrollbar properties, and resize properties so that your frames look and behave exactly as you desire.

Before we begin, however, it's worthwhile to say that the techniques described in the following section apply just to the frames in your frameset and not to the borders between frames. Don't fret; you'll get a chance to explore how to manipulate border properties with the Property Inspector later on in the chapter.

Naming Your Frames

It's no exaggeration to say that when it comes to working with framesets, assigning names to individual frames is probably one of the most important things you can do. As in many other cases, Dreamweaver creates functional HTML code based on unique names you assign to objects. In the case of frames, a unique name allows you to specify the exact frame in which you want a link to load. For instance, you can have a link in one frame that, when clicked, loads a file into a totally different frame. This is all made possible by a simple process:

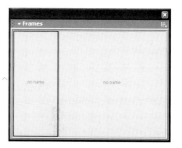

1. Open the Frames panel by choosing Window → Others → Frames. Notice how the Frame panel contains a miniature schematic of your current frameset. If you created your frameset by splitting, you'll notice any previously unnamed frames are given a default name of (no name). However, if you created your frameset using the Insert bar, all of your frames will have been given more specific, yet still generic, names.

2. In the Frame panel, click the frame that you want to name. When selected, the frame in the Frame panel will be highlighted with a black border.

> To select a frame without having to open the Frames panel, you can also Alt+Click (Win)/ Option+Shift+Click (Mac) anywhere within the frame itself in the Document Window.

3. With the frame still selected, open the Property Inspector by going to Window → Properties. Notice that the Property Inspector displays a bevy of options specific to frame properties.

4. Type a name into the Frame Name field.

Frame Name field

> It's wise to keep your frame names simple yet descriptive and avoid using spaces or characters other than letters and numbers, periods, dashes, or underscore.

5. When you finish entering the desired name, either click anywhere off the Property Inspector or press Return (Mac)/ Enter (Win). The name of the frame in the Frames panel will automatically update to reflect the change you made.

Frame Name

Changing the Frame Source

As you've already learned, a frames page is composed of multiple discrete HTML documents each displayed in individual frames, whose configuration is controlled by the frameset file. When you initially create some frames, Dreamweaver automatically generates most of the HTML files that are displayed. You can go right ahead and add content directly to these files from within the Document Window (a process you'll explore later in "Adding Content to Frames"). However, you can also take the HTML files with which Dreamweaver has populated the frames and replace them with existing documents of your choice (that you've already created). To do this, you need to change the frame source:

1. In the Frames panel (Window → Others → Frames), select the frame whose source you want to change. Remember that when any given frame is selected, it will be displayed with a black border.

Frame Source field

2. If it isn't already, open the Property Inspector (Window → Properties) and, with the frame still selected in the Frame panel, type in an absolute URL into the SRC field.

If you want to change the frame's source to a file within your local site (thereby using a relative link), click the browse icon to the right of the Link field. When the Select HTML File dialog box appears, locate and select the file to which you want to link.

For more information on the difference between absolute and relative URLs, see Chapter 6, "Linking Documents with Hyperlinks."

3. When you finish changing the frame's source, either press Return (Mac)/ Enter (Win) or click anywhere off the Property Inspector.

If you are loading an external file (using an absolute URL) into a frame, text will appear in the Document Window indicating this. For example, Remote File: `http://www.captain-primate.com`.

Alternatively, you can change a frame's source directly from within the Document Window:

1. In the Document Window, click in the frame whose source you wish to change—make sure your cursor is blinking away in the desired frame.

2. Go to File → Open in Frame.

3. When the Select HTML File dialog box opens, navigate to the file you want to stick into the frame, select it, and click Select.

Setting Margin Width and Height

Just as with an "unframed" page, you can easily set the margin width (the space in pixels between the frame's content and the left and right frame borders) and margin height (the space in pixels between the frame's content and the top and bottom frame border.)

A frame with a larger margin will have more space between the frame's borders and its content than one that has a lower margin.

A margin width and height of 0 will snuggle your content right up against the left and top of the frame. However, due to the unequal length of each line of text, it will not do the same for the right side of the frame.

To set a frames margin height and width:

1. In the Frames panel (Window → Others → Frames), select the frame whose margins you want to change.

2. If it isn't already, open and expand the Property Inspector (Window → Properties).

3. Type in a value, in pixels, into the Margin Width and Margin Height fields.

4. After you enter the desired margin width and height, either press Return (Mac)/ Enter (Win) or click anywhere off the Property Inspector.

Margin Width field   Margin Height field

Setting Border Properties

While the frames themselves (and their associated content) are the primary focus in any frames page, the areas between the frames themselves (called borders) also contribute to the overall appearance of any frames page, and should therefore be included when you are manipulating your overall design. Luckily for you, the Property Inspector affords you access to several border properties—each of which you'll learn about in the following section.

Turning Borders On and Off

By default, the borders in any frames page have a somewhat simulated 3D beveled appearance. While the presence of the border itself might seem desirable when you first start working with frames, you'll quickly find that it serves no serious design function. In fact, in the world of web design, they are pretty undesirable because they break the visual flow of your design. It's in your best interest to learn early on how to turn your borders on and off:

1. In the Frames panel (Window → Others → Frames), and select the frame whose borders you want to turn on or off.

2. If it isn't already, open the Property Inspector and choose one of the options from the Borders drop-down menu:

Borders drop-down menu

Yes Will make the frame's border visible.

No Will make the frame's border hidden.

Default Will automatically switch the frame's borders to the browser's default—most browsers default to Yes.

You can also set the border visibility for an entire frameset (something you'll learn how to do in "Manipulating Frameset Properties") However, choosing a border visibility option for individual frames overrides border settings defined for the frameset

3. Repeat step 2 on any frames who share the border with the frame whose border visibility you just manipulated.

If you don't synchronize the border visibility settings on all frames that share a common border, you won't see any change.

Setting Border Color

While frame borders, for the most part, are pretty undesirable, you might feel the need (if they are visible in your creation) to change their color. While the process involved with changing border color is quite easy, the result is often somewhat perplexing. When you change the border color of a given frame, all the borders of that frame (even if they are shared with another frame) will change color. The result is that while you can change the color of any given frame's border, you run the risk of affecting other, totally unrelated frames.

> As with changing a border's visibility, you can change border color for an entire frameset (something you'll learn how to do in "Manipulating Frameset Properties"). Making changes to an individual frame's border color will override any change you make to the entire frameset's border color.

To change a frame's border color:

1. In the Frames panel (Window → Others → Frames), select the frame whose borders you want to change color.

2. If it isn't already, open the Property Inspector (Window → Properties).

3. Click the Border Color swatch to open the Color Palette. Select the color you want.

Defining Scrollbar Properties

A scrollbar is an integral part of any HTML document. As the document's content increases beyond the scope of the browser window, a scrollbar (either vertical or horizontal depending on the direction in which your content exceeds the browser window) will automatically be added.

■ ■ ■ ■
DESIGN REMINDER: Horizontal Scrollage

Because of the way web pages have developed, we have been conditioned to absorb information vertically (from top to bottom). So, while vertical scrollbars are quite common, horizontal scroll bars are usually (unless they are explicitly desired) the mark of bad design.

If you think about a frame as a mini browser window, it's only natural to assume that it will react to content in the same way—by adding a scrollbar.

While necessary, however, the frame scrollbar is ironically one of the biggest problems with frames. Think of it this way: If you have three frames, all of which have content that requires scrollbars, you are not only eating up a good chunk of screen real estate, but you are also adding a huge confusion factor for the user. On top of that, it just looks plain messy! Thankfully, in Dreamweaver, you can set whether a given frame gets a scrollbar:

1. In the Frames panel (Window → Others → Frames), select the frame whose scrollbar properties you want to set.

2. If it isn't already, open the Property Inspector (Window → Properties).

3. Choose one of the options from the Scroll drop-down menu.

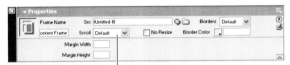

Scroll drop-down menu

Yes Will make a scrollbar (both horizontal and vertical) appear in the frame regardless of whether it requires it or not.

No Will make no scrollbar appear in the frame, even if it is required. The problem with this is that any content that would normally have to be scrolled down to will be inaccessible to users.

Auto Will automatically force the browser to add a scrollbar only when it is needed.

Default Will let the browser decide whether or not to add a scrollbar based on its own rules—for the most part, the browser default for a scrollbar is auto.

Unfortunately, when it comes to scrollbars and frames, it's all or nothing. You either have them or you don't. There is no real way to specify whether you want a horizontal scrollbar, but not a vertical one—or vice versa.

Setting No Resize

By default, users will be able to drag around the borders of your frames page in their browser—much like you did when you went through the process of manually resizing frames earlier in this chapter. This is quite annoying and arguably one of the biggest drawbacks of frames. You've spent a great deal of time getting your page to look exactly right—why would you want the user to come along and fiddle with it?

The user can only resize frames if the borders are visible (they have to click and drag the frame border to resize the frame). This means frames whose border visibility has been turned off cannot be resized in the browser.

Don't worry too much, however, because locking your frames so the user can't drag them around is easy:

1. In the Frames panel (Window → Others → Frames), and select the frame that you want to lock.

2. If it isn't already, open the Property Inspector (Window → Properties).

3. Click the No Resize check box.

No Resize check box

Manipulating Frameset Properties

In the previous section, you explored how to set the various properties for individual frames. Now, you are going to spend some time exploring how to manipulate the properties of the frameset itself.

In some cases, such as border visibility, the frameset properties are identical to frame properties. As mentioned before, many of the settings for frame properties will override their frameset counterparts.

Before you move forward, however, a word needs to be said about how you select the frameset in the Frames panel. Upon close inspection of a frames page in the Frames panel, you'll notice that some of the lines (which serve to either outline or break up frames) are solid, while others have a beveled 3D look. The difference between them is that the solid lines represent the border between frames in the same frameset, while the beveled lines represent the frameset itself.

When you select a regular frame, it is highlighted in black. However, as illustrated in Figure 8.2, when you select a frameset (by clicking the beveled 3D border), it is highlighted in a thicker black line.

Figure 8.2

The left image illustrates what happens when you select a frame. The image on the right illustrates what happens when you select the frameset—note the darker highlight.

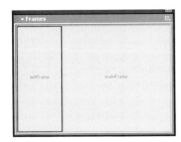 

The Property Inspector will indicate whether you've selected a frame or a frameset.

Selecting the frameset in the Frames panel can be a little tricky—especially when the frameset border is sometimes indistinguishable from the inner edge of the Frames panel itself. It's really in your best interest to have an agile mouse finger and become adept at selecting framesets.

You can also select the frameset by clicking on any border witnn the Document Window. This, however, will only select the frameset associated with the selected border. If you have a nested frameset, you'll need to select it manually before you can gain access to its properties.

This having been said, why don't we move forward and explore the various frameset properties with which you can fiddle.

Setting Border Visibility

As you learned earlier in the chapter, you can easily set the border visibility between frames. So, what exactly is the difference between the visibility of a frame's border and the visibility of a frameset's border? When you set the border visibility of a frameset, all the borders, as opposed to just those associated with the selected frame, are affected. To set the border visibility for a frameset:

1. In the Frames panel (Window → Others → Frames), select the frameset whose border visibility you want to set. Remember that when a given frameset is selected, it will be displayed with a thick black border (opposed to the light one displayed when you select an individual frame).

2. If it isn't already, open the Property Inspector (Window → Properties).

3. Choose one of the options from the Borders drop-down menu:

Borders drop-down menu

Yes Will make the frame's border visible.

No Will make the frame's border lose its 3D beveled look. You will still be left with a small gap (whose default is 6 pixels wide) that will show up as gray in Netscape and white in Internet Explorer.

To lose the border altogether, you not only have to set the border visibility to No, but you also have to set the border width to 0—a process we'll look at shortly.

Default Will automatically switch the frame's borders to the browser's default—most browsers default to Yes.

Setting Border Thickness

You also have control over the thickness of the border itself.

The default thickness of a frameset's border is 6 pixels—if you set it to anything less than 5, you'll lose the 3D look.

To set the frameset's border thickness:

1. In the Frames panel (Window → Others → Frames), select the frameset whose border width you want to set. Remember that when a given frameset is selected, it will be displayed with a thick black border (opposed to the light one displayed when you select an individual frame).

2. If it isn't already, open the Property Inspector (Window → Properties).

3. Enter a value into the Border Width field.

Border Width field

4. When you've entered the desired value, press Return (Mac)/ Enter (Win) or click any-where off the Property Inspector.

Changing Border Color

Changing the color of a frameset's border is just as easy as setting its visibility. Let's take a look at how:

> As you'd expect, if you have the visibility set to No or the thickness set to 0, changing border color will have absolutely no effect.

1. In the Frames panel (Window → Others → Frames), select the frameset whose border you want to change color.

2. If it isn't already, open the Property Inspector (Window → Properties).

3. Click the Border Color swatch to open the Color Palette. From there, select the color you want.

Setting Column and Row Dimensions

Earlier in this chapter, you explored how to resize frames by dragging their respective borders. In this section, you'll also resize frames. However, instead of dragging them, you'll resize them parametrically. You'll also resize blocks of frames organized either in rows or in columns over an entire frameset, as opposed to single frames. This may seem somewhat confusing now, but it'll make sense shortly.

DESIGN REMINDER: Border Thickness

You can set the value of the border thickness to anything you want. Want a border that is 100 pixels wide? Go crazy! The big question is, why would you want a border that thick? Remember, regardless of how thick the framesets border is, the same overall notion of the undesirability of frame borders still applies (and it's magnified the larger your border gets.)

Because frames are square or rectangle shaped and must all fit neatly into a large square (the browser window), they can be thought of being organized into rows and columns—much like tables.

> If you are working with a frameset in which another frameset is nested, you'll only be able to manipulate the frame rows/columns of the currently selected frameset, not any other. To resize the frame rows/columns of a nested frameset, you'll need to select and manipulate it separately.

Using the Property Inspector, you can select any of these frame rows/columns and then resize them in a bunch of different ways:

1. In the Frames panel (Window → Others → Frames), select the frameset whose border you want to resize.

2. If it isn't already, open the Property Inspector (Window → Properties). Notice that on the extreme right side of the Property Inspector there is a simplified schematic of the frame rows/columns in your frameset—remember, nested framesets are not represented.

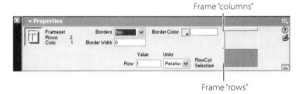

Frame "columns"

Frame "rows"

3. Select either a row or column by clicking its associated tab. The tab, if associated with a frame column, will appear along the top of the schematic or, if associated with a frame row, will appear on the left side of the schematic. Notice that when selected, the frame row or column will be highlighted.

4. From here, you have a number of different options to set the width or height of the selected frame row/column—all of which use the Value field and Units drop-down menu.

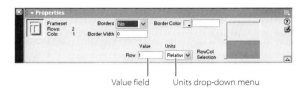

Value field   Units drop-down menu

- Choose Pixels from the Units drop-down menu, and then enter a number into the Value field for the width (or height) of the selected frame row (or column). By doing this, the frame row/column will maintain a fixed size.

Using a fixed width for a frame row/column can be tricky. A frame that has been set at a fixed pixel width that's larger than the resolution of a user's screen will require scrolling to see the entire frame's content. It's usually wisest to stick to relative frame row/column sizing.

- Select Percent, and type a number (from 1 to 100) into the Value field. If, for instance, you enter 25, the selected frame row/column will always expand or contract to occupy 25% of the browser window.
- If you select Relative, the selected frame row/column will always be dynamically expanded or contracted to fill all the remaining space left by any other frame that's been sized using either pixels or percent.

Adding Content to Frames

Earlier in the chapter, you learned how to add content to a frames page by changing the actual source file for a given frame. The process allows you to replace the blank default HTML document that Dreamweaver used to populate the newly created frames with an already existing HTML document that you have previously created.

There is, however, a far easier way to add content to your frames page. Essentially, you edit those default HTML documents that Dreamweaver automatically generates when the frames are originally created.

It's remarkably simple: all you need to do is click in the frame that you want to edit, and then add content as you would with a nonframes page.

Managing Link in Frames with Targets

One of the great things about working with frames is that, by employing something called *link targets*, you can create a link in one frame which, when clicked on, loads up a file in a totally different frame. This means, for example, that you can create a frames page in which one frame consists of a navigation bar whose elements, when clicked, load different documents into a primary content frame, thereby leaving the frame in which the navigation elements reside completely unchanging.

Back in Chapter 6, we looked briefly at link targets. A link target is an instruction to the browser relating to the location where you want a hyperlink loaded.

Overall, this is a pretty handy technique that is rather easy to put into play. The only caveat is that to successfully create hyperlinks that call files into other frames, you have to have previously named each of your frames in your frameset—a process covered earlier in the "Naming Your Frames" section. Beyond this, the process is about as straightforward as they come:

1. First, make sure you've named all of the frames in your frameset.

2. In one frame, include the hyperlinks (either text or images) that will load the desired HTML documents.

3. Select the hyperlink to the document that you want to load up in another frame.

4. Open the Property Inspector (Window → Properties).

5. With the desired link still selected, open the Target drop-down menu (notice that it's populated not only with the standard link targets, but also the names of the frames in your frameset), and choose the name of the frame into which you want the document to load.

Link Target drop-down menu

> By default, if you don't set a target for a link when working in a frames document, the file will load in the same frame in which the link itself resides—something you don't necessarily want to happen.

Beyond any named frames, you also have access to four additional link targets in the target drop-down menu. It's a good idea to become familiar with each:

> You already learned about the _blank and _self targets back in Chapter 6, but we'll go over them again to refresh your memory.

_blank Loads the link up in a totally new browser window, maintaining the window in which the hyperlink was located just below the newly opened window.

_parent The document, when loaded, will occupy the entire area of the frameset document in which the link resides.

_self The default link target, it opens the document in the frame where the link resides.

_top The document will be loaded into the uppermost (hierarchically speaking) frameset, wiping out all frames and nested framesets.

Saving a Frames Page

It's no great intellectual leap to say that you need to save your pages often! However, when you're working with frames pages, primarily because you are dealing with multiple discrete HTML documents, you need to go through several different steps to get everything safely saved.

The first technique involves manually saving each file:

1. With the frames page open in the document which you want to save, click in the first frame—make sure it's blinking in the frame before you continue.

2. Go to File → Save Frame.

3. When the Save As dialog pops up, enter a filename for the frame into the Filename field, navigate to the location where you want the file to be saved, and click Save.

> A frames page can contain anywhere from three to, well, a lot of files, so it's a really good idea to give the HTML file a descriptive filename. This means you'll easily be able to locate and identify any given file in your frameset and edit it independently.

4. Repeat steps 1 through 3 on all the remaining frames in your document.

5. Once you've saved all the frames, you need to save the frameset file itself. To do this, make sure the frames page whose frameset file you want to save is currently open the Document Window.

6. In the Frames panel (Window → Others → Frames), select the frameset you want to save.

7. Go to File → Save Frameset.

8. When the Save As dialog pops up, enter a filename for the frameset into the Filename field, navigate to the location where you want the file to be saved, and click Save.

> Unless you tell Dreamweaver that the source for the HTML file displayed in any given frame is located in another location (by using the procedure described earlier in "Changing the Frame Source"), you'll need to make sure all frames and the frameset file are saved in the same directory.

Manually saving each and every frame can be a little tedious. There is, however, a way in which you can save all the frames in one fell swoop:

1. Make sure the frames page you want to save is open in the Document Window.

2. Go to File → Save All Frames.

3. When the Save As dialog pops up, enter a filename for the frame into the Filename field, navigate to the location where you want the file to be saved, and click Save.

4. After you click the Save button, Dreamweaver will prompt you to save the next frame by re-opening the Save As dialog box—repeat the procedure in step 3.

5. During the process, Dreamweaver will also prompt you to save the frameset file—you'll be able to tell which prompt refers to the frameset file because the default name assigned in the Save As dialog box will be called UntitledFrame (as opposed to Frame or Untitled)

As you go through the process of saving each frame, the frame currently being saved will be highlighted in the Document Window by a hatched border.

Creating NoFrames Content

While frames are supported by the major browsers out there (Netscape Communicator and Internet Explorer), there are browsers that don't support them. For the most part these are text browsers, such as Lynx. However, they are used far more widely than one would expect.

While text browsers are often the most common type of browser that do not support frames, there are also older versions of Internet Explorer and Netscape Navigator that were released before frames were a part of HTML and therefore do not support them.

If you are trying to deliver your content to the widest audience possible, you need to take these nonframes-enabled browsers into account. Thankfully, Dreamweaver lets you integrate content specifically geared for nonframes-enabled browsers into your frames page. This content, called NoFrames (after its HTML tag) will automatically be loaded by the nonframes-enabled browser when it encounters a frames page.

To add NoFrames content to a frames page:

1. Go to Modify → Frameset → Edit NoFrames Content.

2. Dreamweaver will open a special Document Window where you can create the content that will be displayed by a browser that doesn't support frames. Note the there is a bar along the top of the screen indicating that you are currently working on the NoFrames content.

3. Add any content you'd like. Remember, however, that if you are targeting your NoFrames content at a text browser, you'll be limited to text and hyperlinks. If, on the other hand, you are targeting an older browser that is only limited by the fact that it doesn't support frames, you can add images and any other HTML elements that that specific browser supports.

4. When you're finished creating your NoFrames content, go to Modify → Frameset → Edit NoFrames Content to return to the main frames component of the document.

Inspiration: Design and Technique

Founded in August of 2000, Titoonic (`www.titoonic.dk`) is a creative web production company located in Copenhagen, Denmark. Although the company specializes in all manner of web-based multimedia, it is best known for its 3D character animation and design. It was responsible for the design and implementation of numerous 3D Flash characters whose implementation includes visual guides on websites, character-based Flash games, greeting cards, and "webisodes."

Founded by a group of highly creative individuals whose backgrounds include classical animation and graphical storytelling, Titoonic is pushing the boundaries of the cutting-edge of 3D Flash development with their extremely stylish and compelling 3D character design. Titoonic's website (see Figure 8.3) is incredibly well designed and features a healthy dose of zany charm, making it a definite source of inspiration.

Figure 8.3

Titoonic

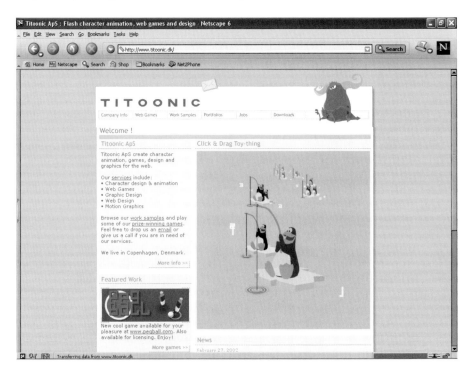

Summary

In this chapter, you explored the intricacies of frames. You started off by learning the fundamentals of frames and the frameset file and moved on to carving a page into frames—either by splitting or using the Insert bar. At that point, you looked at how to bend frames to your will by manipulating both frame properties and frameset properties. Next, you learned to manually add content to frames (a remarkably easy process), how to manage links in frames with targets, and how to save the various components in a frames page. You finished the chapter off by an often overlooked but vitally important topic: adding NoFrames content to your frames page.

In the next chapter, you are going to use some of the most important and useful tools in Dreamweaver (especially if you are designing larger than average sites): Templates and Library Items.

CHAPTER 9

Reusable Elements:
Library Items and Templates

As you've probably figured out by now, web design is a time consuming process that gets even more time consuming as your sites grow in size and sophistication. To fully realize your site, you need many disparate digital assets such as text, images, and multimedia elements. Any tools that provide you with an efficient manner of streamlining the production process or help you manage your ever-increasing cornucopia of digital elements are definitely a boon.

Enter Dreamweaver's reusable elements: Library Items and Templates. Each provides you with invaluable ways in which to make time consuming (and often tedious) website production a far more efficient, effective, and satisfying process.

Topics in this chapter will include the following topics:

- **What is a Library Item?**

- **Creating Library Items and applying them to a page**

- **Managing Library Items**

- **What is a Dreamweaver Template?**

- **Creating and using Templates**

- **Managing Templates**

- **Managing and manipulating site-wide assets with the Assets panel**

What Is a Library Item?

As your websites get larger and larger, you'll incorporate more and more digital assets: more text, more hyperlinks, more multimedia, and more images. You'll also find that many of these elements get used over and over again. Whether it's a copyright statement or a logo that appears on every page, creating (and re-creating) these repeating elements every time they need to be employed can get very tiresome. This is where the Library comes in—and, no, we're not talking about books and late fines.

Essentially, the Library, accessed by going to Window → Assets and then clicking the Library button ⬚ , is a central repository in which you can place any object for future use. What's supremely cool about anything you place in the Library (called Library Items) is that they can be any object (or combination of objects) you can place in a Dreamweaver document. The only real limitation is that you can only include elements that would appear in the body section of the HTML document into a Library Item. This means Timelines, Cascading Style Sheets, or behaviors (because they are associated with the head section of the HTML document) cannot be Library Items.

The Library itself isn't really a discrete panel *per se*; it's a subsection of the Assets panel.

Once you've converted something into a Library Item (a process we'll discuss shortly) the element can be easily added to any page within the local site, thereby avoiding the need to manually re-create the element. For example, say you have a copyright statement that you have to add to every page in a large site. Retyping it each time is a lengthy and time consuming process, even if the copyright statement itself is short. You also run the risk of mistyping something and introducing errors into your creation. If you use the Library, however, all you have to do is type out the copyright statement once, convert it to a Library Item, and then add it to each desired pages with a click of a button.

If the Library *only* served this purpose, it would still be quite useful. However, it has some additional valuable uses. Whenever you add a Library Item to a Dreamweaver document, it maintains a special parent/child relationship with its counterpart in the Library. Essentially, each Library Item (the child) in a document is really just a representation (an instance) of its parent in the Library. As such, it is locked, and cannot be directly edited. However—and here comes the cool part—all instances of any given Library Item in your local site can be changed by changing its parent in the Library. For example, referring back to the copyright statement example, say you created a large site in which each page contains a copyright statement that was an instance of a Library Item. The copyright statement, as most copyright statements do, contains a date. What happens when the year changes and you need to update the date? Well, because you created the copyright statement as a Library Item, all you need to do is change the parent in the Library. All the associated children throughout your local site will automatically change.

I cannot stress strongly enough that there are almost no limits to what can be turned into a Library Item. While my example sticks to the simplest use of the Library, you are not limited to turning simple text into a Library Item. You can turn an entire paragraph in which there are images and multimedia files into a Library Item—any element or combination of elements that you plan on using repeatedly can and should be turned into a Library Item.

Library Items are saved to a special directory (called Library) in the local root folder of your local site. Each exists as a discrete LBI file. If you want to move a Library Item from one local site to another, simply copy the appropriate LBI file and paste it into the Library folder in the target local site.

Creating Library Items

Now that you know what Library Items are and how they work, it's time to dive in and look at the two ways of to creating them: from scratch and from existing page elements.

Creating a Library Item from Scratch

In order to create a Library Item from scratch, you'll be working directly from within the Library itself.

Since Library Items are stored within the directory in the local root folder of a local site, you'll need to be working within a local site before you can create them. All of the examples in this chapter assume that you have already created and are working from a local site.

1. Open the Library by going to Window → Assets, and then clicking the Library button ▥.

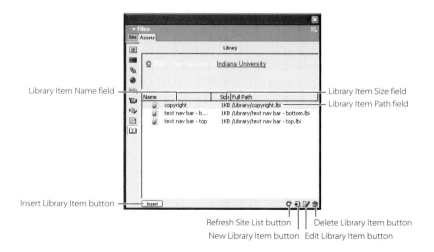

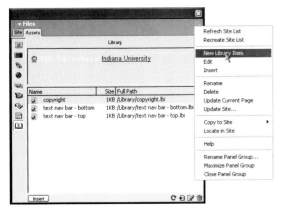

2. When the Library section of the Assets panel pops up, choose New Library Item from the Option menu.

3. A new (blank) Library will be added to the Library. Type a name into the Library Items' name field (by default, any new Library Item is named Untitled). Because this Library Item is blank, nothing shows up in the preview window (besides directions on how to "fill" the blank Library Item.)

4. To "fill" the Blank Library Item, select it and either click the Edit Library Item button or choose Edit from the panel's Option menu.

5. From here, a new document window (we'll call it the Library Item Editor) will open up. The background of the new Document Window is gray and has the name of the Library Item in the title bar. This is where you'll create the Library Item itself.

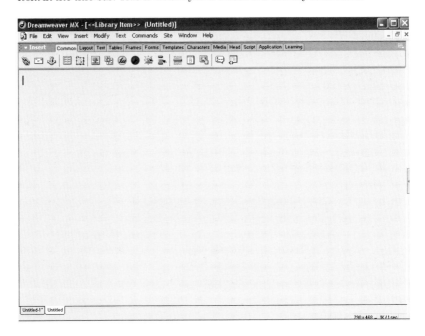

6. With the Library Item Editor open, use any of Dreamweaver's tools to create the Library Item itself. Remember that you can use any element or combination of elements.

As a hands-on exercise, try creating a copyright disclaimer complete with a contact e-mail. While the disclaimer itself will be straight text, you'll need to create an e-mail link (using a mailto: hyperlink) for the e-mail.

7. When you finished composing the Library Item, go to File → Save. The Library Item will automatically be saved to the Library directory of your local site's local root folder.

8. Go to File → Close to exit the Library Item Editor and return to the main Document Window. Notice when you now select the newly created Library Item in the Library, you see a preview in the Library's preview window.

Converting an Existing Page Element into a Library Item

In addition to creating a Library Item from scratch, you can also take an existing element (or combination of elements) in your document and convert it into a Library Item. This is a useful technique, particularly if you have existing content you would like to add to a library.

To convert an existing page element into a Library Item:

1. In the Document Window, select the element (or elements) that you want to convert to a Library Item and open the Library (Window → Assets and click the Library button 📖).

2. Choose one of the following options to convert the selected elements into a Library Item:
   - With the element (or elements) still selected, click the New Library Item button 🗗 .
   - Drag the selected element (or elements) from the Document Window into the Library.
   - With the element (or elements) still selected, go to Modify → Library → Add Object to Library.

3. From here, type a name into the Library Items' name field (by default, any new Library Item is named Untitled).

Applying a Library Item to a Page

After you've created a Library Item (either from scratch or from an existing element), it's simple to add it to your document:

1. Open the Library (Window → Assets and then click the Library button 📖).

2. In the Document Window, place your cursor in the location where you wish the Library Item to be inserted.

3. In the Library, select the item you wish to insert and choose one of the following options:

    -   Click the Insert Library Item button Insert .
    -   Choose Insert from the Library's Options menu.
    -   Click and drag the Library Item from the Library into the Document Window.

Once inserted into the document, the Library Item is locked; the only actions you can take are to change its position within the Document Window or delete it. To edit the Library Item, you'll either have to edit its parent or detach it from the Library, processes we'll discuss later in the chapter.

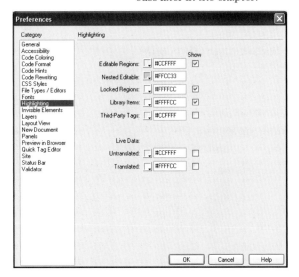

Notice that when it's inserted, the Library Item is highlighted in pale yellow. To change the color:

1. Go to Edit → Preferences.

2. Select Highlighting from the Category list.

3. Click the Library Items color swatch to open the Color Palette. From here, select the color in which you want your Library Items highlighted.

4. Click OK.

If you don't want your Library Items highlighted, uncheck the Show option (to the right of the Library Items color field). However, this is not the best idea, as the color helps show that a given element is a Library Item. These kind of indications help you keep a handle on the design process, especially if you are working on a large site.

Managing Library Items

Library Items are site-wide assets that need to be managed to maximize their usability. Because of this, Macromedia has made it possible to carry out a host of different actions on your Library Items, all of which will be addressed in this section.

Editing a Library Item

Once you've created a Library Item, you can easily go back and edit it. And, as mentioned previously, any changes made to the parent items in the library will automatically affect the children items throughout your local site.

To edit an already exiting Library Item:

1. Open the Library (Window → Assets and click the Library button 📖).

2. Select the Library Item you want to edit and choose from one of the following options:

- Click the Edit Library Item button 📝 .

- Select Edit from the Library's Options menu.

- Double-click the Library Item (either on its preview or its actual name).

3. The Library Item Editor will open. Make any changes you want to the Library Item.

4. When you finish making your changes in the Library Item Editor, go to File → Save.

5. From here, Dreamweaver will ask whether you want to update all the edited Library Item's instances. You have two choices:

- If you want to update all the instances of the Library Item in the entire local site, click Update.

- If you do not want to update all the instances of the Library Item, click Don't Update.

While choosing Update will automatically change all the edited Library Item's instances throughout your local site, what if you clicked Don't Update and later decided you did want to update? Just go to Modify → Library → Update Current Page to update all the instances only on the currently open page, or Modify → Library Update Pages (which will open the Update Pages dialog box) to update all the instances in the entire local site.

Renaming a Library Item

It's quite possible that during the production of your digital marvel, you'll want to rename one (or perhaps more) of the items in your local site's Library. The process is quite easy:

1. Open the Library (Window → Assets and click the Library button 📖).

2. Select the Library whose name you wish to change and either go to Options → Rename or click one of the Library Item names.

3. When the Library Item's name becomes editable, type in a new one.

4. When you finish entering the new name, press Enter (Win)/ Return (Mac) or click your cursor anywhere off the Library.

Detaching an Item from the Library

By this time, I'm sure you've caught on to the fact that if you change the parent Library Item, all the associated children scattered throughout your local site will update to reflect the change. This is an all or nothing kind of process. Unfortunately, it's quite impossible to be selective about which instances are updated. This can be rather frustrating if you find yourself in a situation where you want some but not all of the instances to be updated. Never fear, Dreamweaver features a manageable workaround for this problem. Essentially, individual instances of a Library Item can be detached from their parent, thereby making them fully editable. The drawback to this is that once they are detached, they are no longer included in the sweeping update that occurs when you make changes to their former parent.

To detach an instance from its parent in the Library:

1. With the document open in which the instance resides that you want to detach from its parent, select the instance. (Remember, you can't select subitems within the instance, so the entire instance will be selected.)

2. Open the Property Inspector (Window → Properties).

3. Click the Detach from Original button [Detach from Original] . Now, because the item has reverted back to being "normal," you are free to make any changes you want to the former Library Item.

Copying a Library Item to Another Local Site

As mentioned previously, all Library Items are unique to a given local site, but there will probably be a point when you'll want to use a certain Library Item in another local site. There are a couple ways to do this. You can copy the actual Library Items LBI file to the Library subfolder in the intended local site's local root folder, but this can be cumbersome. To copy a Library Item more efficiently:

1. If you aren't already, make sure you are currently working in the local site which contains the Library Item you want to transfer to another local site.

2. Open the Library (Window → Assets and click the Library button 📖) and select the Library Item you want to transfer.

3. Select Copy to Site from the Library's Options menu and choose the target site from the list of previously defined local sites. The selected Library Item will automatically be copied to the target site's Library folder.

Deleting an Item from the Library

As your site gets larger and larger, you will probably accumulate more and more Library Items. Some Library Items are bound to fall out of use and become obsolete. Even though they take up very little space in the overall scheme of things, Library Items are files that are saved in a directory in the local root folder of your local site. As a result, if you are particularly storage-space conscious, you should always make sure your Library doesn't contain any unused items.

Another good reason for keeping your Library stocked only with those items currently in use is purely organizational: as your site gets larger and your Library Items increase, the sheer number of Library Items can get confusing. Keeping your Library neat and up to date can save you a lot of grief.

To delete items from your Library:

1. Open the Library (Window → Assets and click the Library button 📖).

2. Select the Library Item you want to delete and either choose Delete from the Library's Options menu or click the Delete Library Item button 🗑 .

3. At the prompt, select Yes if you want to delete the item, or No if you don't.

When you delete an item from the Library, the instances that you added to your document(s) are unaffected.

What Is a Dreamweaver Template?

If you are doing your job well as an interactive designer, all of the pages in your site will be closely related variations of the same visual theme. This means you'll be creating page after page with the same basic layout and design. This is especially true in the cases of very large websites. The only real distinction between them will be their content.

Wouldn't it be cool if you could create a framework HTML file and then dump content into it to create each new page? Don't worry, this isn't just wishful thinking, such a thing exists in Dreamweaver: it's called a Template. A Template, which is an amazing time saving device, is a document upon which you can base multiple files with the same design. When you create a Template in Dreamweaver, you create a web page and define areas that are both editable and uneditable (locked). When the Template is applied to a blank document, the areas that were locked cannot be fiddled with, while the areas that were marked as editable can be filled with any kind of content. One of the best things about Templates (much like Library Items) is that they create a parent/child relationship between the file to which the Template was applied and the Template itself. By changing the parent Template, all of the associated linked documents will automatically update to reflect any changes.

Not convinced about the power of Templates? Let's explore Templates with a more real-world example. Say for instance that you are part of a web team at a small university. In the effort to update your university's web presence, the website, which has grown rather haphazardly over the past few years, is to be completely overhauled. One of the primary goals of this endeavor is to bring all the university office's and academic department's websites under the same design umbrella. Without Templates, each person on the web team would have to manually create each department's website after an overall design had been developed. However, with Templates, you only have to create the overall design once, convert it into a Template, and add content, thus guaranteeing a far more streamlined production process. You could also be sure that, because they were all based on the same Template, each of the department's websites would have the same look—instant design continuity!

> Much like Library Items, Templates are saved within their own special directory in the local root folder of your local site; they are saved as DWT files.

Creating Templates

As was the case with Library Items, there are two distinct ways to create Templates in Dreamweaver, and both will be discussed in detail in this section. The first method is to create a Template from scratch, while the second is to turn an existing document into a Template. Both methods have exactly the same result. Which one you use will probably have more to do with your own personal working style than anything else.

For the sake of organization, a process (creating a Template) that is normally pretty linear will be broken up into several distinct sections. Looking at how to create Templates (either from scratch or from an existing page) is only the first step. You'll continue to explore Templates by learning how to set editable regions in your Template and how to save your Template.

Creating Templates from Scratch

To create a Template from scratch:

1. Make sure you've got a blank document open in the Document Window.

2. Go to Window → Assets and click the Templates button 📄 .

> Like the Library, the Templates panel isn't really a panel, it's a subset of the Assets panel.

3. Choose New Template from the panel's Options menu.

4. A new, blank Template will be added to the Template panel. Type a name into the Templates' Name field (by default, any new Template is named Untitled). As this Template is blank, nothing shows up in the preview window (other than directions on how to fill the blank Template).

5. Select the newly created blank Template and either click the Edit Template button 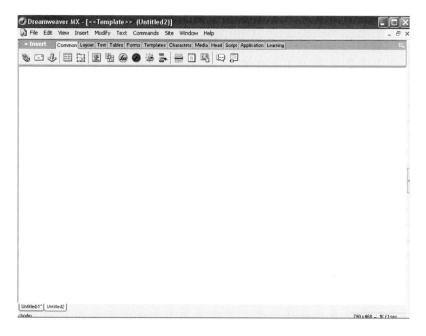 or choose Edit from the panel's Options menu.

6. A new document window (we'll call it the Template Editor) will open up. This is where you create your Template. Unlike the Library Item Editor (discussed earlier), the Template Editor doesn't have a gray background. In fact, it looks almost identical to any other blank document in a Document Window. The only real difference is that the name of the Template appears in the window's title bar.

7. Now you need to create the structure of Template itself. Add images, tables, text, hyperlinks, multimedia—anything you can add to a regular document, you can add to a Template. Remember to think about which areas to make editable and which to leave locked.

> The elements you place in a Template are limited to those things normally integrated into the body section of an HTML document. This means that Cascading Style Sheets, some behaviors, and timeline-based animations can't be included in your Template because their information is stored in the head section of the HTML document.

When you finish creating the structure/design of the Template itself, you need to add editable regions and then save the Template. For the sake of organization, we'll cover these steps in the upcoming sections.

Creating a Template from an Existing Document

While it's quite easy to create a Template from scratch, you may want to turn a document that you've already created (through hours of careful planning and digital sweat) into a Template:

1. Make sure you have the document that you want to convert into a Template open in the Document Window.

2. Go to File → Save as Template; the Save as Template dialog box will open.

3. From the Site drop-down menu, choose the local site to which you want to save the Template.

   When you change the site you want the Template saved to using the Site drop-down menu, a list of all Templates associated with that particular site will pop up in the Existing Templates list.

4. Type in the name for the Template into the Save As field. This name will serve both as the DWT filename and the name listed in the Templates panel.

5. Click Save.

6. The Template will automatically open up in the Template Editor, and you'll be able to set editable and locked regions (something we'll discuss in the following section).

Creating Editable Regions within Your Template

Once you create the actual Template (either from scratch or by converting an existing document), you need to set the regions that will be editable when the Template is applied to a page. It's no exaggeration to say that editable regions are the heart of any Template.

> Remember to mark any areas you want to work with in a Template as editable. By default, any area that you don't mark as editable will be locked when the Template is applied to a document. Locked regions, whether they contain text, images, or any other combination of elements, can not be manipulated in any way, shape, or form—that is, they can't be deleted, moved, or changed.

In the two previous sections, we left off just at the point where you needed to set editable regions in your template. In this section, you'll continue your journey through the wonderful world of Templates and explore how to create the all important editable regions.

To set editable regions in a Template:

1. With the Template open in the Template Editor, select the components (text, images, and so on) that you want to be editable.

2. Go to Insert → Template Objects → Editable Region.

3. When the New Editable Region dialog box appears, type a unique name for the editable region into the Name field. You cannot use angled brackets (<>), single or double quotation marks (' "), or ampersands (&) in an editable region name. The name is used by Dreamweaver to label the editable regions in a document to which the Template has been applied.

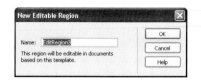

While these steps cover the process of creating editable regions based on existing blocks of text or other elements, you can just as easily create an empty editable region. An empty editable region will appear blank and ready to be filled with content when the Template is applied to a document. A filled editable region, on the other hand, will include the elements you originally selected when you first created the Template in the Template Editor. But don't worry, even if the filled version of an editable region includes some text or other objects, they can be easily deleted when the Template is applied to a document.

To create an empty editable region:

1. With the Template open in the Template Editor, place your cursor in the area where you want the editable region to be located.

2. Go to Insert → Template Objects → Editable Region.

3. When the New Editable Region dialog box appears, type a unique name for the editable region into the Name field. The name is used by Dreamweaver to label the editable regions in a document to which the Template has been applied.

Creating Optional Regions within Your Template

New to Dreamweaver MX is the ability to include optional regions in your Template. An optional region is a section of a Template that is designated to hold content that may or may not appear in the final document.

There are two kinds of optional regions. The first, a regular optional region, contains content that the content author (not the person who originally created the template) can set as visible or invisible in the final template based document. The second type of optional region, the editable optional region, contains content which can be edited by the content author.

To create a regular optional region:

1. With the Template open in the Template Editor, select the components (text, images, and so on) that you want to be optional or place your cursor in the area where you want the optional region to be located.

2. Go to Insert → Template Objects → Optional Region.

3. When the New Optional Region dialog box appears, type a unique name for the optional region into the Name field. The name is used by Dreamweaver to label the editable regions in a document to which the Template has been applied.

4. If you want the region to automatically show (as opposed to being hidden by default), click the Show By Default option.

The options under the Advanced tab let you set the parameters of the optional region—a topic about which you can find more by clicking the Help button in the New Optional Region dialog box.

5. Click OK.

To create an optional editable region:

1. With the Template open in the Template Editor, select the components (text, images, and so on) that you want to be optional or place your cursor in the area where you want the optional region to be located.

2. Go to Insert → Template Objects → Optional Editable Region.

3. When the New Optional Region dialog box appears, type a unique name for the optional region into the Name field. The name is used by Dreamweaver to label the editable regions in a document to which the Template has been applied.

4. If you want the region to automatically show (as opposed to being hidden by default), click the Show By Default option.

5. Click OK.

Creating Repeating Regions within Your Template

A repeating region is a new feature to Dreamweaver MX that lets you designate areas of your Template whose content repeats.

There are two kinds of repeating regions that you can create. The first, a regular repeating region, is a section of content that can be duplicated as often as desired in the final template-based page. The kicker about a regular repeating region is that it cannot be edited unless the template author has included an editable region within it. The second type of repeating region, a repeating table, is a table in which editable regions automatically occupy the individual cells.

To create a regular repeating region:

1. With the Template open in the Template Editor, select the elements (text, images, and so on) that you want to set as a repeating region or place your cursor in the area where you want the repeating region to be located.

2. Go to Insert → Template Objects → Repeating Region.

3. When the New Optional Region dialog box appears, type a unique name for the repeating region into the Name field.

4. Click OK.

To create a repeating table:

1. With the Template open in the Template Editor, place your cursor in the area where you want the repeating table to be located.

2. Go to Insert → Template Objects → Repeating Table to open the Insert Repeating Table dialog box (right).

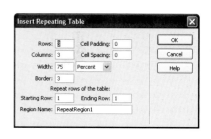

3. Enter the number of rows for the repeating table into the Rows field

4. Enter the number of columns for the repeating table into the Columns field.

5. Enter the repeating table's cell padding into the Cell Padding field.

6. Enter the repeating table's cell spacing into the Cell Spacing field.

7. Set the width of the repeating table into the Width field—remember that you can set whether the table's size is represented in pixels or percent by choosing one of the options from the drop-down menu to the right of the Width field.

8. Set the repeating table's border by entering a value into the Border field.

9. From here, you need to set which rows in the table are included in the repeating region. To do this, enter the row where the repeating region will start into the Starting Row.

10. Enter the last row to be included in the table's repeating region into the Ending Row field.

11. Click OK.

Saving Your Template

Now that you've created your Template and set its editable regions, optional regions, and repeating regions, it's time to save it. Remember, when you save a Template, it is stored as a DWT file in the Template directory located in your site's local root folder.

To save a Template:

1. Make sure the Template you want to save is open in the Template Editor.

2. Go to File → Save As Template.

3. When the Save As Template dialog box appears, select the site to which you want the template saved from the Site drop-down menu. Remember that when you select a site form the Site drop-down menu, that site's existing templates will appear in the Existing Templates list box.

4. Enter the name of the Template into the Save As field.

5. Click OK.

6. After saving the Template, go to File → Close to return to the main Document Window.

If you save a Template without setting any editable regions, you'll get a warning about the possible dire consequences. Actually, the consequences aren't that dire. If you apply the template to a page, you won't be able to add any content. However, it's remarkably easy to go back and edit the template so that it has some editable regions.

Using Templates

Now that you've gone to all the trouble of creating a Template, it's time to start using them. In this section, you'll explore how to apply a Template to a blank page, how to create a page based on a Template from scratch, how to apply a Template to an existing page, and how to detach a Template from a page.

Applying a Template to a Blank Page

To apply a Template to a page:

1. Open a blank document in the Document Window.

2. Go to Window → Assets and click the Templates button ⊟ .

3. Select the Template you wish to apply to the document and choose from the following options:

- Click the Apply button [Apply] .
- Choose Apply from the panel's Options menu.
- Click and drag the Template from the Template panel into the Document Window.

4. The Template, complete with editable regions, will be automatically applied to the blank document. Note that the editable regions are contained within a colored border identified by its unique name.

Creating a Template-Based Page from Scratch

Now that you've learned how to apply a Template to a blank document, let's look at how to create a Template-based page from scratch:

1. Go to File → New.

2. When the New Document dialog box appears, click the Template tab.

3. Select the specific local site from which you want to draw the template from the Template For list box.

4. After you select the site, you'll notice that the list box to the right of the Template For list box (whose name is dynamically generated based on the site you selected) is populated with all of the templates for that site. Select the one you want to use.

   A preview of the template will appear in the Preview section of the New Document dialog box.

5. Click the Create button.

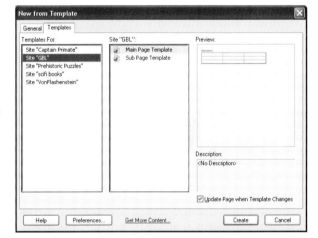

Applying a Template to an Existing Page

You don't have to start off with a blank document when applying a Template—you can also apply one to an existing document:

1. Open the existing document to which you want to apply the Template.

2. Go to Modify → Templates → Apply Template to Page.

3. When the Select Template dialog box opens, choose the local site where the Template you want to use is located from the Site drop-down menu.

4. After selecting a site, a list of Templates for that local site will appear in the Templates list; select the appropriate one.

5. If you want the page to update when the Template itself changes, select the Update Page When Template Changes option.

6. Click Select.

7. When Inconsistent Region Names dialog box opens, choose the regions you want to place the document's existing content.

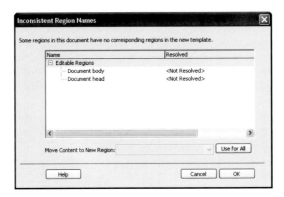

8. If you aren't interested in keeping the page's existing content, choose None and it will be all discarded.

9. Click OK. The Template will be applied to the existing document.

Detaching a Template from a Page

As I'm sure you've noticed, once you apply a Template to a page, the editable/locked regions that you define severely limit what you can do. This is part of the point of a Template. However, there will probably be a point when you decide that you want to change the editable/locked regions you initially defined in a Template. To do this, you much detach the page in question from the Template:

1. Open the document you want to detach from its Template.

2. Go to Modify → Templates → Detach from Template.

3. The page will automatically detach from its parent Template, thereby making all areas editable.

Managing and Manipulating Templates

Now that you've explored how to create Templates and apply Templates, it's time to learn how to manage and manipulate them. Templates are a valuable resource, and it's in your best interest to maximize their usability. In the following section, you'll learn how to edit existing Templates, rename Templates, delete Templates, and copy a Template to another local site.

Editing Existing Templates

Once you've created a Template, it wouldn't do you much good if you weren't able to go back and edit it. To edit a template:

1. Make sure you are currently working in the local site where the Template you wish to edit is located.

2. Go to Window → Asset and click the Templates button 🖹 .

3. Select the Template you wish to edit and choose one of the following options:

   - Click the Edit button 📝 .

   - Choose Edit from the panel's Options drop-down menu.

   - Double-click the selected Template.

4. The Template will open in the Template Editor, where you can make any changes you wish.

5. When you finished editing the Template, go to File → Save and then File → Close.

6. As soon as you resave the Template, Dreamweaver will prompt you, much as with updating a Library Item, to choose whether you want to update all the documents based on the Template.

Renaming a Template

As your digital creation gets larger, you'll probably accumulate more and more Templates, so it's a good idea to give each a fairly descriptive name. As the size of your site increases, your plans might change, and you might need to rename an existing Template. To rename your Template:

1. Make sure you are currently working in the local site in which the Template you wish to edit is located.

2. Go to Window → Assets and click the Templates button 🖹 .

3. Select the Template you wish to rename and either choose Rename from the panel's Options menu or click the Template's name.

4. When the name field becomes editable, type a new name.

5. When you finish typing the name, press Enter (Win)/ Return (Mac) or click anywhere off the Template panel.

Deleting a Template

Like Library Items, Templates are files that are saved in a special directory in your local site's root folder. As such, they do take up a certain amount of memory, though it's pretty insignificant in the grand scheme of things. Still, it's worthwhile, both for the sake of organization and space conservation, to keep the Templates in your Template panel limited only to those which are in use. To delete a Template:

1. Make sure you are currently working in the local site where the Template you wish to delete is located.

2. Go to Window → Assets and click the Templates button 📄 .

3. Select the Template you wish to delete and either click the Delete button 🗑 or select Delete from the panel's Options menu.

4. When prompted, select Yes if you want to delete the Template, and No if you don't.

Once you've deleted a Template from the Template panel, you cannot undo the action with the Edit → Undo command—it's a permanent deletion. Documents that were based on a deleted template are not detached from the template; they retain the structure and editable regions that the template file had before it was deleted.

Copying a Template to Another Local Site

As mentioned previously, like Library Items, all Templates are unique to a given local site, but there will probably be a point when you'll want to use a certain Template in another local site. There are a couple ways to do this. You can copy the actual Template's DWT file to the Templates subfolder in the intended local site's root folder, but this can be cumbersome. To copy a Template more efficiently:

1. Make sure you are currently working in the local site which contains the Template you want to transfer to another local site.

2. Go to Window → Assets and click the Template button 📄 .

3. Select the Template you want to transfer.

4. Select Copy to Site from the panel's Options menu, and then choose the target site from the list of previously defined local sites. The selected Template will automatically be copied to the target site's Templates folder.

If you copy a Template which has hyperlinks relative to the local site in which it was originally created, they won't work properly in the local site to which it is copied.

Managing and Manipulating Site-Wide Assets with the Assets Panel

Websites can be composed of lots of stuff: text, images, Flash movies, Shockwave movies, audio files, and digital video files, as well as lots of other less tangible things like colors, scripts, and hyperlinks. When you stop to think about it, the amount of resources you can use creating a website of any significant size is pretty staggering.

Even more staggering is the thought that the larger your web creations get, the more assets you use and the harder it gets to manage those assets. Short of keeping a running tally of all the colors, hyperlinks, image names and locations, scripts, Flash files, and so on on an enormous piece of paper, it's terribly difficult to keep track of all this stuff. Or is it?

If you think about these digital assets as reusable raw material that should be stored in a safe place for future use, it seems natural that there should be an integrated tool within your visual web design software whose sole task is to help you manage all of your various digital assets. This is exactly what Macromedia created—hoorah!

Back in Dreamweaver 4, the Assets panel was introduced. Acting as a central repository for all sorts of digital resources, the Assets panel lets you manage and manipulate many different types of digital assets for an entire local site.

> Library Items and Templates are also considered assets and therefore have their own section in the Assets panel. Because we've already spent a great deal of time exploring the ins and outs of both, they won't be discussed in any depth in this section of the chapter.

In this section, you'll explore how to manage and manipulate digital assets with the Assets panel. You'll start off by learning how to use the Assets panel to manipulate the various assets within your local site. From there, you'll learn how to add assets to a page and edit them. You'll finish off the last section of the chapter by learning how to manually add assets to the Assets panel.

Because digital assets are associated with a local site, you'll need to define a local site (and create a local cache) before you'll have access to the Assets panel.

Using the Assets Panel

The Assets panel, which is accessible by going to Window → Assets, is the centralized location from which you manage and manipulate all the many digital assets in a local site.

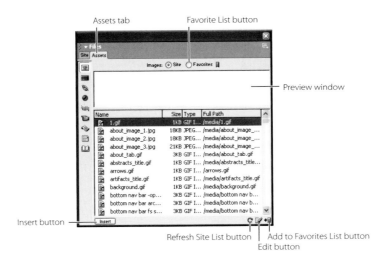

Images ▣   Any web-compatible images (GIF, JPEG, and PNG0 files) in the root folder of your local site will be displayed in this section.

Colors ▦   Any color you've used within your local site, whether it's a background color, a text color, a link color, will be displayed in this section of the Assets panel. Notice that each color is represented by a swatch, a hex value, and an indication as to whether its part of the Websafe Color Palette.

URLs ✎   The URLs section of the Assets panel contains a list of all *external* hyperlinks included in all documents within your local site. These consist of FTP links, links to JavaScript, `mailto (e-mail) links`, gopher links, HTTP links, and links to local files (file://).

Flash ◉   The Flash section of the Assets panel contains all Flash files (SWF files, not FLA files) in your local site.

> If you are interested in learning more about Macromedia Flash, read *Flash MX Savvy* by Ethan Watrall and Norbert Herber (Sybex, 2002).

Shockwave ⅊   The Shockwave section of the Assets panel contains all the Shockwave files (a type of multimedia created by Macromedia Director) in your local site.

Movies 🖼 The Movies section of the Assets panel lists all QuickTime and MPEG files in your local site.

Scripts 🐚 The Scripts section of the Assets panel contains a list of all standalone JavaScript and VBScript files in your local site.

> JavaScript and VBScript embedded in HTML files will not appear in the Scripts section of the Assets panel.

When you create a new local site, the Assets panel is as bare as Mother Hubbard's pantry. However, as you add more digital resources to any page within the local site, the various sections of the Assets panel will fill up.

You can also start off by defining an already existing group of files on your hard drive as a local site, and the various digital assets located in the local site's root folder will automatically populate the Assets panel.

Refreshing the Site List Manually

As mentioned, the Assets panel is automatically populated with all the digital assets located in the root folder of your local site. However, there are a couple of situations in which the list of assets will not automatically update. The first happens when you either remove a digital asset from or add a digital asset to the root folder of your local site. The second happens when you remove the last instance of a color or URL from your local site or add a new color or URL to your local site. Because you always want an accurate accounting of all the digital assets used, it's wise to manually refresh the Asset panels list:

1. Open the Assets panel (Window → Assets).

2. Either click the Refresh Site List button 🔄 or select Refresh Site List from the panel's Options menu.

Previewing Assets

While the list of digital assets in the various sections of the Assets panel is sometimes all you need for a description, sometimes you'll need a little more. To preview an asset:

1. Open the Assets panel (Window → Assets) and select the asset at which you'd like to look.

2. A preview will appear in the preview panel of the Assets panel. Each type of asset appears differently in the preview pane. For example, an image will show up as a small thumbnail, while a URL will simply show up as an enlarged full text path.

Working with the Favorites List

As your site gets larger, you'll find that the number of assets displayed in the Assets panel can get a little overwhelming. Why wade through a list of colors or images, most of which you've used only once or twice, when you are looking for something you use more frequently? This is where the Favorites list comes into the picture. Essentially, the Favorites list is a catalog of your most commonly used digital assets.

VIEWING THE FAVORITES LIST

The Favorites list, which is contained in the Assets panel, is easily accessible:

1. Open the Assets panel (Window → Assets).

2. If it isn't already selected, click the Favorites radio button.

   The Favorites list will be empty until you manually add digital assets to it; we will discuss how to do this shortly.

ADDING AN ASSET TO THE FAVORITES LIST

To add a site's asset to your Favorites List:

> Neither Library Items nor Templates can be added to a local site's Favorite list.

1. Open the Assets panel (Window → Assets).

2. Make sure you are currently in the site list by clicking the Site radio button.

3. Select the asset you want to add to the Favorites List and either click the Add to Favorites List button ➕▣ or choose Add to Favorites List from the panel's Options menu.

   A single item can be added to the Favorites list more than once.

REMOVING AN ASSET FROM THE FAVORITES LIST

You can easily remove assets from your Favorites List as well:

1. Open the Assets panel (Window → Assets).

2. Make sure you are currently in the Favorites List by clicking the Favorites radio button.

3. Select the asset you want to remove from the Favorites List and either click the Remove from Favorites List button ➖▣ or choose Remove from Favorites List from the panel's Options menu.

ORGANIZING ASSETS IN THE FAVORITES LIST WITH FOLDERS

One of the great features of the Favorites List is that you can organize assets into folders:

1. Open the Assets panel (Window → Assets).

2. Make sure you are currently in the Favorites List by clicking the Favorites radio button.

3. Either click the New Favorites Folder button  or choose New Favorites Folder from the panel's Options menu.

4. When the new folder appears, type a title into its name field. When you finish, either click your cursor anywhere off the Assets panel or press Enter (Win)/ Return (Mac).

5. Click and drag any asset into the folder.

Notice that when assets are added to the folder, a plus (+) sign appears to its right. Click it to expand the folder. To collapse the folder, click the minus (-) sign.

COPYING FAVORITE ASSETS TO ANOTHER LOCAL SITE

Just like assets in your regular site list, assets in the Favorites List are bound to a particular local site. However, you can easily copy them to the Favorites List of another local site:

1. Open the Assets panel (Window → Assets).

2. Make sure you are currently in the Favorites List by clicking the Favorites radio button.

3. Select the asset you want to transfer and select Copy to Site from the panel's Options menu.

4. Choose the target site from the list of previously defined local sites.

You can copy entire folders from one local site's Favorites List to another local site's Favorites List.

Adding Assets to a Page

The whole point of the Assets panel is that once a digital asset is used, it can be almost instantly re-accessed and reused without having to go through the steps you underwent the first time it was integrated into the document.

To add assets to a page:

1. Open the Assets panel (Window → Assets).

2. Select the asset you want to add to the page.

3. From here, there are a number of different steps, each specific to the type of asset you want to insert.

Because an asset can be any number of things (including less tangible items like colors and URLs), the process of adding them to a page differs. For instance, in the case of colors, you need to first select the item (text, link, and so on) to which you apply the color, and then insert it. The remaining steps that you need to follow to add an asset to a page will be split into several subsections, each dealing with the separate assets.

2. Select the asset you want to edit and either click the Edit button 📝 or choose Edit from the Asset panel's Options menu.

3. The external editor for that particular file type will open.

4. Make any changes you want to the file and save it.

5. After you finish, close the external editor.

6. Click the Refresh Site List button or select Refresh Site List from the Asset panel's Options menu.

Editing Non-external File-Based Assets

Before editing non-external file-based assets (such as colors or URLs), you'll first need to add them to the Favorites List. To edit non-external file-based assets:

1. Open the Assets panel (Window → Assets).

2. Make sure you are working within the Favorites list by clicking the Favorites radio button located along the top of the Assets panel.

3. Select the asset you want to edit and either click the Edit button 📝 or select Edit from the panel's Options menu.

4. If the asset you selected is a URL, type a new URL into the URL field of the Edit URL dialog box and then type a nickname (if you so wish) into the Nickname field. A nickname is a name you can give to any URL to more easily identify the asset when it appears in the Assets panel.

If the asset you selected is a color, simply choose a new color from the Color Palette. If the color you want is not located in the Color Palette, click the Color Wheel icon to open the Color Picker, where you can mix your own custom color.

5. When you've made the changes to the selected asset, either click the Refresh Site List button or select Refresh Site List from the panel's Options menu.

Manually Adding New Assets to the Assets Panel

As I've mentioned, Dreamweaver automatically populates the Assets panel with all the digital assets you use during the course of creating a local site. While one way to add new assets to the Assets panel is simply to add something to a document within your local site, you can also manually add some types of assets to the Assets panel without having to add them to an actual document.

The four types of assets that can be manually inserted into the Assets panel are colors, URLs, Templates, and Library Items. Because we've already covered Templates and Library Items, this section will focus exclusively on colors and URLS.

> As in the previous section, new colors and URLS can only be manually inserted into the Assets panel when you're working in the Favorites List.

To manually insert a new asset into the Asset panel:

1. Open the Assets panel (Window → Assets).

2. Make sure you are working within the Favorites list by clicking the Favorites radio button.

3. Depending on the type of asset you want to include, click the New URL button ⊡ or the New Color button ⊡ or select New URL or New Color from the panel's Options menu.

4. If the asset you are inserting is a URL, type a new URL into the URL field of the Edit URL dialog box and then type a nickname (if you wish) into the Nickname field.

   If the asset you are inserting is a color, simply choose a new color from the Color Palette. If the color you want is not located in the Color Palette, click the Color Wheel icon to open the Color Picker, where you can mix your own custom color.

5. After you add the new URL or color, click the Refresh Site List button or select Refresh Site List from the panel's Options menu.

Inspiration: Design and Technique

There is nothing more satisfying that a clean, efficient website that just screams understated design. Easily one of the best examples out there of this rare phenomenon is Info 2 Extreme (`www.i2x.net`). Located in Los Angeles, Info 2 Extreme is a full-service, turnkey Internet Application Service Provider. I2X builds websites and web infrastructure for companies worldwide. From initial site architecture to final systems integration, I2X delivers scalable and leverageable Business-to-Business (B2B), Business-to-Consumer (B2C) and Extranet applications to the World Wide Web.

Their corporate site (see Figure 9.1) uses a mix of HTML and Flash for visual design and Cold Fusion for content management. The end result is an elegantly simple site that epitomizes many of the fundamentals of interactive design.

Figure 9.1

Info 2 Extreme

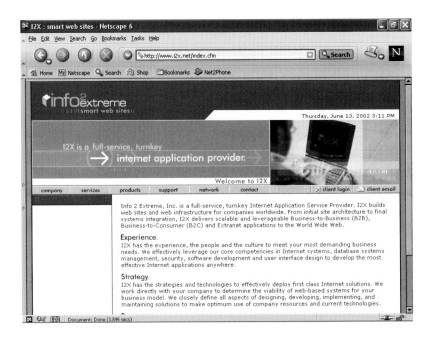

Summary

In this chapter, you explored many of the recyclable and time-saving aspects of Dreamweaver. You started off by learning how to create, apply, and manage Library Items. From there, you learned to create, use, and manage Templates. You finished off the chapter by learning how to use the Assets panel to manage and manipulate site-wide digital assets.

While at this stage of the game you might not see the benefit of these labor saving tools, you will eventually, especially when your projects get larger and more sophisticated and you are looking for any edge on the production schedule. With this in mind, it's a wise idea to thoroughly acquaint yourself with all the subjects discussed in this chapter sooner instead of later.

CHAPTER 10

Working with Forms

While most people think about the Web as a medium used to deliver information (either textual or visual), it has also become a manner of gathering information. Whether it's an e-commerce site that gathers orders, payment information, and customer data, or a site that requires a username and password to enter, the Web has become a two-way street in terms of data flow.

The procedure by which data is sent from a web page to a server (where an infinite amount of stuff can be done to it) involves two separate parts. The first part involves the elements on the web page itself (fields, Submit button, drop-down menus, radio buttons, and so on) used to collect the information from the user. The second part involves a program that sits on the server, takes the data sent from the browser (when the user hits the Submit button), and does something with it—sends it to someone as an e-mail, sticks it in a database, and so on.

In this chapter, we'll focus on the first component: the front-end interface elements, commonly referred to as forms, used to collect the data from the users. One of the terribly cool things about Dreamweaver MX is that you can use it not only to create the front-end form elements (which are used to collect user information), but also to create the back-end server-side component that processes the information—a topic to which you'll get an introduction in Part IV, "Making Dreamweaver Dynamic."

- **Creating forms**
- **Inserting a form**
- **Understanding names and values**
- **Working with text fields**
- **Inserting a check box or radio button**
- **Inserting a radio group**
- **Creating a drop-down menu**
- **Creating a scrolling list**
- **Adding a button**
- **Working with file fields**

Creating Forms

A form on the Web, interestingly enough, is quite like its real-world paper counterpart. It's a structured method of communication that solicits very specific information from the user, whether they are sitting in front of their computer buying books or sitting in the bank applying for a car loan.

The process by which you create the elements that make up a from is relatively easy. The real challenge comes in understanding the nuts and bolts of a form and making sure you've designed your form beforehand so that you'll be able to quickly and efficiently choose those elements that allow you to best serve your data collection needs (for example, using a drop-down menu to collect a user's name is definitely a bad decision—not to mention impossible—when a simple text field will do the trick just fine).

You'll find that one of the great things about Dreamweaver is that it makes creating forms a snap.

Inserting a Form

Before you can start inserting the form objects (text fields, radio button, and so on), you have to insert the actual `<form></form>` tags in which the form objects reside. You can actually have form objects that exist outside the `<form></form>` tags. However, without the tags, they can't interact with back-end component and are therefore pretty useless. Because the form itself, which is inserted just like any other object in Dreamweaver, is an invisible element, it's represented in the Document Window by a dashed red line; this will become a very important visual cue.

> If you do not insert the form first, any form objects you subsequently add will be totally useless. They must reside within the red dashed lines of the form.

To insert a form into your document:

1. Place your cursor in the location where you'd like to insert the form.

2. Open the Insert bar (Window → Insert).

3. Select the Forms tab.

4. Click the Insert Form ⬚ button. Alternatively, you can also go to Insert → Form to insert the form into your Document Window.

Because the form itself is an invisible element, its red dashed line will not show up unless you've got the Form Delimiter element turned on in the Invisible Elements section of the Preferences dialog box (Edit → Preferences). You'll also have to turn the Invisible Elements on using the View Menu (View → Visual Aids → Invisible Elements)

If you've got the document's invisible elements turned on, you'll notice the red dashed box (which is often referred to as the form delimiter)—this is the form itself. Anything within it falls within the `<form></form>` tags.

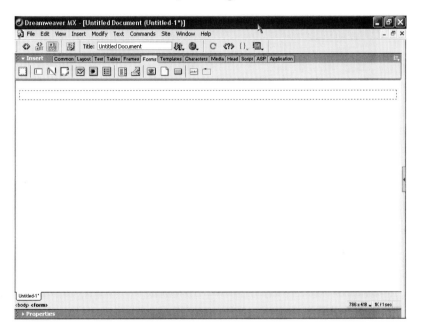

Once you've inserted the form itself, you can move forward and set the form's properties:

1. Open the Property Inspector (Window → Properties).

2. With your cursor inside the form delimiter, select the Form by clicking the `<form>` tab in the Tag Selector.

Remember, the Tag Selector is located in the bottom left-hand corner of the Document Window.

> The form properties are also referred to as a form handler.

3. First, you need to set the Form's method, which is how the form sends the data collected by the form to the server. You have two options:

   - If you use the GET method, the data is sent to the server in the form of a URL. The GET method is rarely used, for two reasons. First, when you pass data in the form of a URL to the server, you are limited in the amount of data that can be moved. Second, because the data is actually visible, sending data in the form of a URL is relatively insecure and therefore not particularly desirable.

   - If you use the POST method, data is encrypted and sent to the server.

4. In the Action field, enter the location (relative or absolute URL) of the script, page, or program that will process the information gathered by the form.

> For more information on processing and using form-submitted data, see Part IV for an introduction on using Dreamweaver MX to create dynamic database-driven sites.

5. When you finish setting the form properties, press Return (Mac)/ Enter (Win) or click anywhere off the Property Inspector.

Understanding Names and Values

Before you can push forward and learn how to insert and manipulate all the types of form widgets that collect user data, there is an important topic that needs to be discussed.

Each of the form objects about which you'll be learning in the upcoming sections are called input items. Each input item, whether it's a radio button, a text box, or a drop-down menu, is represented, both in the HTML source as well as the information that is sent to the server, as two different components: a *name* and a *value*.

In Dreamweaver, the name of an input device is set with the Property Inspector (a process you'll be carrying out each time you insert a new form object into your form). The value of an input device, on the other hand, is generated by the user. For example, say you had a textbox named `DogName` into which the user had to type the name of their dog. If I were to come along and type my dog's name into the textbox, the output to the server would look something like this:

`DogName=Oscar`

What the server does with the output from a form, which is delivered in this name=value structure, is entirely dependent on the type of server-side technology you are using to process the form. It could be stuck into a database along with a whole bucket load of other form-collected information, or it could be e-mailed to the website administrator.

To work properly, it is absolutely necessary that each form object have a name. While Dreamweaver will automatically generate generic names for all of your form objects, it's in your best interest to create your own distinct name so that data delivered to you (if that is how you intend for the form's information to be processed) won't become confusing.

Working with Text Fields

The text field is the most basic of form objects. They are used to collect data that you don't know in advance, such as name, favorite color, favorite cheesy '70s science fiction TV series—you get the picture. Text fields come in several different flavors: single line, multi-line, and password. In the following section, you'll learn how to create each kind of text field, as well as how to set their various properties.

Creating a Single-Line Text Box

A single-line text field is designed to accept—you guessed it—a single line of text. While limited to a single line, the length of the line is quite up to you. To create a single-line text box:

1. Place your cursor in the location within the form delimiter where you wish to insert the single-line text field.

2. Open the Insert bar (Window → Insert) and select the Forms tab.

3. Click the Insert Text Field ☐ button. Alternatively, you can go to Insert → Form Objects → Text Field to insert a text field.

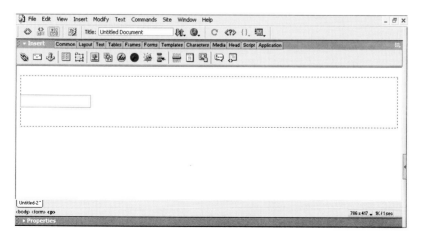

Once the text field itself has been inserted into the document (within the form delimiter), you can set its properties with the Property Inspector:

1. Select the text field whose properties you wish to set. When selected, the text field will be highlighted with a black dashed line.

2. Open the Property Inspector (Window → Properties). Alternatively, you can double-click the text box to open the Property Inspector.

Text field type options

3. If it isn't already, make sure Single Line is selected from the Type options.

4. In the Name field, enter a unique name for the single-line text field.

For this and the other exercises in this chapter, keep in mind how the name/value combination factors into the overall form equation. If you are having trouble remembering how names and values work, see the "Understanding Names and Values" section earlier in this chapter.

5. Enter a numerical value into the Char Width field. As represented in Figure 10.1, the number represents the horizontal size of the text field, not the number of characters that it can accept (that is set by the Max Chars value).

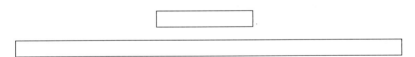

Figure 10.1

The text field on the top has a Char Width of 25, while the one of the bottom has a Char Width of 100—note the difference in size.

6. Enter a numerical value into the Max Chars field. This number represents the maximum number of characters (including spaces) the user will be able to type into the text field.

7. If you want the text field to already have some text in it when the user loads the page, type it into the Init Val field. Any text in the Init Val field, which shows up when the page is initially loaded, can be deleted by the user.

8. When you finish setting the text field's properties, press Return (Mac)/Enter (Win) or click anywhere off the Property Inspector, and the changes will take effect.

Creating a Multiline Text Field

A multiline text field can be used for accepting any kind of text that doesn't fit well on a single line—like the user's favorite Shakespearean soliloquy or their mother's incredible recipe for butter tarts. Note that the multiline text field starts out as a single line text field. To create a multiline text field:

1. Place your cursor within the form delimiter where you wish to insert the multiline text field.

2. Open the Insert bar (Window → Insert) and select the Forms tab.

3. Click the Insert Text Field ▭ button.

4. Select the text field you just created.

5. Open the Property Inspector (Window → Properties) and select Multiline from the Type options. This will change the single-line text field you created into a multiline text field.

   This will also give you access to the multiline text field properties, which you set just as you would for a single-line text field. However, there are some minute differences:

Character Width field   Initial Value field

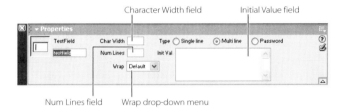

Num Lines field   Wrap drop-down menu

- You must enter a numerical value into the Num Lines field. As shown in Figure 10.2, the Num Lines value controls the vertical size of the multiline text field.

- If you want the text that the user types into the multiline text field to wrap, choose one of the options from the Wrap drop-down menu (which is accessible in the expanded portion of the Property Inspector):

Default The user's browser decides (based on its own rules) whether the text entered into a multiline text field wraps.

Off The text won't wrap (that is, unless the user hits Return (Mac)/ Enter (Win), it will be entered on a single line).

Virtual The text will wrap when it's viewed in the user's browser but won't include any line breaks when it's sent to the server for processing.

Physical The text will include line breaks both on the screen and when it's sent to the server for processing.

Figure 10.2

The multiline text field on the top has a Num Lines value of 2, while the one on the bottom has a Num Lines value of 10—note the difference in size.

Creating a Password Field

A password field is almost the same as the single-line text field; the only difference is that any text typed in by the user is hidden with a generic symbol such as * or •. The Password Field has no other function than to disguise the text from a casual passerby.

To create a Password field:

1. Place your cursor within the form delimiter where you wish to insert the password field.

2. Open the Insert bar (Window → Insert) and select the Forms tab.

3. Click the Insert Text Field ☐ button. Alternatively, you can go to Insert → Form Objects → Text Field to insert a text field.

4. Select the newly created text field.

5. If it isn't already, open the Property Inspector (Window → Properties).

6. Select the Password radio button

7. Set the password text field properties—they are exactly the same as in the case of a single or multiline text field.

> All text entered into the Password text field, including Init Val text, is represented in those snazzy secret symbols.

Inserting a Check Box or Radio Button

Both check boxes and radio buttons (Figure 10.3) let users choose between a series of discrete items.

The difference between radio buttons and check boxes is that check boxes let the user pick as many options as they wish. Radio buttons, on the other hand, let the user choose only one option from a group of options.

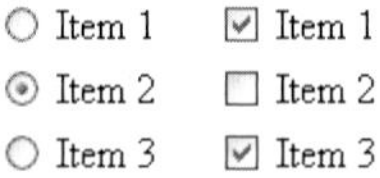

However, the process by which you add and manipulate both check boxes and radio buttons is virtually identical. To insert either check boxes or radio buttons into your form:

1. Place your cursor in the location (within the form delimiter) where you wish to insert the radio button or check box.

2. Open the Insert bar (Window → Insert) and select the Forms tab.

3. Click either Insert Check Box ☑ or Insert Radio Button ⦿ . Alternatively, you can go to Insert → Form Objects → Radio Button or Insert → Form Object → Check Box.

○ Item 1   ☑ Item 1
⦿ Item 2   ☐ Item 2
○ Item 3   ☑ Item 3

Figure 10.3

Radio buttons (left) and check boxes (right) only have two states: on (filled in) or off (left blank).

From here, you can set the properties of either the check box or radio button with the Property Inspector:

1. Select the object whose properties you wish to set.

2. Open the Property Inspector (Window → Properties) and enter a unique name into the Name field.

Checked Value field   Initial value options

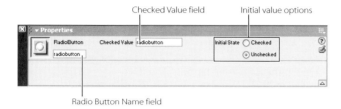

Radio Button Name field

3. Enter a unique name into the Checked Value field. This name will be sent to the server if the user has selected that particular check box or radio button.

4. To determine whether the radio button or check box will be checked or unchecked when the page is initially loaded, choose one of the Initial State options. By default, check boxes and radio buttons are unchecked when a page initially loads.

5. When you finish setting the properties for a check box or a radio button, press Return (Mac)/ Enter (Win) or click anywhere off the Property Inspector.

Inserting a Radio Group

New to Dreamweaver MX is the ability to create a radio group, which is just a group of radio buttons that you insert into your document in one fell swoop through a single dialog box. Beyond that, there are really no differences between a radio group and a regular radio button.

To insert a radio group:

1. Place your cursor in the location (within the form delimiter) where you wish to insert the radio button or check box.

2. Open the Insert bar (Window → Insert) and select the Forms tab.

3. Click the Insert Radio Group button. Alternately, you can go to Insert → Form Objects → Radio Group.

4. When the Radio Group dialog box appears, enter a unique name into the Name field.

> By default, when you create a radio group, it has two radio buttons. You can easily change the number by using the process described here.

5. Click the first item in the Label column. When the field becomes editable, enter a new name for the radio button. This is not the name of the form object but is the text that will appear next to it.

6. Click the corresponding item in the Value column. When the field becomes editable, enter a corresponding value for that radio button.

7. Repeat steps 5 and 6 for the remaining radio buttons.

8. To add additional radio buttons to the radio group, just click the plus (+) **+** button, and repeat steps 5 and 6 for the newly added radio button.

9. To remove a radio button from the radio group, select any of the items in the Label column, and click the minus (−) **−** button.

10. If you want to change the order of the radio buttons in the radio group, select any of the items in the Label field and click the up button **▲** to move it upward in the stack, or click the down button **▼** to move it downward in the stack.

11. Select one of the Lay Out Using options. If you choose Line Breaks, the radio buttons in the radio group will be stacked one on top of the other as if you had pressed Return (Mac)/ Enter (Win) after inserting the radio button. However, if you choose Table, Dreamweaver will create a table in which it places the radio buttons in the radio group.

12. When you finish setting the radio button's properties, click OK

Creating a Drop-Down Menu

A drop-down menu (Figure 10.4) is another way to let the user choose from a number of different options. Unlike radio buttons or check boxes, however, the options are all contained in one menu, thereby saving a fair amount of space.

Figure 10.4

The drop-down menu is designed to let you provide users with a series of options without taking up a great deal of space.

It is also important to note that drop-down menus, like radio buttons, are a "one choice" form object, allowing users to make a single selection (as opposed to several).

To create a drop-down menu object:

1. Place your cursor in the location (within the form delimiter) where you wish to insert the drop-down menu.

2. Open the Insert bar (Window → Insert) and select the Forms tab.

3. Click the Insert List/Menu button ▤. Alternatively, you can also go to Insert → Form Objects → List/Menu.

Notice that when the drop-down menu  is originally inserted, it looks rather small. This is because it's not yet populated with any content. From here, you can populate the drop-down menu as well as set its other properties:

1. Select the drop-down menu whose properties you wish to set.

2. Open the Property Inspector (Window → Properties) and choose Menu.

3. Enter a unique name into the List/Menu Name field.

4. Click the List Values button to open the List Values dialog box. This is where you'll populate the drop-down menu.

5. Click just below the Item Label column header, and an editable field will appear.

6. Type the text you would like to appear in the drop-down menu's first slot.

7. Press Tab to move to the Value column, where an editable field will appear.

8. Type in the value you want associated with the menu item.

9. To add additional menu items (after you typed in the value for the first item), press Tab to return to the Item Label column. Alternatively, you can click the plus (+) button in the top left-hand corner of the List Values dialog box. Repeat steps 7 through 10 until you've added all the items you want to the drop-down menu.

10. When you finished populating the drop-down menu, click OK.

11. With the drop-down menu still selected and the Property Inspector still open, select one of the menu items in the Initially Selected list. This sets the menu item that will be initially selected when the page is loaded.

> To edit a menu item in a drop-down menu, open the Property Inspector, click the List Values button to open the List Values dialog box, and make any changes you want.

12. When you finish setting the drop-down menu's properties, press Return (Mac)/ Enter (Win) or click anywhere off the Property Inspector.

Creating a Scrolling List

Figure 10.5

The scrolling list lets you display the number of menu items that are displayed at any given time.

The scrolling list is to the drop-down menu what the check box is to the radio button. In the case of a drop-down menu, you can only select one item. From a scrolling list, however, the user can choose more than one item by holding down Cmd (Mac)/ Ctrl (Win) and clicking. Also, unlike the drop-down menu, the scrolling list lets you display more than one menu item at a given time (Figure 10.5). In fact, you can control the number of items that are displayed.

The scrolling list starts out as a drop-down menu, so the process to insert one is the same. You transform the drop-down menu into the scrolling list with the Property Inspector. To insert a scrolling list:

1. Place your cursor in the location (within the form delimiter) where you wish to insert the scrolling list.

2. Open the Insert bar (Window → Insert) and select the Forms tab.

3. Click the Insert List/Menu button ▦. Alternatively, you can go to Insert → Form Objects → List/Menu.

4. Select the newly created form object that you want to convert to a scrolling list.

5. Open the Property Inspector (Window → Properties) and select the List option. This converts the drop-down menu to a scrolling list and gives you access to the properties you need to set.

6. Enter a unique name into the Name field.

7. Click the List Values button to open the List Values dialog box. This is where you'll populate the scrolling list.

8. Adding menu items (and their respective values) to a scrolling list is exactly the same process as it is for a drop-down menu. Just follow steps 6 through 10 in the previous section. When you're finished, click OK.

9. If you want the user to be able to select more than one menu item, select the Allow Multiple Selections option.

10. You need to enter a value into the Height field. The number you enter sets the number of menu items that will be visible at any given time in the scrolling list. As illustrated in Figure 10.6, if you enter a value that is lower than the amount of items in the list, a scrollbar will appear, letting the user scroll to the items not currently displayed in the list.

11. When you finish setting the scrolling list's properties, press Return (Mac)/ Enter (Win) or click anywhere off the Property Inspector.

Figure 10.6

The scrolling list on the left has a height value equal to its number of menu items, so there is no scrollbar. The scrolling list on the right has a height value less than the number of its menu items, so there is a scrollbar.

Adding a Button

Buttons are arguably the most important part of a form. While they don't actually collect any information from the user, they act as a bridge between the front-end form and the back-end server. Without a Submit button (the most common type of button), users could diligently fill out your form, but they wouldn't be able to send the data anywhere once they were finished.

Dreamweaver offers you three distinct kinds of buttons that you can add to your form:

Submit Carries out the action (as well as the method) you set when you defined the properties of the form itself.

Reset Clears the form of any entered data and returns it to its initial state.

None Doesn't do a thing. The user can click it to their heart's content, but nothing will happen.

To add a button to your form:

1. Place your cursor in the location (within the form delimiter) where you wish to insert the button.

2. Open the Insert bar (Window → Insert) and select the Forms tab.

3. Click the Insert Button button ▭ . Alternatively, you can go to Insert → Form Objects → Button.

From here, you can set the properties of the button:

1. Select the button.

2. Open the Property Inspector (Window → Properties).

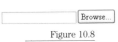

Figure 10.7

Give the button a custom label—anything you want—by entering some text into the Label field.

3. Set the purpose you'd like the button to fulfill by selecting one of the Action options (Submit, Reset, or None)

4. To give your button a custom label, type a name into the Label field. Be wild, be crazy—break out of the mold and give your button a little flare by entering a custom label (see Figure 10.7).

Even if you type in a new label, the button's action won't change.

5. When you finish setting the buttons properties, press Return (Mac)/ Enter (Win) or click anywhere off the Property Inspector.

Working with File Fields

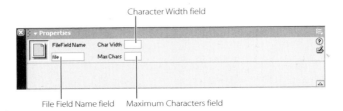

Figure 10.8

The file field, which lets the user browse for and then attach a document to the form and send it to the server, is composed of a text field and a Browse button.

Compared to the other form objects that have been covered thus far, the file field object (sometimes also referred to as the file input field) isn't as commonly used. Essentially, a file field (Figure 10.8) lets the user browse their computer for a file that is then attached to the form and sent to the server with any other data. Say, for instance, you had created a site at which employers could advertise the positions they need filled. You could create a file field that lets the job seeker upload their résumé from their hard drive.

To insert a file field into your form:

1. Place your cursor in the location (within the form delimiter) where you wish to insert the file field.

2. Open the Insert bar (Window → Insert) and select the Forms tab.

3. Click the Insert File Field button ☐. Alternatively, you can go to Insert → Form Objects → File Field.

From here, you can set the (limited) properties of the file field object.

1. Select the button.

2. Open the Property Inspector (Window → Properties).

Character Width field

File Field Name field   Maximum Characters field

3. Enter a numerical value into the Char Width field. Remember, the number represents the horizontal size of the file field's associated text field—not the amount of characters that it can accept (that is set by the Max Chars value.)

4. Enter a numerical value into the Max Chars field—this number represented the maximum of characters the user will be able to type into the text field.

5. When you've finished setting the buttons properties, press Return (Mac)/Enter (Win) or click anywhere off the Property Inspector.

Inspiration: Design and Technique

Prepare yourself for CWD (Canadian World Domination)! Designed as the General Headquarters of the Campaign for Canadian World Domination, CWD (`www.standonguard.com`) was created by General Claire and General Jenny, your future tyrants in the Canadian-dominated new world order. Through the systematic destruction and sublimation of all who oppose their reign, the polite yet horrifically brutal control of our future territories of conquest and the decontamination of non-Canadian influences from the world, the Campaign for Canadian World domination aims to reorganize a New World Society of Canucks to suit their loving, kindly, peaceful, and diabolical aims.

The CWD's web presence (Figure 10.9) which, if you haven't figured out yet, is a typical slice of offbeat Canadian humor, is a testament to clean, inspirational design.

If you don't know what a touque, a chesterfield, or smarties are, you'd better start doing your research because the new world order is coming!

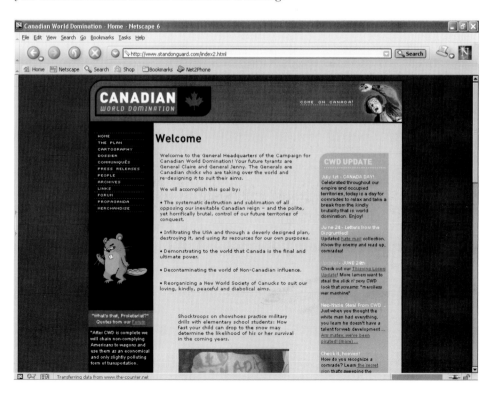

Figure 10.9

The General Head-quarters of the Campaign for Canadian World Domination

Summary

In this chapter, you explored working with forms in Dreamweaver. You learned how to use forms to collect information and how to use some server-side technology to do something with it. You also learned how to insert all the various elements that make up a form in Dreamweaver (text boxes, radio buttons, check boxes, drop-down lists, scrolling lists, and file fields). However, no matter how well Dreamweaver is at creating the front-end component of a form, it's important to remember it cannot generate the back-end component of a form that sits on the server and processes the information sent to it when the user hits the Submit button. Remember, this is only the beginning when it comes to collecting and employing user data. In Part IV, you'll get a solid introduction to how you can use Dreamweaver MX to create dynamic database-driven sites.

In the next chapter, you'll learn how to add some spice to your HTML creations by integrating and manipulating all sorts of multimedia.

CHAPTER 11

Inserting and Manipulating Multimedia

The Web has developed into a medium in which a veritable cornucopia of exciting media can be used to fashion your interactive creation. Whether you want to create a stunning visual experience with Flash, a serious (or fun) interactive application with Shockwave, a rich audio experience with any given sound format, or a marvelous digital video event with QuickTime, the options available for adding that extra oomph to your HTML creation are quite numerous.

In this chapter, you'll explore how to use Dreamweaver to integrate the myriad available multimedia formats into your HTML creation. To start off, we'll discuss some things to keep in mind when designing with multimedia in Dreamweaver. Then we'll get to the good stuff.

This chapter will explore the following topics:

- **Working with Flash movies**
- **Working with Shockwave files**
- **Working with Java applets**
- **Working with Netscape plug-ins**
- **Working with ActiveX Controls**
- **Working with audio files**
- **Controlling inserted media with behaviors**

Before We Get Started

As you'd expect, Dreamweaver can easily handle all of your multimedia needs, from inserting any number of different media types to manipulating them so they look and behave exactly as you wish. But before you get ahead of yourself, with visions of marvelous multimedia creations dancing in your head, it's crucial to note that, except in a single case (Flash text), Dreamweaver can't author any of the kinds of multimedia that will be discussed in this chapter. Instead, just as with images (see Chapter 5, "Inserting and Controlling Images"), Dreamweaver handles how a given media type is displayed and functions within the HTML document itself.

Something else that's important to remember when you're using multimedia of any kind to elevate your HTML creation to the next level: great power comes with great responsibility. Most multimedia files are large, and some are monstrously huge—for instance, even the most basic Shockwave file can easily reach 5MB in size. This means that you'll have to start seriously thinking about bandwidth and accessibility, a topic that's probably not at the forefront of your brain during you creative process. For more information on bandwidth issues, refer to the "Designing with Bandwidth in Mind" section of Chapter 1, "Web Design: The Big Picture."

Working with Flash Movies

There is little doubt that Flash is one of the coolest things to come down the pipe in terms of web design in…well…ever. Essentially, Flash, a file format developed by Macromedia, started out life a few years back as a simple vector animation tool. Because vector-based images are described using mathematical equations (as opposed to bitmap images, which are composed of individual pixels whose color and position take up a fixed amount of computer memory), they are very small (in terms of file size) and appear incredibly crisp and clean. In addition, they can be resized without any image degradation (something that is impossible with bitmaps). All of these characteristics make vectors a wonderful medium to produce animations of all kinds which is what Macromedia Flash was originally designed for.

Several years and several software versions later, Macromedia Flash (the name of both the authoring program and the media itself) has evolved enormously. No longer is Flash suited just for simple vector animations; it is now pretty much the de facto standard for producing highly interactive and visually stunning interactive experiences for delivery both on and off the Web.

Flash has opened up a new world (nay, a new universe) of possibilities for interactive designers. While it would be unfair (and inaccurate) to say that Flash is the future of the Web, it's pretty safe to say that it's *one* of the futures of the Web. Anyone interested in breaking free of the (many) creative constraints of HTML would be wise to roll up their sleeves and dive into Macromedia Flash as soon as possible.

> For those excited about the possibilities of Macromedia Flash, check out Flash MX Savvy by Ethan Watrall and Norbert Herber (Sybex, 2002)

Now that I've gotten you all worked up about the power and possibilities of Macromedia Flash, let's take a look at how to work with Flash files in Dreamweaver. This section will first discuss how you go about inserting a Flash file and will go on to explore how you set that file's properties.

Flash is not natively supported by web browsers. To view a Flash movie (either on or off the Web), you must have the Flash Player installed on your computer. It's a relatively small plug-in for both Mac and PC that's available on the book's accompanying CD-ROM, and is also downloadable from the Macromedia website (`www.macromedia.com/downloads`).

Inserting a Flash Movie

To insert a Flash file into your Dreamweaver document:

1. With the intended HTML file open in Dreamweaver, place your cursor where you wish the Flash movie to be inserted. (A movie is the term most commonly used to refer to something created in the Macromedia Flash authoring program.)

2. Open the Insert bar (Window → Insert), select the Media tab, and click the Insert Flash button ● . Alternatively, you can go to Insert → Media → Flash.

FLASH INSPIRATION

For some great examples of what Flash can do, check out these websites:

> `www.becominghuman.org`
>
> `www.djojostudios.com`
>
> `www.digitalorganism.com`
>
> `www.mnh.si.edu/africanvoices`
>
> `www.rustboy.com`
>
> `www.x15designs.com`
>
> `www.moccu.com`

3. When the Select File dialog box opens up, navigate to where the Flash movie you wish to insert is located, select it, and click Select.

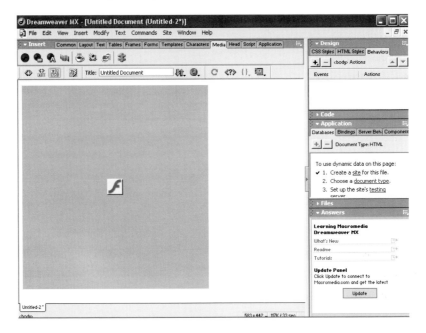

Flash comes in a couple of different file types. FLA is the native file type produced by the authoring program (just as Photoshop produces PSD files). SWF (sometimes pronounced swif) is the file type created when you want to mount your Flash movie on the Web. When inserting a Flash movie, make absolutely sure that you insert the SWF file, not the FLA file. If you don't, the Flash Player won't be able to display it.

You'll notice that when inserted, Flash movies are represented by a gray placeholder. Don't worry—you'll soon learn how to preview the actual Flash file from within the Dreamweaver document.

Manipulating Flash Movies with the Property Inspector

Now that you've learned how to insert a Flash movie into your Dreamweaver document, it's time to set that movie's specific properties with, you guessed it, the Property Inspector. For the most part, the properties you can manipulate are directly related to the way the movie itself is displayed and behaves from within the HTML document.

Changing the Flash Movie's Dimensions

When Flash movies are created, they have a set width and height. However, because they are vector based, they can be easily resized without any loss of image quality To resize an image from within Dreamweaver:

1. Select the Flash movie whose dimensions you wish to change.

2. Open the Property Inspector (Windows → Properties).

Width field

Height field

3. Enter a new value into the Width (W) field.

4. Enter a new value into the Height (H) field.

5. When you're finished changing the movie's dimensions, press Return (Mac)/ Enter (Win) or click anywhere off the Property Inspector for your changes to take effect.

Much like with of an image, you can also resize a Flash movie by using the resize handles:

1. Click the Flash movie you want to resize.

2. Click and hold one of the resize handles located on the movie's sides and corners.

3. Drag the resize handles until your Flash movie is the desired size and release your mouse button. If you hold Shift down while dragging the corner resize handle, your Flash movie will maintain the same proportions.

> If you have the Property Inspector open while you are using the resize handles, you'll notice that the values in the W and H boxes will change dynamically to reflect the increasing size of the image.

Aligning a Flash Movie within the Page

Much like with an image, one of the most basic things you can do with a Flash movie after it's been inserted is to align to the page:

1. Place your cursor anywhere along the line that contains the Flash movie (do not select the movie itself).

2. Open the Property Inspector (Windows → Properties).

3. Click one of the alignment buttons ≣ ≣ ≣ (in the top-right corner).

Aligning a Flash Movie to Text

Once again, just as with an image, you can align a Flash movie to a block of text within your document:

1. For the purposes of this exercise, insert a Flash movie somewhere in a block of text and select the Flash movie.

2. Open the Property Inspector (Windows → Properties).

3. Open the Align drop-down menu and choose one of the options.

For more information on the effect that each option has, see the "Aligning an Image with Text" section in Chapter 5.

Setting the Flash Movie's Background Color

One of the things you do when you author a Flash movie is set its background color. Under normal circumstances, this color remains constant whenever the Flash movie is played. However, after inserting a movie into a Dreamweaver document, you can override the original background color of the movie and replace it with a color of your choice:

1. Select the Flash movie whose background color you wish to change.

2. Open the Property Inspector (Windows → Properties).

3. Click the BG swatch to open the Background Palette and select the color to which you want to change the Flash movie's background.

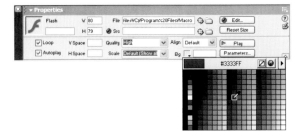

The movie's background color also appears when the movie isn't playing, for example, while it's loading or after it's stopped playing.

Changing the Flash Movie Quality

While Flash movies are relatively compact (compared to other multimedia), they can sometimes get a large in terms of file size. When any movie is created, you have the option of setting the quality at which it plays. Higher quality means that the movie will play slower over a slower connection. Lower quality means that it will play faster over a slow connection. The level of quality you set determines whether your movie sacrifices speed for quality, or vice versa. Ultimately, the choice you make is based on your audience.

For more info on bandwidth and connectivity issues in web design, see the "Designing with Bandwidth in Mind" section of Chapter 1.

One of the great things about Dreamweaver is that you can set the quality of any given Flash movie that you've inserted into your document:

1. Select the Flash movie whose quality you want to set.

2. Open the Property Inspector (Windows → Properties).

3. Open the Quality drop-down menu and choose one of the following options:

   - Low sacrifices speed to visual quality by turning off any anti-aliasing.

   - Auto Low starts the movie playing without anti-aliasing but bumps the quality up to High if the user's computer can cope with the improved quality while still maintaining quick playback.

So, what exactly is anti-aliasing? It's the process by which the edges of text are smoothed out. The kicker is that anti-aliased text, because it is more visually complex, generally results in larger file sizes.

   - Auto High begins playback at High quality but shifts into Low mode if the user's computer can't cope with the increased visual quality and playback speed.

- High forces your movie to be anti-aliased. If the movie contains bitmaps that aren't animated, they will be smoothed. On the other hand, if the bitmaps are animated in any way, they won't be smoothed.

When the Flash movie plays in a browser, the user can dynamically change its quality through the context menu (right-click [Win]/ Option-click [Mac].)

Altering the Flash Movie's Scale

When you learned how to set the width and height of a Flash movie, you weren't really learning how to change the movie's dimension. Instead, you were setting the width and height of the area in which the movie displayed. The manner the movie itself is displayed within that area is set by the scale property. To set the movie's scale:

1. Select the movie whose scale you wish to set.

2. Open the Property Inspector (Windows → Properties).

3. Open the Scale drop-down menu and choose one of the following options:
    - Default (Show All) displays the entire movie (with its correct aspect ratio) in the area defined by the movie's W and H values.

    - No Border expands (without distortion) to fill the entire area defined by the Dimensions setting. As with the Show All option, the movie will maintain its aspect ratio. The difference, however, is that to maintain the movie's aspect ratio with No Border, your movie may expand to be larger than the area defined by the Dimensions settings. As a result, the edges of your movie might appear as if they've been cut off.

    - Exact Fit displays the entire movie in the specified area without reserving the original aspect ratio. Your movie might be slightly skewed.

Looping and Autoplaying the Flash Movie

For the most part, the way a Flash movie plays is determined when the movie itself is initially authored. With Dreamweaver, however, you have a small amount of control over how an inserted Flash movie plays.

To manipulate the manner an inserted Flash movie plays:

1. Select the Flash movie you wish to manipulate

2. Open the Property Inspector (Windows → Properties).

Loop check box —
Autoplay check box —

3. Select one of the following Play options:

   - Loop causes your movie to loop indefinitely

   - Autoplay causes the movie to automatically begin playing when the user loads the HTML file in which it is embedded.

Previewing the Flash Movie From Within Dreamweaver

As mentioned earlier (and as I'm sure you've noticed on your own), when a Flash movie is inserted into a Dreamweaver document, you don't see the movie itself, you see a gray place-holder. This is primarily memory related. If the Flash movie automatically played when it was inserted, it would consume a lot of precious system memory resources. But what happens when you want to see how the changes you've made will affect the way the movie behaves? Well, you could easily preview the entire document in a browser. However, this can get a lit-tle cumbersome if you constantly need to check a rather minute change. Don't worry, Macro-media has provided a way in which to "turn on" the Flash movie so it can be previewed directly from within Dreamweaver:

> To preview the Flash file, *you* must have the Flash Player installed on your computer.

1. Select the Flash movie that you want to preview.

2. Open the Property Inspector (Windows → Properties).

3. Click the Play button [▶ Play] .

4. To stop the movie from playing (which is vital if you want to set any of the movie's prop-erties), click the Stop button [■ Stop] .

Working with Shockwave Files

Shockwave, which is often erroneously confused with Flash, is another web-based multimedia file format developed by Macromedia. The reason for the confusion is understandable: both have their origins at Macromedia, both are used to create stunning interactive experiences, and both are web based. The similarities, however, are less apparent if you drill a little deeper. First, Flash files are created by Macromedia Flash, while Shockwave files are created by Director, Macromedia's flagship portable media (CD-ROM, DVD-ROM, and so on) authoring program. With an astoundingly complex programming language called Lingo, the ability to deal much more efficiently with bitmaps, and the ability to cope far better with audio and video, Director is considerably more full featured than Flash. However, because Director is more of an extensive authoring program than Flash, it is far more difficult to learn. If one were to make a silly analogy, Flash is a spider monkey, graceful and lithe, while Director is a 700-pound gorilla.

For our purposes, the origins and capabilities of Director are neither here nor there. What is really important is that Shockwave files, which are essentially Director movies exported to a format geared toward distribution over the Web (as opposed to on a CD or DVD), are generally more complex multimedia applications than Flash files. Like Flash, for the user to view Shockwave files, they must have a special plug-in (called the Shockwave Player, not to be confused with the Flash Player) on their computer.

Thankfully, the way Dreamweaver copes with Shockwave files is almost identical to the way it copes with Flash files. In fact, both Shockwave and Flash files share almost all of the same properties.

In the following section, you'll learn how to insert Shockwave files into your Dreamweaver document. Unlike with Flash, we won't go through each of Shockwave file's properties. Don't worry—you aren't being shortchanged; it's just a matter of economy. Because Flash and Shockwave share almost all the same properties, you can simply refer back to the previous sections for information on how to manipulate a Shockwave file.

Inserting Shockwave Movies

The process of inserting a Shockwave file into your Dreamweaver document is quite simple:

1. With the intended HTML file open in Dreamweaver, place your cursor where you wish the Shockwave movie to be inserted.

> As was the case with Flash, a movie is the term most commonly used to refer to something created in the Macromedia Director authoring program (whether its exported to Shockwave format or some other format).

2. Open the Insert bar (Window → Insert), select the Media tab, and click the Insert Shockwave button ▯. Alternatively, you can go to Insert → Media → Shockwave.

3. When the Select File dialog box opens up, navigate to the Shockwave movie you wish to insert, select it, and click Select.

Shockwave files have a DCR extension.

You'll notice that, like Flash files, Shockwave files are represented in the document window by a gray placeholder. The process of previewing a Shockwave file within the Document Window is exactly the same as with a Flash file.

Integrating Java Applets

Back in 1990, Sun Microsystems, a company best known for its Unix workstations and Solaris operating system, started a project called Green, whose primary thrust was to create software for consumer electronics—you know, toasters, ovens, microwaves, and the like. One of the results of the project was a programming language called Oak. It soon became obvious to the project participants that while Oak wasn't particularly appropriate for its intended reason (mainly because it was *way* ahead of its time), it would make a great language for Internet programming.

In 1995, Oak was renamed Java and debuted at Sun Microsystems's annual tradeshow, SunWorld. Since then, it has risen tremendously in popularity and is used for the development of all sorts of self-contained lightweight Internet applications, called *applets*. Java applets can be created to do all manner of groovy things, from online multimedia presentations to web-based public-access order-entry systems.

When it comes to using Java applets, there are two general caveats that should be observed. First, most (but not all) browsers natively support Java applets without the aid of a plug-in. Unfortunately, while the most recent version of Java (v2) is quite powerful and has a bucketload of interesting features, it has the least amount of browser support. Second, and perhaps most importantly, primarily for the sake of security, all browsers have the ability to disable Java. Finally, there has been an overall trend to move towards executing programs on the web server and returning only HTML to the user's browser.

Because applets are self contained mini-applications (programs) that are launched from an HTML document into which they are embedded, they are added to a Dreamweaver document much in the same way you'd add a Flash or Shockwave file. In the following sections, you'll look at how to insert a Java applet into an HTML document. Then, you'll proceed to learn how to manipulate the properties of the inserted applet with the Property Inspector.

Java is a fully featured programming language, and a thorough explanation of it would be well beyond the scope of this book. If you are interested in learning more, however, you can get a thorough treatment in Mastering Java 2, JDK 1.4 by John Zukowski (Sybex, 2002). Alternatively, you can go straight to the source at Sun Microsystems's Java applet page at http://java.sun.com/applets.

Inserting a Java Applet

To insert a Java applet:

1. With the intended HTML file open in Dreamweaver, place your cursor where you wish the Java applet movie to be inserted.

2. Open the Insert bar (Window → Insert), select the Media tab, and click the Insert Applet button . Alternatively, you can go to Insert → Media → Applet.

3. When the Select File dialog box opens up, navigate to where the applet you wish to insert is located, select it, and click Select.

The path to your Java applet cannot be expressed absolutely; it must be relative.

You'll notice that, like Flash and Shockwave files, applets are represented in the document window by a gray placeholder. Unfortunately, unlike Flash and Shockwave files, there is no way to preview the applet short of previewing the entire HTML document in a browser.

Manipulating Java Applets with the Property Inspector

Now that you know how to insert Java applets, it's time to roll up your sleeves and set its properties. In the following section, you'll learn how to resize an applet, set an alternate image for an applet, and align an applet to both text and the page itself.

Resizing a Java Applet

When visual Java applets are created, they have a set width and height. However, you can very easily resize them after they've been inserted into your Dreamweaver document:

1. Select the Java applet whose dimensions you wish to change.

2. Open the Property Inspector (Window → Properties).

3. Enter a value (in pixels) into the Width (W) field.

4. Enter a value (in pixels) into the Height (H) field.

5. When you finish changing the applet's dimensions, press Return (Mac)/ Enter (Win) or click anywhere off the Property Inspector for your changes to take effect.

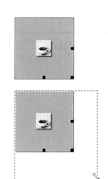

Much as with an Image, you can also resize an applet by using the resize handles:

1. Click the applet you want to resize.

2. Click and hold one of the resize handles located on the movie's sides and corners.

3. Drag the resize handles until your applet movie is the desired size and release your mouse button.

> If you hold Shift down while dragging the corner resize handle, the applet will maintain the same proportions.

Aligning a Java Applet to the Page

One of the most basic things you can do with a Java applet after its inserted is to align to the page:

1. Place your cursor anywhere along the line that contains the applet (do not select the applet itself).

2. Open the Property Inspector (Window → Properties).

3. Click one of the alignment buttons 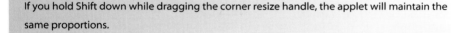 (in the top-right corner).

Aligning a Java Applet to Text

To align an applet to a block of text within your document:

1. For the purposes of this exercise, insert an applet somewhere in a block of text and select it.

2. Open the Property Inspector (Window → Properties).

3. Open the Align drop-down menu and choose one of the options.

Setting a Java Applet's Alt Image or Text

As was mentioned earlier, there are some cases when a browser won't display your Java applet: either the browser doesn't natively support it or, due to security reasons, the user has Java disabled. In cases such as these, you'll want to add some alternate content, such as a static image or text, which will be displayed instead:

1. Select the Java applet to which you want to add some alternate content.

2. Open the Property Inspector (Window → Properties).

3. From here, you can continue two different ways:

   - If you want the alternate content to be textual, type the text into the Alt field. Any text will be represented in the same manner an Alt tag for an image is displayed.

   - If you want instead to display an image, click the Browse to File button. When the Select File dialog box appears, navigate to where the image is saved and click Select.

4. To apply the change you made, press Return (Mac)/ Enter (Win) or click anywhere off the Property Inspector.

Working with Netscape Plug-in Media

So far in this chapter, we've talked about a heck of a lot of different media types (and we'll talk about more). We've talked about Java applets, Flash movies, and Shockwave files. When it comes to media on the Web, these are only the first molecules on the tip of the iceberg. Other media types include digital video, audio, screen-based VR, immersive imaging, and animation. If Dreamweaver were to include a way to insert each individual media type, the Insert bar's Media tab would probably have to be as large as Finland to accommodate them all. The conundrum is that many of the media types that aren't directly covered by Dreamweaver (such as QuickTime) are as popular (or perhaps more popular) than those that are covered. So, what's a visual web designer to do? Well, in an effort to resolve the problem, Dreamweaver lets you insert any kind of media that requires a plug-in (tiny little programs that extend the browser's features) to be displayed in Netscape with the help of one simple process.

For the most part, Internet Explorer doesn't use plug-ins to add extra features, but instead uses something called ActiveX Controls. These will be discussed a little later in the chapter.

It's important to note that, despite what Dreamweaver's menus and dialog boxes say, you are not actually inserting the plug-in itself, you're inserting a file that requires a plug-in. When the plug-in media is inserted, a reference to the file is included in its <embed> tag. When the HTML page is loaded by the browser, the reference indicates the type of file and which plug-in must be used to display it.

In the following sections, you'll explore first how to insert Netscape plug-in media. From there, you'll learn how to set the plug-in media's properties.

Inserting Netscape Plug-in Media

The process to insert Netscape plug-in media in your document is as remarkably easy:

1. With the intended HTML file open in Dreamweaver, place your cursor where you wish to insert the Netscape plug-in media.

2. Open the Insert bar (Window → Insert), select the Media tab, and click the Insert Plug-in button . Alternatively, you can go to Insert → Media → Plug-in.

3. When the Select File dialog box opens up, navigate to where the Netscape plug-in media file is located, select it, and click Select.

You'll notice that, like Flash and Shockwave files, the Netscape plug-in media file is represented in the document window by a gray placeholder.

Setting Netscape Plug-in Media Properties

Now that you've inserted the Netscape plug-in media (not that it was particularly hard), you can learn how to set the media's properties. It's important to remember that because the inserted media can be any number of things, the Property Inspector only lets you set the most general of properties. In the following section, you'll learn how to resize the media, align it to both the page and text, add a plug-in URL, add a border, and preview it from within Dreamweaver.

Resizing Netscape Plug-in Media

Just like all the other media types we've discussed, the various file types that fall under the Netscape plug-in media category (which is just about every other media type in the universe not incorporated into Dreamweaver) are initially authored with a set width and height. However, you can very easily resize them after they've been inserted into your Dreamweaver document:

1. Select the Netscape plug-in media whose dimensions you wish to change.

2. Open the Property Inspector (Window → Properties).

3. Enter a value (in pixels) into the Width (W) field.

4. Enter a value (in pixels) into the Height (H) field.

5. When you're finished changing the media's dimensions, press Return (Mac)/ Enter (Win) or click anywhere off the Property Inspector for your changes to take effect.

You can also resize the Netscape plug-in media by using the resize handles:

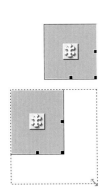

1. Click the media you want to resize.

2. Click and hold one of the resize handles located on the media's sides and corners.

3. Drag the resize handles until your Netscape plug-in media is the desired size and release your mouse button.

> If you hold Shift down while dragging the corner resize handle, the media will maintain the same proportions.

Aligning Netscape Plug-in Media to the Page

One of the most basic things you can do with Netscape plug-in media after it's inserted is to align it to the page:

1. Place your cursor anywhere along the line that contains the media (do not select the applet itself).

2. Open the Property Inspector (Window → Properties).

3. Click one of the alignment buttons ≣ ≣ ≣ (in the top-right corner).

Aligning Netscape Plug-in Media to Text

You can align Netscape plug-in media to a block of text within your document:

1. For the purposes of this exercise, insert some Netscape plug-in media somewhere in a block of text and select the media.

2. Open the Property Inspector (Window → Properties).

3. Go to the Align drop-down menu and choose one of the options.

Adding a Plug-in URL

Because Netscape plug-in media requires an actual plug-in to be displayed, it's a good idea to provide a link to the location where the user can download it. To add the necessary link:

1. Select the Netscape plug-in media to which you wish to add the plug-in link.

2. Open the Property Inspector (Window → Properties).

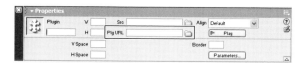

3. Enter a URL (such as `www.quicktime.com`) into the Plg URL field.

4. Press Return (Mac)/ Enter (Win) or click anywhere off the Property Inspector for your changes to take effect.

Adding a Border

You might find yourself in a situation where you'd like to set the Netscape Media plug-in further apart from the rest of your page's content. This can be accomplished by giving the media a border.

To add a border:

1. Select the media to which you wish to add a border.

2. Open the Property Inspector (Window → Properties).

3. Enter a value (in pixels) into the Border field; the value you enter represents the thickness of the border.

4. Press Return (Mac)/ Enter (Win) or click anywhere off the Property Inspector for your changes to take effect.

Previewing Netscape Plug-in Media from within the Document Window

Thankfully, Dreamweaver lets you preview the media directly from within the Document Window. This means you don't have to preview the document in a browser everytime you want to see how the media looks/plays.

Just as with both Flash and Shockwave, Dreamweaver can't play the media unless you have the plug-in installed on your computer.

To preview a media file, just follow these steps:

1. Select the Netscape plug-in media that you want to preview.
2. Open the Property Inspector (Window → Properties).
3. Click the Play button ▷ Play .
4. When you want to stop the media file from playing, click the Stop button ■ Stop .

Working with ActiveX Controls

ActiveX Controls are to Internet Explorer what plug-ins are to Netscape. They function by allowing Internet Explorer to play multimedia content that isn't natively supported.

Unfortunately, due to the specific software architecture of ActiveX Controls, they can only be used with Internet Explorer 3.0 or above. In addition, Mac users are out of luck, as ActiveX Controls only work on Windows—bummer.

As with Netscape plug-in media, Dreamweaver provides you with a relatively easy way to include ActiveX Controls into your document. However, unlike Netscape plug-in media (where you insert the media, not the actual plug-in, directly into the document), you do insert the ActiveX Control directly into your Dreamweaver document. From there, with the Property Inspector, you configure the ActiveX Control to load the specific type of media and file you wish to display.

In the following sections you will learn how to add an ActiveX Control to your Dreamweaver document. From there, you'll explore how to set the properties of the ActiveX Control.

If you are interested in leaning more about ActiveX Controls, go to www.activex.com or www.active-x.com.

Inserting an ActiveX Control

The process by which you insert an ActiveX Control into your Dreamweaver Document is quite easy:

1. With the intended HTML file open in Dreamweaver, place your cursor where you wish to insert the ActiveX Control.

2. Open the Insert bar (Window → Insert), select the Media tab, and click the Insert ActiveX button ![icon]. Alternatively, you can go to Insert → Media → ActiveX.

You'll notice that instead of opening up a Select File dialog box, a small placeholder ![icon] is inserted. This is as it should be. Later, you'll learn how to tell Dreamweaver which file will be accessed and played by the ActiveX Control.

Setting the ActiveX Properties with the Property Inspector

If you were to line up all the different media types that are discussed in this chapter and decide which is the most Property Inspector–intensive (that is, which requires the most work with the Property Inspector), it would definitely be ActiveX Controls. As you've already learned, the process of inserting the ActiveX Control results only in a placeholder being inserted into the document. You must use the Property Inspector to set the location of the file, the media type, and myriad other properties.

In this section, you'll learn how to set the Class ID, include the necessary CodeBase, set the actual file's path, combine the `<embed>` and `<object>` tags, and add an alternate image.

> As we've already explored how to align media (both to text and to the page itself), we'll skip that process for an ActiveX Control—the process is exactly the same as with the other media types.

Setting an ActiveX Control's Class ID

The Class ID is a unique code that identifies the specific ActiveX Control needed to play/display the media file. Without it, the ActiveX Control you inserted into your Dreamweaver document is totally useless and will not display the file properly. A Class ID is a complex string of numbers and letters; it is best to copy and paste it into the appropriate place in the Property Inspector so that you can avoid mistyping it.

When attempting to integrate the Class ID, you'll find yourself running into a rather large wall. Unfortunately, there isn't a central location where the most commonly used Class IDs are listed. They need to be painstakingly gleaned from the documentation when the ActiveX Control is acquired.

To set the ActiveX Control's Class ID, just follow these steps:

1. Select the placeholder of the ActiveX Control whose Class ID you need to set.

2. Open the Property Inspector (Window → Properties).

3. Enter the Class ID into the Class ID field, seen to the right of the Width field in the above graphic.

> If you've already entered a Class ID for another ActiveX Control it will appear in the Class ID drop-down menu.

4. To apply your changes, press Return (Mac)/ Enter (Win) or click anywhere off the Property Inspector.

Setting an ActiveX Control's CodeBase

The CodeBase is a URL that provides a location where the ActiveX Control can be downloaded if it isn't installed on the user's computer.

> If the user doesn't have the necessary ActiveX control to display a certain type of media, the browser will automatically go to the CodeBase URL.

For example, the CodeBase for the QuickTime ActiveX Control is `www.apple.com/quicktime/download/qtcheck/`.

Like the Class ID, there is no real central location where you can find the various CodeBase URLS for all the most commonly used ActiveX Controls. You'll either have to glean the information from the ActiveX Control's documentation or visit the manufacturer's website.

To set an ActiveX Control's CodeBase:

1. Select the placeholder of the ActiveX Control whose CodeBase you need to set.

2. Open the Property Inspector (Window → Properties).

Codebase field

3. Enter the necessary URL into the Base field.

4. To apply your changes, press Return (Mac)/ Enter (Win) or click anywhere off the Property Inspector.

Setting a File's Path

As you probably remember, when you insert an ActiveX Control into your Dreamweaver Document, you aren't actually inserting the media file itself. One of the steps you need to go through after you insert the ActiveX Control is to point it in the direction of the media file it needs to play (an MPEG file, for example). Unfortunately, the process itself, which is absolutely necessary if you want the ActiveX Control to work properly, is a little counterintuitive and not particularly user friendly.

To set the path of file you want the ActiveX Control to play/display:

1. Select the placeholder of the ActiveX Control with which you are currently working.

2. Open the Property Inspector (Window → Properties).

3. Click the Parameters button $\boxed{\text{Parameters...}}$ to open the Parameters dialog box.

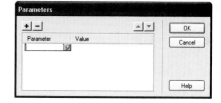

4. Type **Filename** into the first position of the Parameters columns, which is automatically an editable field.

5. Press Tab to move to the first position in the Value column, which automatically becomes an editable field. Alternatively, instead of pressing Tab, you can click the first position in the Value column.

6. Type the path (either relative or absolute).

> If the path you enter into the Value column is absolute, make sure to include the http:// portion of the address, or it might not work.

7. When you finish, click OK.

Combining the *<embed>* and *<object>* Tags

When you insert the ActiveX Control, the `<object>` tag is used, as opposed to the `<embed>` tag, which is used by Netscape to integrate plug-in media. This causes a bit of a problem, as Netscape doesn't recognize the `<object>` tag 100 percent of the time, nor does Explorer recognize the `<embed>` tag 100 percent of the time. Fortunately, Dreamweaver lets you combine both tags (as if you were sticking the Netscape plug-in media and the ActiveX Control in the same space) so that both browsers are covered:

1. Select the ActiveX Control that you wish to work with.

2. Open the Property Inspector (Window → Properties).

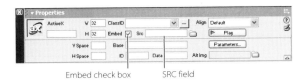

Embed check box   SRC field

3. Select the Embed option. This includes the `<embed>` tag, which is needed if you want to add Netscape accessibility. When you do this, the SRC field goes live.

4. Because the `<embed>` tag requires that you directly reference the file you are including, a path must be entered into the SRC field. To do this, just click the Browse to File button (to the right of the SRC field). When the Select File dialog box appears, navigate to where the file is located, select it, and click Select.

Adding an Alternate Image

Usually, if you opt not to combine both the `<embed>` and `<object>` tags so that both Explorer and Netscape will be covered, you run the risk of your ActiveX Control–enhanced HTML document being loaded by a browser that cannot cope with ActiveX. Fortunately, Dreamweaver provides a way to avoid this kind of painful situation. As with Java applets, you can add an alternate image that will display in the event that your audience is using a non-ActiveX Control–enabled browser:

1. Select the ActiveX Control to which you wish to add an alternate image.

2. Open the Property Inspector (Window → Properties).

3. Click the Browse to File button.

4. When the Select File dialog box opens, navigate to where the image is located, select it, and then click Select.

Adding Audio to Your Site

Digital audio is often overlooked as a potential type of multimedia you can include in your document. This is unfortunate, as audio is an amazingly powerful medium with which you can very effectively affect the emotions of your audience.

Don't be fooled, however: digital audio (as it's used on the Web) is far more than a constantly looping drum/bass track that plays (rather incessantly, I might add) in the background of a Flash movie. There is a lot that goes into digital audio, and I'm not talking just about composition. There are many different digital audio formats with different properties, each of which are suited to different situations.

Digital audio has a rather complex system that affects quality and file size. I won't go into the inner technical aspects of digital audio here, but you do need to know this: the wisest (and simplest) way to approach the file size and quality issue is that better quality means larger file sizes (sometimes significantly larger). Conversely, less quality usually means smaller file sizes.

Something else you need to know is that despite the fact that digital audio files are not visible elements (like a Flash movie or a QuickTime file), they consume a heck of a lot of bandwidth. Good, CD quality audio consumes an enormous amount of bandwidth, so you always have to keep the bandwidth consumption/accessibility equation in mind that was discussed way back in Chapter 1.

So, what about digital audio on the Web? Well, without getting too involved with the ins and outs of the topic (this is a book about Dreamweaver, remember), let's take a brief look at the formats you might want to consider incorporating into your creation. Remember, the following list is hardly exhaustive (I haven't included Quicktime Audio and RealAudio to name a few); it's designed to give you only a brief introduction.

For more information about digital audio, see the Indiana University Electronic Music Studio website at www.indiana.edu/~emusic.

AU Associated with the UNIX platform, AU files were one of the first web-based audio formats. AU files are fairly well compressed and are therefore generally smaller in terms of file size than many other audio file formats. The great thing is that, because they've been around for so long, AU files can be played by the vast majority of browsers without the aid of a plug-in.

AIFF Standing for Audio Interchange File Format, AIFF was originally developed by Apple and is thus seen most often associated with the Apple QuickTime environment.

WAV WAV files are one of the rock-solid standards of digital audio on the Web. Featuring a good level of compression and sound quality, WAV files, which were actually originally developed for use on Windows machines, are playable by most browsers without the use of a plug-in.

MP3 Definitely one of the highest profile digital audio formats around (let's call it the "rock star who drives their motorcycle out of the seventh floor of a hotel into the pool" of the audio world), MP3, which is less commonly known as Motion Picture Experts Group Audio or MPEG-Audio Layer-3, offers an amazingly high level of quality (CD-level quality, in fact) in a very small package (relatively speaking.) This makes it highly desirable as an audio format. The unfortunate thing is that MP3 isn't natively played by any browser. Don't let this get you down, however, as lots and lots of media players and plug-ins (such as QuickTime, Windows Media Player, or RealPlayer) play MP3 files. Another drawback about MP3 files is that a user must wait until the entire file has been downloaded before they can play it (that is, it doesn't stream).

MIDI MIDI (Musical Instrument Digital Interface) is as much a standard as it is an audio file format, by virtue of the fact that it facilitates communications between electronic instruments, processors, and computers from different manufacturers. The format itself is pretty much only appropriate for electronic instrumental music, so use it very wisely.

Now that you've briefly explored some of the different types of files that you can use to add audio to your HTML creation, it's time to come back down to earth, take a breath, and get back to how Dreamweaver deals with digital audio. There are two primary ways to incorporate digital audio into your document with Dreamweaver. The first involves directly linking to an audio file; the second involves embedding the audio file directly into you document. Both methods will be discussed in the upcoming sections.

Linking to an Audio File

One of the simplest ways to include audio in your web page is to create a link to the desired file. Essentially, a standard hyperlink points to the file. When the user clicks the link, the audio file is loaded up in the appropriate player (either the browser itself or the necessary third part plug-in). Yup, it's as easy as that:

1. Select either the text or image you wish to link to the audio file.

2. Open the Property Inspector (Window → Properties).

> If you need a refresher on hyperlinks, see Chapter 6, "Linking Documents with Hyperlinks."

3. Click the Browse to File button .

4. When the Select File dialog box opens, locate the audio file, select it, and click Select.

Embedding an Audio File

The second option to include audio is to embed it directly in the document itself. When you embed the audio file, the appropriate player (or plug-in) will be stuck in a fixed location in the page (as opposed to floating freely above the page as it does when you link to a file using the previously described process.)

To embed an audio file:

1. Place the cursor where you wish to embed the audio file

2. Open the Insert bar (Window → Insert), select the Media tab, and click the Insert Plug-in button 🧩 . Alternatively, you can go to Insert → Media → Plug-in.

3. When the Select File dialog box opens, navigate to where the audio file is located, select it, and then click Select.

> If you are swift (which I'm sure you are), you've noticed that the process of embedding an
> audio file is exactly the same as inserting some Netscape plug-in media. Just to make things
> even easier, the process of setting an embedded audio file's properties are exactly the same
> as setting the properties of some Netscape plug-in media—refer back to the earlier section of
> the chapter for a refresher.

Inspiration: Design and Technique

Located in Berlin, Moccu (`www.moccu.com`), which was founded in 2000, is a full-featured digital design studio that specializes in Flash-based web design, interfaces, animation, applications, entertainment, and interactive storytelling. Their projects have included interface and animation design for a proposed touch-screen gas pump, an online recruiting game for Challenge Unlimited, and an online banking portal.

Moccu's website (see Figure 11.1) is bursting with multimedia goodness. Beyond the stylish graphic design, Moccu's most interesting feature is its 3D environmental interface. While the vast majority of advanced Flash interface design conforms to a 2D computer-like GUI model, Moccu has created an innovative interface that emulates an integrated 3D space.

Figure 11.1

Moccu

Summary

In this chapter, you explored how to use Dreamweaver to add that extra oomph to your HTML creation by using multimedia files. You started off with Flash, how to insert Flash movies into your document, and how to set the properties of Flash files. From there, you learned how to work with Shockwave movies, Generator objects, Java applets, Netscape plug-in media, ActiveX Controls, and digital audio—your basic, all-around whirlwind tour of sound and motion on the Web. As I mentioned numerous times throughout the chapter, there is a lot more to many of the multimedia file formats than was discussed here. If any of them especially pique your interest, you should sally forth and indulge your curiosity.

CHAPTER 12

Managing and Publishing your Site with Dreamweaver

Creating a website, whether large or small, can be a complicated process. You not only have to consider website design issues, but you also need to consider logistical and mechanical issues such as asset management, site organization, and server management. On top of this, if you are working as one member of a team, such things as access and project management become an issue as well. For those who are relatively new to web design, the realization that creating a website is far more than just placing text and images can be a little daunting. Don't worry; Dreamweaver can handle it, and so can you.

As has been mentioned a couple of times previously, Dreamweaver is as much as website design tool as it is a web page design tool. And as such, it contains a whole host of tools intended to help you manage and manipulate not only a site on which you are the sole creative force, but also a site on which you are simply one member of an entire web design team.

In this chapter, you'll get a chance to explore the following topics:

- **Using the Site panel to manipulate a local site**
- **Using the Site panel to manipulate a remote site**

Using the Site Window to Manipulate a Local Site

Back in Chapter 2, "Starting Up Dreamweaver," you learned how to set up a rudimentary local site (something that is absolutely vital if you want to take advantage of Dreamweaver's true power and potential). You also learned the absolute rudiments of the Site panel, focusing primarily on how you can create and manipulate a site map.

> Because the process of creating a local site has already been covered, it will not be covered in this chapter. If you are having trouble remembering how to set up a local site, it's important to refresh your memory before continuing: see the "Setting Up a Local Site" section in Chapter 2.

In this section, you will explore how to use the Site panel to manage and manipulate a local site. Included will be a discussion on how to open files, create new files, move files, check the integrity of your local site's links, repair broken links, search your local site, create Design Notes, and switch to another local site, all from within the Site panel.

Opening Files from Within the Site Window

While you can manually open files using the File → Open command, you can also open HTML documents in your local site directly from within the Site panel. This is particularly handy if you are doing other things from within the Site panel and need to quickly open up a document.

> While the Site panel offers you easy access to the files in your local site, you can use its built-in file explorer to access any of the files on your hard drive without having to leave the Dreamweaver MX workspace. However, remember that if you don't save the file to the local site, it won't be included when you upload to your remote server

Site drop-down menu

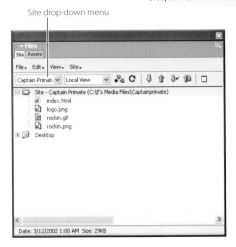

Date: 3/12/2002 1:00 AM Size: 29KB

To open a document from within the Site panel:

1. If you aren't already working in a defined local site, open the Site panel (Window → Site), and select a site from the Site drop-down menu. Alternatively, if you are already working within a defined local site, but the Site panel isn't open, go to Site → Site Files.

2. When the local site appears in the Site panel, navigate to the location where the file is located and select it.

> To drill down into a local site, simply click on the expand (+) icon just to the left of a folder to open it.

3. Choose one of the following options to open the selected document:

- Go to File → Open.

- Double-click the file's icon (to the left of the actual filename)

- With your cursor over the file, open the context menu (right/Option-click) and choose Open.

Creating New Documents

While you can create new HTML documents in Dreamweaver by using the File → New command, you might find it helpful to know that you can also create them easily directly from within the Site Window itself. This is quite helpful if you want to create *placeholder* documents, that is, HTML files which are located within your local site, but to which no content has yet been added.

To create a new document from within the Site Window:

1. From within a defined local site, select the folder (or subfolder) where you want the newly created file to be created.

2. Open the context menu (right/Option-click) and choose New File or go to File → New File.

3. From here, a new HTML file (called `untitled.html` by default) will appear in the selected folder; notice that the name of the newly created file is an editable field.

> The extension (either HTML or HTM) with which the new file is created is determined by the Add Extension When Saving option, which is located in the General category of the Preferences dialog box (Edit → Preferences).

4. Without clicking anywhere, type the desired name for the newly created file. If you don't enter a file extension (.htm or .html) when you are typing a newly created file's name, Dreamweaver will not be able to open it.

5. When you finish typing the name, click anywhere off the newly created file or press Enter (Win)/Return (Mac).

> You cannot create a new file that doesn't have a name. If you attempt to do so, Dreamweaver will give you an error message.

Creating New Folder

For the sake of organization and orderliness, your local site should be separated into a series of folders and subfolders. When you initially define a local site (in an area where there aren't any existing files), you'll only have one folder in your local site, your local root folder. However, as you progress in your creative endeavors, you'll want to create additional subfolders. This can easily be done from directly within the Site panel.

The way you create and organize folders and subfolders within your local site is often at least partially determined by your site's information architecture. For a review of information architecture, see Chapter 1, "Web Design: The Big Picture."

1. In a defined local site, select the folder (or subfolder) where you want the newly created folder to be located.

If you are starting with a new local site in which no files are located, you'll need to select the Local Root folder (the topmost folder in the right side of your Site Window).

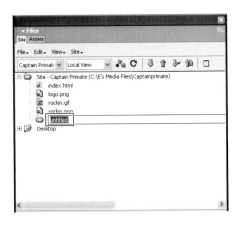

2. Open the context menu (right/Option-click) and choose New Folder, or go to File → New Folder.

3. A new folder (called `untitled` by default) will appear in the selected folder; notice that the name of the newly created folder is an editable field.

4. Without clicking anywhere, type the desired name for the newly created folder. Because folders aren't HTML documents, they don't need an extension, just a name.

5. When you finish typing the name, click anywhere off the newly created file or press Enter (Win)/Return (Mac). (You cannot create a new folder that doesn't have a name. If you attempt to do so, Dreamweaver will give you an error message.)

■ ■ ■ ■

DESIGN REMINDER: Keeping Things Neat and Tidy

As you've figured out by now, websites can get extremely complicated. In a site that is even marginally complex, you can have hundreds and hundreds of HTML files and images. On top of this, you can have innumerable multimedia files. As a result, it's a good idea to organize each section of your website into discrete folders. Another good tactic is to have a single folder in which all your site's images reside. This way, all of your HTML files can reference that one folder, and you'll always know where to find one of your site's images.

Moving Files

One of the coolest features of the Site Window is that you can move a file to any location within the local site. This doesn't sound like much on the surface, but when you drill down a little deeper, it's quite significant. As you already know, a website is a series of files that are connected together using links. For instance, when you create a hyperlink from one document to another, a path (whether it's absolute or relative) references the document to which you are linking and provides the browser with the exact location of it. Without the correct path, the browser won't be able to locate the document to which you are linking and will spit out the dreaded 404 Error message.

Likewise, when you insert an image (or any other media file) into a Dreamweaver document, you create a reference to the file itself (you don't actually embed the file into the document). In order for the browser to properly display the media file (image, Flash movie, and so on) the path has to remain unchanged. If either file is moved (either the referencing HTML document or the media file itself), the path will change, and the media file won't display.

This is where the power of the Site Window shines. If you move any file, folder, or subfolder, Dreamweaver automatically scans your entire local site, locates any file that references the moved document(s), and makes the necessary changes to all associated paths. This is a phenomenally powerful feature: it saves you the embarrassment of possibly having a broken link whenever you reorganize your site, and it saves you from having to tediously update link upon link upon link (especially if your site is particularly large).

> Dreamweaver will only update paths from within the Site Window. If, for instance, you move some stuff around using your operating system's file management feature (Windows Explorer, for example) the paths of the files within your local site will *not* be updated.

To move files around in your local site:

1. In a defined local site, select the file that you want to move.

2. Click and drag it to the location where you want it to be moved and release your mouse button. Notice that your cursor changes, and the location over which the cursor is located is highlighted with a blue box.

   To move a file to a specific location, you can either click, drag, and release it over the actual folder (or subfolder) in which you want it moved or release it over one of the other files within the target folder/subfolder (the result will be the same, whichever method you use).

If you are moving the file to a location deep within the structure of your site, make sure you've already expanded all of the appropriate folders and subfolders so that the file can be placed exactly where it needs to go.

3. After you move the file, the Update Files dialog box will open. Within it, you'll see a list of all the documents that include a link to the file you've just moved.

4. To update all the associated files, click the Update button. A progress bar along the bottom will indicate the updating progress. When the process is finished, the Update Files dialog box will automatically close, returning you to the Site Window.

Using these steps, you can also move entire folders complete with all their contents.

Checking Links Sitewide

During the process of creating a site of any significant size, you can end up with a certain amount of broken links. Maybe you accidentally mistyped the path of a Flash movie you inserted into a document, or you moved some of your local site's files without using the Site Window's handy dandy tools. You can also accumulate a number of orphaned files (files that still exist in the local site but are no longer linked to any file). Both broken links and orphaned files can be a serious problem—broken links because they are unprofessional and serve as a major turn-off for your audience, and orphaned files because they consume disk space. However, if you were to manually sift through an entire sire looking for broken links and orphaned files, you'd potentially spend a lot of time in front of your computer. Fear not, fellow traveler in the land of web design, Dreamweaver MX provides you the ability to check for broken links and orphaned files:

1. From within a local site, open the Site panel (Window → Site).

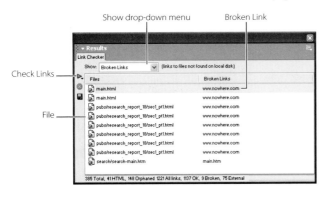

2. In the Site panel, go to Site → Check Links Sitewide.

3. The Link Checker panel will open, and your entire local site will be scanned for broken links, orphaned files, and external links.

4. When your local site has been scanned, the total number of files, number of broken links, number of orphaned files, and number of external links will be displayed in the Link Checker panel.

The Link Checker panel reports on the number of external links in your site. It doesn't, however, have the ability to determine whether the external file to which you are linking is still in the same location as when you originally created the link.

4. To view a list of the broken links, orphaned files, or external links, choose the appropriate option from the Show drop-down menu (in the top left-hand corner of the Link Checker panel).

If you want to re-run the search, click the Check Links button, which acts as a drop-down menu from which you can decide whether you want to check the links for the entire site, or just for the currently open document.

From here, you can fix the broken links that Dreamweaver found, a process that will be covered in the next section. Unfortunately, you can't do a bulk delete of all the orphaned files that were discovered by the Link Checker dialog box. You have to delete them individually in the Site Window—bummer!

Fixing Broken Links

Now that you've learned how to locate all the broken links within your local site, it would be wise to learn how to fix them. Remember, a broken link can refer to either a hyperlink to a document whose position (or name) has changed or an image whose position or name has changed. Let's pick up where we left off in the previous section:

1. Follow steps 1 through 5 as described the previous section.

2. Choose Broken Links from the Show drop-down menu. Notice in the Site Checker dialog box's Files column, there is a list of all the files in which broken links were found. In the Broken Links column, you'll see the specific broken link (path) within that document.

3. Select the broken link you want to fix. Notice that the path becomes an editable field and a Browse to File button appears just to the right of the link.

4. Click the Browse to File icon to open the Select File dialog box.

5. Relocate either the image or file referenced in the broken link, and click the Select button. The link will update in the Broken Links column.

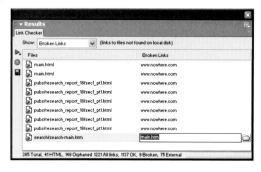

6. Press Enter (Win)/Return (Mac) or click anywhere off the editable Broken Link field. If there are other broken links to this file, Dreamweaver will ask you whether you want to fix all references. Click Yes, and you'll save yourself a lot of time. If you click No, only the single link will be fixed, and all the remaining broken links to that particular file will need to be fixed separately.

7. Once you've updated the link, Dreamweaver will remove it from the Link Checker dialog box.

8. Continue to repeat steps 3 through 7 until you've fixed all the broken links in your local site.

Working with Design Notes

Design Notes are easily one of the coolest site management features in Dreamweaver. In a situation where more than one person is working on a given site, there has to be some behind-the-scenes communication about any number of topics; Design Notes provide that.

> Even though they are geared toward working in a group, Design Notes are also useful for leaving yourself helpful reminders in a situation where you are the sole designer on a project.

Essentially, Design Notes are tiny little files that work like digital post-it notes, attaching themselves to any file in a local site. When the file is moved (or uploaded to a remote site), the Design Note moves with it, remaining permanently attached until it is deleted.

> Design Notes are saved with a MNO extension in a subfolder (called _notes) that is automatically created in the root folder of your site.

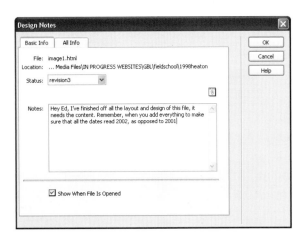

For example, say you're working on a file in which the primary content has yet to be added by your content manager (let's call him Ed). You can attach a Design Note to the file in question that says something like, "Hey Ed, I've finished off all the layout and design of this file, it needs the content. Remember, when you add everything to make sure that all the dates read 2002, as opposed to 2001." When Ed opens the file in question, the Design Note automatically opens.

Whether in a remote site or local site, Design Notes are displayed in the same way, as a little yellow bubble to the right of a file.

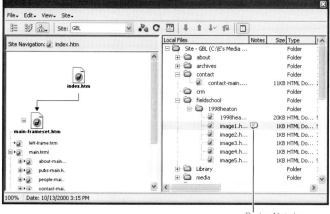

Design Note icon

The Design note icon will *only* be displayed after you click the Site panel's Expand/Collapse button.

In the following sections, you are going to explore how to set up and configure Design Notes, as well as how to create, attach, and view them.

Configuring Design Notes

Before you can take advantage of Design Notes, your local (or remote) site needs to be configured to deal with them

1. Open the Edit Sites dialog box (Site → Edit Sites).

2. Select the site for which you want to enable Design Notes, and click Edit.

3. From here, the Site Definition dialog box will open. If it isn't already, make sure you open the advanced section by selecting the Advanced tab. From there, click the Design Notes option in the Category list box.

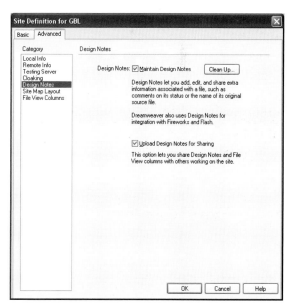

If you're already using Design Notes, you can click the Clean Up button to delete any Design Notes that aren't associated with a file.

4. Click the Maintain Design Notes check box.

5. If you want your Design Notes uploaded to the remote site (something we'll talk about creating shortly), click the Upload Design Notes for Sharing option.

6. Click OK.

Creating Design Notes

Once you've configured your site to deal with Design Notes, the process of attaching them to a file is easy:

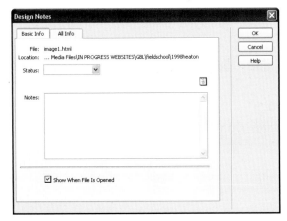

1. With the Site panel open, select the file to which you want to attach a Design Note.

2. Open the context menu and choose Design Notes or go to File → Design Notes. This will bring up the Design Notes Dialog box.

3. If you want to include the status of the file, select one of the options from the Status drop-down menu.

4. If you want to add the current date to the Design Note (in mm/dd/yy format), click the Add Date button.

5. In the Notes field, type in the text for the Design Note.

6. If you want the note to automatically open when the file to which it is attached opens (as opposed to having to be opened manually), select the Show When File Is Opened check box.

7. Click OK.

To make more detailed custom Design Notes, use the All Info section of the Design Notes dialog box.

Viewing Design Notes

There are a couple of different ways to open a Design Note. The first way happens automatically if you've enabled the Show When File Is Opened option described in the previous section. The second way involves manually opening the note:

1. With the Site Window open, select the file with the attached Design Note you want to open.

2. Choose from the following options:

- Double-click the Design Note icon.
- Go to File ➔ Design Notes.
- Open the file's context menu and choose Design Notes.

3. Any of these options will automatically bring up the Design Notes dialog box, and the Design Note in question will be displayed.

Cloaking Files

A new feature to Dreamweaver MX is the ability to cloak specific file types or complete folders—and for you Trekkies out there, we're not talking about Romulans and Klingons (make it so, Number One). Cloaking lets you exclude folders or specific file types from sitewide operations such as Put/Get, Synchronization, inclusion in the Assets panel, and site-wide link checking. It's a pretty handy feature if you are working on a large site and are trying to work on one specific area of the site without affecting the other areas.

Enabling Cloaking

Before you can cloak folders in your site, you must first enable the cloaking feature for your local site. To do so:

1. Go to Site ➔ Edit Sites to open the Edit Sites dialog box. Select the site for which you want to enable cloaking, and click Edit.

2. Select the Cloaking option in the Category list box.

3. Select the Enable Cloaking checkbox.

4. If you want to cloak specific file types, click the Cloak Files Ending With checkbox, and then enter the specific extensions associated with the files you want to cloak into the text field.

5. When you're finished, click OK.

Cloaking Site Folders

Now that you've enabled cloaking for your site,. You can go ahead and cloak any folder or subfolder (and by extensions, all of its contents). To cloak a site folder:

1. Open the Site panel (Window ➔ Site).

2. Navigate to the location of the specific folder you want to cloak.

3. In the Site panel, go to Site → Cloaking → Cloak.

4. Dreamweaver will automatically cloak the selected folder (see Figure 12.1).

To uncloak a folder, select it in the Site panel and go to Site → Cloaking → Uncloak. You can also uncloak all cloaked folders in your local site by going to Site → Cloaking → Uncloak All.

Switching to Another Local Site

All of the procedures that have been discussed thus far are pretty cool. The only problem is that they can only be carried out on the currently open local site. What happens if you want to stop working on the currently open site and start working on another? The process of switching from local site to local site from within the Site Window is really easy:

Site drop-down menu

1. Make sure the Site panel is open (Window → Site).

2. Select another local site from the Site drop-down menu.

Figure 12.1

When a folder has been cloaked, it and all of its associated files are crossed out with a red hatch-mark.

Using the Site Window to Manipulate a Remote Site

Remember that managing and manipulating your local site is really only half of what the Site Window is used for. You can also use it to manage and manipulate your remote site, which is the online counterpart of your local site that sits on a web server somewhere and can be accessed by anyone with a web browser and an Internet connection. One of the neatest things about Dreamweaver is that the line between a local site and a remote site is very transparent. With many other visual web authoring tools you can create your website, but you must then employ an FTP client to upload it to your intended web server.

With Dreamweaver, however, the FTP client is built right into the Site panel. As a result, some very tricky, time consuming, or seemingly impossible procedures can be pulled off effortlessly.

In the following sections, you'll learn how to use the Site Window to create, manage, and manipulate a remote site. You'll start off by leaning how to configure a remote site and go on to explore how to connect to the remote site, upload and download files, use the Check In/Check Out feature, synchronize your local and remote sites, and refresh your remote site. Finally, you'll learn how to use Site Reports to improve your overall workflow.

> An FTP client (File Transfer Protocol) is a program with which you move files from your computer to another computer somewhere else on the Internet.

Setting Up a Remote Site

Before you get too much ahead of yourself thinking of all the groovy things you can do with the Site Window, you need to configure your remote site. The process itself is actually part of setting up a local site; Macromedia assumes that when you configure a local site, you will also configure its complementary remote site. As a result, it's just a matter of setting some additional properties for your remote site:

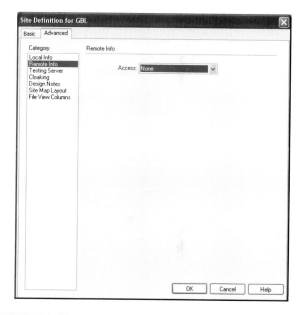

1. Open the Edit Sites dialog box (Site → Edit Sites).

2. Select the local site whose remote component you want to configure and click Edit.

3. Choose Remote Info from the Category list. You'll notice that the Remote Info section is pretty bare: it's just a single drop-down menu. Don't worry; this is as it should be.

> The Testing Server option in the Category list box comes into play when you use Dreamweaver MX to create a dynamic database-driven site—a topic to which you'll get an introduction in Part IV, "Making Dreamweaver Dynamic."

From here, you'll need to use the Access drop-down menu to determine how you access your remote site. For a description of the two most common methods (FTP and LAN), as well as their associated properties, continue on to the next sections.

Connecting to Your Remote Server Using FTP

As mentioned previously, FTP is how you connect and transfer files to a computer somewhere else on the Internet to which you do not have direct access. Chances are, unless you find yourself in the fortunate position of having access to a web server over a LAN (local area network), you'll use FTP to access your remote server. To set up your remote site so that it's accessed by FTP:

1. Follow steps 1 through 3 as described in the previous section.

2. Select FTP from the Access drop-down menu.

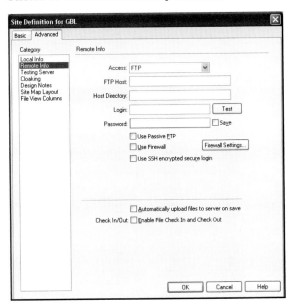

3. Now you have access to all the properties specific to FTP access. In the FTP Host field, enter the name of the FTP host.

> If, for some reason, you aren't sure of the exact host name of your web server (or any of the other associated necessary info), contact the company that is providing you with server space; they'll be able to tell you exactly what you need to know.

4. In the Host Directory field, type the exact path (for example, `usr/www/htdocs`) of the location where publicly accessed documents reside on your web server. .

5. Enter your login into the Login field.

6. Enter your password into the Password field.

> Because a web server is a secure computing environment, a unique login and password is required each time you wish to upload files to or download files from your remote site. If you want to avoid having to retype your login and password each time you connect to your remote site, check the Save option. However, this can cause some security problems: anyone who has access to that PC will automatically have access to your server.

7. If your remote site resides on a server that uses a firewall, make sure you've got the Use Passive FTP option selected. If you don't, you might not be able to connect to your remote site.

8. If you are working from behind a firewall (software that increases security on a computer network), make sure you have the Use Firewall option selected. From here, you'll need to enter the information for a proxy server in Preferences dialog box (Edit → Preferences).

For help with firewall-related issues, contact the system administrator for your Internet Service Provider.

9. If you want your files to be automatically uploaded to your remote site when they're saved, select the Automatically Upload Files to Server on Save option. Remember, in order for this option to function, you need to be connected to the Internet whenever you save.

10. If you want to enable the Check In/Check Out feature, select the Enable File Check In and Check Out option. Don't worry too much about what Check In/Check Out does right now—you'll get a chance to explore it in depth later in the chapter.

11. When you're finished inputting the settings for FTP access, click the Test button. Dreamweaver will attempt to connect to your remote side based on the information you provided. If the test is successful, Dreamweaver will tell you.

In order for Dreamweaver to test an FTP connection, you need to be connected to the Internet.

12. When you're finished, click OK.

Connecting to Your Remote Server Using a LAN

If you are lucky enough to work somewhere that owns and maintains their own web server (to which you have direct access), you don't need to use FTP. Instead you'll use the Local/Network option. The Local/Network is extremely easy to configure because it assumes that you'll have direct access (through a LAN) to the computer that is acting as your web server.

To set up the connection to your local site using Local/Network:

1. Follow steps 1 through 3 described previously in the "Setting Up a Remote Site" section.

2. Choose Local/Network from the Access drop-down menu.

3. Click the Browse to File button (to the right of the Remote Folder field).

4. When the Choose Remote Folder dialog box opens, navigate to the folder in which the publicly accessible documents reside on the web server, open it, and click Select.

5. If you want the list of files on the remote site to automatically update whenever Dreamweaver (or any other program) adds a new file, select the Refresh Remote File List Automatically.

6. If you want to enable the Check In/Check Out feature, select the Enable File Check In and Check Out option (we'll explore in depth what Check In/Check Out does later in the chapter).

7. If you want your files to be automatically uploaded to your remote site when they're saved, select the Automatically Upload Files to Server on Save option. Remember, for this option to function, you need to be connected to the Internet whenever you save.

8. When you're finished inputting the settings for Local/Network access, click OK.

Connecting to a Remote Site

Now that you've properly configured your remote site, it's time to learn how to connect to it using Dreamweaver's built-in FTP client.

Because the vast majority of Dreamweaver users don't have direct access to a web server, this section of the chapter will focus exclusively on using FTP to connect to your remote site (as opposed to Local/Network).

To connect to your remote site using the FTP client:

1. From within the Site panel (Window → Site) of the local site to whose remote server you wish to connect, click the Connect button 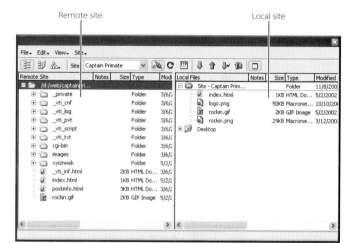 .

> In order to successfully connect to the web server (remote site) by FTP, you must be hooked up to the Internet and must have properly configured the remote site via the Site Definition dialog box, as discussed in the section "Setting Up a Remote Site."

2. Dreamweaver opens a session (that's a fancy term for a connection) with the web server on which your remote site is sitting. If you didn't select the Save Password and Login option when you configured the remote site, you'll be prompted to input your login and password.

3. If everything has been configured properly (and your web server isn't experiencing any problems), a dialog box will appear relating the progress of the connection, and then the remote site will appear in the left side of the Site panel.

4. As soon as you connect to your remote site, you can disconnect by clicking the Disconnect button (which replaces the Connect button).

> To view both your local and remote site in the Site panel, click the Expand/Collapse button.

Uploading to a Remote Site

The whole point of having a built-in FTP client in Dreamweaver is to upload files to your web server (remote site) so that the entire web world can experience your glorious site. Because of this, you might assume that the Site panel makes it easy to upload files, and you'd be right! Macromedia has made a sometimes difficult process into something quite effortless:

1. Make sure you're connected to the remote site to which you wish to upload (remember to click the Expand/Collapse button).

2. From the Local Site section of your Site panel, select the file you want to upload to your remote site.

3. Choose from the following options:

- Click and drag the file from the local site section of the Site Window to the remote site section of the Site Window.

If there is an identically named file in the same directory to which you are uploading your file, the one on the remote site will be overwritten.

- Click the Put Files button 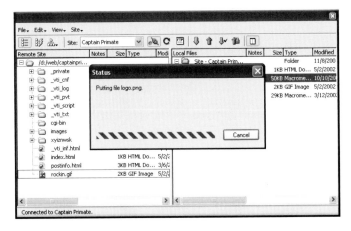 .
- Go to Site → Put.

4. If the document you are uploading has any associated files (inserted Flash movies or images, for example), Dreamweaver will prompt you with the Dependent File dialog box. To upload all documents' associated files, click Yes. If you don't want to upload all the associated files, click No.

5. A window will appear showing the progress of your upload. When the upload is complete, the file will appear in the remote site section of the Site panel.

You can upload any number of files in one fell swoop. Just select all the files you want to upload and follow the procedures just outlined, beginning with step 3.

Downloading from a Remote Site

To download a file or files from a remote site is just as easy as uploading:

1. Make sure you're connected to the remote site to which you wish to download (remember to click the Expand/Collapse button to display both the local and remote site in the Site panel).

2. From the Local Site section of your Site panel, select the file you want to download from your remote site.

3. Choose from the following options:

   - Click and drag the file from the remote site section of the Site Window to the local site section of the Site panel.
   - Click the Get Files button ⬇ .
   - Go to Site → Get.

4. If the document you are downloading has any associated files (inserted Flash movies or images, for example), Dreamweaver will prompt you with the Dependent File dialog box. To download all documents' associated files, click Yes. If you don't want to download all the associated files, click No.

5. A window will appear showing the progress of your upload. When the upload is complete, the file will appear in the remote site section of the Site panel.

Using the Check In/Check Out Feature

Back when you were learning how to configure your remote site, one of the steps was to choose whether you wanted to enable the Check In/Check Out feature. In this section, you'll learn more about that feature as well as how to put it to good use.

Here is a horrible scenario for you to consider. Say you are one member of a distributed web design team working on a project. Say you download a file from the remote server that requires the addition of some content, a task for which you are responsible. Remember, when you download a file from a server, you aren't really taking the file, *per se*; you're only making a copy of the file. The file itself still hangs out on the server, while the copy is stuck on your hard drive. In our scenario, unbeknownst to you, a short time after you download the file, the graphic designer of the project downloads the same file to make some changes to the layout. When you're finished adding the necessary content to the file, you upload it to the server. Unfortunately, when the graphic designer finishes her changes, she uploads the file and replaces the one on the server, which has all the changes you've made, with her version of the file. The humanity! Hours of work down the tube!

As simplistic as this scenario is, this kind of tragedy happens quite often. How can it be avoided? This is where Dreamweaver's Check In/Check Out feature comes in to the picture: when you enable the Check In/Check Out feature, you can check files out from the remote site. When they're checked out, the file on the server becomes locked, prohibiting anyone else from downloading it and making changes to it. When you're finished editing the file, you check it back into the server, and it then becomes accessible again to other individuals.

The Check In/Check Out feature only works for those who are accessing the remote site with Dreamweaver. If one of your team members is accessing the web server with another FTP client, they can upload and download files with no restrictions.

When a file has been checked out, a small checkmark appears next to it in the remote site portion of the Site Window, indicating that it is locked to all other users.

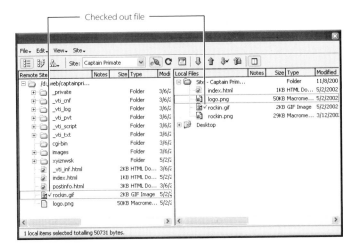

Another cool thing about the Check In/Check Out feature is that it can be configured to display the name of the individual (as well as the e-mail address) who checked out a particular file.

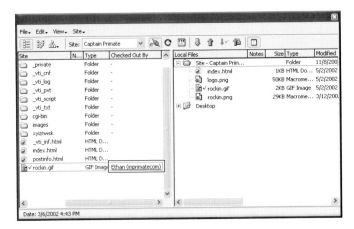

To configure a remote site's Check In/Check Out feature:

1. Open the Edit Sites dialog box (Site → Edit Sites).

2. Select the local site whose Check In/Check Out feature you want to configure, and click Edit.

3. Choose Remote Info from the Category list.

4. If it isn't already, select the Enable File Check In and Check Out option. Once this is done, a series of additional options will appear.

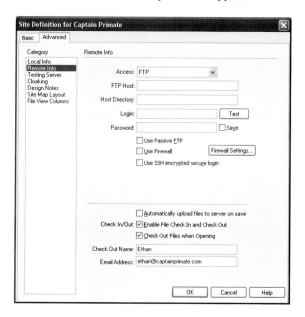

5. If you want the file to be automatically checked out when the user downloads it, select the Check Out Files When Opening option.

6. If you want your name displayed next to the checked out file, enter a name into the Check Out name field.

7. If you want your e-mail displayed next the checked out file, enter it into the E-mail Address field.

> Users accessing the same remote site through Dreamweaver can click the address of the individual who checked out a given file to launch their e-mail program.

8. When you're finished configuring the Check In/Check Out features, click OK.

Now that you've configured Check In/Check Out, you can take advantage of its features. To check out a file:

1. From within the local site from which you want check out a file, select the file in the remote site section of your Site Window.

2. Click the Check Out Files button ⬇∨ or go to Site → Check Out.

To check a file back into the remote site, just follow these steps:

1. In the local site section of the Site Window, select the file that needs to be checked back into the remote site.

2. Click the Check Files In ![icon] button or go to Site → Check In.

> Sometimes when you check a file back into a server, the copy in your local site becomes Read-Only (represented by a small padlock icon to the right of the filename in the Site panel). To turn this feature off, select the file, right-click/ Cmd-click to open the context menu and select Turn Off Read Only.

Synchronizing Files Between a Local and Remote Site

Sometimes you get into a situation where you aren't exactly sure whether the files on your remote site or your local site are the most up to date. It would be a painful process to go through all of your directories to check which files have the most recent time/date stamp. Fortunately, Dreamweaver provides a one-step way to ensure that both local and remote sites have all the most up-to-date versions of the files: Synchronize.

> When you synchronize a local and remote site, you can also automatically delete the files on one site that do not appear on another.

To synchronize a local and remote site:

1. Make sure you are connected to your remote site (and both are showing in the Site panel).

> You can also synchronize only selected files or folders, as opposed to an entire site.

2. In the Site panel (Window → Site), go to Site → Synchronize.

3. When the Synchronize File dialog box appears, choose the scope of the synchronization from the Synchronize Scope drop-down menu:

   • If you want to sync the entire site, choose Entire *Site Name*.

   • If you want to sync only selected files or folders, choose Selected Local Files Only.

4. From the Synchronize Direction drop-down menu, choose the direction in which the synchronization process will flow:

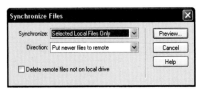

   • If you choose Put Newer Files to Remote, Dreamweaver determines the newest versions of files in the local site and uploads them to the remote site.

- If you choose Get Newer Files from Remote, Dreamweaver finds the newest versions of files on your remote site and downloads them to your local site.

- If you choose Get and Put Newer Files, the newest versions of files will flow from your local server to your remote server, and vice versa.

5. If you want to delete files from the remote site that aren't located in the local site, select the Delete Remote Files Not on Local Drive option.

6. When you're finished setting all the options in the Synchronize Files dialog box, click the Preview button. Dreamweaver will open a dialog box displaying all the files that are slated to be included in the synchronization.

7. Deselect any files you don't want included in the synchronization by clicking the check box directly to its left, and then click OK.

8. When the process is finished, you'll be prompted to keep a record of the changes. If you want to, click the Save Log button. Dreamweaver will provide a dialog box to set the location where you want the log saved. If you don't want to save a log, click the Close button.

Refreshing a Remote Site

When you refresh a site (either local or remote), Dreamweaver will reread the contents of any selected directory to see if the contents have changed. If they have, it will automatically update the view. This is particularly helpful if files have been added or removed by other users during the course of your FTP session.

> If you enabled the Refresh Local Files Automatically option in the Site Definition dialog box, you'll only have to refresh a remote site, as your local site will automatically refresh when any changes are made.

To refresh a site, just follow these steps:

1. With a local and remote site open in the Site Window, select the topmost folder of the site (local or remote) you wish to refresh.

2. Click the Refresh button **ℂ** .

Inspiration: Design and Technique

Widely recognized as one of the most talented and creative digital design firms in the industry, Terra Incognita (`www.terraincognita.com`) believes that effective websites are planned story-spaces that employ interactive narratives to engage people's imagination. To help the development of vibrant interactive projects, their staff combines expertise in strategy, design, and technology with a strong foundation in the liberal arts.

Terra Incognita's website (see Figure 12.2) uses colors and images that encourage a feeling of exploration and discovery. Their portfolio, which includes award-winning websites for National Geographic and the Smithsonian Museum, embodies this feeling and encourages the user to embark on an exhilarating intellectual journey.

Figure 12.2

Terra Incognita

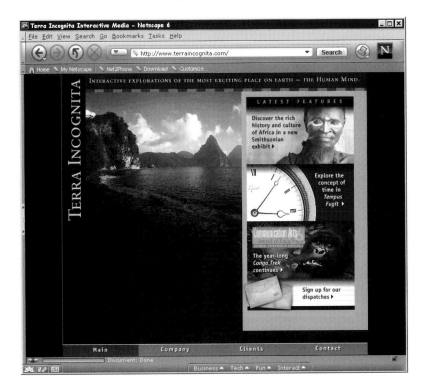

Summary

In this chapter, you explored how to use Dreamweaver's tools, primarily the Site Window, to manage and manipulate your HTML creation. You started off by learning how to use the Site Window to work with a local site. You looked at how to open and create new files, create new folders, move files, check links sitewide, and repair broken links, all from within the Site Window.

From there, you investigated how to use the Site Window to work with a remote site. Included was a look at how to set up a remote site, how to connect to a remote site, how to upload and download files, how to take advantage of the Check In/Check Out feature, how to sync a remote and local site, and how to refresh a site.

PART III

Working with Dynamic HTML

While each successive version of HTML offered unparalleled opportunities for publishing hypertext documents, the medium was not as malleable as many would have liked. Text could only be arranged in a limited number of ways, making it hard to create a compelling visual experience. In addition, the way HTML treated graphics made laying out a document even harder. Finally, the interactivity in HTML documents was limited to the actual hypertext. It was not until the release of Dynamic HTML that many of these problems were solved.

First, DHTML features Cascading Style Sheets (CSS), which allow designers to exert a far greater degree of control over the way their document appears. Second, with DHTML you can far more efficiently integrate HTML with JavaScript, thereby creating some genuinely interesting interactive features on your web page. Finally, DHTML allows you to position elements exactly as you wish using a system of x and y coordinates.

Here is the cool thing: Dreamweaver MX gives you the power to efficiently create and manage DHTML—like this is a big surprise!

CHAPTER 13

Working with Cascading Style Sheets

One of the chief frustrations when using HTML, as you've probably already figured out, is that it is limiting in terms of content layout and design. There is almost no typographic control to speak of, which is extremely frustrating to print designers who've become used to being able to exert total control over how their textual content appears. This all changed with Cascading Style Sheets (CSS). With it, you can really split content and appearance so that it truly has *style*.

In this chapter, you are going delve deep into Dreamweaver and learn how to use CSS to do all sorts of groovy things:

- **What are Cascading Style Sheets?**

- **Understanding styles and their attributes**

- **Creating a style sheet**

- **Applying a style sheet**

- **Editing a style sheet**

- **Converting CSS styles to HTML**

- **Working with external style sheets**

What Are Cascading Style Sheets?

For those designers who grew up in the print world, Cascading Style Sheets (CSS), one of the features of Dynamic HTML (DHTML), is one of the exciting new developments to come to HTML in recent years. As has been mentioned numerous times, HTML is not a designer's medium. The inherent limitations of the markup language make it very difficult to get a document looking exactly as you want. However, with CSS, you have a far more printlike control over an HTML document.

> Generally speaking, a style is a group of characteristics (like font, position, color, and so on) that are referred to by a single name. A style sheet is a group of these styles.

Basically, a CSS is a list of rules governing the way the elements of an HTML document are displayed. While HTML already is filled with rules that are designed to dictate how things are displayed (that is what tags are for), Cascading Style Sheets is cool for two basic reasons. First, with the help of DHTML's ability to access a document's DOM (Document Object Model), CSS lets you manipulate a greater range of the document's features than ever before.

Second, with the help of CSS, you can actually redefine the way the browser displays a whole range of HTML tags.

Strictly speaking, there are two different kinds of styles in CSS: a style class and a redefined tag. A redefined tag style involves an HTML tag whose properties have been changed. For instance, you can create a redefined tag style in which the <b> (bold) tag is altered so that when it is applied, the text is not only bolded, it also changes to green. The second type of style, called a style class, involves a style that has many different attributes. This style is then applied to a block of selected text to change the text's look. The great thing about both types of styles is that they can be changed well after they are created, and all of the elements to which they were applied will update.

After you create a style (something we'll talk about shortly), there are a couple of different ways the information is stored. The first way, called inline, involves sticking the style information in the HTML document itself (see Figure 13.1).

THE DOCUMENT OBJECT MODEL (DOM)

The Document Object Model, which is part of the World Wide Web Consortium's (W3C) HTML 4.0 standard, makes every element in an HTML document a discrete and editable object. Because the DOM contains the specs for all elements in an HTML document, you can use a scripting language to edit them to your heart's content.

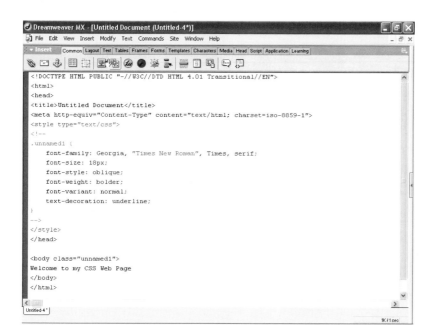

Figure 13.1

An inline style is stored in the <head> section of an HTML document.

The second way to store CSS information is to create an *external style sheet*. A discreet file with a CSS extension, the external style sheet is a document with nothing more than the style information (Figure 13.2).

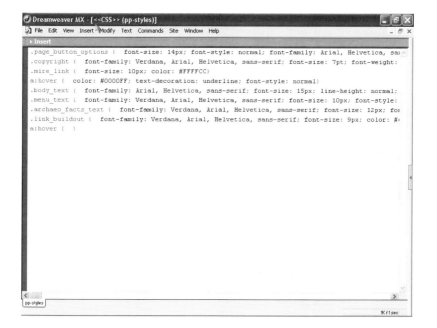

Figure 13.2

An external style sheet is a document that only contains the style information.

While style information that is saved inline applies only to the document in which it is located, an external style sheet can be linked to any number of HTML documents.

Now, don't get me wrong, CSS is pretty darned groovy, but it isn't all sunshine and roses. First, because it is a feature of Dynamic HTML, at the very minimum, it is only supported by 4.0 browsers and above. In addition, many aspects of CSS are supported by only one browser, and some don't even work with any browsers. Wait, it gets even worse than this: some CSS attributes that, theoretically, are supposed to be supported by both Netscape and Internet Explorer are often unpredictable. So, what is one supposed to do? Well, when you're using Dreamweaver MX to leverage the power of CSS, always preview your document to see if it works properly in your target browser—a process that was discussed in Chapter 3, "Setting Up and Managing Your Page."

Understanding Styles and Their Attributes

There are more than 70 different style attributes that you can manipulate, and it's well worth your while to become at least passingly familiar with each so that you can truly leverage the power of CSS.

The information in the following section will become useful only after you learn how to create a style sheet, something that will be covered a little later in the chapter. Because of this, there will be no real indication of how to get to the dialog boxes that are displayed— that will be looked at later. For now, it's important to become familiar with each of the styles, where they reside in the Style Definition dialog box, and how they can be used.

In many cases, Dreamweaver can't display a given attribute. These cases will be noted in the following sections; they are also marked in the Style Definition dialog box with an asterisk (*).

Type

As you'd expect, the Type styles primarily affect how type appears in your document.

Font The Font drop-down menu lets you set the specific font of the style you are creating. With it, you can choose from the run-of-the mill HTML fonts as well as additional fonts. To do so, just click the Edit Font List option and add the desired font(s) when the Edit Font List dialog box appears.

Size With the Size drop-down menu, you can choose the size of your text. You can choose a numerical value or choose from a series of preset size options. When you choose a numerical value, the unit's drop-down menu becomes accessible, and from it you can choose the specific unit (the default is points) of the numerical size value.

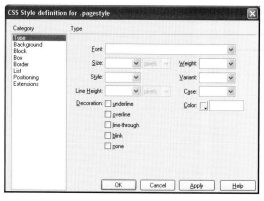

Style The Style drop-down menu lets you choose from three options: normal, italic, or oblique.

Line Height The Line Height drop-down menu lets you set the distance between individual lines in a block of text. The line height, traditionally referred to as leading, can be set by choosing `[value]` from the drop-down menu, typing a value into the drop-down menu, and choosing the units in which the value will be expressed from the unit's drop-down menu.

Weight The Weight drop-down menu, which lets you choose from a series of numerical values or relative settings (normal, bold, bolder, or lighter), affects the "boldness" of text.

Variant The small-caps variant option switches the style's text from the way it would normally look to a style in which all the characters are uppercase with the capital letters being slightly larger. Be wary, however: the variant option is neither previewable in Dreamweaver nor supported by the vast majority of browsers.

Decorations The various text decoration options (underline, overline, line through, blink, or none) let you add extra style to the way text appears. Choosing underline will underline the style's text. Overline will insert a line along the top of the text. Line-through strikes the text with a line running straight through its middle. Blink will make your text appear and then disappear repeatedly.

DESIGN REMINDER: Blink, the Bane of Web Design

While creating blinking text might be attractive to those who want to create a movement-filled website, using the Blink decoration option is a surefire way to annoy your audience. Blinking text, which can also be created using the `<blink>` tag, is probably one of the most universally hated HTML options.

Case The options in the Case drop-down menu let you set whether the text is displayed in lowercase or uppercase characters. Be advised, if you manipulate the style's case, it won't be displayed in Dreamweaver.

Color You can choose a text color for the style by clicking the Color swatch to open the Color Palette.

Background

As you've probably noticed, you can only apply a background color or image to an entire page, table, or cell. This is rather frustrating if you want to exercise a little more control over how background colors or images are used in your design. With the CSS background attributes, however, you *can* exert more power background colors and images.

Unfortunately, only Netscape 6 and Internet Explorer 6 fully support all the CSS background attributes

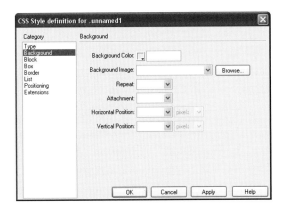

Background Color Click on the color swatch to open the Color Palette. From here, you can choose the color of the style's background.

Background Image You can set the style's background image by clicking the Browse button to open the Select Image Source dialog box. Navigate to where the image is located, select it, and click Select.

As with all other cases in Dreamweaver, you are limited to GIFs, JPEGs, and PNGs for a style's background image.

Repeat The options in the Repeat drop-down menu (no-repeat, repeat, repeat-x, repeat-y) determine the way the style's background image tiles. Choosing no-repeat displays the selected image only once. If you select repeat, the image will tile both vertically and horizontally to fill the style's entire area. Choosing repeat-x causes the image to tile only horizontally (as a single line), while choosing repeat-y causes the image to tile vertically (as a single line.)

Attachment The attachment attribute really comes into play when you apply a style to the <body> tag of an HTML document (which effectively applies it to the entire visible portion of the page.) Choosing scroll from the Attachment drop-down menu will make the background image behave as it would under normal circumstances: it will move in or out of view when the page is scrolled. If you choose fixed, the background image remains and will move when the page is scrolled, thereby remaining in the position where it was originally placed. Unfortunately, only Internet Explorer supports the fixed attribute. Netscape will treat it as scroll. The Attachment attribute will not be displayed within Dreamweaver.

Horizontal Position The Horizontal Position attribute lets you set the location of the background image relative to the element to which you are applying the style. You can choose left, center, or right, and they work the same as any alignment options. Alternatively, you can set a value by selecting [value] from the drop-down menu, typing a number into the drop-down menu, and then choosing the units in which the value will be expressed from the Units drop-down menu.

Vertical Position The Vertical Position works exactly the same as the Horizontal Position attribute, except it affects the vertical position of the background image relative to the element to which you applied the style

Block

The various Block attributes affect the typographic characteristics of all text within a selected element.

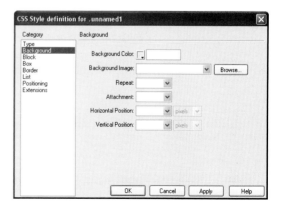

Word Spacing The Word Spacing attribute lets you set the amount of space between words in a selected block. Word Spacing isn't displayed in the Dreamweaver environment.

To alter the spacing, just select [value] from the drop-down menu, type a number into the drop-down menu, and choose the units in which the value will be expressed from the Units drop-down menu.

The only browser that currently supports word spacing is Netscape 6.*x*.

Letter Spacing While Word Spacing affects the distance between individual words, Letter Spacing affects the distance between individual characters within a block. Letter Spacing isn't displayed in the Dreamweaver environment.

To set Letter Spacing, select [value] from the drop-down menu, type a number into the drop-down menu itself), and choose the units in which the value will be expressed from the Units drop-down menu to the right.

Letter Spacing is currently only supported by Explorer 6.x and Netscape 6.*x*.

Vertical Alignment The Vertical Alignment attribute sets the vertical position of an image within a selected block.

> For more information on the present options, check out the "Organizing and Laying Out Text" section in Chapter 4, "Adding and Manipulating Text."

Text Align The Text Align attribute lets you set the alignment of the text within the selected block. Your alignment options include left, center, right, and justify (which stretches the lines so that they are both right and left justified).

Text Indent With the Text Indent attribute, you can set a tab-like space in the first line of any block of text. To do this, type a value into the Text Indent Field, and when the Units drop-down menu goes live, select a unit in which you want the indent expressed.

Whitespace The Whitespace attribute, which isn't displayed in Dreamweaver, controls the way the tabs and spaces appear in a block of text. Selecting the Normal option causes any *additional* whitespaces to collapse. Choosing the Pre option will preserve all whitespaces. If you select the Nowrap option, the line will only break if a line break (
 tag) is used.

Display The Display attribute lets you set whether an element is displayed and how that item is displayed.

Box

When working with CSS, think of the selection to which styles are applied as an invisible box. The Box attributes let you control the way in which the elements within the selection (box) act in relation to the box itself.

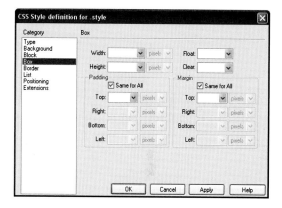

Width The Width attribute set the width of the selected element's box. To leave the box as is, leave the field blank (don't choose anything from the drop-down menu) or choose Auto. To alter the width of the box, select [value] from the drop-down menu, type a number into the drop-down menu, and choose the units in which the value will be expressed from the Units drop-down menu.

> If the selection is wider than the value of the box itself, it will wrap to fit within the box.

Height The Height attribute sets the height of the selected element's box. To leave the height as is, leave the field blank or choose Auto. To change the height of the box, select [value] from the drop-down menu, type a number into the drop-down menu, and choose the units in which the value will be expressed from the Units drop-down menu.

Float By setting the Float attribute, you can take the element to which you are applying the style and stick it on either the left or right side of the page. If any other text encounters the floating object, it wraps itself around the element's box.

> Unfortunately, Dreamweaver will only properly display floating images and not other elements such as text.

Clear The Clear attribute determines the way floating objects interact with the element to which you're applying the style. If you choose Left, floating objects won't be able to occupy the margin to the left of the selected object. Choosing Right prohibits floating objects from occupying the right margin of the selected object. If you want floating objects to be able to occupy both left and right margins of a selected object, choose both. To prohibit floating objects from occupying both the left and right margins of the element to which you are applying the style, you must manually enter **both** into the clear field.

Padding The Padding attributes work almost the same as they do with tables. Essentially, each value (top, right, bottom, left) determines the distance between the element to which the style was applied and the inside edge of its box. To change any of the padding values, select [value] from the specific drop-down menu, type a number into the drop-down menu itself, and choose the units in which the value will be expressed from the units drop-down menu. If you want the value for each padding attribute, click the Same for All check box. The Padding attribute only works if the box's border is set to visible.

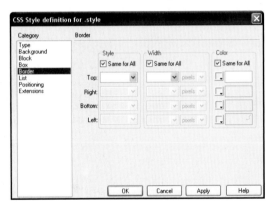

Margin The Margin attributes let you set the distance (top, right, bottom, or left) between the element to which you applied the style and all other elements in a page. To leave the margin unchanged, select Auto from any of the four drop-down menus. If you want to set a specific margin on any of the four sides of the object, select [value] from the drop-down menu, type a number into the drop-down menu, and choose the units in which the value will be expressed from the Units drop-down menu. As with the Padding attributes, if you want all the Margin attributes to be the same, check the Same for All check box.

Border

The various Border attributes are closely related to the Box attributes. By default, the box of an element to which you've applied a style is invisible. However, with the Border attributes, you can control the way the edge (border) of the box looks.

If you want the border invisible, leave all of the Border attributes unchanged from their default state.

Width The four independent Width attributes (top, bottom, right, left), which do not display in Dreamweaver, determine the *thickness* of the element's border. To set a specific value for any of the edges, select [value] from the drop-down menu, type a number into the drop-down menu itself), and choose the units in which the value will be expressed from the Units drop-down menu. In addition, you've got several preset options (thin, medium, thick) from which you can choose.

> Remember, you can set the width value for any edge independently of any other.

If you want all of the Width values to be the same, click the Same for All check box.

Color The four independent Color attributes (top, bottom, right, left) let you set the color of the element's border. Just click the Color swatch to open the Color Palette and choose a border color for the style. As with all of the Border attributes, you can set the color of all the borders to be the same by clicking the Same for All check box.

Style The various Style attributes let you change the look of the element's border. As with all of the Border attributes, you can set the style of all the borders to be the same by clicking the Same for All check box.

List

As you probably remember, the way lists (either ordered or unordered) look is pretty limiting and thereby frustrating. If you are having trouble remembering how lists work, see Chapter 4.

However, with the CSS List attributes, you can exert a more control over how an ordered or unordered list appears.

Type The Type drop-down menu lets you select from a preset list of bullets or numbers that are used in a list. The Type attribute doesn't display in Dreamweaver.

Bullet Image Even with the additional types available, bullets can be pretty humdrum and boring. You can add a little extra "oomph" with the Bullet Image attribute, which lets you choose an image that will be used in place of the regular bullet. Click the Browse button. In the Select Image Source dialog box, navigate to the place where the image is located, select it, and click Select.

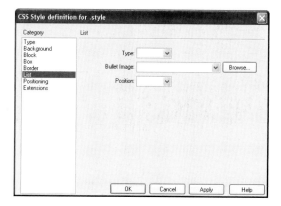

The Bullet Image attribute doesn't show up in Dreamweaver.

Position The Position attribute lets you determine how the text wraps in relation to the bullet. Choosing inside will line up all the text with the bullet point; choosing outside will line the text up with the page's margin.

The Position attribute doesn't display in Dreamweaver.

Positioning

One of the coolest things about CSS is that you can use it to position elements on your page using an absolute coordinate system.

In Dreamweaver, there are two ways that this can be accomplished: with the Positioning attributes in the Style Definition dialog box, or with Layers. Because there is an entire chapter (Chapter 14, "Absolute Positioning with Layers") devoted to Layers, we're going to skip over the Positioning attributes in the section.

Extensions

The Extensions attributes section of the Style Definition dialog box is where Macromedia has placed the most advanced CSS features. The kicker is that currently, the Extensions attributes have extremely spotty browser coverage.

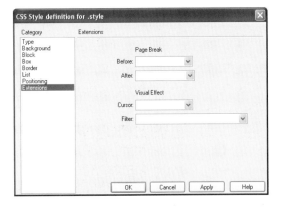

Page Break While all of the attributes we've discussed thus far have been supported by either Netscape or Explorer, the Page Break attribute isn't currently supported by either—it's still in the "recommendation" phase. When (and if) it is adopted, it would let you set a page break either before or after a block of text for the purposes of printing.

Cursor The Cursor attribute (which is only supported by Internet Explorer 4.0 or above and Netscape 6.x) lets you change the user's cursor. Simply choose an option from the drop-down menu.

Filter The Filter attribute is a proprietary (Microsoft owns it lock, stock, and barrel) doohickey/widget, which only functions with Explorer 4.0 or above, that lets you apply a special effect to a selected object. However, don't be too surprised that some Filter attributes won't even work in Explorer—they are pretty unreliable.

Creating a Cascading Style Sheet

Now that you've spent some time exploring the various attributes you can set for a given style, it's time to put that knowledge to work and learn how you use Dreamweaver to actually create Cascading Style Sheets.

As mentioned earlier, there are two different kinds of styles (redefined tags and style classes) and two kinds of style sheets (inline and external) you can create. While not exactly accurate, for the purposes of this section, I'll refer to all of these as CSS (or simply "style sheets").

The following sections are going to cover all the bases. You'll learn how to create a style class, redefine an HTML tag, and redefine hyperlink properties with selectors. For the purposes of this section, however, you're going to focus exclusively on how to create an inline Cascading Style Sheet. A little later on in the chapter, you'll take what you learned here and apply it to creating an external Cascading Style Sheet.

Defining a Style Class

A style class is a style with many different attributes that can be applied to any block of text. In this section, you'll explore how to create a style class:

1. Make sure the document in which you want to create the style sheet is open.

2. Open the CSS Styles panel by going to Window → CSS Styles.

3. Click the New Style  button to open the New Style dialog box.

4. If it isn't already, select the Make Custom Style (class) option from the Type list.

5. You'll notice that the words `.unnamed1` will appear in the name field. This is the name of the style that will appear in the CSS Styles panel. Since you probably don't want to use this default name, click anywhere in the Name field and type a new name. The name that you give shouldn't have any spaces and it must begin with a period (.). If you don't add one yourself, Dreamweaver will automatically do it for you.

6. From the Define In options, choose This Document Only.

Remember that the style created using the process outlined in this section only applies to the document from which it is being created. If you want to create a style that can be applied to many different documents, you'll need to create an external CSS—something we'll talk about later in this chapter.

7. Click OK.

8. The Style Definition dialog box will appear. Note that the name of the style sheet appears in the title bar of the Style Definitions dialog box (below left).

9. Set all the attributes of your style.

If you are having trouble remembering what each attribute does, see the previous section, "Understanding Styles and Their Attributes."

10. Click OK. The style class will appear in the CSS Styles panel (below right).

After having gone though the above steps, you'll be faced with a totally blank page because you need to actually *apply* it to something for it to affect that way your page looks. If you want to put that newly created style to work, see the "Applying a Style Sheet" section later in this chapter.

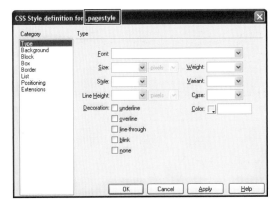

New style

Changing an HTML Tag

The process by which you redefine an HTML tag is just as easy as creating a style class:

> It's important to remember that even though you change the properties of an HTML tag, it will always retain its original characteristic: the new one(s) will just be added on.

1. In the document for which you want to change an HTML tag, open the CSS Styles panel (Window → CSS Styles).
2. Click the New Style button ▣ to open the New Style dialog box.
3. From the Type list, choose the Redefine HTML Tag option.
4. From the Tag drop-down menu, choose the tag that you wish to redefine. The items that populate the Tag drop-down menu depend on the type of CSS being used.
5. Choose the This Document Only from the Define In options.

> Remember, we'll discuss creating external CSS later in this chapter.

6. Click OK.
7. In the Style Definitions dialog box, select the attributes you'd like to add to the tag and click OK.

Unlike a style class, the redefined tag will not appear in the CSS Styles panel. Instead, it will appear in the Edit Style Sheet dialog box (which is accessible by clicking the Edit Style Sheet button in the CSS Styles panel). Of course, after having gone though the above steps, you'll be faced with a totally blank page because, again, you need to actually apply it to something for it to affect the way your page looks. To put that newly created style to work, see the "Applying a Style Sheet" section later in this chapter.

> Don't worry too much about editing a redefined tag (or a style class, for that matter); we'll cover that later in this chapter.

Redefine Hyperlink Properties with Selectors

CSS Selectors let you create a *pseudoclass* (not really a class, but close enough) that combines a style class with a redefined HTML tag. Affecting only the <A> tag, CSS Selectors are most commonly used to change the way a hyperlink looks when a user moves their mouse over it. Say, for instance, you wanted a hyperlink not to have its typical underline and for it to change to a different color when the user moves their mouse over it: this would be done with a CSS Selector.

To redefine hyperlink properties with a CSS Selector:

1. In the document for which you want to change hyperlink properties, open the CSS Styles panel (Window → CSS Styles).

2. Click the New Style button ☐ .

3. Choose the Use CSS Selector option from the Type list.

4. From the Selector drop-down menu, choose the hyperlink state whose properties you want to change:

   - Choosing a:active will let you change the properties of the hyperlink when it's active (that is, when it's clicked by the user).

   - By selecting a:hover, you'll be able to manipulate the properties of the hyperlink when the user's mouse is over the link itself.

   - By Choosing a:link, you can change the properties of the hyperlink as it would appear normally (just hanging out on the page doing its thing).

   - Selecting a:visited lets you manipulate the way the hyperlink looks after it has been clicked by the user.

5. From the Define In options, choose This Document Only.

6. Click OK.

7. In the Styles Definitions dialog box, select the attributes you want applied to the hyperlink.

8. Click OK.

As with a redefined tag, the CSS selector will not appear in the CSS Styles panel and will appear instead in the Edit Style Sheet dialog box, which is accessible by clicking the Edit Style Sheet button in the CSS Styles panel. The CSS Selector will apply to all the hyperlinks on the page.

Applying a Style Sheet

Now that you've gone through all the trouble of creating a style sheet, it's time to learn how to apply it to a page. Because both a redefined tag and a CSS Selector are automatically applied to the document in which they're created, you can't apply them manually. However, you can (and are supposed to) manually apply style classes to selected items:

> You can apply a style class to an entire page by selecting the <body> tag with the Tag Selector and then following the steps listed here.

1. Select the element(s) in your page to which you wish to apply the style class.

2. Open the CSS Styles panel (Window → CSS Styles) and click the style that you would like applied to the selected element(s). The style class will automatically be applied.

New to Dreamweaver MX is the ability to apply styles using the Property Inspector's CSS mode. The process is extremely easy:

1. Select the text in your page to which you wish to apply the style class.

2. If isn't already, open the Property Inspector (Window → Properties).

3. Click the Toggle HTML/CSS Mode icon 🄰 (located just to the left of the Font drop-down menu).

> Beyond the methods described here, you can choose a predesigned Cascading Style Sheet when you create a new document. Just go to File → New. When the New Document dialog box appears, click the CSS Styles Page option from the Category list box. From there, select one of the predesigned CSS styles pages from the CSS Style Sheets list box (of which there are many), and then click Create.

4. This will switch the Property Inspector into CSS Mode.

5. To apply a style to the selection, choose one from the CSS Style drop-down menu, which will be populated with the same styles in the CSS Styles panel.

> When you select some text to which a style has been applied while the Property Inspector is in CSS Mode, the style's attributes will appear to the right of the CSS Style drop-down menu.

6. To switch the Property Inspector back to HTML Mode, just click the HTML/CSS Mode icon Ⓢ (which changes when you witch to CSS Mode).

Removing a Style

You may find yourself in a situation where you want to remove a style class from an element:

1. Select the element from which you want to remove the style class.

2. Open the CSS Styles panel (Window → CSS Styles) and click the None option.

3. If the Auto Apply option isn't selected, click the Apply button ; if it is selected, the style class will automatically be removed.

Editing a Cascading Style Sheet

Style classes, redefined tags, or CSS selectors are by no means fixed in stone. One of the best features of CSS is that you can create a style and apply it to any number of elements and then go back and change that style and have all of the elements to which it was applied change accordingly. There's a quick and easy way to edit a style sheet:

> Remember, we're still working with inline styles here; we'll explore how to work with external style sheets a little later in the chapter.

1. In the document whose style sheet you wish to edit, open the CSS Styles panel (Window → CSS Styles).

2. Select the style you want to edit.

3. Click the Edit Style Sheet button 📝 . Alternatively, you can click the Edit Styles radio button at the top of the CSS Styles panel, select the style class, redefined HTML tag, or CSS selector that you want to edit, and click the Edit Style Sheet button.

4. In the Style Definitions dialog box, make any changes you want and click OK.

5. Click the Edit Style Sheet dialog box's Done button.

> You can also use the Edit Style Sheet dialog box to create a new style sheet, duplicate an existing style sheet, or delete a style sheet.

Converting CSS Styles to HTML Markup

Because CSS is only supported by 4.0 browsers and above, you might find that you might want to alter your CSS-enabled HTML file so that it can be viewed by those who aren't using the necessary technology. To do this, you need to save your HTML file in a format accessible by older browsers:

1. Open the page you want to convert.

2. Go to File → Convert → 3.0 Browser Compatible.

3. In the Convert to 3.0 Compatible Browser dialog box, select the CSS Styles to HTML Markup option, and click OK.

4. Dreamweaver will convert the document and open it up in a new window.

> The new CSS-free document is unsaved. As a result, you'll need to save it before you exit.

Working with External Style Sheets

Now that you've got a handle on how CSS (and specifically inline styles) works, it's time to explore the second type of style sheet: external. An external style sheet is a discrete file with a CSS extension that is composed of nothing more than the actual style information (see Figure 13.3).

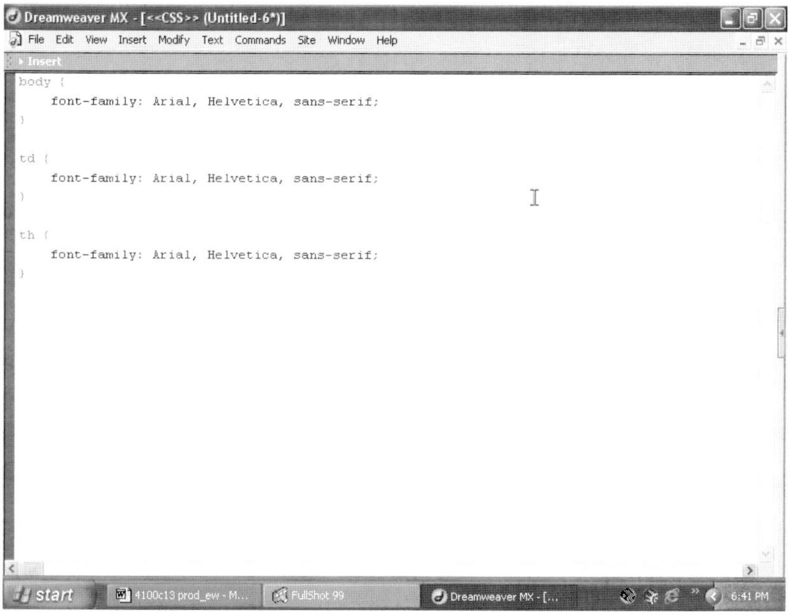

Figure 13.3

An external style sheet is incredibly simple, containing only the style information.

The primary benefit of an external style sheet is that it only needs to be created once. It can be reapplied *ad infinitum* to page after page without having to recreate the same styles, which is what you have to do if you use inline styles.

In the following section you are going to explore two separate topics: how to create external style sheets and how to link an external style sheet to an HTML document.

Creating an External Style Sheet

The process of creating an external style sheet is alomst identical to creating an inline one—*almost*. There are a few differences that warrant a full exploration of the process.

If you remember, a style class is a style with many different attributes that can be applied to any block of text. To create a style class:

1. In the document for which you want to create the external style sheet, open the CSS Styles panel (Window → CSS Styles).

2. Click the New Style button ⊡ .

3. From the type options, choose either Make Custom Style (class), Redefine HTML Tag, or Use CSS Selector.

4. Select the Define in (New Style Sheet File) option.

5. Click OK.

6. In the Save Style Sheet File As dialog box, navigate to the location where you want to save the CSS file (remember, an external style sheet is a discrete file), type a name into the File Name field, choose Style Sheet Files (*.css) from the Save As Type drop-down menu, and click Save.

7. In the Styles Definition dialog box, select the attributes you'd like applied to that style.

8. Click OK.

By default, the external style sheet you created will automatically be applied to the currently open document.

Linking to an External Style Sheet

As mentioned many times, one of the grand benefits to an external style sheet is that it can be created once and then applied to any number of HTML documents. When you do this, all the redefined HTML tags, CSS Selectors, and style classes will either be automatically applied (as in the case of a redefined HTML tag) or be available for application (in the case of style classes).

To link an external style sheet to a Dreamweaver document:

1. In the document to which you want to link the external style sheet, open the CSS Styles panel (Window → CSS Styles).

2. Click the Attach Style Sheet button ↵.

3. When the Link External Style Sheet dialog box appears, click the Link radio button. From there, click the Browse button.

4. In the Select Style Sheet File dialog box, navigate to the CSS file you wish to attach, select it, and click Select.

5. After the external style sheet has been attached to the document, notice that all of its style classes are accessible through the CSS Styles panel.

Redefined tags and CSS Selectors will automatically be applied to the document when the external style sheet is attached.

Inspiration: Design and Technique

Easily one of the oldest and most respected web design and development resources on the web, Webmonkey (`http://hotwired.lycos.com/webmonkey`) is not only a great place to go when you want to get the latest word in design, it's also a top-notch example of a content-heavy website whose design and layout is managed by Cascading Style Sheets (CSS).

Part of the Lycos network, Webmonkey (see Figure 13.4) features extremely useful and insightful articles, tutorials, and other resources on authoring, design, multimedia, e-business, programming, and back-end development. In addition, Webmonkey has cool features such as a library of downloadable JavaScript code, an HTML cheat sheet, and an extensive list of hex color codes.

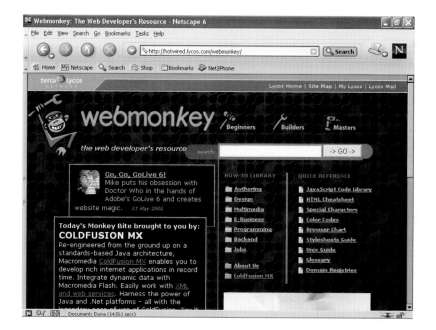

Figure 13.4

Webmonkey is not only a phenomenal design resource, but also an excellent example of a content-heavy site whose lay-out and design is managed by CSS.

Summary

In this chapter, you explored Cascading Style Sheets. You started off with a introductory dis-cussion about the nature, capabilities, and applications of style sheets and learned that there are some serious obstacles to complete adoption of CSS, primarily browser support issues.

From there, you jumped right in and engaged in a rather lengthy exploration of styles and their attributes. After that, you learned how to create, apply, and edit style sheets. You fin-ished off the chapter with a look at converting CSS styles to HTML markup, and finally, learned how to leverage the incredible power of external style sheets.

CHAPTER 14

Absolute Positioning with Layers

As has been mentioned before, the Web is not particularly well suited as a design medium. It's pretty difficult to get things looking exactly as you would like. This, however, was not much of a problem for the vast majority of the people who were using the Web in the early days of HTML. However, things started to change as more and more traditional print designers, who were accustomed to total control over their creations, began migrating into the world of web design. This is where DHTML comes into the picture. As you've already learned in previous chapters, Dynamic HTML has three very powerful features, one of which is the ability to position elements on a page using an absolute system of coordinates. This feature alone, which makes web design much more like traditional print design than ever before, is tremendously exciting.

As with many of the DHTML features that we've already discussed (and those that will be discussed in furture chapters), Dreamweaver makes the absolute positioning of elements, something that would be very time consuming and tedious if you had to hand-code the DHTML, quite effortless through the use of a great feature called layers.

In this chapter, you are going to explore the following topics:

- **Understanding layers**
- **Creating layers**
- **Manipulating layers**
- **Working with the Layers panel**

Creating Layers

The process of creating layers is quite easy, and, like many features in Dreamweaver, can be accomplished a number of different ways. In the following sections, you will look at how to create layers using the Insert menu and with the Insert bar.

Because layers are made possible by Dynamic HTML, they are only supported by browsers that are version 4.0 or above.

Creating a Layer with the Insert Menu

A layer can be inserted into your Dreamweaver Document using the Insert menu:

1. In the document into which you want to insert the layer, place your cursor where you'd like the layer to be initially placed.

2. Go to Insert → Layer. The top left-hand corner of the layer (which is created with a default size) is automatically inserted where your cursor is.

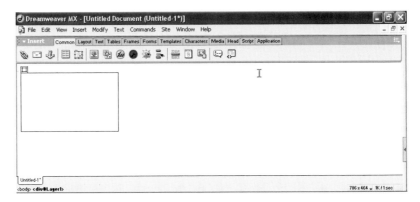

Creating a Layer with the Insert Bar

Because a layer is a specific kind of object within Dreamweaver, it can also be inserted into a document with the Insert bar. However, unlike with the Insert menu, you can also use the Insert bar to draw a layer:

1. In the document into which you want to insert the layer, open the Insert bar (Window → Insert) and select the Common tab (if it isn't already).

2. Click the Draw Layer button 🔲 . The Draw Layer button is also located under the Layout tab of the Insert bar.

3. Move your cursor to the location in your page where you want to create the layer—notice that your cursor has changed to crosshairs.

4. Click and drag so that the outlines are equal to the desired size of the layer.

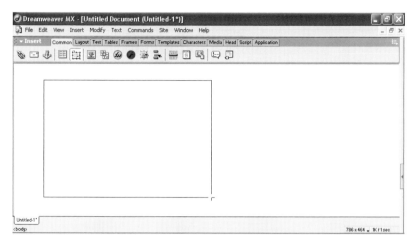

5. When the outlines are the dimensions you want the layer to be, release your mouse button.

If you have your document's invisible elements turned on, you'll notice that a small yellow icon is also inserted into the document. This represents the actual layer tag and can be clicked to select the particular layer. As with other invisible elements, this icon only appears when you're working within Dreamweaver. It won't be visible when your page is viewed in a browser.

Manipulating Layers

As you'd assume, the process of creating the layer is only the first step you need to take. While relatively simple looking, layers are fairly complicated objects that need a certain amount of massaging and manipulating to get the maximum use out of them. It behooves you to get intimately familiar with the different ways in which they can be manipulated

In this section, you'll get a chance to explore a bucket load of topics geared toward helping you get the most of layers.

Adding Content to a Layer

One of the benefits of layers is that content can be placed exactly where you want it within your page, and any content that can be added to a normal Dreamweaver document can be inserted into a layer. Thus, the first step in learning how to work with layers is to learn how to add content to them. To add content to a layer:

1. In the document where the layers reside, click your cursor any-where within the layer. When you do this, it will go from being *dormant* to being *live*: its edges turn solid black and a handle appears in the upper left-hand corner.

Dormant layer 　　　Live layer

2. After you confirm the cursor is inside the confines of the layer, follow the same procedure you'd follow to insert content into a page under normal circumstances. Remember, you can insert anything into a layer (text, images, multimedia, and so on).

> As has been mentioned before, the Web is not particularly well suited as a design medium. It's pretty difficult to get things looking exactly as you would like. This, however, was not much of a problem for the vast majority of the people who were using the Web in the early days of HTML. However, things started to change as more and more traditional print designers, who were accustomed to total control over their creations, began migrating into the world of web design. This is where DHTML comes into the picture.

Selecting a Layer

To manipulate a layer (whether it has any content or not), you must first select that layer:

1. In the document that has the layer you wish to select, choose one of the following options:

   • Click the edge of a dormant layer. If the layer is active (that is, you've clicked somewhere within it), but not selected, click its handle.

   • Click the layer's icon , which represents the layer's code and appears when the layer is initially inserted.

> If the layer's marker isn't visible, it's more than likely that your document has its invisible elements turned off (of which the layer marker is one). To turn them back on, go to View → Visual Aids → Invisible Elements. If it doesn't become visible, you might also have to turn the layer marker on using the Edit Preferences dialog box: go to Edit → Preferences, select Invisible Elements from the Category list, and click Anchor Points for Layers option.

2. When selected, the layer's resize handles will appear.

   In addition to the options described below, you can select a layer by going to Window → Others → Layers and clicking its name in the Layers panel. If you want to learn more about the Layers panel, see the section "Working with the Layers Panel" later in this chapter.

Deleting a Layer

You will probably reach the point where you'll want to delete a layer. While the process itself is pretty easy, it's extremely important to remember that if you delete a layer, all of its content goes in the garbage as well.

To delete a layer:

1. In the document that has the layer you wish to delete, select the layer using one of the methods described in the previous section.

2. Either press Delete/Backspace, or right/Cmd-click and choose Cut from the pop-up context menu.

Resizing a Layer

While when layers are created (whether with the Insert menu or the Insert bar), they have an initial width and height. Don't worry, their dimensions are hardly fixed: they can be changed on a whim using a number of different techniques. In this section, you'll look at how to change the dimensions of a layer both by dragging and with the Property Inspector.

A layer will automatically increase in size to accommodate new content.

Resizing a Layer by Dragging

One of the most intuitive and user friendly ways to resize a layer is by manually dragging its resize handles:

1. Select the layer that you want to resize and choose from the following options:

    - Click the handles in the middle of the layer's left or right sides to resize horizontally (top right).

    - Click and drag the handles in the middle of the layer's top or bottom to resize vertically (bottom right).

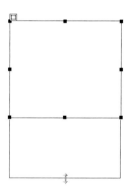

    - Click and drag the handles on any of the layer's four corners to resize both horizontally and vertically at the same time.

2. When the layer has reached the desired size, release your mouse button.

Resizing a Layer with the Property Inspector

While dragging is a great way to quickly and easily resize a layer, it doesn't offer you pixel-precise control. Say, for instance, you need a layer whose dimensions are 121×54. If you resized by dragging, it would be hit or miss. With the Property Inspector, however, you can set the exact dimensions of a layer:

1. Select the layer whose dimensions you want to change and open the Property Inspector (Window → Properties).

Layer width

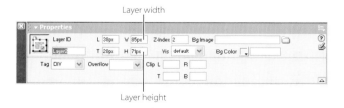

Layer height

2. Enter a value for the layer's width (in pixels) into the W field.

3. Enter a value for the layer's height (in pixels) into the H field.

4. Press Return (Mac)/ Enter (Win), or click anywhere off the Property Inspector to apply the changes.

> If your layer is populated with a fixed-size object (like an image), its size cannot be changed to be smaller than the object itself.

You can also resize the layer by using the keyboard. Just select the layer and press Option/Cmd+arrow, and it will be resized incrementally in the direction of the arrow key you're pressing.

Moving a Layer

Another benefit of layers is that they can be used to position content anywhere on your page. This means you have to be able to easily change their location. Once again, Dreamweaver provides you with two primary ways to move a layer: by dragging and with the Property Inspector.

Moving a Layer by Dragging

One of the easiest and most intuitive ways to move a layer is by dragging it:

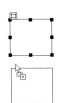

1. Select the layer you wish to move, click the layer's handle and drag it to its new location.

2. When it is in the location you wish, release your mouse button.

Moving a Layer with the Property Inspector

You can also move your layer using absolute units (pixels) relative to the top (Y) and left (X) of the page in which it resides:

1. Select the layer you want to move and open the Property Inspector (Window → Properties).

2. Enter a value (in pixels) into the L field for the distance from the left side of your page.

3. Enter a value (in pixels) into the T field for the distance from the top of the page.

4. Press Return (Mac)/ Enter (Win) or click anywhere off the Property Inspector.

Changing a Layer's Background Color

A cool feature of layers (which can be used in many different creative ways) is that their background color can be changed.

A layer's background color will always be overridden by a layer's background image.

To change a layer's background color:

1. Select the layer whose background color you wish to change and open the Property Inspector (Window → Properties).

2. Click on the Bg Color swatch to open the Color Palette.

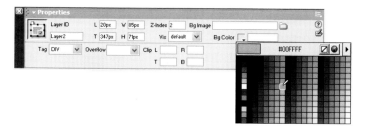

3. Click the color you wish to use for the layer's background. Remember, to mix your own custom color, you can always open the Color Picker by clicking the color wheel icon in the Color Palette.

Adding a Background Image to a Layer

You certainly aren't just limited to changing the background color of a layer; you can also add a background image.

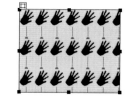

A layer's background image will tile to fill the entire layer.

To add a background image to a layer:

1. Select the layer to which you want to add a background image and open the Property Inspector (Window → Properties).

2. Click Browse to File.

3. When the Select Image Source dialog box appears, navigate to the location where the image is located, select it, and click Select.

Setting the Layer Overflow

A little earlier, we discussed how to resize a layer. I mentioned that, under normal circumstances, a layer will expand to accommodate content. However, there are situations when the layer's dimensions will have been set to be smaller than the content itself. In situations such as these, what happens to the extra content that is outside the confines of the layer? This is where something called *layer overflow* comes into the picture. Essentially, the four layers overflow settings determine how the browser copes with that extra content.

> If you are using any of Netscape's proprietary tags (`<layer>` and `<ilayer>`), a layer's overflow property will be totally ignored.

Unfortunately, layer overflow has pretty spotty browser support. Currently, only Netscape 6.x and Internet Explorer 4.0 or above can properly cope with layer overflow.

Keep in mind that Dreamweaver won't display a layer's overflow property. To see it, you'll need to preview the page in a browser.

To set the layer's overflow property:

1. Select the layer whose overflow property you wish to set and open the Property Inspector (Window → Properties).

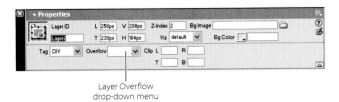

Layer Overflow
drop-down menu

2. From the Overflow drop-down menu, select one of the following options:

Visible The layer's dimensions will be totally ignored and all the content will be displayed.

Hidden The content that falls outside the layer will be cut off and not displayed.

Scroll Horizontal and vertical scrollbars will appear in the layer regardless of the layer's dimensions and the size of the content.

Auto Scrollbars will appear only if the size of the content exceeds the dimensions of the layer.

Setting Layer Visibility

Another cool feature of layers is that you can determine whether or not they are visible. On the surface, this might seem somewhat of a useless property over which to have control. Why create layer content only to make it invisible? However, when you think about the fact that the visibility of a layer can be controlled in Dreamweaver with behaviors (little snippets of JavaScript code, which will discuss more in Chapter 15, "Adding Advanced Interactivity with Behaviors"), the ability to control their visibility makes a lot more sense. For instance, you could have a layer appear when the user moves their mouse over a certain area in your web page, and then have it disappear when their mouse is moved away.

> Whether a layer is visible or not doesn't impact the amount of time it takes for it to load (or the amount of computer memory it consumes): invisible content loads at the same rate as visible content.

To set the visibility of a layer:

1. Select the layer whose visibility you want to set and open the Property Inspector (Window → Properties).

Visible drop-down menu

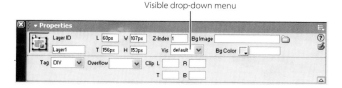

2. Select one of the options from the Visible drop-down menu:

Default Lets the browser determine whether or not the layer is visible. Most browsers use Inherit as their default setting for a layer's visibility.

Inherit Causes the visibility of all layers nested in one layer to be determined by the parent layer in which they are embedded.

Visible Causes the layer to be visible in the browser.

Hidden Forces the layer and all of its contents to be invisible in the browser.

Manipulating a Layer's Clipping Area

The clipping area is an interesting but not often used layer feature. Essentially, the clipping area acts as a mask that hides (and doesn't delete) the layer's contents outside a predefined square. The square is defined by four values: top, bottom, left, and right. The L (left) and R (right) sides of the clipped area are measured from the left side of the layer. The T (top) and B (bottom) sides of the clipped area are measured from the top of the layer.

To set a layer's clipping area:

1. Select the layer whose clipping area you wish to set and open the Property Inspector (Window → Properties).

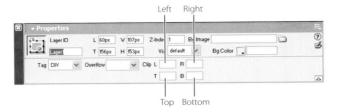

2. Enter a value (in pixels) for the left side of the visible area into the L field.

3. Enter a value (in pixels) for the right side of the visible area into the R field. If the value for the right side of the visible area is not larger than that of the left side, the layer's content will be totally invisible.

4. Enter a value (in pixels) for the top of the visible area into the T field.

5. Enter a value (in pixels) for the bottom of the visible area in the B field. If the value for the bottom of the visible area is larger for that of the top, the layer's content will be invisible.

6. Press Return (Mac)/ Enter (Win) or click anywhere off the Property Inspector.

Understanding and Changing a Layer's Tag

Just like any other element in a web page, a layer is represented by a specific HTML tag. However, unlike many other elements, a layer can actually be represented by one of four different tags, each of which has specific characteristics.

To change a layer's tag:

1. Select the layer whose tag you wish to change and open the Property Inspector (Window → Properties).

2. Choose one of the tags from the Tag drop-down menu:

<div> Sanctioned by the World Wide Web Consortium (W3C), it uses absolute positioning and an integrated paragraph break.

<span> Also sanctioned by the W3C, it uses relative positioning without an integrated paragraph break.

<layer> Not sanctioned by the W3C, it is *only* supported by Netscape 4.0.

<ilayer> Also not sanctioned by the W3C and also *only* supported by Netscape 4.0.

> Both <layer> and <ilayer> have a series of additional properties. First, you can choose among two types of X/Y relationships between a nested layer and its parent. Top & Left refers to the regular relationship of nested layer to the top-left corner of its parent layer. PageX/PageY, on the other hand, alters a nested layer's location so that it is located in relation to the top left-hand corner of the page rather than to the parent layer.

Working with the Layers Panel

While the vast majority of the stuff you can do to layers is carried out with the help of the Property Inspector, there is an additional tool with which you can manipulate and manage the layers in your document: the Layers panel.

Accessible by going to Window → Others → Layers, the Layers panel lists all of the current layers in your document and lets you rename a layer, prevent layer overlap, set the stacking order of your layers, nest layers, and set layer visibility.

Layer visibility

Naming a Layer with the Layers Panel

By default, when you create a layer (either with the Insert menu or the Insert bar), it is created with a standard default name: Layer1, Layer2, Layer3, and so on. To give the layers in your page a new name:

> If you want to use a behavior to control the way a given layer behaves, it will need a unique name.

1. From the document where the layer you wish to rename resides, open the Layers panel (Window → Others → Layers).

2. Double-click the layer name.

3. When the Layer Name field becomes active, type in a new name.

4. Press Return (Mac)/ Enter (Win) or click anywhere off the Layers panel.

Preventing Layer Overlap

Another cool feature of layers is that, because they can be positioned anywhere on a page, they can be placed on top of one another (see Figure 14.1). The relationship between layers in a stack (that is, which one is on top) is set by the Z Index, something we'll discuss shortly.

Figure 14.1

Layers can be placed on top of one another, creating an overlap.

However, you'll probably encounter a situation in which you'll want to prevent the layers from overlapping. To do this:

1. In the page in which you wish to prevent layer overlap, open the Layers panel (Window → Others → Layers).

2. Click Prevent Overlaps option. The Prevent Overlap option affects all layers on the page.

Setting Layer Stacking Order

When two or more layers overlap, a spatial relationship is instantly established determining the position of all the layers in an imaginary three-dimensional stack. You can think about overlapping layers as a stack of papers. If one of the sheets of paper is at the bottom of the pile, its content might only be partially visible, depending on how the remainder of the sheets are positioned. On the other hand, the sheet on the top of the stack will have all of its content visible.

The order of each layer in the stack, called the *Z-Index* (which is represented by a numerical value), can be manipulated to your heart's content using the Layers panel:

1. From the page in which you wish to prevent layer overlap, open the Layers panel (Window → Others → Layers).

2. Double click the layer's Z-Index.

3. When the Z-Index field becomes editable, enter a new value (remember, a high number means a higher place in the stack).

4. To apply your changes, press Return (Mac)/ Enter (Win) or click anywhere off the Layers panel. The layers displayed in the Layers panel will automatically reorganize themselves in the new stacking order.

The lower a layer's Z-Index, the lower it will be in the stack.

You can also change a layer's Z-Index by using the Property Inspector.

Nesting Layers

When you nest layers, you place one layer within another. The layer in which the other is placed acts as a parent, partially controlling the nested layer's properties. When you move the parent layer, the nested child layer moves as well.

To nest two layers using the Layers panel:

1. From the document that contains the layer you wish to nest, open the Layers panel (Window → Layers).

2. In the Layers panel, holding down Cmd/Ctrl, click and drag the layer you wish to nest and move your cursor over the layer you wish to act as the parent. Notice that the cursor will change to a document icon, and the target parent layer will be highlighted with a faint blue box.

3. When your cursor is over the layer that will act as the parent, release your mouse. Notice that an expand/collapse icon will appear to the left of the parent layer, and the child layer will be represented as a subset of the parent.

Setting Layer Visibility

Earlier in this chapter, we discussed how to set the visibility of a layer using the Property Inspector. You can also change the visibility of a layer with the Layers panel:

1. From the document which contains the layer you wish to nest, open the Layers panel by going to Window → Others → Layers.

2. Click the "eyeball" column to set a layer's visibility:

   - A closed eye (bottom left) indicates that the layer's visibility has been set to hidden.

   - An open eye (bottom right) means that the layer's visibility has been set to visible.

   - No eyeball means that the layer's visibility has been set to Inherit, which causes the visibility of all layers nested in one layer to be determined by the parent layer in which they are embedded.

Inspiration: Design and Technique

Jump aboard the Mojovator, baby! Mojovator? What the heck is a Mojovator? It's one of the landmarks in Mojotown (www.mojotown.com), a terribly groovy Flash-based virtual talent agency specializing in anything digital, interactive, or just plain cool.

Mojotown's website (see Figure 14.2) is not *just* a website; it's pretty close to a life-altering experience. Featuring incredibly stylish and sophisticated environment and character design, the website is a definite must for anyone looking for a bucketload of inspiration. Besides, anyone who could come up with the title *Superphonic Rockonauts* for a series of web-animated shorts can't be all that bad!

Summary

In this chapter, you embarked on an exploration of layers. As mentioned, layers, which are a feature of Dynamic HTML, allow you to position elements on your page according to a set of absolute coordinates. You learned how to create layers using both the Insert menu and the Insert bar, how to manipulate layers, and how to use the Layers panel.

In the next chapter, you'll continue your voyage in the land of Dreamweaver and Dynamic HTML with an exploration of behaviors.

Figure 14.2

The groovy streets of Mojotown

CHAPTER 15

Adding Advanced Interactivity with Behaviors

One of the most important features of Dynamic HTML (DHTML) is the ability to tightly integrate a scripting language (most commonly JavaScript or VBScript) with HTML. Granted, people were using JavaScript in web pages before DHTML hit the scene. However, this cool new relationship between HTML and JavaScript lets you create some cool eye-candy as well as some genuinely useful widgets that were previously impossible.

In Dreamweaver, a behavior is a small little JavaScript program that, through the help of some pretty snazzy tools, can be easily integrated into your document and used to extend the interactivity and usability of your HTML creation. The great thing about behaviors is that, with a relative minimum of effort, they can immediately be put to work without you having to learn how to hand-code JavaScript. This alone makes them one of the most exciting features in Dreamweaver.

In this chapter, you'll explore the following topics:

- **Understanding behaviors**
- **Inserting behaviors**
- **Modifying and manipulating a behavior**
- **Working with standard Dreamweaver behaviors**
- **Integrating new behaviors**

Understanding Behaviors

Interactivity is a buzzword that is often used in conjunction with the Web. Well, truth be told, until recently, straight HTML design (as opposed to Flash or Shockwave) wasn't particularly interactive. Generally speaking, one clicked a hyperlink, and a new HTML document was loaded into the browser, and that was it—not particularly interactive. However, this changed a fair amount when DHTML started being used.

One of the most important features of DHTML is the ability to tightly combine JavaScript (and sometimes VBScript) with standard HTML to create truly interactive features in a website (relative to what was available previous to DHTML). While this feature was great, it was still well out of reach of most casual (or even experienced) designers. JavaScript, while certainly easier to write than other computer languages such as C, C++, or Pascal, was hardly a walk in the park. JavaScript is an object-oriented scripting language that definitely takes a good deal of dedication and brainsweat to learn.

Never one to follow, Dreamweaver was the first visual web design software to integrate a highly user-friendly way to insert tiny little JavaScript programs, which they call behaviors, into HTML documents. The program takes care of all the back-end JavaScript structure, leaving the designer free to focus on the best way to integrate a given behavior's interactive features into their document.

Structurally speaking, when you insert a behavior into your document (which is done with the use of Dreamweaver's Behavior panel), the bulk of its JavaScript is inserted into the <head> portion of the HTML document. However, if the behavior is associated with an object (an image, etc.), you'll see some JavaScript in the <body> portion of the HTML source code.

While not often referred to in this manner, there are really only two types of behaviors: those that function in concert with the page itself (page behaviors) and those that are associated with a specific object (object behaviors). This doesn't mean that there are specific page behaviors and specific object behaviors—quite the contrary. Whether a behavior is a page behavior or an object behavior depends solely on the HTML tag to which they are attached. For instance, if a behavior is attached to a page's <body> tag, it becomes a page behavior. However, if the same behavior is associated with the <img> tag of one of the page's images, for example, it becomes an object behavior.

DESIGN REMINDER: Behaviors and Browser Madness

As you already learned in the "Browser Madness" section of Chapter 1, "Web Design: The Big Picture," all browsers don't universally support DHTML (and therefore don't support behaviors). Generally speaking, because behaviors take advantage of DHTML's integration of HTML and JavaScript, you'll find that most require a 4.0 browser or above to function properly. This, however, isn't always the case. Some pre-4.0 browsers had better integrated JavaScript HTML support than others. The bottom line is that you always need to test your behavior-enhanced document in various browsers to ensure it works.

The Action/Event Equation

A behavior is made up of two discrete parts, an *event* and an *action*. On the whole, the event/action equation is a fairly simple concept to understand. For a behavior to work, the user must first do something (this is the event): load a page, move their mouse over a certain object, press a key on their keyboard, or click a certain object. When that event has happened, the JavaScript behavior (the action) executes. It's a basic cause and effect kind of relationship. The event (which is user driven) must happen for the action to occur.

When you insert a behavior into your document, you must set the event, which is represented in the Behavior panel by something called an *event handler*. Basically, an event handler is JavaScript code for a specific user action. But don't worry too much, event handlers, even though they are syntactically JavaScript, are pretty self explanatory and easy to work with.

There are, however, a few other details you should know when it comes to understanding event handlers. First, some events are browser specific. Don't worry about having to know which ones work with which browsers: Dreamweaver will provide a list of all the appropriate events based on the behaviors' target browser (which you can set in the Behavior panel). Second, because behaviors are associated with specific HTML elements (something we'll discuss in a bit), different event handlers will be made available depending on the way the behavior is being used.

Even though it may seem a little boring, it's wise for you to get familiar with all the most commonly used event handlers:

onAbort Occurs when the user clicks Stop or presses Esc before a page or an image loads. The onAbort event, which works with Netscape 3.0 or above and Internet Explorer 4.0 or above, can be associated either with the <body> (a page) and <img> (an image) tags.

onAfterUpdate Occurs when the content of a text or form field changes. onAfterUpdate is only compatible with Internet Explorer 4.0 or above.

onBeforeUpate Occurs when the content of a text or form field changes before the element loses focus.

onBlur Occurs when the given object is no longer the focus of the user's attention—for example, when the user clicks elsewhere after having clicked in a form's text field. The onBlur event, which functions with Netscape 3.0 or above and Internet Explorer 3.0 or above, can be associated with images and form elements.

onChange Occurs when the user changes the default selection or content in a form element, such as a drop-down menu or a text field. Compatible with Netscape 3.0 or above and Internet Explorer 3.0 or above.

onClick Occurs when the user clicks an object within a page. The event will not take place until the mouse button is released. Compatible with Netscape 3.0 or above and Internet Explorer 3.0 or above.

onDblClick Occurs when a user double-clicks an object within a page. Compatible with Netscape 4.0 or Internet Explorer 4.0 or above.

onError Occurs when a browser or JavaScript error occurs when either a page or an image is loading. Compatible with Netscape 3.0 or above and Internet Explorer 4.0 or above.

onFocus Occurs when a page element, such as a form element, becomes the focus of the user's attention. For example, a form's text field comes into focus when the user clicks within the field. Compatible with Netscape 3.0 or above or Internet Explorer 3.0 or above.

onHelp Occurs when the user clicks their browser's help button or chooses the Help function from the browser's menu. Compatible only with Internet Explorer 4.0 or above.

onKeyDown Occurs when the user presses any key on their keyboard. The key itself does not have to be released for the event to occur. Compatible with Netscape 3.0 or above and Internet Explorer 3.0 or above.

onKeyPress Occurs when the user presses and releases any key on their keyboard. Compatible with Netscape 3.0 or above and Internet Explorer 3.0 or above.

onKeyUp Occurs when any key on the user's keyboard is released after it's depressed. Compatible with Netscape 4.0 and Internet Explorer 4.0 or above.

onLoad Occurs when a page or image has finished loading. Compatible with Netscape 3.0 or above and Internet Explorer 3.0 or above.

onMouseDown Occurs when the user depresses their mouse button. The mouse button does not have to be released for the event to occur. Compatible with Netscape 4.0 or above and Internet Explorer 4.0 or above.

onMouseMove Occurs when the user points their cursor at the object to which the behaviors are attached (an image, for example) and moves their mouse. Compatible with Netscape 6.0 and Internet Explorer 3.0 or above.

onMouseOut Occurs when the user moves their cursor off the object to which the behavior has been attached. Compatible with Netscape 3.0 or above and Internet Explorer 4.0 or above.

onMouseOver Occurs when the user moves their cursor over the object to which the behavior has been attached. Compatible with Netscape 3.0 or above and Internet Explorer 3.0.

onMouseUp Occurs when a depressed mouse button is released. Compatible with Netscape 4.0 or above and Internet Explorer 4.0 or above.

onReset Occurs when a user clicks a forms' Reset button. Compatible with Netscape 3.0 or above and Internet Explorer 3.0 or above.

onResize Occurs when the user resizes their browser window. Compatible with Netscape 3.0 or above and Internet Explorer 3.0 or above.

onScroll Occurs when the browser's scrollbar is used. Compatible only with Internet Explorer 4.0 or above.

onSelect Occurs when the user selects text within a form field. Compatible with Netscape 3.0 or above and Internet Explorer 3.0 or above.

onSubmit Occurs when the user clicks a form's Submit button. Compatible with Netscape 3.0 or above and Internet Explorer 3.0 or above.

onUnload Occurs when a user leaves a page by clicking another hyperlink or hitting the Back button. Compatible with Netscape 3.0 or above and Internet Explorer 3.0 or above.

There are some additional esoteric event handlers that are not covered in this list. If you are interested in finding out how they work, refer to Dreamweaver's help function: Help → Using Dreamweaver.

Inserting Behaviors

Now that you've spent ample time exploring the mechanics of behaviors, it's time to learn how to integrate them into your document.

The following section will not focus on behavior-specific settings. Instead, it will give you the general, step-by-step process you need to go through to insert a behavior (any behavior) into your document. You'll learn about specific behaviors, and how to work with their properties, later in this chapter.

To insert a behavior into your document:

1. In the document into which you wish to insert the behavior, open the Behavior panel by going to Window → Behaviors.

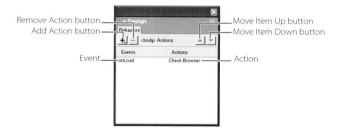

2. Depending on what you wish to attach the behavior to (the page or an object), choose from the following options:

- If you wish to attach the behavior to an object, select the specific object. The selected object's tag shows up in the title bar of the Behavior panel.

- If you wish to attach the behavior to the page itself, click your cursor anywhere in the document window, making sure you don't select anything or click within a table. Alternatively, you can select the <body> tag in the Tag Selector (located in the Document Window). Once you do this, the <body> tag will show up in the Behavior panel's title bar.

3. Click the Add Action button ▢, go to Show Events For, and choose the intended target browser. This sets the available events for the behavior. Remember, some events don't work with certain browsers.

4. Click the Add Action button again, and choose the specific action (behavior) you'd like attached to the selected object.

5. When the dialog box for that specific action pops up, set the necessary properties and click OK.

> For a detailed description of what each behavior does and how you can set its properties, see the "Working with Standard Dreamweaver Behaviors" section later in this chapter.

6. To set the behavior's event, click the small down pointing arrow just to the behavior's event to open the Event drop-down menu.

7. Select a specific event to trigger the action (behavior). Remember, the list of available events was limited when you chose the target browser in step 3.

You can easily add more than one action for a single object. Just select the object again and repeat steps 3-7. You can also easily add multiple events for a single action by selecting the same object, repeating steps 4-7, and choosing an additional event for the same action.

Managing and Manipulating Behaviors

As with most elements you work with in Dreamweaver, behaviors would be pretty useless if you weren't able to go back and edit them. In this section, you'll explore how to go back and fiddle with behaviors after you insert them into your document. Topics that will be covered include how to change the properties of a behavior, how to delete a behavior, and how to change the order of actions.

Changing the Properties of a Behavior

There are certain behaviors that have detailed properties that are set when they're initially inserted into a document. You'll explore specific Dreamweaver behaviors in the "Working with Standard Dreamweaver Behaviors" section later in this chapter.

During the course of your design, you'll probably find yourself in a situation where you'll need to go back and change the properties of a behavior you used previously. To change the properties of a behavior:

1. Select the object to which the behavior you wish to edit is attached. If you are editing a page behavior (a behavior that's been attached to the <body> tag), place your cursor anywhere in the document (don't select anything or place the cursor in a table). Alternately, you can select the <body> tag in the Document Window's Tag Inspector.

2. If it isn't already, open the Behavior panel (Window → Behavior).

3. Double-click the action you wish to edit.

4. When the action's dialog box appears, make your changes and click OK.

Deleting a Behavior

When you insert a behavior into your document, you certainly aren't stuck with it—you can quite easily delete it. To delete a behavior:

1. Select the object to which the behavior you wish to delete is attached. If you are deleting a page behavior (a behavior that's been attached to the <body> tag), pace your cursor anywhere in the document (don't select anything or place the cursor in a table). Alternately, you can select the <body> tag in the Document Window's Tag Inspector.

2. If it isn't already, open the Behavior panel (Window → Behavior).

3. Select the action (behavior) you would like to delete.

4. Click the Remove Action button ▬. Alternatively, you can press Backspace/Delete.

Changing the Order of a Behavior

As I mentioned earlier, you can have multiple actions attached to an object or multiple actions attached to a single event. In cases like these, the actions themselves will execute from top to bottom in the Behavior panel. While the default sequence is established by the order you attach the individual actions, you can easily change it to suit your needs.

When would you need to reorder the actions (behavior) attached to a specific object? Say, for instance, you had a splash page in which you had placed an Enter My Site button. When the user clicks the button, your site opens in a browser window with fixed dimensions (created and controlled by using Dreamweaver's Open Browser Window behavior). Now, because your site also has DHTML elements, you used the Check Browser behavior to make sure the user's browser is 4.0 or above. This behavior also executes when the user clicks the Enter My Site button. However, for this system to work properly, you need to check the user's browser before you launch your site. As a result, you would have to be absolutely sure the Check Browser action is placed above the Open Browser Window behavior in the Behavior panel.

To change the order of a behavior in the Behavior panel:

1. Select the object to which the behavior you wish to reorder is attached. If you are reordering a page behavior (a behavior that's been attached to the <body> tag), place your cursor anywhere in the document (don't select anything or place the cursor in a table). Alternately, you can select the <body> tag in the Document Window's Tag Inspector.

2. If it isn't already, open the Behavior panel (Window → Behavior).

3. Select the action (behavior) you would like to reorder and choose from the following options:

    - Click the Up arrow ▲ to move the action up in the stack. Each time you click the Up arrow, the action will be moved one position upward.

    - Click the Down arrow ▼ to move the action down in the stack. Each time you hit the Down button, the action will be moved one position downward.

Working with Standard Dreamweaver Behaviors

Dreamweaver comes with a host of behaviors that let you do a whole range of interesting things. Want to check the user's browser for a certain plug-in or make sure they are using a specific version or browser? How about creating a pop-up message or a rollover? All of these things and many more are possible with standard Dreamweaver behaviors.

In this section, you'll learn how to work with the most common standard Dreamweaver behaviors. For the sake of economy, it's assumed that you're already familiar with how to insert a behavior and set its event. The following discussion will pick up at the point in the process of inserting a behavior where you choose the action from the Behavior panel's Add Action drop-down menu and will not rehash how you set the action's event.

Because a thorough and exhaustive exploration would be outside the scope of this chapter, some behaviors have been excluded—most notably the Change Property and Set Navbar behaviors. In addition, how to create a Jump Menu (which is controlled by the Jump Menu behavior) was covered in Chapter 10, "Working with Forms." Also, because they'll be discussed in Chapter 16, "Animating with the Timeline Tool," timeline-specific behaviors will be skipped over as well.

Calling JavaScript

JavaScript is a very versatile scripting language that lets you do far more than is available with Dreamweaver's prepackaged JavaScript behaviors. You can just as easily open up Code View and write your own JavaScript directly into the HTML source code. However, for those who might be just starting to learn JavaScript, the prospect of hand coding might seem a little daunting. This is where the Call JavaScript action comes in. It lets you enter some JavaScript into a dialog box that will be executed when a given event occurs.

To use the Call JavaScript action:

1. With the item to which you wish to attach the Call JavaScript behavior selected and with the Behavior panel open, click the Add Action button.

2. Select Call JavaScript.

3. When the Call JavaScript dialog box pops up, type the code into the JavaScript field.

4. When you finish entering the JavaScript into the field, click OK.

5. Click the small down-pointing arrow to the right of the behavior's event to open the Event drop-down menu.

6. Select the specific event you'd like to trigger the Call JavaScript action. Remember, you can limit the available events by selecting a target browser from the Add Action drop-down menu's Show Events For submenu.

Checking for a Plug-in

As you learned back in Chapter 11, "Inserting and Manipulating Multimedia," There are many types of media you can use that aren't natively supported by most browsers and that therefore require a plug-in to display properly.

Plug-ins are a double-edged sword. With them, you are free to incorporate incredibly cool stuff like Flash, Shockwave, or digital video into your page. However, because they aren't part of the browser itself, you can never be absolutely sure whether the user has the necessary plug-in to view your content. If they don't, they'll need to download it, a prospect which can often be particularly frustrating.

What if you could get your website to check the user's browser for necessary plug-ins and then automatically direct them to your main site (if they've got the plug-in necessary) or an alternate page (if they don't)? Well, if you hadn't figured it out by the title of this section, Dreamweaver has a behavior to do just that!

To use the Check Plug-in action:

1. With the item to which you wish to attach the Check Plug-in behavior selected and with the Behavior panel open, click the Add Action button.

2. Select Check Plug-in

3. From here, the Check Plug-in dialog box will open.

4. At this point, you've got a couple of options:

   - Click the Select Plug-in option, and then choose the specific plug-in from the Plug-in drop-down menu.

   - If the plug-in for which you'd like to check is not available in the Plug-in drop-down menu, choose the Enter Plug-in option and type in the name of the plug-in *exactly* as it appears in Netscape's About Plug-ins page. To open Netscape's About Plug-ins page, go to Navigator's Help → About Plug-ins command (on a Windows machine) or select About Plug-ins from the Apple menu (on a Mac).

5. Click the Browse button to the right of the If Found, Go to URL field. When the Select File dialog box appears, navigate to the location of the page you wish to load if the browser confirms the presence of the desired plug-in, select it, and click Select.

6. Click the Browse button to the right of the Otherwise, Go To URL field. When the Select File dialog box appears, navigate to the location of the page you wish to load if the user's browser doesn't have the necessary plug-in, select it, and click Select.

7. Select the Always Go to First URL if Detection Is Not Possible option.

8. When you finish setting all of the Check Plug-in behavior's properties, click OK.

Checking the Version of a Browser

As you've learned at various points throughout this book (especially in Chapter 1), there are many different browsers out there that have varying levels of support for different web technologies. Given the fact that at some point during the design process, you are going to want to take advantage of some of the groovier web technologies, such as Cascading Style Sheets, behaviors, or absolute positioning, how do you cope with users who don't have the most up-to-date browsers? It's an incredibly bad move to create a website which isn't accessible or doesn't offer a lower tech alternative. What's the solution? Well, as was the case with the

Check Plug-in behavior, Dreamweaver offers you the Check Browser behavior, which will check the version of the browser and send the user to an appropriate page.

Logistically speaking, it's a good idea to attach the Check Browser behavior to the link which leads to your site proper. This way, you can check the version/make of the user's browser *before* they get to the place where they actually need specific software. Alternatively, you could also attach the Check Browser behavior to the page (the <body> tag) itself.

To use the Check Browser behavior:

1. With the item to which you wish to attach the Check Browser behavior selected and with the Behavior panel open, click the Add Action button.

2. Select Check Browser

3. From here, the Check Browser dialog box will open.

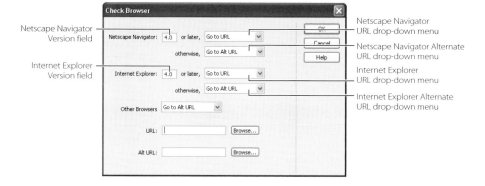

4. Enter the earliest version of Netscape that supports the features you are employing in your web page into the Netscape Navigator Version field.

5. Choose the location (Stay on the Page, Go to Alt URL, or Go to URL) you'd like to send users whose browser is the version of Netscape you indicated (or later) from the Netscape URL drop-down menu.

6. Choose the location (Stay on the Page, Go to Alt URL, or Go to URL) you'd like to send users whose browser is lower than the version of Netscape you indicated from the Netscape Alternate URL drop-down menu.

7. Enter the earliest version of Internet Explorer that supports the features you are employing in your web page into the Internet Explorer Version field.

8. Choose the location (Stay on the Page, Go to Alt URL, or Go to URL) you'd like to send users whose browser is the version of Internet Explorer you indicated (or later) from the Internet Explorer URL drop-down menu.

9. Choose the location (Stay on the Page, Go to Alt URL, or Go to URL) you'd like to send users whose browser is lower than the version of Internet Explorer you indicated from the Internet Explorer Alternate URL drop-down menu.

10. Choose the location (Stay on the Page, Go to Alt URL, or Go to URL) you'd like to send users who are using any browser other than Netscape Navigator or Internet Explorer from the Other Browsers drop-down menu.

11. Now you need to establish which file will act as the primary URL and Alt URL. First, click the Browse button to the right of the URL field.

12. When the Select file dialog box opens, navigate to the location where the page that will act as the primary URL is to be found, select it, and click the Select button. Alternatively, you can type an absolute URL into the URL field.

13. Now, click the Browse button to the right of the Alt URL field.

14. When the Select file dialog box opens, navigate to the location where the page that will act as the Alt URL is to be found, select it, and click the Select button. Alternatively, you can type an absolute URL into the Alt URL field.

15. When you finish, click OK.

You can also use the Check Browser behavior to redirect the user's browser to a version of your site that has been tailored specifically for either Netscape or Internet Explorer, depending on which one the user is using.

Controlling Shockwave or Flash Movies

With the help of the Control Shockwave or Flash behavior, you can play, stop, rewind, or jump to a specific frame of a Flash or Shockwave movie.

> To use the Control Shockwave or Flash behavior, a Shockwave or Flash movie must have been inserted into your page using the <object> or <embed> tag. For more information on working with Flash and Shockwave movies, see Chapter 11.

To use the Control Shockwave or Flash behavior:

1. With the item to which you wish to attach the Control Shockwave or Flash behavior selected and with the Behavior panel open, click the Add Action button.

2. Select Control Shockwave or Flash

3. From here, the Control Shockwave or Flash dialog box will open.

4. Select the Flash or Shockwave movie you wish to manipulate from the Movie drop-down menu.

The names that appear in the Movie drop-down menu are not the actual filenames. Instead, they are the unique names that were given by using the Property Inspector's name field, which is located in the extreme left-hand side of the Property Inspector (to the right of the Flash/Shockwave icon) when a Flash or Shockwave movie is selected.

5. Depending on what exactly you want to do, select one of the options (Play, Stop, or Rewind). If you wish the movie to jump to a specific frame, select the Go to Frame option and enter a specific frame number into the field.

6. Click OK.

Dragging a Layer

One of the coolest things about Layers (which were discussed in Chapter 14, "Absolute Positioning with Layers") is that they don't have to be static, fixed elements on your page. With the help of the Drag Layer behavior, you can create a layer that your user can interactively move around their browser. If you aren't sure how to either create or name a layer, see Chapter 14.

Unfortunately, the Drag Layer behavior is not compatible with Netscape 6.0.

To use the Drag Layer behavior:

1. Make sure you have a named layer inserted in your document.

2. Because the Drag Layer behavior will only work if it's attached to the page, you need to select the page's <body> tag with the Tag Inspector or click your cursor anywhere within the page itself (but be careful not to select anything or place your cursor in a tab).

3. With the Behavior panel open, click the Add Action button.

4. Select Drag Layer.

5. From here, the Drag Layer dialog box will open.

6. Make sure the Basic tab is open and then choose the Layer you wish to make dragable from the Layer drop-down menu.

Because each layer is a unique item with unique coordinates, you need to add a new Drag Layer behavior for each individual layer.

7. From here, you have a couple of choices:

    - If you want the user to be able to drag the layer anywhere within the browser window, choose Unconstrained from the Movement drop-down menu.

    - If you wish to restrict the movement of a layer, choose Constrained from the Movement drop-down menu.

      When you do this, you'll notice that four additional fields appear (Up, Down, Left, Right). The values you enter into these fields represent (in pixels) the edges of the constrained area and are relative to the original position of the layer's top left-hand corner.

8. From here, you can set a drop target. Essentially, a drop target is a specific location in the page where you want the user to drag the layer. A layer is considered to have reached the drop target when its left and top coordinates match the coordinates you enter.

9. Enter a value into the Left field. This represents the distance in pixels of the drop target from the left side of the Document Window.

10. Enter a value into the Top field. This represents the distance in pixels of the drop target from the top of the Document window.

> If you wish to get the current coordinates of the layer's drop target (its top left-hand corner), click the Get Current Position button, and the Top and Left fields will be automatically filled in.

11. If you want the layer to automatically snap to its drop target within a certain area (as opposed to just the coordinates themselves), enter a value (in pixels) for the distance into the Snap if Within field.

12. From here, you can move into the more advanced properties of the Drag Layer behavior. If you are interested in creating a simple puzzle or manipulatable scene, you don't have to delve into the Advanced properties. However, if you wish to, start off by clicking the Advanced tab in the Drag Layer dialog box. This will give you access to the Advanced section of the Drag Layer dialog box.

13. To start off with, you have two choices for the location of the layer's handle. (A layer's handle is the specific area that can be used to click and drag the layer itself.)

- To make the entire layer act as the handle (that is, to allow the user to click and drag anywhere in the layer itself), choose Entire Layer from the Drag Handle drop-down menu.

- If you wish to define a specific area in which the user needs to click to drag the Layer, choose Area Within Layer from the Drag Handle drop-down menu.

  When you do this, you'll notice that four additional fields appear (L, T, W, and H). The values you enter into these fields represent (in pixels) the left (L), top (T), width (W), and height (H) of the drag handle area. The values themselves are measured from the top and left of the layer.

  Remember, if you define a specific handle within the layer, it won't be visible. You might want to include some sort of visual indicator (for example, a button) that is placed exactly in the same location at the defined drag handle area so the user will know where to click and drag.

14. If you wish the layer's Z-Index to change when the user drags it, select the When Dragging, Bring Layer to Front option.

15. From here, you need to decide what happens to the layer (in terms of its Z-Index) once it's released:

- If you want it to be placed on the top of the layer "stack" (and therfore overlay all other layers), choose Leave on Top from the When Dragging drop-down menu (to the right of the When Dragging Bring to Front check box).

- If you want the layer to be stuck back in its original place in the Z-Index, choose Restore Z-Index from the When Dragging drop-down menu.

16. If you want some JavaScript to be executed while the layer is being dragged, enter the code or function name into the Call JavaScript field.

17. If you want some JavaScript to be executed when the layer is released, enter the code or function name into the When Dropped Call JavaScript field. The JavaScript entered into the When Dropped Call JavaScript field will execute regardless of where the layer is released by the user.

18. If you wish the JavaScript that you entered into the When Dropped Call JavaScript field to be executed when the layer is released in the drop target area, select the Only if Snapped option.

19. When you finish setting the Drag Layer behavior's properties, click OK.

Going to a URL

One of the biggest drawbacks of using standard hyperlinks (either with text or an image) is that it's impossible to load multiple documents into multiple frames or windows with a single click of the mouse. Granted, the one click/one load document equation isn't usually that limiting. However, if you are doing anything moderately complex with frames, it's vital that you be able to load different files into different frames with a single click. This is where the Go to URL behavior enters the picture. With it, you can load up any number of documents in any number of frames with a single click of the mouse.

To use the Go to URL behavior:

1. With the item to which you with to attach the Go To URL behavior selected and with the Behavior panel open, click the Add Action button.

2. Select Go To URL

3. When the Go To URL dialog box pops up (shown below-left), select the frame into which you'd like to load the URL from the Open In list box. (If you don't have any frames in your document, the only option in the Open In: field will be Main Window.)

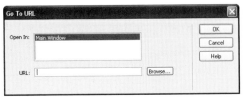

4. Now, you need to select the actual file which is loaded into the selected frame. To do this, click the Browse button (to the right of the URL field). When the Select File dialog box opens, navigate to where the desired file is located, select it, and click the Select button.

5. Repeat steps 3 and 4 to load additional files into additional frames.

6. When you finish, click OK.

Opening a Browser Window

I'm sure in your travels on the Web you've noticed sites (there are quite a few) that will load up a page into a browser window that has a fixed size. In addition, these fixed-size windows often aren't adorned with the usual browser window accoutrements (like scrollbar, navigational toolbar, drop-down menu, and son on). When used properly, this is definitely a cool design technique. Well, with the help of Dreamweaver's Open Browser Window behavior, you can do it also:

1. Select the item to which you would like to attach the Open Browser Window Behavior (it can be text, an image, or even the page itself).

2. If it isn't already, open the Behavior panel (Window →
   Behaviors).

3. Click the Add Action button and select Open Browser
   Window.

4. This will open the Open Browser Window dialog box (shown
   to the right).

5. The first thing you need to do is set the actual file that will be loaded up into the opened
   browser window. To do this, click the Browse button (to the right of the URL to Display
   field). When the Select File dialog box pops up, navigate to the location of the intended
   file, select it, and click Select. Alternatively, you can type the URL (either absolute or
   relative) into the URL to Display field.

6. Enter a value (in pixels) for the width of the browser window into the Window Width field.

7. Enter a value (in pixels) for the height of the browser window into the Window Height
   field.

8. From here, select the attributes you would like *included* (as opposed to those you
   would like to exclude) in your opened browser window.

9. Enter a unique name for your window into the Window Name field. For the behavior to
   work properly, it must have unique name that contains no spaces or special characters.

10. When you finish, click OK.

Playing a Sound

Back in Chapter 11, you learned that you could either embed or link to an audio file. But
what if you wanted to create a more interactive audio experience, such as a sound playing
when someone moved their mouse over a particular object? This is where the Play Sound
behavior comes in. As its name suggests, it can be used to play an audio file.

> It's important to remember that the only types of audio that are natively supported by *most*
> browsers is WAV, AIFF, and AU. If you want to use the behavior to play another type of audio
> file, your user will require a plug-in of one type or another.

To use the Play Sound behavior:

1. With the item selected to which you'd like to attach the
   behavior and with the Behavior panel open, click Add Action
   and select Play Sound.

2. From here, the Play Sound dialog box will appear.

3. Click the Browse button (to the right of the Play Sound field). When the Select File dialog box appears, navigate to where the audio file you with to play is located, select it, and click Select.

4. When you finish, click OK.

Creating a Pop-Up Message

A JavaScript pop-up message is a cool way to provide your users with a little extra information. You can easily create one using the Pop-up Message behavior (below left):

1. With the item selected to which you'd like to attach the behavior and with the Behavior panel open, click Add Action and select Pop-up message.

2. From here, the Pop-up Message dialog box will appear (below right).

3. Type the text of the pop-up message into the Message field.

4. When you finish, click OK.

Preloading Images

A great way to streamline your user's experience is to preload your site's images so that they'll load quickly (as opposed to loading slowly).

To preload an image:

1. With the item selected which you'd like to trigger the Preload Images action and with the Behavior panel open, click Add Action and select Preload Images.

A good strategy is to attach the Preload Image action to the page itself (the <body> tag). This way, the user doesn't have to do anything for the behavior to be executed.

2. This will open the Preload Image dialog box.

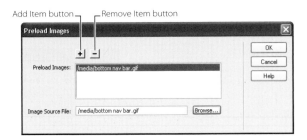

3. Now you'll need to add the first image to be preloaded. To do this, first hit the Browse button (to the right of the Image Source File field).

4. When the Select File dialog box opens, navigate to where the image you want to preload is located, select it, and click Select.

5. After you add the first image to preload, you can go ahead and add others. To do this, click the Preload Image dialog box's Add Item button .

6. Now click the Browse button (to the right of the Image Source File field). When the Select File dialog box opens, navigate to where the image you want to preload is located, select it, and click Select.

7. To add more images, just repeat steps 5 and 6.

8. When you finish adding all the images to be preloaded, click OK.

Setting Status Bar Text

Like a JavaScript pop-up message, integrating Status Bar text into your page is a great way to provide the user with some extra information.

To use the Set Text of Status Bar behavior:

1. With the item selected which you'd like to trigger the Set Text of Status Bar action and with the Behavior panel open, click Add Action and go to Set Text → Set Text of Status Bar.

2. This will open the Set Text of Status Bar dialog box.

3. Type the text you'd like to appear in the status bar into the Message field.

4. When you finish, click OK.

Set the Text of a Frame

Under normal circumstances, if you want to change the content of a frame, you need to load a new document. However, through the use of the Set Text of Frame behavior, you can dynamically change the textual content of a frame:

1. With the item selected which you'd like to trigger the Set Text of Frame action and with the Behavior panel open, click Add Action and go to Set Text → Set Text of Frame. If you don't have any frames in your document, you won't be able to access the Set Text of Frame behavior.

2. This will open the Set Text of Frame dialog box (bottom left).

3. Select the frame whose text you wish to manipulate from the Frame drop-down menu.

4. From here, you can enter new content into the New HTML field. If you want to populate the New HTML field with the page's existing content (which you can then change), click the Get Current HTML button (bottom right).

Unless you edit the existing content (by clicking the Get Current HTML button), any content you enter into the New HTML field will automatically overwrite the frame's code.

5. If you wish to preserve the background color of the frame, click the Preserve Background color option.

6. When you finish, click OK.

Set the Text of a Layer

If you aren't using frames in your document, but you still want to be able to dynamically change the text in your page, a good alternative is to use the Set Text of a Layer behavior. With it you can dynamically change a layer's content and formatting while retaining layer attributes.

To use the Set Text of Layer behavior:

1. With the item selected which you'd like to trigger the Set Text of Layer action and with the Behavior panel open, click Add Action and go to Set Text → Set Text of Layer. (This may seem obvious, but if you don't have any layers in your document, you won't be able to access the Set Text of Layer behavior.)

2. This will open the Set Text of Layer dialog box.

3. From here, select the layer whose text you wish to manipulate from the Layer drop-down menu. If you haven't named your layer, it will show up in the Layer drop-down menu with its default name (Layer1, Layer2, and so on).

4. From here, you can enter new content into the New HTML field. If you want any HTML formatting, you'll need to add the proper tags yourself.

> The content you place in the New HTML field can be any valid HTML source code, including images.

5. When you finish, click OK.

Setting the Text of a Text Field

With the help of the Set Text of a Text Field behavior (whoa, that's a mouthful), you can dynamically change the text within a text field (either single or multiline).

To use the Set the Text of a Text Field behavior:

1. With the item selected which you'd like to trigger the Set Text of a Text Field action and with the Behavior panel open, click Add Action and go to Set Text → Set Text of Text Field. If you don't have any Text Fields in your document, you won't be able to access the Set Text of Text Field behavior.

2. This will open the Set Text of Text Field dialog box.

3. From here, select the text field that you wish to manipulate. Individual text fields will be listed in association with their particular form. So, if you have multiple forms on a single page, you'll be able to easily select the specific text field you want to work with.

4. Enter the desired text into the New Text field. Remember, if you have multiple lines in the New Text field, a single-line text field won't be able to display them in the same way a multiple-line text field will. It will simply compress the multiline text into a single line.

5. When you finish, click OK.

Showing and Hiding Layers

If you'll cast your mind back to Chapter 14, you'll remember that one of the layer properties you learned how to set was visibility. You also learned that you can use behaviors to dynamically control the visibility of a layer. Well, in this section, you'll learn how to do this using the Show-Hide Layers behavior:

1. With the item selected that you'd like to trigger the Show-Hide Layers action and with the Behavior panel open, click Add Action and go to Show-Hide Layers.

2. This will open the Show-Hide Layers dialog box.

3. Select the layer whose visibility you want to manipulate from the Named Layers list box. Remember that if you haven't named your layer, it will show up in the Layer drop-down menu with its default name (Layer1, Layer2, and so on).

4. From here, you have a few options:

- If you wish to show a layer whose visibility was previously set to Hide, click the Show button [Show].

- If you wish to hide a layer who visibility had previously been set to Show, click the Hide button [Hide].

- If you want to return the layer to its default visibility, click the Default button [Default].

5. When you finish, click OK.

Validating a Form

When you create a form, you assume that the user will fill out all the forms and, if need be, constrain their data entry to a certain format, such as a two-character province/state code or a complete e-mail address.

Under normal circumstances, a user can fill a form out any way they please (either intentionally or by accident), and then submit it to you. This can be pretty frustrating if the point of the form is to collect some very specific data. So, aside from standing over the user with a big stick and whacking them whenever they make an error, how can you prevent this type of thing from happening? By using the Validate Form behavior, that's how! Essentially, the Validate Form behavior works by checking the data entered into any text field against a standard you've already set. If the data doesn't conform, the form will simply not submit.

If you don't have a completed form on your page (in which all the text fields have been properly labeled), you won't be able to access the Validate Form behavior.

To use the Validate Form behavior:

1. With the item selected that you'd like to trigger the Validate Form action and with the Behavior panel open, click Add Action and go Validate Form.

   There are a couple of different elements to which you can attach the Validate Form behavior. You can attach it to the Submit button using an onClick event. Alternatively, you can attach the behavior to each individual field you'd like to validate and then execute it with an onBlur event. Finally, you can attach it to the form (`<form>` tag) itself and then execute it with an onSubmit event.

2. This will open the Validate Form dialog box.

3. From here, select the specific field to which you'd like to add a validation from the Named Fields list.

4. If you wish the field to be required (that is, the user must fill it out in order to submit the form), select the Value Required option.

5. From here, you've got a couple of different options:

   • If you aren't concerned with exactly what kind of data is entered into the field but you want to make sure *something* has been added to the text field, select the Anything option in the Accept section of the Validate Form dialog box.

   • If you want to make sure that the field is only filled with numbers, select the Numbers option in the Accept section of the Validate Form dialog box.

   • If you want to make sure that the data entered into the field is a syntactically correct e-mail address (something@something.something), select the E-mail Address option in the Accept section of the Validate Form dialog box.

The Validate Form will not check whether the e-mail address entered is real, only whether it conforms to the expected e-mail syntax.

   • If you want the data entered to be a number that falls within a certain range, select the Number From option in the Accept section of the Validate Form dialog box. From there, enter the beginning number in the range into the first field and the ending number in the range into the second field.

6. When you finish, click OK

Creating a Rollover

A rollover (an image which changes when it's moused over and then reverts back to the original when it's moused out) is arguably one of the most popular effects in web pages these days.

In Dreamweaver MX, the most popular way to make a rollover is with the Swap Image behavior:

1. With the image to which you'd like to apply the Swap Image behavior selected, and with the Behavior panel open, click the Add Action button and select Swap Image.

2. This will open the Swap Image dialog box.

3. Select the image you wish to turn into a rollover from the Images list box. If you selected the image before opening the Swap Image dialog box, it will be automatically highlighted. If you haven't named any of your images, they will all show up with the same default name (unnamed <img>). To avoid confusion, if you are creating a number of different rollovers on the same page, you should name all of your images.

4. Now, you need to set the image that will replace the selected image. To do this, click the Browse button (to the right of the Set Source To field).

5. When the Select File dialog box appears, navigate to where the image is located, select it, and click Select.

6. If you want the second image to be preloaded when the page itself loads (which is definitely a good idea if you want the rollover to be smooth), click the Preload Images option. This will automatically attach a Preload Image behavior to the <body> tag of the page itself.

7. If you want the image to switch back to the original when the user moves their mouse off it, click the Restore Images onMouseOut option. This will add a Swap Image Restore behavior to the image (which doesn't have much use beyond this situation).

8. When you've finished, click OK.

You can also create a rollover by going to Insert → Interactive Image → Rollover Image and then entering the necessary properties in the Insert Rollover Image dialog box.

Creating a Pop-Up Menu

Arguably one of the coolest new features of Dreamweaver MX is the ability to create graphical JavaScript pop-up menus—a feature that was previously only available if you were working with Macromedia Fireworks. With the help of the Show Pop-Up Menu behavior, you can easily create a complex (and terribly cool) navigational element, the creation of which otherwise might prove somewhat complicated and beyond the reach for someone starting out in the world of web design. Before you begin, know that the Show Pop-Up Menu behavior can only be attached to a named image. Also, if the document in which you are working has yet to be saved, you will be unable to use the Show Pop-Up Menu behavior.

> The Show Pop-Up Menu behavior can also be used to edit a pop-up menu that was created in Fireworks and imported into Dreamweaver MX.

To create a pop-up menu using the Show Pop-Up Menu behavior:

1. With the item selected that you'd like to trigger the Show Pop-Up Menu action and with the Behavior panel open, click Add Action and go to Show-Hide Layers.

2. When the Show Pop-Up Menu dialog box appears, first make sure the Contents tab is open.

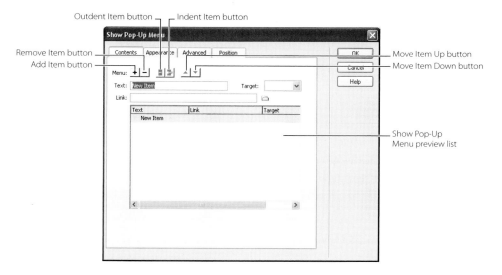

3. Enter the text (that will appear in the drop-down menu) for the first item into the Text field.

4. Enter the menu item's corresponding URL into the Link field. If you want to link to another page in your site, click the Browse to File button 📁. When the Select File dialog box appears, navigate to where the file is located, and select it.

5. Select the location where you want the link to load from the Target drop-down menu.

6. To add additional menu items, click the Add Item button ➕ , and repeats steps 3-5.

7. If you want one of the items in your menu items to be nested below the primary menu (see Figure 15.1), select the item from the Show Pop-Up Menu preview list, and click

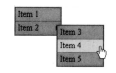

Figure 15.1

A menu item can be nested below the primary pop-up menu.

the Indent Item button ⊞ . If you want to un-nest the menu item, click the Outdent button.

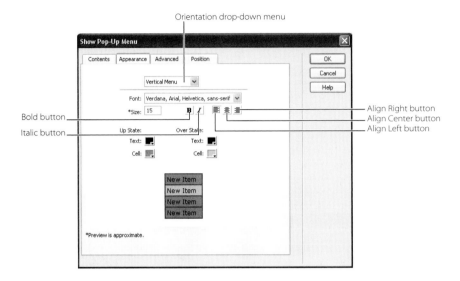

8. If you want to change the position of an item in the menu, select it, and click either the Move Item Up button ▲ or the Move Item Down button ▼ .

9. When you finish adding all the items to your pop-up menu, click the Appearance tab. From here, you will configure the way your menu looks. As you change the properties in the Appearance tab, the preview at the bottom of the dialog box will change accordingly.

10. Select the direction which the menu will flow (either Horizontal or Vertical) from the Orientation drop-down menu.

11. Select the font for the menu's items from the Font drop-down menu.

12. Click one of the text style buttons (Bold or Italic) to change the appearance of your menu's text.

13. From here, you can click one of the Align buttons ▤ ▤ ▤ to align the items within the menu.

14. To choose a color for the text when the user's mouse isn't over the menu item, Click the Up State Text Color swatch and choose a color from the color palette.

15. To choose a color for the cell (in which the text of each individual menu item resides) when the user's mouse isn't over the menu item, Click the Up State Cell Color swatch and choose a color from the color palette.

16. To choose a color for the text when the user's mouse is over the menu item, Click the Over State Text Color swatch and choose a color from the color palette.

17. To choose a color for the cell when the user's mouse is over the menu item, Click the Up State Cell Color swatch and choose a color from the color palette.

18. When you've finished setting the appearance of the pop-up menu, click the Advanced tab (shown below-right)—this is where you'll fine-tune how your pop-up menu looks.

19. To set the width of the cells in your menu, either select Automatic or Pixels from the Cell Width drop-down menu. If you choose Automatic, the cell width is automatically set by the widest item in the menu. If, however, you choose Pixels, you can set the width manually by inputting a value into the Cell Width field.

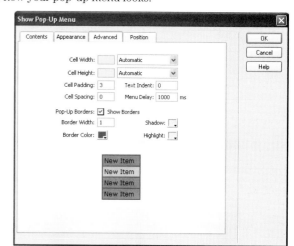

20. To set the height of the cells in your menu, either select Automatic or Pixels from the Cell Height drop-down menu. If you choose Automatic, the cell height is automatically set by the tallest item in the menu. If, however, you choose Pixels, you can set the height manually by inputting a value into the Cell Height field.

21. Enter a value for the cell padding of each of your menu items into the Cell Padding Field.

22. Enter a value for the cell spacing of each of your menu items into the Cell Spacing Field. (If you are having trouble remembering how cell padding and cell spacing affects how content in a cell is displayed, see Chapter 7, "Working with Tables.")

23. If you want to change the distance between the menu item and the left side of the cell, enter a value (in pixels) into the Text Indent field.

24. To set the delay between the time when the user moves their mouse over the object to which the Pop-up menu behavior has been attached and when the menu actually appears, enter a value into the Menu Delay field. The value you enter is in milliseconds; for example, 1000 is 1 second, 2000 is 2 seconds, and so on.

25. If you want your pop-up menu to have a solid border, click the Show Borders option.

26. Enter the value for the width of the menu's border into the Border Width field.

27. To set the color for the border, click the Border Color swatch and make your choice from the color palette.

28. To set the menu's shadow color, click the Shadow Color swatch and make a choice from the color palette.

29. To set the menu's highlight color, click the Highlight Color swatch and make a choice from the color palette. Neither the highlight color nor the shadow color are displayed in the Show Pop-Up Menu dialog box.

30. When you finish setting the pop-up menu's advanced properties, click the Position tab— this is where you'll manipulate the position of the pop-up menu when it's opened.

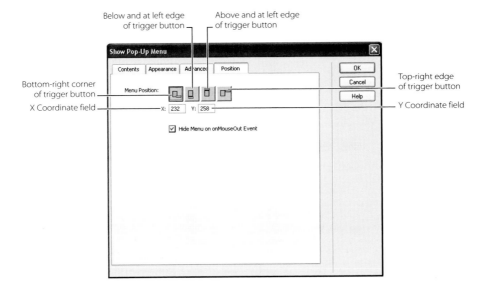

31. Click one of the preset Menu Position option buttons to set the location where the menu will appear when the user triggers the event.

32. If you want to manually set the location of the menu, enter a value (in pixels) into the X Coordinate and Y Coordinate fields—the position is relative to the top left-hand corner of the menu itself.

33. If you want the menu to disappear when the user moves their mouse off it, click the Hide Menu on MouseOut Event. When you do this, Dreamweaver MX adds an additional behavior (Hide Pop-Up Menu).

Integrating New Behaviors

As you've probably figured out by now, behaviors are really cool tools that let you extend the power of Dreamweaver MX. The great thing is that, much like plug-ins for other programs, an entire community of behavior developers has sprung up. The definite added bonus is that, unlike the plug-in industry, the vast majority of developers distribute their behaviors free for anyone to download.

The most complete resource for downloadable behaviors is the Macromedia Exchange (`www.macromedia.com/exchange`), where you'll not only be able to download behaviors for Dreamweaver MX, but also free components, extensions, and add-ons for a host of other Macromedia programs including Flash MX, ColdFusion MX, JRun, and HomeSite.

All you need to take advantage of this virtual wealth of free downloadable behaviors is an Internet connection and small (free) program called the Macromedia Extension Manager. Designed to let you install and manage downloaded components over multiple Macromedia programs, the Extension Manager is vital if you want to take advantage of free downloadable components.

A copy of Macromedia Extension Manager has been included on this book's accompanying CD.

To use the Extension Manager to add new behaviors to Dreamweaver:

1. After having installed and opened the Extension Manager, go to File → Install Extension. Alternatively, you can click the Install New Extension button 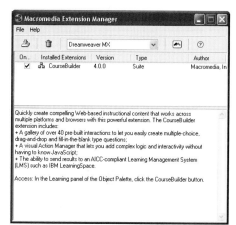 .

2. When the Select Extension to Install dialog box appears, navigate to where you downloaded the extensions, select it, and click Install.

3. After the extension is installed, it will be visible in the Extension Manager's list (and available for use in the program for which it was designed).

Inspiration: Design and Technique

For those readers of legal drinking age who yearn for a top-notch martini recipe, you must check out the Virtual Cocktail Hour (`www.virtualcocktailhour.com`). Featuring over 350 martini recipes, wine/food pairing advice, seasonal Bailey's recipes (yum!), and trade secrets of some of the worlds most renowned chefs, the Virtual Cocktail Hour (see Figure 15.2) not only provides you with almost everything you need to know about the subtle art of cocktails, but does so in an extremely stylish and well-designed manner. Employing straight HTML and a very simple layout, Virtual Cocktail Hour is a definite feast for the eyes (and the palette).

Figure 15.2

Virtual Cocktail Hour

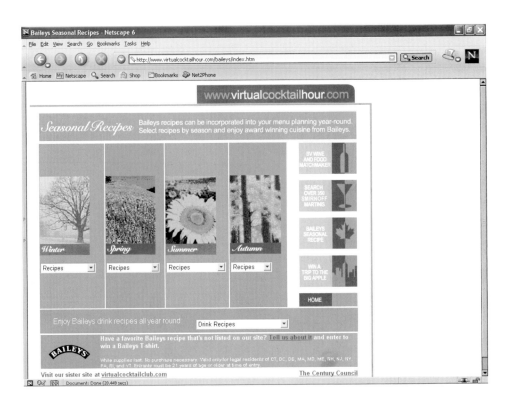

Summary

In this chapter, you thoroughly explored one of the most powerful aspects of Dynamic HTML: JavaScript and HTML integration. You began by exploring the general ins and outs of behaviors (JavaScript code inserted into your Dreamweaver MX document). Included was a very important discussion about event handlers. From there, you learned how to insert behaviors into your Dreamweaver MX document and how you modify them once they've been inserted. You finished the chapter by looking at the vast majority of the standard Dreamweaver MX behaviors available to you and how to go about acquiring and integrating new behaviors.

In the next chapter, you'll finish off the exploration of Dynamic HTML with a look at how to animate with the Timeline Tool.

CHAPTER 16

Animating with the Timeline Tool

As we discussed in Chapter 11, "Inserting and Manipulating Multimedia," media elements, such Flash movies or digital video, can add a powerful extra *oomph* to your HTML creation. However, in the vast majority of cases, these media elements require a special plug-in in order to display properly. Well, what if you want to add some multimedia animation to your web page, but you don't want to open the Pandora's Box of plug-ins? This is where Dreamweaver's Timeline panel comes in.

Essentially, a timeline is a "cost-effective" way to create relatively complex animations using JavaScript and layers that don't require a plug-in to be viewed—pretty cool, huh?

In this chapter, you'll spend time exploring all aspects of timelines in Dreamweaver; included will be a discussion of the following topics:

- **Understanding timelines**
- **Creating a timeline**
- **Animating layers**
- **Adding Frame behaviors to your timeline**
- **Using behaviors to control a timeline**
- **Making animations go**

Understanding Timelines

As has been mentioned numerous times before, one of the most powerful aspects of DHTML is the ability, with the help of a scripting language (most commonly JavaScript), to change the properties or position of most given elements in an HTML document. By taking advantage of this feature, you can actually create relatively complex animations without the need for plug-ins.

In Dreamweaver, this DHTML characteristic is controlled and manipulated by the Timeline panel, and any animation created with it is called a timeline. Unlike many other elements in Dreamweaver (such as an image or a Flash movie), a timeline isn't an object *per se*, but a complex manipulation of the HTML document's source code facilitated by a number of lines of JavaScript that get inserted when the timeline itself is created.

In this way, it's more like a behavior. However, unlike a behavior, a timeline is controlled and manipulated by a fairly complex standalone tool—the Timeline panel.

As you'll find out soon enough, when you learn to actually create a timeline in your document, the only elements you can actually animate are layers. However, given the fact that you can insert almost anything into a layer, this is no great hindrance to your grand animation schemes.

To be completely honesty, timelines aren't used that often on the web. They are limited in terms of interactivity and visual quality compared to such plug-in dependent media such as Macromedia Flash or Apple Quicktime. This, however, doesn't mean they should be totally discounted. They definitely have some unique advantages over other multimedia elements. First, because they are composed entirely of JavaScript in the HTML source code, they don't increase the size of your document like a Flash movie does, for example. Neither do they require that the user has a particular plug-in to be properly viewed. One of the other interesting features of timelines is that you can use them in concert with behaviors. For example, you can create an animation, the end of which features a Go To URL, that sends the user to another page entirely.

Timelines, however, have some drawbacks. The most prominent being that, because they use JavaScript and layers (both DHTML features), they require a 4.0 browser or above to be properly viewed. So, while they don't require a plug-in like Macromedia Flash or Apple Quicktime, they do call for your audience to have some specific software.

Knowing Your Way around the Timeline Panel

The Timeline panel is the primary instrument with which you create and manage timelines. However, due to the nature of timelines, the Timeline panel is somewhat more complicated than many of Dreamweaver's panels that have been discussed thus far. Because of this, before we launch into actually creating a timeline, we will fully explore the tool itself.

One of the cool things about timelines is that they can contain any number of individually animated layers.

To open the Timeline panel, go to Window → Others → Timelines.

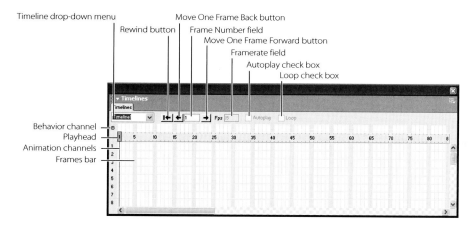

Once opened, the Timeline panel can be a little daunting, but once you break it down into its components parts, you won't feel quite so intimidated:

The Behavior channel The portion of the timeline into which you place behaviors. Like the Animation channels, the Behavior channel is composed of individual frames.

The Animation channels The portion of the Timeline panel where the animations of individual layers are controlled. The Animation channels are composed of individual frames. Each individually animated layer occupies a single Animation channel.

The Timeline Controls Include the tools by which you name your timeline, move the Playhead forward and backward, set the framerate, and play the animation itself.

The Frames Bar Gives a set and sequential numbering of the frames and includes the Playhead (which controls which frame is displayed at any given time).

Understanding Frames and Keyframes

Any animation, whether it's the latest Hollywood 3D animated blockbuster, Walt Disney's original *Fantasia*, or your humble timeline, is composed of frames. Each frame contains one static image that, when displayed in succession with other images in other frames, creates the illusion of movement.

> A timeline isn't composed of static images *per se*. Instead, it is composed of the same layer (populated with content), whose position changes from frame to fame over time.

In the Timeline panel, as you've already learned, frames are displayed horizontally in each animation channel as small white boxes. The beige frames aren't different from the rest of the frames in an animation channel—they are colored differently to indicate every fifth frame.

As the Playhead passes through each successive frame, the changed position of the animated layer is displayed, thereby creating something of a digital flipbook.

Animated layers are represented in the Timeline panel as solid blocks through which a black line runs. When a layer is initially added to the Timeline panel (a process that will be covered later in the chapter) you'll notice that its beginning and end are not your average-looking frames. Instead, they are small empty circles.

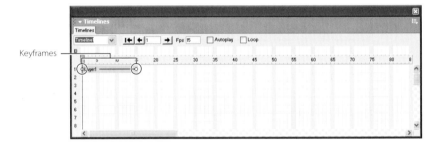

These special frames, which are referred to as keyframes, represent the point in an animation where a change is defined. Keyframes are extremely important if you want your animation to be anything more than a layer (with its associated content) moving along a straight line. By inserting keyframes, you can set points in the animation where the layer is in a different position on your page, thereby creating an animation that follows a nonlinear path.

Creating and Manipulating a Timeline

When you create a timeline, you don't actually insert a discrete timeline object with the Insert bar (as you would an image object or Flash movie object). Instead, you take a layer (or layers) that you've already created (with their associated content), and add it to the Timeline panel. By doing this, you're telling Dreamweaver: "Hey, I'd like to animate this layer." Dreamweaver will then add the necessary JavaScript into the HTML source code that represents the characteristics of the animation itself, and can then be edited with the Timeline panel.

Having said this, let's take a look at how you go about adding a layer to the Timeline panel, thereby creating a timeline:

1. If it isn't already, open the Timeline panel by going to Window → Others → Timelines.

2. When the Timelines panel opens, select the layer in the Document Window that you would like to add to the timeline.

3. From here, you've got a couple of different options. Regardless of which of the following options you take, a small pop-up message will appear, giving you some information about what layer attributes the Timeline panel (which is also sometimes referred to as an inspector) can animate. If you don't want the message to pop up every time you add a layer to a timeline, select the Don't Show Me This Message Again check box.

   • Go to Modify → Timeline → Add Object to Timeline.

   • Click and drag the selected layer directly into the directed animation channel in the Timeline panel. If you click and drag the layer into the Timeline panel, you can place it in whichever channel you want and have it start in any frame.

   • Cmd-click (Mac)/ Right-click (Win) on the selected layer and choose Add to Timeline from the context pop-up menu.

4. Notice that, be default, when the layer is added to the timeline, its animation bar (which you will learn to edit later to exert greater control over the animation itself) is 15 frames in length.

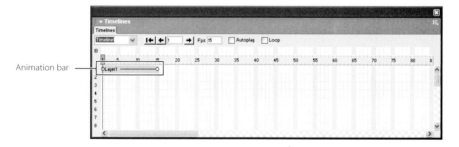

In addition, notice that the animation bar displays the name of the layer itself.

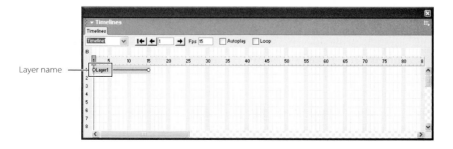

You'll also notice that in its default state, the animation bar has only two keyframes—one at the beginning and one at the end.

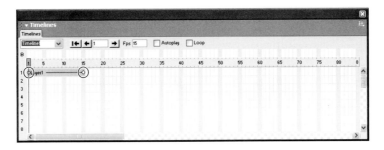

5. From here, if you desire, you can add additional layers (which will occupy successive channels) into the Timeline panel by repeating steps 2 and 3.

> The initial location where the layer is placed (animation channel and starting frame) in the Timeline panel is temporary—you'll learn how to move it around later in this chapter.

Remember, the process of adding a layer (or layers) to the Timeline panel (thereby creating a timeline) is just the first step. From here, you need to learn how to do some minor manipulation of the timeline itself before you go on to learn how to actually animate the layer.

Naming a Timeline

One of the cool things about timelines is that you can easily have more than one, each of which can feature more than one animated layer, in a given document. Given this, you need a quick and easy way to name the individual timelines so that they can be distinguished. Dreamweaver will give each successive timeline you create a default name: Timeline1, Timeline2, Timeline3, and so on.

To name a timeline:

1. Make sure the document in which you have inserted more than one timeline is open.

2. If it isn't already, open the Timeline panel by going to Window → Others → Timelines.

3. Select the timeline you want to rename from the Timeline drop-down menu.

4. Once it's selected, highlight its name in the Timeline drop-down menu (which acts as an editable field when the menu itself isn't open).

5. When the name is highlighted, type a new one.

Because you can't open more than one timeline at a given time, you use the Timeline drop-down menu to switch between the various timelines in your document.

Changing the Length of an Animation

As you learned before, a timeline animation (just like any other kind of animation) is made up of frames. The number of frames in the animation (coupled with the actual frame rate) determines its actual length. You can very easily stretch out the animation bar so that it occupies more frames, and therefore more time.

Remember, because we have yet to explore how to animate an object (changing its position over time), stretching the animation bar so that it occupies more frames won't have any visible effect on the animation itself.

To stretch the animation bar to occupy more frames:

1. Make sure the document in which the timeline you want to manipulate is open.

2. If it isn't already, open the Timeline panel by going to Window → Others → Timelines.

3. If you have more than one timeline in the document, select the appropriate one from the Timeline panel's Timeline drop-down menu.

4. Click and hold the final keyframe of the animation bar whose length you wish to change.

5. With your mouse button still held down, drag the keyframe to the right to increase the length of the animation bar or to the left to decrease the length of the animation bar.

6. When the animation bar has reached the length you desire, release your mouse button.

If you want to increase the size of the animation bar one frame at a time, you can go to Modify → Timeline → Add Frame. Alternatively, to decrease it one frame at a time, go to Modify → Timeline → Remove Frame.

Moving an Animation Bar

As I mentioned earlier, the position in the animation channel where a layer's animation bar is initially placed isn't fixed. You can very easily move it around.

There are a couple of reasons you might want to do this. First, if you shift it to the right in its animation channel, the animation itself won't actually start until the Playhead reaches the firs keyframe (see Figure 16.1).

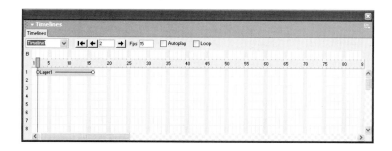

Figure 16.1

An animation's bar can be shifted so that its first keyframe is not located in frame 1, but a later frame.

Second, you could move a series of animation bars into one animation channel so that their animations happen one after another (see Figure 16.2).

Figure 16.2

You can have a number of animation bars occupying the same animation channel, one after another.

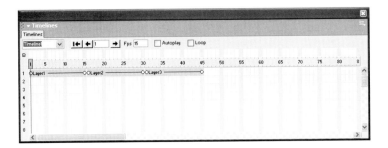

Different animation bars cannot occupy the same frame in the same animation channel.

To move an animation bar:

1. Make sure the document is open in which the timeline is located and the Timeline panel itself is open (Window → Others → Timelines).

2. Select the entire animation bar by clicking any of its frames. Don't click one of its keyframes; this will select only that individual keyframe, not the entire animation bar.

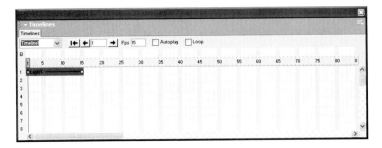

3. Once it's selected, click and drag the animation bar to the desired location and release your mouse button.

Removing an Object from the Timeline

Just as you added a layer to the timeline, you can easily remove it:

1. Make sure the document is open in which the timeline is located and the Timeline panel itself is open (Window → Others → Timelines).

2. Select the entire animation bar by clicking any of its frames. Don't click one of its keyframes; this will select only that individual keyframe, not the entire animation bar.

3. Once it's selected, you have a number of options:

- Press the Delete key on your keyboard.
- Go to Modify → Timeline → Remove Object.
- Cmd-click (Mac)/ right-click (Win) and choose Remove Object from the context pop-up menu.

When you remove a layer from the Timeline, you aren't deleting the layer itself from the page. Instead, you are removing that layer from the timeline's associated JavaScript.

Setting the Timeline's Frame Rate

Framerate determines the rate at which an animation plays. Represented in frames per second (fps), the framerate of an animation, which is set in the control section of the Timeline panel, is related to both the speed and quality of the animation. Look at it this way. If you have a high framerate, more frames will be displayed in the space of a second, thereby making the animation appear smoother. The lower your framerate, the less frames will be displayed in a given second, thereby decreasing the quality of your animation by making it appear more jerky.

The framerate itself is not an absolute value *per se*; instead it is the optimum number that the user's browser attempts to reach. The default value of 15 is a good framerate for both Macs and PCs.

> Each individual timeline in your document can have its own separate framerate. However, all animated layers in a Timeline have the same framerate.

To set a timeline's framerate:

1. Make sure the document is open in which the timeline is located and the Timeline panel itself is open (Window → Others → Timelines).
2. If you have multiple timelines in your document, choose the one whose framerate you wish to change from the Timeline drop-down menu.
3. Enter a value into the fps field.

Animating an Object

Now that you've learned about the different components of the Timeline panel, how to add a layer to your page's timeline, and how to manipulate the various properties of animation and the animation bar, it's time to learn how to make the layer(s) move over time.

9. With the newly created keyframe still selected, click and drag the layer to the location in the document where you'd like it to be at that point in the animation. Notice that, like before, the animation path will curve to accommodate the layer's position at that particular keyframe.

You can move keyframes around within the animation bar by clicking and dragging. This effects the packing of the overall animation.

Adding Frame Behaviors

As mentioned earlier, you can add behaviors to your timeline in order to add a little extra interactivity. These behaviors, which are placed directly into the Timeline panel's Behavior channel are triggered by the Playhead itself, and not the user.

To add behaviors to your timeline:

1. Make sure the document is open in which the timeline is located and the Timeline panel itself is open (Window → Others → Timelines).

2. If you have multiple timelines in your document, choose the one to which you'd like to add a frame behavior from the Timeline drop-down menu.

3. Select the specific frame in the Behavior channel to which you'd like to add a behavior.

4. From here, you've got a number of different options:

    -   Cmd-click (Mac)/ right-click (Win) and choose Add Behavior from the context pop-up menu.

    -   Double-click the selected frame.

    -   Go to Modify → Timeline → Add Behavior to Timeline.

5. This will open the Behavior panel. From here, you can choose the behavior you'd like to attach to the frame. Use the process described throughout Chapter 15, "Adding Advanced Interactivity with Behaviors." You will have access to only those behaviors that don't require a physical object be inserted into your document, such as the Jump menu or Swap Image behaviors.

6. Once you finish selecting and configuring the behavior, it's important to note that the event handler (onFrame1, onFrame2, onFrame3, and so on) used is determined by the frame to which the behavior was attached and is completely fixed.

7. When you finish fiddling with the behavior, you can close the Behavior panel. Note that the frame in the Behavior channel to which you attached the behavior has been filled.

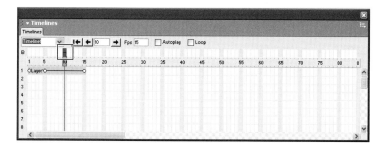

Using Behaviors to Control a Timeline

Back in Chapter 15, you spent a great deal of time going over almost every behavior that Dreamweaver had to offer. Conspicuously absent from the that discussion was a series of behaviors whose functionality related solely to timelines. Never fear, in this section of the chapter, we'll explore each in detail.

Playing a Timeline

The Play Timeline behavior is perhaps one of the most important timeline-related behaviors. While its name is pretty self-explanatory (it plays the timeline), it can be used to integrate some user timeline control functionality into your HTML creation. You can attach it to another element (such as an image or a rollover), thereby allowing the user to initiate the timeline at their will.

To use the Play Timeline behavior:

1. With the item selected which you'd like to trigger the Play Timeline action and with the Behavior panel open, click Add Action and go to Timeline → Play Timeline.

2. This will open the Play Timeline dialog box.

3. Select the timeline upon which you'd like the Play Timeline behavior to work from the drop-down menu.

4. Once you finish, click OK.

5. From here, you can select the appropriate handler to trigger the action.

If you are having a difficult time remembering how to set the action's event handler, see the "Inserting a Behavior" section in Chapter 15.

Stopping a Timeline

The opposite of the Play Timeline behavior, the Stop Timeline behavior, lets you stop a timeline that has already begun playing. Like the Play Timeline behavior, it can be used to include some user timeline control into your web page.

To use the Stop Timeline behavior:

1. With the item selected which you'd like to trigger the Stop Timeline action and with the Behavior panel open, click Add Action and go to Timeline → Stop Timeline.

2. This will open the Stop Timeline dialog box.

3. Select the timeline upon which you'd like the Stop Timeline behavior to work from the drop-down menu. If you want all of the timelines in your document to stop, select **ALL TIMELINES**.

4. Once you finish, click OK.

5. From here, you can select the appropriate handler to trigger the Stop Timeline behavior.

You can also add the Stop Timeline behavior to a timeline's Behavior channel, thereby causing the animation to stop in midstream without the user doing anything.

Going to a Specific Frame in a Timeline

If you are using the Play Timeline behavior, the animation initiates at the very beginning. However, what if you want to send the animation to a specific frame? This is where the Go to Timeline Frame behavior comes in. With it, you can jump the Playhead to any frame in the target timeline:

1. With the item selected which you'd like to trigger the Go To Timeline Frame action and with the Behavior panel open, click Add Action and go to Timeline → Go To Timeline Frame.

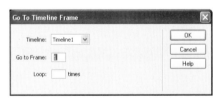

2. This will open the Go To Timeline Frame dialog box.

3. Select the timeline upon which you'd like the Go To Timeline Frame behavior to work from the drop-down menu.

4. Enter the frame to which you'd like the Playhead to jump into the Go To Frame field.

5. If you want that section of the animation to loop (from the behavior to the end), enter the number of times into the Loop field.

6. When you finish, click OK.

You can also add the Go To Timeline Frame behavior to a timeline's Behavior channel, thereby causing the animation to skip to another frame without the user doing anything.

Making the Animation Go (Vroom)

Now that you've gone to the trouble of creating a timeline, animating a layer (or layers), and perhaps even integrating frame behaviors, it's time to learn how to get the animation to go.

> To test your Timeline, all you need to do is preview the page in the browser of your choice.

I know this might seem to be the simplest step in the whole procedure, but there is a little more to it than meets the eye. Most notably is the fact that once the web page is opened in a browser, the timeline will not automatically play unless you've taken some steps beforehand.

In the previous section, you explored how you can use the Play Timeline behavior to allow the user to initiate the animation. In the following section, you'll learn how to automatically play the timeline without any user interaction.

Autoplaying a Timeline

The simplest way to make sure that your animation plays when it's viewed in a browser is to set its autoplay feature. As the name suggests, the autoplay feature ensures that the timeline will automatically start running as soon as the page loads in a browser.

To set the autoplay feature:

1. Make sure the document is open in which the timeline is located and that the Timeline panel itself is open (Window ➔ Others ➔ Timelines).

2. Click the Autoplay check box located in the Timeline Control section of the Timeline panel.

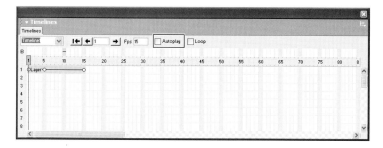

If you want the animation to play over and over again (as opposed to just once), select the Loop option, located to the right of the Autoplay check box.

Inspiration: Design and Technique

Founded in Fall 2000 by Guthrie Dolin, Matthew Carlson, and Raul Diaz, Dept 3 (www.dept3.com) is a full-featured San Francisco-based design house that specializes in identity design, brand strategy, interactive design, interface design, information design, and all manner of print design. Dept 3's website (Figure 16.3) is an incredibly cool example of simple, stylish, and straight HTML design.

Figure 16.3

Dept 3

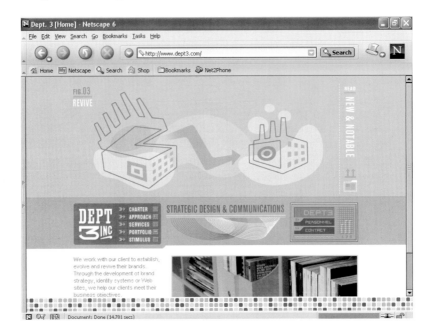

Summary

In this chapter, you learned how to create animations that don't require plug-ins with the help of Dreamweaver's Timeline tool. To start off with, you rolled your sleeves up and dug into the guts of what exactly a timeline is and how it works. From there, you explored the benefits and drawbacks of using timelines. Next, you looked at how to insert and manipulate a timeline into your Dreamweaver document, how to animate objects, and how to use frame behaviors. You finished the chapter off with a look at how to get a timeline animation to run. In the following chapter, you'll take your first steps towards creating a dynamic database-driven website using Dreamweaver MX's cool new dynamic tools.

PART IV

Making Dreamweaver Dynamic

Under normal *circumstances, web pages are pretty static things. The information they contain remains absolutely the same after they are authored and uploaded to a server. If you want them to change, you have to change them yourself and then re-upload them to the web server. This is not a bad state of affairs if your site was designed to deliver a rarely changing set of information. However, what happens if your site features up-to-the-minute information that requires almost constant updating? Worse still, what if you want to offer your audience the ability to actively change the way they interact with your website by allowing them to customize the type of information displayed or even how the pages themselves appear? With regular HTML, this would be completely impossible.*

Don't despair, though: there is a host of incredibly exciting technologies that let you meld traditional HTML, databases, and specialized application servers to create websites that are truly dynamic, and all of the tools to do so are available right at your fingertips in Dreamweaver MX! In the following section, you'll get a solid introduction to the complexities of conceiving, creating, and deploying dynamic database applications.

CHAPTER 17

Setting the Groundwork for Your Dynamic Database-Driven Application

So you want to make your web pages dynamic, do you? Well, before you launch into the world of endless dynamic possibilities, there are some very important topics that must first be discussed. As with all things of any consequence, a good and solid foundation is necessary for a successful learning experience. Creating dynamic database-driven applications with Dreamweaver MX is hardly any different. First, you need to have a good understanding of how dynamic database-driven applications actually work. From there, you need to explore the different types of database-driven technologies available in Dreamweaver MX that can help you realize your creative ideas. At that point, you'll be in a great position to jump into Dreamweaver MX and look at what to do in order to lay the groundwork for your dynamic database-driven application.

- Understanding dynamic database-driven applications
- Working with an application server
- Introduction to the dynamic Dreamweaver
- Setting your testing server
- Setting your document type
- Connecting to a database
- Working with a database connection
- Viewing your database's structure

Understanding Dynamic Database-Driven Applications

Before you dive into creating dynamic content with Dreamweaver MX it's a good idea to get a solid theoretical background in a number of different topics. This background will not only help you better understand what you're getting into, but also help you make better choices when it comes to actually building your grand dynamic creation. In this section of the chapter, you'll hunker down and sample such digital morsels as how dynamic applications work, what dynamic database-driven technologies exist for your use, which dynamic technology best suits your needs, and how to choose and work with a database. While many of the following topics may lack the necessary applied context right now (and are perhaps a little dry), you must at least have a cursory understanding of them if you want to successfully design and deploy dynamic database-driven sites.

How a Dynamic Application Works

As you learned back in Chapter 1, "Web Design: The Big Picture," the Web works on a client-server model. A client, the web browser in this case, is a piece of software that runs on a local computer that communicates with a server in another location, which is a computer that performs tasks for other computers, such as sending out e-mail. When you type a URL into a browser (or click a hyperlink), a request is sent to a specific web server (which is determined by the actual URL being used) through a router. When the request reaches the proper destination, the web server decides (based on the URL itself) which document is being requested. From there, the server locates and retrieves the document from somewhere within its directory structure and sends it back along the route that the request came. On the way back, the router makes sure the requested document is sent to the client that originally made the request. The last leg happens when the client (the web browser) receives the requested document and displays it for the users' reading (or viewing) pleasure. Pretty simple, huh?

Dynamic database applications function on the same general client-server model. There are, however, some extra details. One of the pivotal differences between the way static web pages work (as just described) and the way dynamic web applications work is the notion of server-side scripting. Essentially, server-side scripts are code (not HTML) the author (you) inserts into the HTML document that acts as commands to the server itself. When the web server receives a request for a document in which there are some server-side scripts, it will first retrieve the document from within its directory, much as it does in the case of regular nondynamic pages. However, before it sends the document back to the client (the browser), it will recognize and execute the server-side code.

The whole point of the dynamic tools in Dreamweaver MX is to create all of the necessary server-side code in a relatively easy-to-use visual authoring environment so that those among us who are either not interested or not experienced in learning another scripting language aren't shut out of the groovy world of dynamic database-driven applications.

Under most circumstances, the server-side code tells the server to populate the HTML page with content that is drawn from a database. This leads us to the second aspect of dynamic database-driven applications: the database.

The second pivotal aspect of a dynamic database-driven application is the database itself. The whole point of creating a dynamic application is that the content in your site can change based on user interaction—and a database is usually the source of the dynamic content. So, where does the database fit into the equation just described? Well, for the most part, the database itself (which can range from Microsoft Access to MySQL) will sit in a directory on your web server with all your other site files. The server will pull information out of the database and stick it into the HTML document as needed, based on the commands it receives from the server-side code. This leads us to the third pivotal component of the database-driven application: the server application.

For the most part, your average web server isn't equipped to understand the server-side code that makes this whole dynamic content thing possible. Think of it this way: the server speaks French, but the document that it receives is partially written in Arabic. For it to understand the Arabic (which contains the actual commands) in the document, it needs a translator of sorts. In the world of dynamic database-driven applications, this translator is a piece of software called an application server. Installed on the web server, the application server will translate server-side code and then execute the commands contained therein. It kind of works this way: the web server retrieves a file for which it got a request from a browser. It takes a look at the server-side code in the file, scratches its head, turns to the application server and says, "I haven't the faintest clue what this says, do you know?" The application server then takes a look at the server-side code, and says, "Yeah, I know what this says, why don't you let me deal with it?" The application server then executes the server-side code, populates the HTML file with content grabbed from a database, hands the file back to the web server which, very happy with itself because it didn't have to do the work, sends it back to the browser to be displayed as pure HTML.

Some web servers double up as application servers. The most common example is Microsoft IIS or PWS, which act both as a web server and application server for Active Server Pages and ASP.NET.

So, let's recap: what exactly do you need for a dynamic database-driven application to work properly?

- Code in the HTML file that gets executed by the server (server-side code)
- A web server that accepts the request from the browser and returns the HTML file after it has been filled with content grabbed from a database
- The database from which the dynamic content is taken
- An application server that interprets and executes the server-side code

Your Dynamic Choices

Now that you know how dynamic database-driven applications work, it's time to look at the various technologies out there that allow you to create dynamic websites—and there are many. The dynamic database technologies discussed next are all available to use in Dreamweaver MX.

Active Server Pages

Active Server Pages (ASP) is a server-side scripting technology developed by Microsoft. ASP is based on an HTML-like syntax in which custom-made VBScript, JScript (Microsoft's version of JavaScript), or JavaScript code resides in specialized tags within the actual HTML document.

While the most common way to deploy ASP is with Microsoft's Internet Information Server, there are a number of other methods (mainly Sun's Chili!soft) to deploy ASP on other platforms such as Linux or Solaris.

One of the great joys of ASP is that it can store site information in a database. As users visit the site, the information is called from the database on a case-by-case basis. Because of this, you can effect all manner of changes to your layout (font, color, and so on) by changing the ASP itself and not the actual HTML page. In addition, ASP, like many server-side technologies, can draw upon information within a database to continuously repopulate a web page with dynamic data.

One of the other great things about ASP is that it can work with any ODBC (Open Database Connection) compliant database. As a result, you can create your database in a wide range of programs. This, coupled with the fact that it runs on Microsoft IIS or PWS (both of which are web servers that come with your Windows operating system), makes ASP very attractive to grass roots developers.

ASP.NET

ASP.NET, which is the newest kid on the block in terms of dynamic database-driven technologies, is the next step in the evolution of ASP. Back in 1998, a fellow at Microsoft by the name of Scott Guthrie created a prototype of a new version of ASP that he called ASP+.

Essentially, he thought that ASP was a little too cumbersome for really cool application development. Three years later, what started out as a side project to improve upon an existing technology has, depending on who you ask, turned into one of the most talked-about technologies to emerge in a long time, ASP.NET.

Structurally speaking, ASP.NET-based pages function similar to regular ASP-based pages. However, for ASP.NET Microsoft has combined the page-based model of ASP with some of the best features of compiled languages like Visual Basic and C++. In fact, Microsoft even created a new language, C# (pronounced "C Sharp"), to help C++ developers take advantage of ASP.NET

It's important to note that ASP.NET doesn't really replace ASP. The two technologies work just fine side-by-side. You can easily run your ASP.NET applications alongside your existing ASP applications on the same machine. Further, ASP.NET is backward-compatible, meaning that most of your ASP pages will work just fine from within the ASP.NET environment.

For more information on ASP.NET, see Microsoft's website at `www.microsoft.com` or go directly to the source at `www.asp.net`. You can also check out `www.4guysfromrolla.com` for some additional material.

ColdFusion

Originally developed by Allaire (which was acquired by Macromedia in 2001), ColdFusion is a dynamic database-driven application technology that uses a unique tag-based server scripting language, CFML (ColdFusion Markup Language), in conjunction with a specialized server, ColdFusion Server, to deliver powerful dynamic web applications. Because CFML is quite similar to HTML, it is fairly easy to learn and use.

Here's how ColdFusion works. When a user requests a ColdFusion document (which is called a template and has a CFM extension), the web server passes the file first to the ColdFusion Server (which sits on the web server itself) before passing it to the user's browser. The ColdFusion Server looks at the template and interprets any of the embedded CFML. The ColdFusion Server then generates the output from the CFML in the template and returns the file to the web server to be passed back and displayed in the user's browser.

Let's take a look at a short example. Say, for instance, that you've created a ColdFusion template with all the necessary CFML to create a list of the current books you are reading. When a user tries to load that file (remember, it's called a template) into their browser, the server notices the CFM extension and passes the request onto the ColdFusion Server. When the ColdFusion Server receives the request, it pulls the list of the current books you are reading from a database (which you keep constantly updated), sticks the data in the appropriate places in the template (which are designated using CFML), and passes the file back to the web server. The web server then sends the file to the user's browser and lets them view the list of the books that you are currently reading.

You've probably noticed that the ColdFusion Server has been mentioned several times. Unlike ASP (which only requires a specific type of web server), ColdFusion needs another specific piece of software that sits on the web server to work properly. This piece of software is called ColdFusion Server, and without it, ColdFusion will not work. The kicker is that the ColdFusion server costs about $5000 (for the Enterprise version) or $2000 (for the Pro version). This price tag alone makes ColdFusion somewhat prohibitive for the average user. To learn more about ColdFusion, go to `www.macromedia.com/coldfusion`.

You can generate CFML a number of ways. The first is to write it from scratch as you would HTML. You can also use either Macromedia Dreamweaver MX or ColdFusion Studio MX, both of which are obtainable from Macromedia.

PHP

Back in 1994, a fellow named Rasmus Lerdorf developed a series of Perl scripts that allowed him to monitor the users who accessed his website. Word got around about Rasmus' interesting invention, and people started asking to use his scripts on their pages. Shortly thereafter, Rasmus released them as a package that he called Personal Home Page (PHP) Tools.

By 1995, PHP, whose name was changed from Personal Home Page Tools to Hypertext Preprocessor (go figure), had quickly gained an enormous amount of steam. The sheer popularity of PHP prompted Rasmus to release a scripting engine and additional scripts designed to process data from forms.

When the third incarnation of PHP (PHP3) was released, it included a far more efficient scripting engine. The syntax of PHP was changed so that it looked like a cross between C/C++ and Perl instead of just straight Perl (which isn't an object-oriented programming language). To allow third-party developers to further extend PHP by developing their own modules, PHP3 included an API (Application Programming Interface).

The current release of PHP (PHP4) was completely reworked to give users more control over their PHP creations. In addition, the API more efficiently integrates third-party PHP modules.

PHP's benefits lie in several different areas. First, you can write PHP with a simple text utility like Notepad, SimpleText, or Emacs. Like many server-side scripting technologies (including all those discussed in this section of the chapter), PHP can draw information from any ODBC-compliant database on the server. PHP can be installed on most web servers, whether Windows based or Unix based. Generally speaking, PHP is reported to be faster and more stable than both ASP and Cold Fusion. All of these benefits are great, but you haven't heard the best: *it's free!*

To download a copy of PHP, go to `www.php.net`.

Not only will it work on almost any server in existence and generally run faster and more efficiently than ASP or Cold Fusion, but it also doesn't cost a single penny. You can use it for noncommercial or commercial applications, trade it with friends, hang it on your wall, or burn it on a CD and use it to play fetch with your dog. Further, because PHP is open source, there are tens of thousands of developers in the known universe working hard to develop modules that do new and groovy things. Being open source and free are important, given the fact that new and successively financially unattainable application servers are hitting the market. To find out more about PHP, go to the source at `www.php.net`. You can also go to `www.phpbuilder.com`. If you are interested in open source software, go to `www.opensource.org`.

JSP

Back in 1990, Sun Microsystems, a company best known for its Unix workstations and Solaris operating system, started a project called *Green* whose primary thrust was to create software for consumer electronics—you know, toasters, ovens, microwaves, and the like. One of the results of the project was a programming language called Oak. It soon became obvious to the project participants that while Oak wasn't particularly appropriate for its intended reason (mainly because it was *way* ahead of its time), it would make a great language for internet programming.

In 1995, Oak was renamed Java and christened at Sun Microsystems's annual tradeshow, SunWorld. Since then, it has risen tremendously in popularity and is used for the development of all sorts of self-contained lightweight Internet applications—including dynamic database-driven applications.

Essentially, JSP pages are a mix of server-side code and regular HTML. The only real difference between JSP and other aforementioned technologies is that JSP, as one would expect, uses Java for the server-side code.

Although Java was developed by Sun Microsystems, JSP is hardly an exclusively Sun-dominated technology. In fact, there is a huge number of JSP application servers on the market these days: Macromedia JRun, IBM Websphere, Apache Tomcat, and BEA Weblogic. In addition, many JSP servers are compatible with both Windows and Unix platforms.

Making the Right Choice for Your Dynamic Application Needs

So, now that you've been bombarded with a discussion of all the dynamic database-driven technologies available for use in Dreamweaver MX, what is the best choice? Well, if you read the previous sections in detail, you'll notice a couple of trends emerging that will influence your decision. First, the application server. What does it cost? Is it compatible with the web server you (or your ISP) is using? Second, the database. Is the database you are planning on using compatible with the dynamic database-driven technology you are planning on using? If you are planning on mounting your dynamic website on a remote server, is your type of database supported? Third, the web server. What does the intended web server cost? Is your intended application server compatible with your intended web server? Fourth, the dynamic database-driven technology itself. Are the intended features of your dynamic site supported by your application technology of choice?

> While all of the previously discussed technologies have similar features, they each have different strengths and weaknesses in terms of what they can do. While Dreamweaver MX lets you access a huge amount of these specialized features, the introductory nature of this section prohibits me from specializing in one particular technology. As a result, the chapters that follow will stick to the more generic features that all of the technologies have in common.

Ultimately, your decision is going to be based on a combination of different factors. This having been said, let's do a quick rundown of each technology so that you can make a better decision:

ASP Active Server Pages work with an ODBC or OLE DB–compliant database (of which there are many). As a result, you have many options for the particular database you want to use. Further, ASP is most commonly deployed on the Microsoft IIS or PWS web server (both come with your Windows operating system), so you don't have to buy a web server. Finally, because IIS and PWS double both as application servers and web servers, you won't have to put out any extra money for an application server. This means that you'll find many commercial server space providers that support ASP. All of these factors make ASP one of the most widely chosen dynamic database-driven technologies.

ASP.NET ASP.NET is almost the same as ASP in terms of features that would influence your dynamic database-driven technology decision at this introductory stage of the game. While ASP.NET does feature some fairly hefty tools for working with SQL, the only real difference of which you should be aware right now is that ASP.NET will run only on Windows 2000 or a Windows XP Pro computer upon which the IIS 5 server is running and the .NET frame has been installed (this can be downloaded from Microsoft at `www.asp.net/download.aspx`). If you are using the PWS web server on a Windows 95 or 98 machine, you will be unable to deliver ASP.NET applications.

> SQL, which stands for Structured Query Language, is not a database per se. Instead it's a type of language used to formulate complex database queries (questions).

ColdFusion One of the most attractive features of ColdFusion is that the application server can function both on a Windows platform and a Unix platform. Further, ColdFusion works with an ODBC or OLE DB–compliant database (of which there are many). In addition, while you can use Dreamweaver MX to author ColdFusion applications, CFML is a markup-based language, and is therefore easier to learn than a scripting language such as JavaScript or VBScript. However, give the fact that the application server costs anywhere from $2000 to $5000, it is not the choice of many smaller developers or companies.

PHP   PHP is an interesting technology that has gained a huge amount of support in recent years. Chief among the reasons is the fact that the application server (which, as mentioned before, can be acquired at `www.php.net` and runs on both Unix and Windows server) is free. Because of this, many commercial server space providers support PHP. In addition, while MySQL is the database of choice for PHP, it, like the PHP application server, is free (for more information on MySQL, go to `www.mysql.com`).

While Microsoft Access doesn't natively support MySQL export, MyAccess, a free utility that allows you to manage MySQL databases directly from within Access, can be downloaded from `www.mysql.com/Downloads/Win32/myaccess2000_1_4.zip`.

JSP   While quite powerful and accessible, JSP is one of the least used dynamic database-driven technologies. There are a fair amount of JSP application servers that run on both Windows and Unix server, but most are commercial and quite expensive. For example, Macromedia's JRun server ranges in price from $1000 to $5000, depending on the version you buy. The only exception is the Jakarta Tomcat server, which can be downloaded for free at `http://Jakarta .apache.org/tomcat`. The second issue is that since JSP uses JDBC to let the application "talk" to the database, the number of different databases that you can employ are somewhat limited.

Working with an Application Server

As has already been mentioned, an application server is a vital part in a dynamic database-driven application. While the role it plays in getting your wonderful dynamic creations onto the World Wide Web is obvious, an application server can also be used to test and preview your dynamic database-driven pages during the authoring process. Test, you say? I bet you're thinking to yourself that you can easily test a page using the preview in browser function that was discussed back in Chapter 3, "Setting Up and Managing Your Page."

Unfortunately, unlike regular static HTML pages, you cannot use the preview in browser function for documents that contain dynamic content pulled from a database. Why? Well, when Dreamweaver MX previews a document in a browser, it uses your computer as the web server. When it comes to dynamic database-driven pages, the link that Dreamweaver MX creates between the file itself and the browser when the document is previewed lacks the vital translation of the server-side code that is handled by the application server. Just because Dreamweaver MX can author the server-side script and place it in the HTML document doesn't mean it can preview the results in a browser. For that, you need to have the application server itself installed on your computer.

What I've neglected to say thus far is that, aside from Microsoft PWS and IIS, which serve both as application server and web server, all of the applications previously discussed need a web server (which should be installed on the computer from which you are testing) to work properly. I strongly suggest that, if you are working on a Windows platform, you install and use either PWS or IIS, depending on which OS version you are using. Both servers are free, easy to install, and easy to configure. Obviously, if you are developing on a Mac, you don't have this option.

Granted, you don't necessarily have to install the application server for the dynamic database-driven technology you are using (see Table 17.1) on your computer. You could certainly upload all your site's files to the remote server (where an application server resides) to preview your dynamic pages within a browser. This, however, can prove to be a little time consuming and cumbersome when you are trying to rapidly develop and test your dynamic application. It's in your best interest to have a copy of the application server you are using installed on your computer.

Dreamweaver MX lets you view dynamic data extracted from a database using something called Live Data (a topic that will be discussed in detail in Chapter 18, "Displaying and Manipulating Data from Your Database"). The kicker is that the dynamic content is displayed in the Document Window and not within a browser. This alone can prove to be somewhat frustrating to someone who wishes to see how their dynamic pages will appear when viewed in their intended medium: the web browser.

Table 17.1 Dynamic Database-Driven Technologies and Their Associated Application Servers	DYNAMIC DATABASE-DRIVEN TECHNOLOGY	APPLICATION SERVER
	ASP	Microsoft PWS (also acts as web server)
		Microsoft IIS (also acts as web server)
		Sun ChilliSoft ASP
	ASP.NET	Microsoft IIS 5 with .NET framework (also acts as web server)
	JSP	BEA WebLogic
		IBM WebSphere
		Apache Tomcat
		Macromedia JRun
		ColdFusion MX ColdFusion MX
	PHP	PHP Server

So, how do you go about getting the appropriate application server? In certain cases, such as Microsoft PWS and IIS, the server comes with your operating system, and all you need to do is install is from your operating system's program disk. In other cases, such as Macromedia ColdFusion, JRun, or WebSphere, you'll have to purchase the server. Thankfully, many of the commercial application servers are available as a time-limited demo (usually 30 days or so). In cases such as the PHP server or Apache Tomcat, you can download the application server for free, no strings attached (the joys of open source software!). Table 17.2 provides a list of the application servers we've discussed, as well as the location from which they can be downloaded.

APPLICATION SERVER	LOCATION
Microsoft PWS (doubles as web server)	Windows 95 and 98 application CD
	(`setup.exe` file located in the add-ons\pws folder)
Microsoft IIS (doubles as web server)	Windows 2000, XP or XP Pro application CD
	(from the Control Panel, open the Add or Remove Programs dialog box and select the Add/Remove Components option)
BEA WebLogic	`http://commerce.bea.com/downloads/weblogic_server.jsp`
IBM WebSpehre (demo)	`www-4.ibm.com/software/webservers/appserv/download.html`
Apache Tomcat (free)	`http://jakarta.apache.org/tomcat`
Macromedia JRun (demo)	`www.macromedia.com/jrun`
ColdFusion MX (demo)	`www.macromedia.com/coldfusion`
PHP Server (free)	`www.php.net`

Table 17.2

Application Servers and Their Download Locations

Once you install the application server on your computer, you are only halfway finished. From there, you'll need to tell Dreamweaver MX where the application server is located so the content will display properly when you preview your dynamic pages, a process we'll explore in the "Setting Your Testing Server" section later in this chapter.

Introduction to Dynamic Dreamweaver

Now that you've gotten a solid introduction to the "theory" behind dynamic database-driven applications and, hopefully, made the choice for which technology you'll use, its time to start exploring Dreamweaver MX's dynamic related tools. Granted, you were already introduced to some of the things discussed here in Chapter 2, "Starting Up Dreamweaver." However, it's really good to re-familiarize yourself—especially now, since many of Dreamweaver MX's dynamic tools will have a better context.

As you've already guessed, creating dynamic database-driven applications are a fairly specialized undertaking. As a result, you have to have some pretty specialized tool with which you can develop, test, and deploy your dynamic creations—all of which Dreamweaver MX provides. In the following section, you are going to get a brief refresher in the dynamic tools you'll be using. From there, you'll get a brief introduction to how server behaviors and objects are used to create server-side code in Dreamweaver MX.

Dreamweaver's Dynamic Tools

Like with many other creative processes in Dreamweaver, when you author dynamic database-driven applications, you are going to use a set group of tools—primarily panels. In order to continue laying the groundwork for your dynamic database-driven application, it's a really good idea to refresh your memory a little by revisiting some of the panels to which you were briefly introduced back in Chapter 2.

Insert Bar

When you click the Application tab of the Insert Bar (Window → Insert), you get access to a set of generic dynamic content and server behaviors that can be inserted into your document (see Figure 17.1).

Figure 17.1

The Insert bar's Application tab

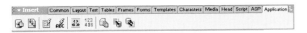

While many of the available options are also available in the Server Behavior panel, the Insert bar is a handy way to insert some of the most common server behaviors and types of dynamic content.

In addition, you'll notice that, depending on the type of document (ASP, JSP, ColdFusion, etc.) with which you are currently working, there is an additional tab in the Insert bar that contains a series of different code elements (see Figure 17.2) that, when clicked on, will be inserted into the Code View of your document.

> Because of the introductory nature of this section of the book, we aren't going to be going into the different document specific code elements. Instead, we'll be sticking to the server behaviors accessible under the Insert bar's Application tab and the Server Behavior panel.

Figure 17.2

The Insert bar features an additional tab that contains code elements specific to the type of document with which you are currently working.

Databases Panel

The Databases panel (see Figure 17.3), which is accessibly by going to Windows →
Databases, is the tool through which all of your database connections are made (a
process we'll discuss later in this chapter) and where all connections are then displayed.

In addition, you can use the Databases panel to view the entire structure of
your database—including tables, columns, and individual data types.

Figure 17.3

The Databases panel

Binding Panel

The Bindings panel (see Figure 17.4), which can be accessed by going to Window → Bindings,
is the location where all of the sources of dynamic content are displayed—a topic that will be
discussed in detail in Chapter 18.

Server Behaviors Panel

The Server Behaviors panel (see Figure 17.5) is the primary tool for adding discreet blocks of server-side code to your pages. Accessed by going to Windows →
Server Behaviors, the Server Behaviors panel is one of the most important tools
for creating dynamic content in Dreamweaver MX.

If you are interested in learning more about server behaviors, see the "Server
Behaviors and Objects" section below.

Figure 17.4

The Bindings panel

The Components panel

The Components panel, which is accessible by going to Windows → Components,
lets you add and manipulate ASP.NET and ColdFusion based components. In
addition, it allows you to add and manipulate JSP based JavaBeans.

Understanding Server Behaviors

Server behaviors are probably one of the most important aspects of authoring
dynamic database-driven applications in Flash MX. Even at this early stage of your
journey through the world of dynamic Dreamweaver, you've already learned that
code is a pivotal and vital part in creating dynamic database-driven applications.
This is all fine and good if you leave, breath, and think code. However, what if you are kind of
person who still wants to develop dynamic database-driven applications, but aren't able to
code your way out of a wet paper bag? Never, fear, this is where server behaviors come into
the picture.

Essentially, Server Behaviors, which are accessible through both the Server Behavior
panel and the Insert bar, are pre-written blocks of code that are designed to do specific
things: create a user login, navigate through dynamic data, update a database record, etc.

Figure 17.5

**The Server Behaviors
panel**

The bottom line is that with Server Behaviors, you don't ever have to do any hand coding at all. Multiple behaviors can be added to any page, thereby allowing you to create some genuinely complex dynamic applications without ever having to think about the code. Dreamweaver MX takes care of everything behind the scenes so you can focus on what is most important—creativity.

As you'll find out in later chapters in this section of the book, Dreamweaver MX ships with a set of default Server Behaviors. The terribly cool thing is that you don't have to make due with just what ships with the program. There is a whole community of developers who create and distribute their own home-made Server Behaviors (which are generically referred to as extensions)—the vast majority of which are totally free. One of the largest resources is located at the Macromedia Exchange (`http://www.macromedia.com/exchange`)where you can download all sorts of incredibly cool components that let you extend the power of Dreamweaver MX. In order to download and install additional Server Behaviors, you'll need to get a little free piece of software from Macromedia called the Extension Manager.

Setting Your Document Type

As you've already learned, you have many different options when it comes to choosing a database-driven application technology. As a result, one of the first things you need to when you're starting to create your dynamic site is to tell Dreamweaver the type of document you'll be working with. There are actually two ways of doing this: when creating a new document and from within an existing document—let's take a look at both.

Setting Your Document Type from Scratch

One of the new features in Dreamweaver MX is the ability to set the type of document when you start a new page:

1. Go to File → New to open the New Document dialog box.

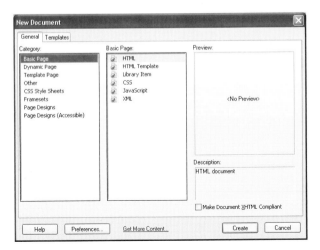

2. If it isn't already, click the General tab.

3. Select the Dynamic Page option from the Category list box.

4. From here, choose the specific page type you would like your new document to be from the Dynamic Page list box.

5. When you're finished, click Create.

6. From here, not only will the Dreamweaver MX workspace be configured to work with the selected document type (by displaying that server technology's tab in the Insert bar, for example), but the proper extension (.asp, .php, .jsp, etc.) will be attached to the document once its saved.

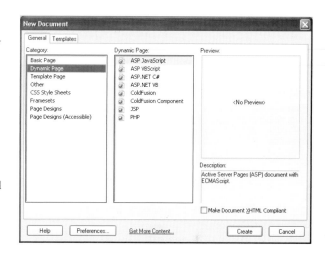

If you are working on a page whose document type has already been set to one type of dynamic database-driven technology or another, you will actually be unable to convert it to another dynamic document type. Instead, you'll need to create a new document type from scratch using the process described above.

Setting Your Document Type from Within an Existing Page

While creating a specific document type from scratch is a relatively easy process, what happens if you already have an existing static HTML page that you want to convert to a different document type? Fear not, the process is equally easy.

1. With the document open whose document type you wish to change, open either the Databases panel (Window → Databases), the Bindings panel (Window → Bindings), the Server Behaviors panel (Window → Server Behaviors), or the Components panel (Window → Components).

2. Notice that instead of the usual content, the panel you opened will have a numbered list of instructions—each with a blue link.

3. Click the document type link in step #2 to open the Choose Document Type dialog box.

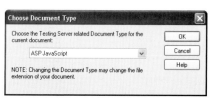

4. Open the drop-down menu and select the document type to which you want to convert the existing page.

5. Click OK.

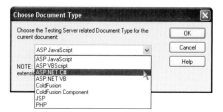

Setting Your Testing Server

Now that you've set your document type, it's time to explore how to set your testing server. I've already mentioned that if you have a web server and an application server installed on your computer, you can test your site and see how it would appear in a user's browser. Before you do this, however, you have to tell Dreamweaver MX the location of the server itself:

1. Open the Site Definition dialog box (Site → Edit Sites).

2. When the Edit Sites dialog box appears, select the specific site whose testing server you wish to set and click Edit.

3. When the Define Site dialog box opens, click the Advanced Tab.

4. Select the Testing Server option from the Category list box.

5. Select the type of server model you're using from the Server Model drop-down menu.

6. Choose how you will access the testing server from the Access drop-down menu. If you have direct access to the testing server (either over a LAN or because it's on your own computer), select Local/Network. If you are accessing your testing server remotely via FTP, select FTP. When you select FTP as the manner to access your testing server, you'll need to enter the name of the FTP host, the host directory, the login/password, and firewall information.

7. From here, you need to tell Dreamweaver MX where on your web server it is going to temporarily transfer the page so that it can be processed by the application server and displayed by the browser. You can easily set the root folder of the web server. Alternatively, you can create your own subfolder. If you do create your own subfolder, it's important to remember that it *must* be within the root folder of your web server, or Dreamweaver MX will not be able to properly display the page in a browser.

    By default, Dreamweaver MX assumes that there is an application server running on your web server.

8. Click the Browse to File button (to the right of the Testing Server Folder field). When the Choose the Remote Folder dialog box appears, navigate to the root folder of your web server and click Select.

9. Enter the correct URL prefix into the URL Prefix field. The structure of the URL prefix must match that of the Testing Server Folder field. For instance, with Microsoft PWS or IIS, if your testing server folder is `C:\Inetpub\wwwroot\scifi\`, your URL Prefix would be `http://localhost/scifi`. If you don't enter the correct URL prefix, you won't be able to properly test your dynamic pages.

10. Click OK.

11. When you are returned to the Edit Sites dialog box, click Done.

> Because it happens in the Site Definition dialog box, the process of setting your testing server is one that can be carried out when you are initially setting up a local site.

Connecting to a Database

Before you can actually begin integrating content from a database into your web page, you need to tell Dreamweaver MX where the intended database is located. The kicker is that databases and web applications don't really speak the same language. As a result, they need an intermediary of sorts, a "translator," to properly communicate. In the world of database there are three types of translators that exist: ODBC (Open Database Connectivity), OLE DB (Object Linking & Embedding Database), and JDBC (Java Database Connectivity).

The good thing for those who are just starting out in the world of dynamic web applications is that the type of dynamic database-driven technology you select usually automatically dictates the type of translator that is used. For instance, because ASP "speaks" ODBC, the choice is automatically made. On the other hand, if you choose to create a ColdFusion MX or JSP-based site, JDBC will be used as the translator.

The translator that is selected functions through the use of a database driver. Essentially, a database driver is a tiny piece of software that facilitates the communication between your database and your application—without it, you won't even be able to connect to your database in Dreamweaver MX. It's important to understand that database drivers are database specific (Table 17.1). So, for instance, if Microsoft Access is your database of choice, the Access driver needs to be installed on your computer.

Database drivers are written and distributed be a host of third-party developers, including Microsoft and Oracle. However, if you are planning on using an ODBC-based dynamic database-driven technology, Microsoft offers a number of free downloadable drivers for the most popular databases (including MS SQL Server, MS Access, and Oracle). These drivers, which unfortunately run only on the Windows operating system, are automatically installed with Microsoft Office and Windows 2000.They are also included in the MDAC (Microsoft Data Access Components) packages, the latest version of which can be acquired by going to`www.microsoft.com/data/download.htm`.

	DYNAMIC DATABASE-DRIVEN TECHNOLOGY	TRANSLATOR TECHNOLOGY	COMMON DATABASE DRIVERS
Table 17.3 **Dynamic Database Application Technologies, Their Translators, and Common Database Drivers**	ASP	ODBC or OLE DB	Microsoft Access Driver
			Microsoft SQL Server Driver
			Microsoft SQL Server Provider
			Microsoft ODBC for Oracle
	ASP.NET	OLE DB	Microsoft Access Driver
			Microsoft SQL Server Driver
			Microsoft SQL Server Provider
			Microsoft ODBC for Oracle
	JSP	JDBC	Sun JDBC-ODBC Driver
			i-net Sprinta JDBC Driver
			Oracle Thin JDBC Driver
	ColdFusion MX	JDBC	Sun JDBC-ODBC Driver
			i-net Sprinta JDBC Driver
			Oracle Thin JDBC Driver
	ColdFusion 4/5	ODBC or OLE DB	ColdFusion Drivers
			Microsoft Access Driver
			Microsoft SQL Server Driver
	PHP	MySQL default	MySQL Drivers

To recap, here's what you need to make a connection to a database in Dreamweaver MX:

- A database to which you are going to connect.

- The specific driver associated with that database needs to be installed on your computer.

CROSS-PLATFORM WOES

It's at about this time that problems with developing dynamic database-driven applications with Dreamweaver MX on a Mac start creeping into the picture. Actually, they won't really creep in: they'll hit you full force upside the head and potentially drop you dead in your tracks. Unfortunately, because Macs have not been traditionally used for database development, the number of ODBC drivers (the most commonly drivers used in grass roots dynamic database development) available are few and far between. The result is that in many cases, Mac users aren't going to be able to find the necessary drivers they need, thereby preventing them from making the database connection in Dreamweaver. Bummer.

This may all seem a little overwhelming and confusing, but it really isn't. As long as you've got the correct database driver installed on your machine, you are in good shape.

This having been said, in the following sections, you'll walk through the process of establishing a database connection for each of the various dynamic database-driven technologies available to you in Dreamweaver MX.

Creating a Database Connection for ColdFusion MX

Creating a database connection for ColdFusion MX is a little different from setting a regular database connection. First, it's not called a database connection, but a data source. Second, most of the work of defining a data source is done in the ColdFusion Administrator (the server's management tool) not Dreamweaver MX. As a result, the steps outlined here are somewhat on the light side, as they neglect what you'll need to do while in the ColdFusion Administrator, a topic which is outside the scope of the chapter. If you've chosen ColdFusion as your database-driven technology, you'll want to become intimately familiar with its management tools.

CHECKING YOUR SYSTEM'S DATABASE DRIVERS IN WINDOWS

If you aren't exactly sure which database drivers you've currently got installed on your computer, there is an easy way to tell. If you are working on Windows NT, 98, or 95, go to Start → Settings → Control Panel and then double-click the ODBC Data Sources icon (which might also be called 32-Bit ODBC Data Sources, depending on your system). If you are using Windows 2000, choose Start → Settings → Control Panel → Administrative Tools → Data Sources. If you are Using Windows XP, go to Start → Control Panel → Performance and Maintenance → Administrative Tools → Data Sources (ODBC).

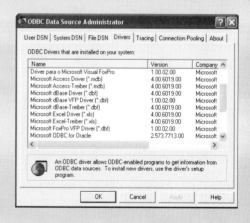

When the ODBC Data Source Administrator dialog box opens, click the Drivers tab and you'll see a list of the database drivers installed on your system.

To set up a data source for ColdFusion:

> If you are using ColdFusion Server 4 or 5 (as opposed to ColdFusion MX), you can set up a DSN (Data Source Name), as will be described in the "Creating a Database Connection for ASP" section next, and it will be treated as a data source.

1. Make sure you are working from within a site whose server model/document type has been set to ColdFusion MX.

2. Open the Database panel (Window ➔ Databases).

3. Click the Modify Data Sources button [icon] (in the top right-hand corner of Database panel).

   If you haven't set ColdFusion as your Document Type/Server Model, you won't have access to the Modify Data Sources button.

4. The ColdFusion Administrator will open in a browser window. Log in and create a new data source. (For more information of working with the Cold Fusion Administrator, refer to the product documentation.)

5. When you've finished creating the new data source, close down the Cold Fusion Administrator.

6. Make sure a ColdFusion document is open in Dreamweaver MX. You'll note that the newly created data source will be located in the Databases panel (Window ➔ Databases).

Creating a Database Connection for ASP

There are two steps to creating a database connection when you're using ASP. First, you have to create something called a DSN (Data Source Name). A DSN is a single word that identifies a set of database parameters such as the name and location of the database itself, the specific database driver that is used, and the login/password (if any) required to access the data. Setting up a DSN is relatively easy. However, like setting up a data source for a ColdFusion connection, it happens outside of Dreamweaver MX—and therefore is out of the scope of this book (sorry). Second, you'll have to tell Dreamweaver MX which DSN you'll be using, a process that is also pretty painless.

This having been said, there are two different types of DSNs you can create: Local and Remote. In the following sections, you'll look at how to create both, as well as the differences between them.

If you've installed an application server (PHP, PWS, IIS, ColdFusion, and so on,) on your local machine for the purposes of testing, you can either create a remote DSN or a local DSN. It really makes no difference, as your machine is serving as both the local computer on which the application is developed as well as the server to which it is deployed.

Creating a Connection with a Local DSN

When you create a local DSN, you're telling Dreamweaver MX that the DSN you're using has been (or will be) defined on the local machine. Note that Macs are unable to natively generate DSNs. If you are developing an ASP application on a Mac, you will have to use the remote DSN option.

To create a Local DSN:

1. Open your operating system's ODBC Data Source Administrator (see Figure 17.6) by choosing the appropriate option:

   - If you are using Windows XP, go to Start → Control Panel → Administrative Tools → Data Sources (ODBC).

   - If you are Using Windows 2000, go to Start → Settings → Control Panel → Administrative Tools → Data Sources.

   - If you are using Windows 95, 98, or NT, go to Start → Control Panel. When the Control panel opens, double-click the ODBC Data Sources icon (which might also be called 32-Bit ODBC Data Sources, depending on your system).

2. Click the System DNS tab—this is where all the DSNs currently on your system are displayed.

3. Click the Add button.

4. When the Create New Data Source dialog box appears (see Figure 17.7), select the specific driver (that is, the database) you want to use, and click the Finish button.

   If the driver for the specific type of database you're using does not show up in the Create New Data Source dialog box, you'll need to download it from the vendor's website and install in on your machine.

Figure 17.6

The ODBC Data Source Administrator

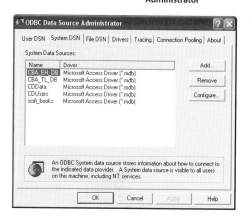

Figure 17.7

The Create New Data Source dialog box

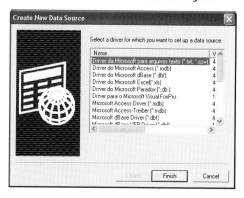

5. When the ODBC Microsoft Access Setup dialog box (see Figure 17.8) opens, enter a descriptive name into the Name field.

6. To tell your computer where the database associated with that particular DSN is located, click the Select button.

7. When the Select Database dialog box appears, navigate to where your database is located (presumably in the root folder of your local site), select it, and click OK.

8. When you are returned to the ODBC Microsoft Access Setup dialog box, click OK.

9. When you are returned to the ODBC Data Source Administer, your newly created DSN will be listed under the DSN System tab.

10. Now you need to go back into Dreamweaver MX and establish the actual database connection. Before you get started, make sure you are working from within a local site whose server model/document type has been set to ASP. Then, if it isn't already, open the Databases panel (Window → Databases).

11. Click the plus (+) button (in the panel's upper left-hand corner) and select Data Source Name (DSN) from the subsequent drop-down menu (see Figure 17.9).

12. When the Data Source Name (DSN) dialog box (see Figure 17.10) opens, enter a unique name into the Connection field. This name will serve to identify the connection to the DSN you created and will be displayed in the Databases panel.

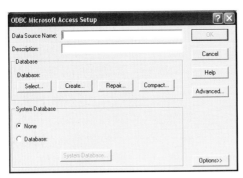

Figure 17.8

The ODBC Microsoft Access Setup dialog box

Figure 17.9

Click the Databases panel's plus (+) menu to get access to the Data Source Name (DSN) option.

13. Now you need to point Dreamweaver MX to your newly created DSN (which contains all the information about your database). Open the Data Source Name (DSN) drop-down menu and select the DSN you created.

    Here is a bit of a shortcut. If you want to create the DSN from within Dreamweaver MX, click the Define button (to the right of the Data Source Name (DSN) drop-down menu) in the Data Source Name (DSN) dialog box to open the Create New Data Source dialog box. From there, you'll be able to easily define your local DSN.

Figure 17.10

The Data Source Name (DSN) dialog box

14. Click the Using Local DSN radio button.

15. Click the Test button. Dreamweaver will then see if, based on the parameters you supplied, it can locate and connect to your database. If the test is successful, a dialog box will pop up giving you a big old thumbs up.

16. When you've finished creating the connection, click OK.

17. Your DSN will be added to the Databases panel (see Figure 17.11).

Creating a Connection with a Remote DSN

When you create a remote DSN, you're telling Dreamweaver MX that the DSN you're using has been (or will be) defined on a remote machine—usually the web server itself.

Figure 17.11

Once you've successfully established a connection to your database, the name will appear in the Databases panel.

Mac users who are developing ASP-based pages have no other choice than to use a remote DSN. This is because, as discussed previously, Macs, not being particularly well suited for database development, don't have the ability to create a local DSN.

For the most part, you'll find that you'll use a Remote DSN in a situation where your site is being hosted on a web server to which you don't have direct access (that is, it's not located on the machine on which you are authoring the site). It's important to remember that, because DSNs and ASP are Windows-specific, the remote server upon which you'll be mounting your site will have to be Windows based.

To connect to a database using a remote DSN:

1. Make sure a DSN has been defined on the remote server upon which you will be hosting your site.

If you are hosting your site with a commercial server provider, you'll need to first make sure they support the type of database you'll be using and then request that they define a DSN for you. Depending on the company, this could possibly take some time. Make sure you plan well in advance.

2. Make sure you are working within a site where ASP has already been defined as the server model/document type.

3. Open the Databases panel (Window → Databases).

4. Click the plus (+) button in the panel's upper left-hand corner and select Data Source Name (DSN) from the subsequent drop-down menu.

5. When the Data Source Name (DSN) dialog box appears, enter a name for the new connection into the Connection Name field—don't use any spaces or special characters.

6. Select the Using DSN on Testing Server option (at the bottom of the Data Source Name [DSN] dialog box).

7. Enter the Name of the DSN into the Data Source Name (DSN) field. Make sure you enter the name exactly as it was defined on the remote server. If you want, you can click the DSN button (to the right of the Data Source Name [DSN] field) to get a list of all the DSNs defined on the remote server.

   When you click the DSN button, Dreamweaver attempts to connect to the testing server you set in Testing Server section of the Site Definition dialog box. If, for some reason, Dreamweaver is unable to connect to the remote server, it will give you an error message and you will be unable to see the list of defined DSNs.

8. If a login and password were set when the DSN was originally defined, you'll need to enter the information into the User Name and Password fields.

   Remember, if you don't provide the login/password that you set when the DSN was originally defined, Dreamweaver MX will be unable to connect to the database.

9. When you finish setting all the necessary information, click the Test button. Dreamweaver MX will attempt to connect to the database. If you are successful, Dreamweaver MX will tell you so.

10. When you finish, click OK to exit the Data Source Name (DSN) dialog box.

11. When you are plopped back into the main work space, you'll note that the connection will be added to the Databases panel.

Creating a Database Connection for ASP.NET

Creating a database connection for ASP.NET is somewhat different than it is for ASP. This is primarily because ASP generally uses a different "translator"—OLE DB—to connect to a database. This means you'll have to jump though some extra hoops to set up your connection.

As with ASP, you need to define a DSN to properly connect to a database when you're working with ASP.NET. If you are having difficulty remembering how to define a DSN, see the "Creating a Database Connection for ASP" section earlier in the chapter. The only real difference is that instead of an ODBC driver, you'll specify an OLE DB driver.

Figure 17.12

Click the Databases panel's plus (+) menu to get access to the OLE DB option.

1. Make sure you are working from within a local site whose server model/document type has been set to ASP.NET.

2. If it isn't already, open the Databases panel (Window → Databases).

3. Click the plus (+) button in the panel's upper left-hand corner and select OLE DB Connection from the subsequent drop-down menu (see Figure 17.12). (If you are planning to connect to a Microsoft SQL Server database instead, choose the SQL Server Connection from the Database panel's plus [+] menu.)

4. When the OLE DB Connection dialog box appears (see Figure 17.13), enter a unique name for the connection into the Connection Name field.

5. From here, you need to create the connection string that contains all the necessary info your ASP.NET application needs to connect to the database (something like a DSN). To do this,

Figure 17.13

The OLE DB Connection dialog box

click the Template button in the OLE DB Connection dialog box. This opens the Connection String Template dialog box (see Figure 17.14), where you'll be able to select a string template for the specific type of OLE DB provider you need to use.

6. Select the template for the specific OLE DB provider you are using and click OK. Notice that the connection string is entered into the OLE DB Connection dialog box's Connection String field. From here, you'll need to configure the template (which contains only the structure of the string itself, not the information specific to your database).

7. Click the Build button.

Figure 17.14

The Connection String Template dialog box

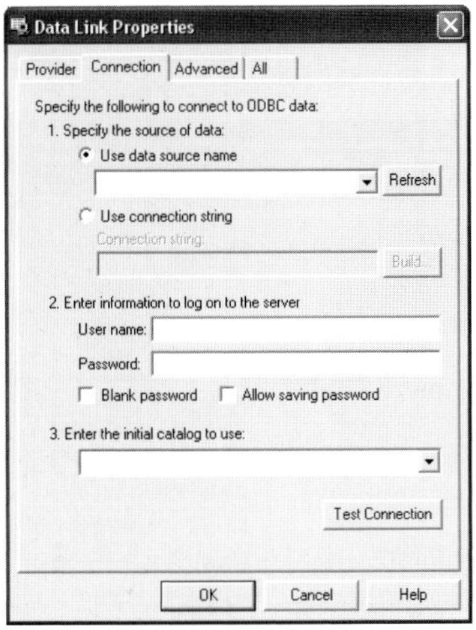

Figure 17.15

**The Data Link Proper-
ties dialog box**

8. When the Data Link Properties dialog box appears (see Figure 17.15), click the Connection tab.

9. Click the Use Data Source Name radio button.

10. Open the Use Data Source Name drop-down menu and select the DSN that you previously defined.

11. If a login and password was set when the DSN was originally defined, you'll need to enter the information into the User Name and Password fields.

12. If you want, you can test the connection by clicking the Test Connection button.

13. When you finish, click OK.

14. When you return to the OLE DB Connection dialog box, you'll notice that the particulars of your connection string have been added to the Connection String field.

15. Click OK to return to the main program workspace.

Creating a Database Connection for JSP

Like all of the other cases discussed thus far, the process of creating a database connection for JSP is determined by the technology itself. As mentioned previously, the database connection is facilitated by the JDBC translator, which works through the use of a database-specific driver. Because of this, the most important step in making a database connection for JSP is to make sure the appropriate database driver is installed on your machine.

USING ODBC FOR A JSP DATABASE CONNECTION

You can connect to a database for JSP by using ODBC instead of JDBC. If you do this, you only need to set up a DSN like you did in the "Creating a Database Connection for ASP" section earlier in this chapter. However, for this to work you need a special driver called a JDBC-ODBC bridge driver. There are also a couple of additional issues of which you should be aware. First, the JSP application server upon which you are mounting your JSP site *must* be running on a Windows platform. Second, the Windows server upon which the JSP application server is running *must* have the ODBC driver for the database you are using. Third and most importantly, the Windows server *must* have the JDBC-ODBC bridge driver installed. This driver is part of the Java 2 SDK downloadable from Sun Microsystems at http://java.sun.com/j2se/.

Sun Microsystems provides an online a searchable database of JDBC drivers; to see it, go to http://industry.java.sun.com/products/jdbc/drivers.

Once you do this, making the database connection is easy. The only thing that you might find irksome is that you need to know some rather specific and specialized information about your particular driver that is obtainable only from the vendor.

To make a database connection in JSP:

1. Make sure you are working from within a local site where the server model/document type has been set to JSP.

2. Open the Databases panel (Window → Databases).

3. Click the plus (+) button (in the panel's upper left-hand corner) and select the database driver you are using from the subsequent drop-down menu (see Figure 17.16). If the driver you are using is not included in the drop-down menu, select Custom JDBC Connection.

4. When the subsequent dialog box (whose name will depend on the specific driver you selected) appears, enter a unique name for the connection into the Connection Name field.

5. If you selected the Custom JDBC option, you'll need to enter the full name of the driver into the Driver field now—you'll be able to get this name from either the driver documentation or by contacting the vendor.

6. Now, things get a little dicey. Regardless of whether you chose the Custom JDBC Connection option or one of the other available drivers, you need to enter the location for the database into the URL field (whether on a remote testing server or your local machine). The problem is that the structure of the path itself is particular to the type of driver/database you're using. As you will notice, depending on the type of driver you selected, Dreamweaver has entered the structure of the URL itself complete with placeholders (the square brackets), which you will need to fill in yourself. The parameters can be acquired from either your driver documentation or the vendor.

7. From here, insert the login and password, if needed, for the database into the Username and Password fields.

Figure 17.16

Click the Databases panel's plus (+) menu to get access to all the available JDBC drivers.

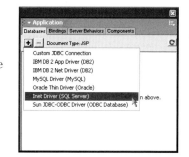

Figure 17.17

Figure 17.17

Click the Databases panel's plus (+) menu to get access to the MySQL Connection option.

8. Select either the Using Driver on Testing Server or Using Driver on this Machine option to set how Dreamweaver MX will connect to the database.

9. When you've finished setting all the parameters of the connection, click the Test button. If Dreamweaver successfully connects to the database, you'll get a message indicating so.

10. Click OK to return to the main workspace. Notice that your connection is added to the Databases panel.

Creating a Database Connection for PHP

Creating a database connection for PHP is probably the easiest of all those we've discussed. All you need to do is make sure that MySQL database (which, as mentioned before, is open source and free) has been installed on the application server (either a remote host or your local machine) upon which you are mounting your website:

1. Make sure you are working from within a local site whose server model/document type has been set to PHP.

2. Open the Databases panel (Window → Databases).

3. Click the plus (+) button (in the panel's upper left-hand corner) and select MySQL Connection from the subsequent drop-down menu (see Figure 17.17). If the driver you are using is not included in the drop-down menu, select Custom JDBC Connection.

4. When the MySQL Connection dialog box opens (see Figure 17.18), enter a unique name in the Connection Name field.

5. Enter the name of the server that is hosting MySQL into the MySQL Server field—you can enter either an IP address (for example, 129.63.123.15) or the actual host name (for example, generichost.com). If you are running MySQL on your local machine, you can enter localhost.

Figure 17.18

The MySQL Connection dialog box

6. If a login and password are required to make the connection to your database, enter them in the Username and Password fields.

7. Enter the name of the database itself (including its extension) in the Database field. You can also click the Select button (to the right of the Database field) to get a list of MySQL databases on the host that is specified.

8. Click the Test button to see if Dreamweaver can make the connection to the database you're using.

9. Click OK to return to the main workspace.

10. Note that the connection has been added to the Databases panel.

Working with a Database Connection

Now that you've learned how to make the essential database connection for your server technology of choice, it's time to explore how to manipulate that connection. In the following sections, we'll briefly look at how you can go about editing an already established database connection. From there, we'll move on to how you can delete a database connection entirely.

Editing a Database Connection

Once a database connection has been established, it's an extremely easy process to go back and alter any of its various parameters:

1. If it isn't already, open the Databases panel (Window → Databases).

2. Select the specific connection you want to edit.

3. Cmd-click/right-click to open the context menu.

4. Select Edit Connection.

5. The dialog box particular to the server technology your connection employs will open. For instance, if you want to edit an ASP database connection, the Data Source Name (DSN) dialog box will open.

6. When you finish editing the database connection, click OK to return to the main workspace.

Deleting a Database Connection

Any given local site can have any number of discrete database connections. As a result, if your site is particularly large or complex, you might end up accumulating a fair number of database connections. So, what happens when you want to get rid of a database connection? You'll have to delete it:

1. If it isn't already, open the Databases panel (Window → Databases).

2. Select the connection you want to delete.

3. Cmd-click/right-click to open the context menu.

4. Select Delete Connection

5. When the dialog box appears warning you that the action cannot be undone, click Yes.

Viewing the Structure of Your Database

Arguably one of the coolest features in Dreamweaver MX is the ability to easily view the entire structure of your database—right from within the program itself. You'll find this feature extremely handy in situations where, for instance, you do not want to exit Dreamweaver MX and open up your database to figure out exactly what you named a given table or column.

1. Make sure you are working from within a site in which a database connection has been defined—you won't be able to view the structure of a database in a site where a connection hasn't already been made.

2. If it isn't already, open the Databases panel (Window → Databases).

3. Click the plus (+) icon (to the left of the connection name whose database structure you wish to view). The will expand the database connection and let you see any associated tables, views, or stored procedures.

4. Click the plus (+) icon to the left of Tables to view all the tables within that database.

5. You can expand the table you want to view by clicking its plus (+) icon. You'll notice that a list of each column in the table appears, and the specific data type of each is indicated by a small symbol just to its left (see Figure 17.19)

6. To collapse the database, follow the procedure just described (but in reverse): click the associated minus (–) icons rather than the plus (+) icons.

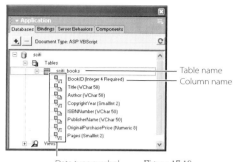

Table name
Column name

Data type symbol

Figure 17.19

Once you fully expand the Tables category, you can view all the associated columns, each of whose data type is represented by a small symbol.

Inspiration: Design and Technique

Zonecomics.com is your portal to the persistent noir world of The Zone, a mysterious and corrupt city in which different powerful factions secretly vie for power. Through the use of branching Flash movies, Zonecomics.com (see Figure 17.20) was originally conceived to tell multiple linear stories in a nonlinear fashion—a process the creators of the site have called contextual storytelling. Developed using Dreamweaver, Zonecomics.com is an extremely exciting experiment in nonlinear storytelling that uses PHP/mySQL to store and track user preferences, customize the interface (based on the "faction" with which the user affiliates when they register), and actually change the content of the Flash movies.

Figure 17.20

Zonecomics.com is an exciting experiment in nonlinear storytelling that employs Dreamweaver, Flash, and PHP/mySQL to create a remarkably immersive and inventive interactive experience.

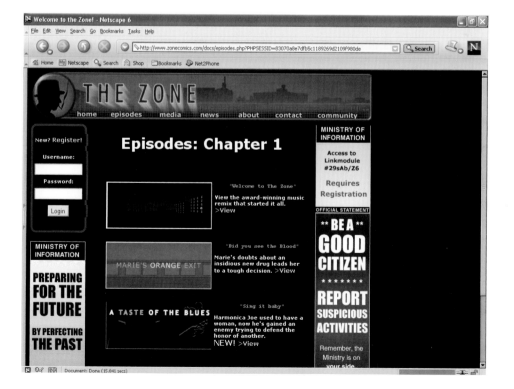

Summary

In this chapter, you took your first steps in the wide and wonderful world of dynamic database-driven applications. You started off by exploring how dynamic database-driven applications actually work. From there, you learned about the myriad technologies available to you for developing dynamic websites. After that, you looked at working with an application server. From there, you rolled your sleeves up and jumped into Dreamweaver MX with an introduction to Dreamweaver MX's dynamic working environment. This was followed with an exploration of how to set your document type, set a testing server, and connect to a database. You finished off the chapter with investigating how you can use the Databases panel to view the entire structure of your database.

In the coming chapter, you'll expand upon this knowledge and learn how to display dynamic information drawn from a database.

CHAPTER 18

Displaying and Manipulating Data from Your Database

As the name suggests, dynamic database-driven applications need dynamic content to function. Without dynamic content, they would be, well, static. And, what the heck would be the point of having dynamic websites that were static? In the following chapter, you will use all of the knowledge you've acquired about laying the groundwork for a dynamic database-driven application and start leaning how you can create something dynamic.

As mentioned in the frontmatter, the vast majority of task-oriented content presented in this section of the book will be geared toward developing ASP-based applications.

Topics that will be covered in this chapter include:

- Creating a source of dynamic content for your application
- Adding dynamic content to your page
- Formatting dynamic content
- Dynamically displaying multiple records
- Navigating through dynamically generated database records
- Creating a record counter

Creating a Source of Dynamic Content

One of the most important steps in creating a dynamic database-driven application is to tell Dreamweaver MX where it will draw its content. In Chapter 17, "Setting the Groundwork for Your Dynamic Database-Driven Application," you learned how to create a database connection. This process is only the first step in getting content from a database onto your page. In this section, you'll learn how to create a source of dynamic content that will act as a store of information from which dynamic content can be retrieved and displayed on your web page. You'll start off by learning how to create and test a Recordset, one of the most ubiquitous sources of dynamic content. From there, you'll look at how to use another source of dynamic content, user submitted form data, to generate dynamic content.

Using a Recordset

Despite the fact that you've learned that the application server acquires information from your database, the truth of the matter is that it can't communicate with your database directly. Instead, it uses an intermediary, called a Recordset, which contains a set of information retrieved using a database query and is stored within the server's memory. Not only does a Recordset facilitate communication between the application server and the database, but it also allows the application server to retrieve the desired information quite rapidly. You can think of a Recordset as a container between the application server and the database that is filled with the specific information from the database that your dynamic application needs to function. When the application requires some specific information, it goes and rummages through the Recordset, not the database, to find it If you are using a database to store and retrieve your dynamic information, you *must* use a Recordset.

Because Recordsets are one of the most ubiquitous sources of dynamic content, you'll find that you'll be using them quite often. In the following section, you'll look at how to create a Recordset. From there, you'll learn how to test your Recordset.

Before you can create a Recordset, you must have already made a database connection. In addition, the database to which you connected must have some information in it.

Creating a Recordset

As mentioned previously, before you can create a Recordset, you must have already established a database connection. Once you've done that, follow these steps:

1. Make sure the document that will use the Recordset is open.

2. If it isn't already, open the Bindings panel by going to Window → Bindings. The
   Bindings panel where all your sources of dynamic content are displayed.

3. Click the plus (+) button (in the panel's top left-hand corner) and choose Recordset (Query) from the subsequent drop-down menu.

4. From here, the Recordset dialog box will appear. If you aren't
   already, make sure you are working from within the Simple
   Recordset dialog box by clicking the Simple button (which only
   appears if you're working from within the Advanced Recordset
   dialog box).

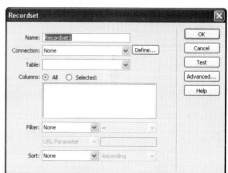

5. Enter a unique and descriptive name for your Recordset into the
   Name field. Don't use any spaces or special characters other than
   the underscore (_).

6. Select the database connection for which you are creating the
   Recordset from the Connection drop-down menu.

7. From here, choose the specific table in your database from which you want to create the
   Recordset.

8. Once you choose the database table, you'll notice that the Columns list box fills up with
   a list of all the columns in your database. From here, you can choose which information
   you want included in the Recordset. The cool thing is that you can select only the information that your application will use and leave the rest out. If you want all of the database columns included in the Recordset, click the All radio button. If, however, you only
   want a limited number of columns included in the Recordset, click the Selected radio
   button. Then, select those columns you want included—remember, you can hold down
   the Cmd/Ctrl key to select multiple items.

9. Click the Test button to see if the intended information can be retrieved.

10. When you're finished, click the OK button.

11. You'll notice that the Recordset has been added to your Bindings panel. You can expand the Recordset (by clicking on the plus [+] icon just to the left of its name) to see a list of all the columns that you included.

The Advanced Recordset dialog box, which is accessible by clicking the Advanced button, allows you to handcraft a more complex Recordset using SQL (Structured Query Language), a language that allows you to retrieve, add, and remove data from a database. While almost everything even remotely dynamic that you do in Dreamweaver MX generates SQL, you don't have to worry about creating any yourself (unless you want to, that is).

Using Form-Submitted Data

While using a database in conjunction with a Recordset as your source of dynamic content is probably one of the most common techniques when it comes to creating database-driven applications, you do have some additional options. One of the most interesting is to use information submitted by a user via a form. The difference between using form-submitted information instead of a Recordset as a source of dynamic content is that form-submitted data is stored in the server's memory and is used to create a dynamic content. For instance, on one page you could have a form that asks the user to fill in their name. When they do so and click the Submit button, they are taken to a second page in which their name (or at least, what they entered into the form) is used to generate some dynamic text—something like "Hi Ethan!"

> If you've forgotten how to create and work with forms, refresh your memory by checking out Chapter 10, "Obtaining User Information with Forms."

There are, however, a couple of caveats you should be aware of before you get into using form-submitted data as a source of dynamic content. First and most importantly, because form-submitted data is not stored in a database, it only has a one-time use. In addition, under normal circumstances, you can only pass form-submitted data from one page to a second page. You can't hold onto the form-submitted data and use it three or four pages down the line.

There are two primary methods by which data can be sent from a form to a server: POST and GET. Because the way you use them as dynamic content varies for each, you'll explore both types in the following sections. You'll also learn how to store form-submitted data in the server's memory (thereby allowing it to be used repeatedly) using something called a session variable.

Remember that while the following examples discuss ASP, the general principle outlined can be easily applied to any other document type.

Employing the *POST* Method

Back in Chapter 10, you learned that when you use the POST method to send information to a server, the data itself is included in the body of the message sent to the server. You can pass that information to a second page and use it to generate some sort of dynamic response based on the text entered into the form by the user:

1. Make sure you have a page open whose document type has been set to ASP.

2. If it isn't already, open the Insert bar (Window → Insert). Select the Forms tab.

3. Click the Form button ⬚ . Alternatively, you can go to Insert → Form. This will add the `<form></form>` tags to the page's code and the form delimiter in design view.

   If you have your invisible elements turned off, you won't be able to see the form delimiter. To make it visible, go to View → Visual Aids → Invisible Elements and make sure the particular element is "turned on" in the Invisible Elements section of the Edit Preferences dialog box (Edit → Preferences).

4. Make sure your cursor is still within the form delimiter and enter **Name:**.

5. Without moving your cursor anywhere else, insert a text field by either clicking the Text Field button ▭ in the Forms section of the Insert bar or going to Insert → Form Objects → Text Field.

6. Press Return (Mac)/ Enter (Win), and enter **Where Were You Born:**. Repeat the previous step so that you have another Text Field directly after the word address.

7. Press Return (Mac)/ Enter (Win) again and enter a Submit button by clicking the Button button ▭ in the Forms section of the Insert bar or by going to Insert → Form Objects → Button.

8. At this point, your form should look something like this:

Name: [   ]

Where Were You Born: [   ]

[**Submit**] |

9. Now that you have the form to collect some information from the user, you need to set the properties of the individual form elements as well as of the form itself. First, select the first Text Field. If it isn't already, open the Property Inspector (Window → Properties).

10. Enter **name** into the TextField field.

11. Select the second Text Field and enter **born** into the TextField field.

12. With your cursor still within the form delimiter, click the `<form>` tab in the Tag selector at the bottom of the Document Window. This selects the form itself and grants you access to its properties in the Property Inspector.

13. In the Property Inspector, select `POST` from the Method drop-down menu.

14. Enter **response.asp** into the Action field. This will be the name of the file (which you've yet to create) that will use the form submitted data to create a dynamic response.

15. Save the file (File → Save) as **submit.asp**.

16. Now it's time to create the page that will take the form-submitted data and use it to produce a dynamic response. First, create a new file (File → New) and make sure its document type is ASP.

17. Before you go any further, save the new file (File → Save) in the same directory as the previous file and name it **response.asp**.

18. Insert a form by clicking the Form button  in the Forms section of the Insert bar or by going to Insert → Form.

19. With your cursor still in the form delimiter, enter **Welcome**.

20. Press Return (Mac)/ Enter (Win) and type **We're glad to have someone from   visiting our website!** Nope, the sentence isn't a typo—and note that you need three spaces between the words "from" and "visiting." The reason for this will become clear in a few steps.

21. Now it's time to integrate the data submitted by the form in the `input.asp` file. First, if it isn't already, open the Bindings panel (Window → Bindings).

22. Click on the panel's plus (+) button and choose Request Variable from the subsequent drop-down menu. This will open the Request Variable dialog box.

23. Select Request.Form from the Type drop-down menu, and enter **name** into the Name field.

The text you enter into the Name field must be *exactly* the same name you assigned to one of the text fields in the `input.asp` field—it doesn't really matter which one at this stage of the game, but I chose to do the one called name first.

24. Repeat the process described in steps 22 and 23 for each of the remaining form elements for which you wish to gain access—in this case, you only need to do a single one (called **born**).

25. When you finish, you'll have two entries in the Bindings panel.

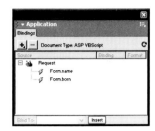

26. Now drag the first `Request.Form` element (`Form.name`, in this case) just to the right of the word "Welcome" on the first line.

27. Drag the second `Request.Form` element (`Form.born`) so that it is between the words "from" and "visiting."

28. You might find that you'll need to add a space either before or after (or both) the `Form.born Request.Form` element to ensure that the sentence, when previewed, has the necessary spaces between words. At this point, the text should look something like this:

> Welcome (Form.name)
>
> We are glad that someone from (Form.born) is visiting our website!

29. Save the `response.asp` file. Now it's time to test it out. For the application to work properly, however, both pages need to be copied to your testing server. If you were to preview the `input.asp` file in a browser, only that file would get copied to the testing server. The second file (`response.asp`) doesn't go anywhere. The result is that when the `input.asp` file gets copied to the testing server, it will search in vain for the `response.asp` file and be unable to find it, and you'll get an error message. To avoid this, you need to manually copy the `response.asp` file to the location on your testing server that you set as your Testing Server Folder when you were setting up your site. After you do this, preview the `input.asp` file in a browser, fill out the form, and marvel at your creative ingenuity!

Employing the *GET* Method

Now that you know how to use the `POST` method to pass form-submitted data from one page to another, let's look at how you can use `GET` to do the same thing. Remember, `GET` functions by sending the form-submitted data to the server in the form of a URL (see Figure 18.1).

http://www.amazon.com/exec/obidos/search-handle-url/index=books&field-keywords=watrall&bq=1/104-4842437-0249533

Figure 18.1

When you use the *GET* method, your information is sent to the server in the form of a URL.

In this section, you'll repeat the exercise carried out in the previous section using the two files you previously created (`input.asp` and `response.asp`). However, you'll have to fiddle with them to make one to send the data using GET and the other to display data sent with the GET method:

1. Make sure the `input.asp` file you created in the previous section is open.

2. Click on the `<form>` tag in the Document Window's Tag Selector.

3. If it isn't already, open the Property Inspector (Window → Properties).

4. Choose GET from the Method drop-down menu.

5. Open the `response.asp` file.

6. For the `response.asp` file to be able to use the form-submitted data, you have to switch to a different type of Request Variable that can come with form-submitted data that uses GET (`Request.QueryString`, to be exact). So, to start off with, if it isn't already, open the Bindings panel by going to Window → Bindings.

7. Now you need to remove all of the `Request.Form` elements from both the page proper and the Bindings panel. To do this, select each one independently and click the Delete button. At this point, your Bindings panel should be empty and there shouldn't be any `Request.Form` elements on the page.

8. In the Bindings panel, click the plus (+) button and select Request Variable.

9. When the Request Variable dialog box appears, select `Request.QueryString` from the Type drop-down menu.

10. Enter **name** into the Name field.

11. As in the previous section, repeat steps 9 and 10 for each form element whose data you wish to use—in this case, you only need to do one more (called **born**).

12. When you finish, you'll have two entries in the Bindings panel.

13. Now drag the first `Request.QueryString` element (`QueryString.name`, in this case) to the right of the word "Welcome" on the first line.

14. Drag the second `Request.QueryString` element (`QueryString.born`) so that it is between the words "from" and "visiting."

15. You might find that you'll need to add a space either before or after (or both) the QueryString elements to ensure that the sentence, when previewed, has the necessary spaces between words. At this point, the text should look something like this:

```
Welcome {QueryString.name}

We are glad that someone from {QueryString.born} is visiting our website!
```

16. Now you can test your page—but remember what I said about manually copying the response.asp file to the location of your Testing Server Folder on your testing server.

Creating and Using a Session Variable

Using either POST or GET in conjunction with either Request.Form or Request.QueryString is all fine and good for passing data from one page to another. The kicker, as mentioned before, is that form-submitted data has only a one shot use—once it's used in the manner just described, it's gone. In addition, it can only be passed directly from one page to another. You can't pass it from the first page to the fifth page. What if you wanted to hold onto the submitted data and use it over and over again? That's where a session variable comes in.

Essentially, you can store data in a session variable until the user leaves the site—after that, the information is disposed of. This is made possible by the use something called a Session ID, which acts as a unique identifier for all the users currently viewing your site. So, for instance, you can use a session variable to store the user's name (which they submitted using a form in the site's initial page). Then, you could repeatedly dynamically display their name in all the other areas of your site.

Creating and using a session variable involves two steps. The first step is to manually enter the session variable's syntax directly into your page's source code (don't worry, it's a pretty painless operation); the second step involves turning the code you manually entered into a drag-and-droppable object so that it can be used in Dreamweaver MX's visual authoring environment.

In the following exercise, you'll use the two files you created in the previous "Using the POST Method" section.

> The syntax used to establish the session variable in the following section is geared exclusively toward ASP and ASP.NET.

Because you'll only be using the user's name to generate some dynamic content, you can delete the second line of text (Where Were You Born) and the second Text Field from the `input.asp` file. In addition, remove the second line of text from the `response.asp` file.

1. Make sure the `response.asp` file is open. Then, if it isn't already, open the Bindings panel (Window → Bindings).

2. Delete all of the Request objects from within the Bindings panel.

3. Remove all the Request elements from the page proper that you had dragged from the Bindings panel.

4. Enter into Code View by clicking the Show Code View button ◆▷.

5. Now you need to hand-enter the syntax for the session variable. At the very top of the document (just below the `<%@LANGUAGE="VBSCRIPT"%>` line), enter the following code:
   `<%Session("user_name")=Request.Form("name")%>`

   This sets up a session called `user_name` that is "filled" with the data entered into the Text Field called name in the `input.asp` file.

   If you were using form-submitted data that employed the GET method, you would replace `Request.Form` in the line of code with `Request.QuerString`.

6. Now you need to turn the session variable you created into an element that is held in the Bindings panel so that it can be dragged and dropped onto your page (much as you did with the Request elements you created in the previous two sections). Switch back to Design View by clicking the Show Design View button.

7. Click the Binding panel's plus (+) button and select Session Variable from the subsequent drop-down menu.

8. When the Session Variable dialog box appears, enter **user_name** into the Name field and click OK. This will add the Session Variable to the Bindings panel.

9. Now, drag the `user_name` session variable from the Bindings panel to the right of the first line of text. Right about now, your `response.asp` file should look something like this:

   Welcome {Session.user_name}

10. As it stands now, the session variable isn't that useful—you could easily use the Request object to pass the data from one page to another, as you did in the two previous sections. To make it more useful, you're going to add a third page that uses the same session variable as the `response.asp` page. To do this, create a new ASP file and save it as `response2.asp`.

11. Add a form by clicking the Form button ⬚ in the Forms section of the Insert bar (Windows → Insert). Alternatively, you can go to Insert → Form.

12. With your cursor still within the form delimiter, enter **Are you still here?**

13. Now, drag the `user_name` session variable from the Bindings panel, and place it right after the "here" and the "?" At this point, your `response2.asp` file should look something like this:

Are you still here {Session.user_name} ?

14. Open the `response.asp` file, and add a link to the `response2.asp` file. This lets you see the session variable used in the `response.asp` file. It also lets you click the link and see the session variable used in the `response2.asp` file.

15. From here, test out your creation. Remember to copy the `response2.asp` and `response.asp` files to the location of your Testing Server Folder on your testing server.

Adding Dynamic Content to Your Page

Now that you've learned how to set up a source of dynamic content, it's time to look at how you can start using that content. You've already looked at how to use dynamic content when you explored how to take form-submitted data and create a dynamic response. In this section, you'll go back to working with databases and Recordsets as a source of dynamic content.

You'll find the Microsoft Access database (called `scifi_books`) discussed in the following section in the `Chapter 18` folder of the book's accompanying CD. While you are certainly welcome to use your own database, you might find it easier to use the provided database.

In this section, you'll first explore how to add dynamic text to your page using a Recordset and a database. From there, you'll look at how you can add dynamic images to your page.

As with the previous section, this section of the book will focus on working with ASP. However, if you are working with another server technology, the general concept is still the same.

Adding Dynamic Text to Your Page

Once you make a database connection and created a Recordset, the process of adding basic dynamic text to your page is quite easy. I say "basic" because the process outlined next is only a foundation for many of the other techniques you can use to add dynamic text to your page, some of which we'll discuss later in the chapter.

1. Make sure you've created a local DNS for the `scifi_books` database. (If you are having trouble remembering how to create a DNS, refer back to Chapter 17, "Setting the Groundwork for Your Dynamic Database Application.")

2. Make sure you have a page open in Dreamweaver MX whose document type has been set to ASP.

3. Create a database connection to the `scifi_books` database. (If you forgot how to create a database connection, see Chapter 17.) In the following exercise, I gave the connection the same name as the database itself (`scifi_books`).

4. Now that you've established a connection to the database, it's time to create the necessary Recordset. If it isn't already, open the Bindings panel by going to Window → Bindings.

5. Click the Binding panel's plus (+) button and select Recordset (Query) from the subsequent drop-down menu.

6. When the Recordset dialog box appears, enter **rsScifi_books** into the Name field. You can give the Recordset any name you with; however, for consistency's sake, I always use the same name as the database, except that I add *rs* at the beginning.

7. Select the previously created DSN for the `scifi_books` database from the Connection drop-down menu.

8. Because there is only one table in the `scifi_books` database, you won't have to select from which the Recordset will draw it information. The only table will be automatically selected in the Tables drop-down menu.

9. Click the Selected radio button. When the Columns list box activates, select the Title, Author, CopyrightYear, PublisherName, and Pages columns. Remember that you can hold down the Cmd/Ctrl key to select multiple items.

10. When you're finished, click OK.

11. Now it's time to add some dynamic content to your page. First, with the Binding panel open (Window → Bindings, if it isn't already open), expand the **rsScifi_books** Recordset by clicking the plus (+) icon directly to its left. This will give you access to the different fields in the Recordset.

12. Click and drag any of the fields in the Recordset from the Bindings panel to your page. Alternatively, you can also select the field and click the Insert button in the bottom right-hand corner.

13. Congratulations, you've just added some dynamic text to your page! Yes, at it's most basic, it's really as simple as that! From here, you can preview your page in a browser and, if you've correctly set up your testing server, the placeholder in the page will be replaced with dynamic content drawn from your database.

While the process is described above is very simple, you could easily add additional dynamic text by dragging additional fields from the Bindings panel to the page. You can integrate the fields themselves into your page layout any way you want. For instance, you can create a table in whose cells you insert one of the fields from the Bindings panel. This way, you could get a linear representation of a single record in the database.

If you are astute, you will have noticed a couple of things about the dynamic content that replaces the placeholder when you preview your page in a browser. First, despite the fact that there are 30 fields (that is, entries) for each column in the `scifi_books` database, only one gets displayed. Further, if you looked a little closer at the database, you'll notice that the field that actually gets displayed is the first one in the particular column. The bottom line is that each "block" of dynamic text you drag from the Bindings panel to the page is linked to a single field in the database. While the field itself can be changed (thereby changing the actual content that is displayed in the browser), you can only display *one* field.

This could prove to be somewhat problematic and limiting when it comes to displaying multiple database records. However, as mentioned before, the process just described is only a foundation for many other techniques you can use to add dynamic text to your page, some of which we'll discuss later in this chapter.

Adding Dynamic Images to Your Page

Now that you know how to add dynamic text to your page, it's time to explore how to add dynamic images to your page. While the theory behind adding a dynamic image is quite similar to adding dynamic text, there are some noteworthy differences. First, as you learned in the previous section, the dynamic text that is displayed on your web page is drawn from a database. However, in the case of dynamic images, the images themselves are not stored in the database. Instead, the *path* to the image is stored in the database. The images themselves can be stored absolutely anywhere, as long as their path in the database correlates to their actual location.

You'll find the Microsoft Access database (called `dynamic_images`) discussed in the following section (as well as the accompanying image files) in the `Chapter 18` folder of the book's accompanying CD. While you are certainly welcome to use your own database, you might find it easier to use the provided database.

To add a dynamic image to your site:

1. Make sure you've created a local DNS for the `dynamic_images` database. (If you are having trouble remembering how to create a DNS, see Chapter 17.)

2. Make sure you have a Dreamweaver MX page open whose document type has been set to ASP.

3. Create a database connection to the `dynamic_images` database. (If you forgot how to create a database connection, see Chapter 17.) In the following exercise, I've given the connection the same name as the database itself (`dynamic_images`).

4. Now that you've established a connection to the database, it's time to create the necessary Recordset. If it isn't already, open the Bindings panel by going to Window ➝ Bindings.

5. Click the Binding panel's plus (+) button and select Recordset (Query) from the subsequent drop-down menu.

6. When the Recordset dialog box appears, enter **rsDynamic_images** into the Name field.

7. Select the previously created DSN for the `dynamic_images` database from the Connection drop-down menu.

8. Because there is only one table in the `dynamic_images` database, you won't have to select from which one the Recordset will draw its information. The only table will be automatically selected in the Tables drop-down menu.

9. Click the Selected radio button. When the Columns list box activates, select the ImageName and ImageSource columns. Remember, you can hold down the Cmd/Ctrl key to select multiple items.

10. When you finish, click OK.

11. Click the Image button in the Common section of the Insert bar (Window ➝ Insert). Alternatively, go to Insert ➝ Image. This will open the Select Image Source dialog box.

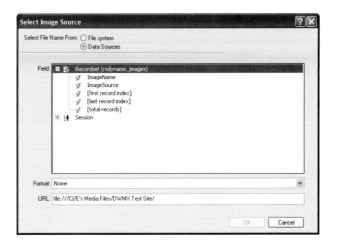

Figure 18.2

When you click the Data Sources radio button, the Select Image Source dialog box changes so that you can select the particular field in the Recordset that contains the path to the image.

12. Instead of navigating to where the image was located (as you would if you were inserting a regular static image into your page), click the Data Sources radio button at the top of the Select Image Source dialog box.

13. When the Select Image Source dialog box changes (see Figure 18.2), select the Image-Source field in the Field list box. This tells Dreamweaver MX that the ImageSource field is the location in the `dynamic_images` database that has the path to the particular image.

14. Click OK.

15. When you are returned to the Document Window, you'll notice that a small placeholder icon has been added to represent the location and presence of a dynamic image (see Figure 18.3).

16. When you finish, if your application server and web server are on your local machine, you can test out your page by previewing it in a browser. As with previous cases, you'll need to copy all of the images to the location of your Testing Server Folder on your testing server.

Figure 18.3

A small placeholder icon represents the presence and location of a dynamic image.

The `dynamic_images` database was created so that the path stored in the ImageSource column necessitates that the page itself *must* be in the same folder as the images. If you want to put the images in another directory, that's fine. However, you will need to change the paths in the database to reflect the image's new location.

Formatting Dynamic Text

In the "Adding Dynamic Text" section earlier in this chapter, you probably noticed that when you previewed your page in a browser, the dynamic content was rendered in the default Dreamweaver MX font (Times/Times New Roman, Size 3). This is fine for the purposes of testing, but what if you want the dynamic text to be formatted so that it fits in with your design/typographic scheme? It's easy to format dynamic text:

1. Create or open a page that contains dynamic textual content, similar to that which you created in either the "Using Form Submitted Data" or "Adding Dynamic Text" sections earlier in this chapter. The important thing is that the page has dynamic content which you've dragged from the Bindings panel.

2. Click any of the instances of dynamic content on your page—notice how the entire thing is selected.

3. If it isn't already, open the Property Inspector (Window → Properties).

4. From there, you can make any typographic changes you want—style, size, font, color, and so on.

5. If your machine is acting both as web server and application server, preview your page in a browser. Notice the dynamic text that is pulled from the database.

Dynamically Displaying Multiple Records

In the "Adding Dynamic Text to Your Page" section earlier in this chapter, you learned that when you drag an instance of dynamic content from the Bindings panel onto the page and preview it in a browser, only the first field in that particular column is displayed. Even if you continue to add instance after instance, all you would get would be a repetition of the same content from the first field in that particular column. So what happens when you want to display the content from multiple fields within a column? The process is quite easy.

 In this section of the chapter, you'll go back to using the `scifi_books` database in the Chapter 18 folder on the book's accompanying CD.

In the following section, you'll use the Dynamic Table server behavior to create a table that Dreamweaver MX will populate with multiple records from the `scifi_books` database:

1. Make sure you've created a local DNS for the `scifi_books` database. (If you are having trouble remembering how to create a DNS, refer back to Chapter 17.)

2. Make sure you have a page open in Dreamweaver MX whose document type has been set to ASP.

3. Create a database connection to the `scifi_books` database. (If you have forgotten how to create a database connection, see Chapter 17.) In the following exercise, I gave the connection the same name as the database itself (`scifi_books`).

4. Now that you've established a connection to the database, it's time to create the necessary Recordset. If it isn't already, open the Bindings panel by going to Window → Bindings.

5. Click the Binding panel's plus (+) button and select Recordset (Query) from the subsequent drop-down menu.

6. When the Recordset dialog box appears, enter **rsScifi_books** into the Name field. You can give the Recordset any name you wish, but for consistency's sake, I always use the same name as the database; the only difference is that I add *rs* at the beginning.

7. Select the previously created DSN for the `scifi_books` database from the Connection drop-down menu.

8. Because there is only one table in the `scifi_books` database, you won't have to select from which one the Recordset will draw its information. The only table will be automatically selected in the Tables drop-down menu.

9. Click the Selected radio button. When the Columns list box activates, select the Title, Author, CopyrightYear, PublisherName, and Pages columns. Remember that you can hold down the Cmd/Ctrl key to select multiple items.

10. When you finish, click OK.

11. If it isn't already, open the Insert bar (Window → Insert).

12. Open the Applications tab and click the Dynamic Table button . Alternatively, you can go to Insert → Application Objects → Dynamic Table.

13. When the Dynamic Table dialog box appears, select the specific Recordset whose fields you wish to display from the Recordset drop-down menu. In this exercise, since you only have one existing Recordset, `rsSciFi_books` will be automatically chosen.

14. From here, select from the following options:

    - If you want all of the records to be displayed on a single page (30, in the case of the `scifi_books` database), click the All radio button.

    - If you only want a certain percentage of the database records displayed on the page at any given time, click the Show radio button and enter the number of records you want displayed in the field.

15. In the Border field, enter a value for the border width of the table that Dreamweaver MX will generate— remember, entering 0 means your table will be invisible.

16. Enter a value for the table's cell padding into the Cell Padding field.

17. Enter a value for the table's cell spacing into the Cell Spacing field.

    If you are having trouble remembering how a table's border, cell padding, and cell spacing affect how the table looks, see Chapter 7, "Laying Out Your Document with Tables."

18. Click OK.

19. Voila! Dreamweaver MX will create a table and populate it with dynamic content drawn from the `scifi_books` database.

Repeat	Author	CopyrightYear	PublisherName	Pages
{rsSciFi_books.Title}	{rsSciFi_books.Author}	{rsSciFi_books.CopyrightYear}	{rsSciFi_books.PublisherName}	{rsSciFi_books.Pages}

You'll notice, however, that the table itself only has one row (the cell's of which are populated with fields from the Recordset). How will multiple records be displayed if there is only one row of dynamic content in the table? If you preview your dynamic page in a browser, you'll notice that the number of records you set is displayed. How does this work? Well, when you create a dynamic table, Dreamweaver MX inserts a Repeat Region server behavior. The Repeat Region server behavior dynamically expands the table so that each row is populated with the content from another record in the database—cool, huh?

> The table that is generated is just like any other table you create manually. As a result, you can manipulate its properties (size, border, background color, and so on) to your heart's content.

Navigating through Dynamically Generated Database Records

A couple times in this chapter (the "Adding Dynamic Text to Your Page" and "Dynamically Displaying Multiple Records" sections, in particular) when you inserted dynamic content from a database that had multiple records, only the content from a single field was actually displayed. In the case of adding dynamic text or dynamic images, you had no way of viewing the rest of the records in the database. In the case of the previous section where you learned how to dynamically display multiple database records, there was no way of viewing the next batch of records (if you chose only to display a limited number of records on the page at one time).

So, what happens if you want your users to be able to navigate through all of the dynamic content in the database? This is where a Recordset Navigation Bar comes into the picture. Essentially, it lets you create a navigational system (including first, last, next, and previous links) in which the user can cycle through all of the dynamic content (be it text, images, or multiple records). When creating a Recordset Navigation Bar, you have a couple of options as to how you want the links that comprise the system to look. You can create text links:

Or you can use images:

To create a Recordset Navigation Bar:

1. Create a page that displays only 10 records at a time using the process described in the previous section.

2. Click just below the dynamic table (if you can't, place your cursor directly to the right of the table and press Return [Mac]/ Enter [Win]).

3. If it isn't already, open the Insert bar by going to Window → Insert and click the Application tab.

4. Click the Recordset Navigation Bar button ⟨⟩ .

5. When the Recordset Navigation Bar dialog box appears, select the Recordset with which you are currently working from the Recordset drop-down menu.

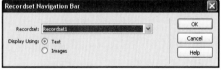

6. Click the Text radio button if you want your links to be text based. Alternatively, if you want your links to be images, click the Images radio button. The page on which you are working must be saved before you can insert image-based links.

7. When you finish, click OK. Dreamweaver MX inserts a Recordset Navigation Bar into your document.

8. Now, if your application server and web server are on your local machine, you can test out your page by previewing it in a browser.

When you preview the page in your browser, you'll notice that the specific links that appear will change depending on what portion of the Recordset is currently being viewed.

For example, if you are at the very beginning of the Recordset, the First and Previous links will not be displayed. Similarly, if you are at the very end of the Recordset, the Next and Last links will not be displayed. This helpful feature comes courtesy of a special server behavior that Dreamweaver automatically adds when it generated the Recordset Navigation Bar.

If you want all of your navigational elements to be visible, regardless of where the user is in the Recordset, you'll need to remove the server behaviors:

1. Make sure you have the page open that has the Recordset Navigation Bar you want to change.

2. If it isn't already, open the Server Behavior panel by going to Window → Server Behaviors.

3. Select the Show if Not First Record server behavior.

4. Click the Server Behavior panel's minus (–) button to remove the behavior.

5. Repeat steps 3 and 4 for all the remaining Show If Not First Record server behaviors.

Creating a Record Counter

Up until this point, everything that you created hasn't displayed much information. The largest database you worked with was the `scifi_books` database, which had a grand total of 30 records—not a terribly large database. However, when you start creating applications in which lots of information is displayed, your users can easily lose their point of reference as they cycle through page after page of records. You need to provide a sort of dynamic feedback, a reference point, allowing them to easily pinpoint the relative position of the record they are currently viewing in regard to all the other records in the database. In Dreamweaver MX, this is where a record counter enters the picture. For example, if the Recordset is comprised of 100 records, and 10 are currently being displayed on the page, the record counter would say "Displaying Records 10–20 of 100." Essentially, when you create a record counter, Dreamweaver MX inserts some specially formatted dynamic text.

To create a record counter:

1. Create a page that only displays 10 records at a time using the process described in the "Dynamically Displaying Multiple Records" section earlier in this chapter.

2. Click just below the dynamic table (if you can't, just place your cursor directly to the right of the table and hit Return [Mac]/ Enter [Win]).

3. If it isn't already, open the Insert bar by going to Window → Insert and click the Application tab.

4. Click the Recordset Navigation Status button .

5. When the Recordset Navigation Status dialog box appears, select the Recordset of which the dynamically generated content is a part.

6. Click OK.

7. Dreamweaver MX will insert the Recordset Navigation Status dialog box.

Records {Recordset1_first} to {Recordset1_last} of {Recordset1_total}

Remember, because the Recordset Navigation bar is just some dynamic text to which Dreamweaver MX has made some alterations, you can format it so it looks however you want using the Property Inspector (Window → Properties).

Inspiration: Design and Technique

Designed by Djojo Studios (whose site appears in this book's color section), Langlevelator (`www.langlevelater.nl/en`) is easily one of the most innovative, immersive learning environments on the Web today. Built entirely using Flash and Dreamweaver, the site (see Figure 18.4) was designed for the Floriande Dutch Horticultural Exhibition to teach kids about environmental issues.

Figure 18.4

Djojo Studios' Langlevelator

Melding Djojo Studios' easily recognizable stylish illustration with an incredibly immersive Flash-based environment, Langlevelator lets kids navigate through a series of virtual pavilions, each of which mirrors an actual pavilion at the horticultural exhibition. Each pavilion contains topical quizzes, the successful completion of which awards kids with tiles to build their own interactive urban landscapes.

Summary

In this chapter, you took some very important steps along the path of dynamic database-driven websites. First, you looked at how to create a source of dynamic content, which included an exploration of how to create a Recordset and how to use user-submitted form data. From there, you investigated how to use all of your hard fought knowledge and add dynamic content (both text and images) to a page. At that point, you looked at how to format dynamic text, dynamically display multiple database records, and create a custom navigation scheme for cycling through multiple records. You finished off the chapter by learning how to create a dynamic record counter.

In the next chapter, you'll take all of the knowledge you've gained in this chapter (as well as Chapter 17) and start creating some more useful and complex dynamic database-driven applications.

CHAPTER 19

Developing Common Dynamic Applications

Dynamic database-driven sites are more than just the sum of their parts—they are applications that *do* things. Whether they display an ever-changing listing of the latest and greatest films at your local theater, restrict access to the content of a site based on membership or registration, or display the number of students who've registered for a given course at a local university, they all have a point and a purpose.

Until this point, you've looked at the building blocks of dynamic database-driven applications. In this chapter, you'll use that knowledge and take a step-by-step tutorial-based approach to constructing some of the more common dynamic applications. While the tutorials in this chapter will be project based (don't worry, all the necessary files are provided on the CD), the skills you learn can easily be applied to your own stunning dynamic creations.

This chapter, like the previous one, will focus on creating applications using ASP. While I would love to cover all of the various database driven technologies available in Dreamweaver MX, ASP is probably one of the easiest to work with at the level of experience to which this book is targeted. Don't worry too much if you're using another technology, though, as the techniques described here are fairly general and can be easily adapted if you so desire.

The following topics will be covered in this chapter:

- **Building a Master/Detail page**
- **Building an Insert Record page**
- **Building a User Registration page**
- **Creating a Login page**
- **Creating a simple search engine**

Building a Master/Detail Page Set

A Master/Detail page is a cost-effective way to provide users with an efficient way to browse and access large, similar blocks of information. The Master page contains a list of dynamically generated records (like those you learned how to create in Chapter 18, "Displaying and Manipulating Data from Your Database"). When the user clicks one of the records, the user is transported to a second page (the detail page), which displays more of the information in the database related to that given record. For instance, a company could have a page that features a list of all of their employees. If the user clicked any of the individual employees, a page would load that included a great deal more information about the specific employee (department, phone number, fax number, e-mail address, favorite type of cheese, and so on).

All of the files that you'll need to complete this tutorial can be found in the `Chapter 19` folder of the book's accompanying CD. What you won't find, unfortunately, is a copy of the finished pages. Don't worry, you aren't getting short changed. Because the application is based on a Recordset, which is based on a DSN that is unique to the computer upon which it is created, if I did provide files they would be totally useless to you (because they were based on a DSN and a Recordset created on my computer). This tutorial assumes that you have an application server capable of processing ASP files installed on your local machine. If you don't, disregard the next step. You will also need to disregard all the steps that ask you to preview your page in Live Data View or in a browser.

THE PROJECT

I'll admit it: I'm a science fiction nut. I watch it, I read it, and I even have a running science fiction novel that I write in my spare time (which really isn't that often— resulting in a very short novel thus far). Hey, I've even developed a university class designed to use science fiction stories and novels to introduce undergraduate students to the principles of socio-cultural anthropology! In this section of the book (as well as several other sections that follow), you'll be using an Access database filled with 40 complete records of science fiction novels pulled from my own (rather large) collection. The premise is that you are creating a web page designed to provide an audience with information about the books in your collection. To start off with, you'll create a Master/Detail page combination in which the Master page lists a series of records from the database, each of which contain limited information (title, author, copyright year) about a particular book. The detail page, on the other hand, will feature more in-depth information about the book such as page count, original purchase price, and ISBN number.

To create a Master/Detail Page Set:

1. Copy the `scifi_books.mbd` database from the `Chapter 19` folder of the book's accompanying CD to the location on your hard drive where you'll set up the local site for this exercise (yes, you'll need to set up a local site).

2. Set up a DSN for the database as described in Chapter 17, "Setting the Groundwork for your Dynamic Database-Driven Application."

3. From here, set up a local site whose Testing Server's server model is ASP VBScript. Make sure you've properly configured your testing server (as outlined in Chapter 17).

4. Go to File → New.

5. When the New Document dialog box opens, select Dynamic Page from the Category list box, choose ASP VBScript from the Dynamic Page list box, and click Create.

> As you've noticed, when Dreamweaver MX starts, it automatically opens a generic HTML page in the Document Window. Because you aren't going to use this document, you can leave it in the background after you create a new document. Alternatively, you can close it down (File → Close).

6. First, you need to make the necessary database connection. If it isn't already, open the Databases panel (Window → Databases).

7. Click the Database's plus (+) button 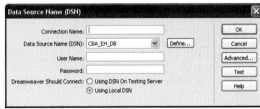 and select Data Source Name (DSN) from the subsequent drop-down menu.

8. When the Data Source Name (DSN) dialog box appears, enter **scifi_books** into the Connection Name field.

9. Select the DSN you established for the `scifi_books.mbd` database from the Data Source Name (DSN) drop-down menu.

10. If the database connection requires a login/password, enter them into the User Name and Password fields, respectively.

11. If it isn't already, click the Using Local DSN radio button. (If you want to make sure Dreamweaver MX can make the connection based on the information you entered, click the Test button.)

12. Click OK.

13. Now, for the Recordset. If it isn't already, open the Bindings panel (Window → Bindings).

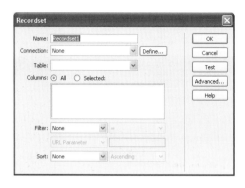

14. Click on the Binding panel's plus (+) button and select Recordset (Query) from the subsequent drop-down menu.

15. When the Recordset dialog box appears, enter **rsScifi_books** into the Name field.

16. Choose the `scifi_books` connection from the Connection drop-down menu.

17. Make sure the All radio button is selected (just above the Columns list box). This ensures that all of the columns in the database are included in the Recordset.

You can click the Test button to make sure that Dreamweaver MX is able to properly create the Recordset.

18. Click OK.

19. Now that you've laid the groundwork, it's time to actually build the Master/Detail Page Set. The first thing you need to do is save the current page. Go to File → Save. When the Save As dialog box appears, navigate to the location in your local site where you want to save the file, enter **booksMaster** into the File Name field, choose Active Server Pages (*.asp) from the Save As Type drop-down menu, and click Save.

20. Now, you'll use the Master/Detail Page Set server object to create your snazzy dynamic web application. First, place your cursor in the Document Window.

21. If it isn't already, open the Insert bar (Window → Insert) and click the Application tab.

22. Click the Master/Detail Page Set button .

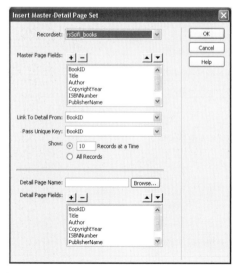

23. The Master Detail Page Set dialog box will appear. Make sure `rsScifi_books` is selected in the Recordset drop-down menu.

24. Now, you need to set which fields from the database will be visible on the master page. Select BookID and click the Remove Item button (the minus icon [–]) at the top of the Master Page Fields list box.

25. Repeat the process for CopyrightYear, ISBNNumber, Publisher-Name, OriginalPurchasePrice, and Pages. At this point, the Master Detail Page Set dialog box should look like this:

26. Now you need to create a link that will allow the user to jump to the detail page and view the expanded information for each of the records. To do this, select Title from the Link to Detail From drop-down menu (if it isn't already). This means that the title of each book on the Master page will automatically become the link to the detail page.

27. Select BookID from the Pass Unique Key drop-down menu. The number in the BookID column uniquely identifies each record and will be used to properly construct the detail page.

28. If it isn't already, click the top radio button (to the right of the word Show), and enter 10 in the Records at a Time field. This will ensure that only 10 records from the database will be displayed at any given time on your master page.

29. Go ahead and create the detail page. Enter **bookDetail.asp** into the Detail Page Name field. The totally cool thing about Dreamweaver MX is that it will automatically generate the detail page for you. However, if you want to use an existing page, all you need to do is click the Browse button, locate the desired file, and select it.

30. Select BookID from the Detail Page field list box, and click the Remove Item (the minus icon [–]) button ▬ . This will ensure that the information in the BookID field (which is simply a unique identifier for each book) isn't displayed in the detail page. Other than that, you'll want all the other fields to appear in the detail page, so leave them alone.

31. At this point, the Master Detail Page Set dialog box should look like this:

32. Click OK.

33. From there, Dreamweaver inserts the necessary code into the bookMaster page (as well as a Recordset navigation bar and a Recordset status bar) and automatically generates the bookDetail page (see Figure 19.1).

Figure 19.1

Dreamweaver automatically generates the necessary code for both the bookMaster and bookDetail pages.

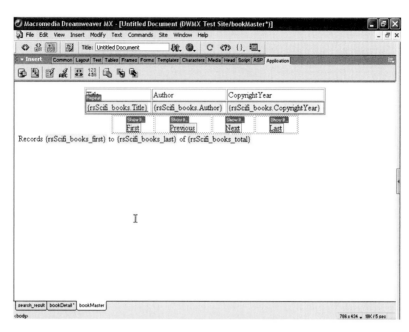

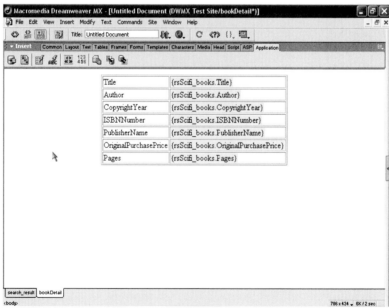

34. Now there is only one thing left to do: test the application. As you learned in Chapter 18, "Displaying and Manipulating Data from Your Database," you need to copy all the supporting files to the root folder of your testing server. In the case of this tutorial, this not only includes the `bookMaster.asp` and `bookDetail.asp` files but also the `Connections` folder that Dreamweaver MX automatically created in the root folder of your local site. After you've done that, you can preview your beautiful creation in a browser, sit back, and marvel at your ingenuity!

> Here is a neat trick. Try setting up a remote site in which the Remote Folder is the same as the Testing Server Folder on your local machine (which you'll access using Local/Network instead of FTP). This means that you'll be able to upload the files for the application simply by using the Site panel.

Building an Insert Records Page

For the most part, all of the topics we've discussed thus far have dealt with drawing information from a database. When you initially create your dynamic website, the databases you employ will be populated with some information, but you'll definitely want to add additional information as time goes on. There are two ways you can do this. The first is to add information to the database using the program in which it was originally created and then upload the new copy to your web server. This can prove to be a little clunky and time consuming, however. Alternately, you can create a web page that interfaces directly with the database on the server and lets you add new records. This is a cool technique, as it allows you to update the database directly from within a browser without having to go through the process of updating the database on your machine and then uploading the new copy to the server.

> **THE PROJECT**
>
> You're going to continue working on the science fiction book website. Now that you've created the Master/Detail Page Set, you are ready to create a page that allows you to add additional books to the database.

As with the previous section, you'll continue to work with the `scifi_books.mbd` database located in the `Chapter 19` folder of the book's accompanying CD.

This tutorial will start from scratch as if you hadn't already created a Master/Detail Page Set. As a result, it will go through the process of setting up a new database connection. However, if you went through the previous tutorial, you'll already have the proper database connection in place.

As with all the other tutorials in the chapter, this tutorial assumes that you have an application server capable of processing ASP files installed on your local machine. If you don't, disregard the next step. You will also need to disregard all the steps that ask you to preview your page in Live Data View or in a browser.

To create an Insert Records page:

1. If you haven't already, copy the `scifi_books.mbd` database from the `Chapter 19` folder of the book's accompanying CD to the location on your hard drive where you'll set up the local site for this exercise.

2. Set up a DSN for the database as described in Chapter 17.

3. From here, set up a local site whose Testing Server's server model is ASP VBScript. Make sure you're properly configured your testing server as outlined in Chapter 17.

4. Go to File → New.

5. When the New Document dialog box opens, select Dynamic Page from the Category list box, choose ASP VBScript from the Dynamic Page list box, and click Create.

> As with the previous tutorial, when Dreamweaver MX starts, it automatically opens a generic HTML page in the Document Window. Because you aren't going to use this document, you can leave it in the background after you create a new document. Alternatively, you can close it down (File → Close).

6. First, you need to make the necessary database connection. If it isn't already, open the Databases panel (Window → Databases).

If you already did the previous tutorial, the necessary database connection will already have been established. If so, just skip steps 7–12.

7. Click the Databases panel's plus (+) button ⊞, and select Data Source Name (DSN) from the subsequent drop-down menu.

8. When the Data Source Name (DSN) dialog box appears, enter **scifi_books** into the Connection Name field.

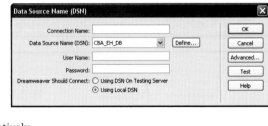

9. Select the DSN you established for the `scifi_books.mbd` database from the Data Source Name (DSN) drop-down menu.

10. If the database connection requires a login/password enter them into the User Name and Password fields, respectively.

11. If it isn't already, click the Using Local DSN radio button.

   If you want to make sure Dreamweaver MX can make the connection based on the information you entered, click the Test button.

12. Click OK.

13. Now, for the Recordset. If it isn't already, open the Bindings panel (Window → Bindings).

14. Click the Binding panel's plus (+) button and select Record-set (Query) from the subsequent drop-down menu.

15. When the Recordset dialog box appears, enter **rsScifi_books** into the Name field.

16. Choose the `scifi_books` connection from the Connection drop-down menu.

17. Click the Selected radio button.

18. When the Columns list box goes live, select all of the fields *except* BookID.

   You can click the Test button to make sure that Dreamweaver MX is able to properly create the Recordset.

19. When you finish, click OK.

20. Now it's time to create the form that will be used to add a new record into the database. If it isn't already, open the Insert bar (Window → Insert) and click the Forms tab.

   If you don't want to go through the process of creating the actual form (described next), a completed example (*without* the necessary server behaviors), `bookInsert.asp`, is included in the `Chapter 19` folder of the book's accompanying CD.

21. Click the Form button ▭ .

> Because the form itself is an invisible element, its red dashed line will not show up unless you've got the Form Delimiter element turned on in the Invisible Elements section of the Preferences dialog box (Edit → Preferences). You'll also have to turn the Invisible Elements on using the View menu (View → Visual Aids → Invisible Elements).

22. With your cursor inside the form delimiter, open the Common tab and click the Insert Table button ⊞.

23. When the Insert Table dialog box opens, create a table that has a cell padding of 3, a cell spacing of 3, 2 columns, 8 rows, a width of 50%, and a border of 0.

24. In the first cell of the first column, enter the text **Title**.

25. Move your cursor to the first cell of the second column. Open the Insert bar's Forms tab, and click the Insert Text Field button ▭.

26. Select the newly created Text field, and, if it isn't already, open the Property Inspector (Window → Properties).

27. Enter **50** into the Char Width field.

28. Enter **bookTitle** into the Label field (in the left-most portion of the Property Inspector, just below the words "TextField").

29. Move your cursor to the second cell in the first column. Enter the text **Author**.

30. Move your cursor to the second cell in the second column, and insert a new Text field.

31. With the newly created text field still selected, use the Property Inspector to set the Char Width value to 50, and the Label value to bookAuthor.

32. Move your cursor to the third cell in the first column. Enter the text **Copyright Year**.

33. Move your cursor to the third cell in the second column, and insert a new Text field.

34. With the newly created text field still selected, use the Property Inspector to set the Char Width value to 50, and the Label value to bookCopyrightYear.

35. Move your cursor to the fourth cell in the first column. Enter the text **ISBN Number**.

36. Move your cursor to the fourth cell in the second column and insert a new Text field.

37. With the newly created text field still selected, use the Property Inspector to set the Char Width value to 50, and the Label value to bookISBN.

38. Move your cursor to the fifth cell in the first column. Enter the text **Publisher Name**.

39. Move your cursor to the fifth cell in the second column and insert a new Text field.

40. With the newly created text field still selected, use the Property Inspector to set the Char Width value to 50, and the Label value to bookPublisher.

41. Move your cursor to the sixth cell in the first column. Enter the text **Original Purchase Price**.

42. Move your cursor to the sixth cell in the second column and insert a new Text field.

43. With the newly created text field still selected, use the Property Inspector to set the Char Width value to 50, and the Label value to bookPrice.

44. Move your cursor to the seventh cell in the first column. Enter the text **Pages**.

45. Move your cursor to the seventh cell in the second column, and insert a new Text field.

46. With the newly created text field still selected, use the Property Inspector to set the Char Width value to 50, and the Label value to bookPages.

47. Move your cursor to the eighth cell in the second column, and click the Button button 🔲 in the Insert bar's Forms tab.

48. With the newly inserted button still selected and the Property Inspector open, enter **Add to Database** to the Label field. At this point, the form should look like this:

New Science Fiction Book Insert Form

Title	
Author	
Copyright Year	
ISBN Number	
Publisher Name	
Original Purchase Price	
Pages	
	Add to Databse

49. Now it's time to integrate the Insert Record server behavior that will make the whole application possible. First, if it isn't already, open the Server Behavior panel (Window → Server Behaviors).

50. Click the Add Item button ＋ , and choose Insert Record from the subsequent drop-down menu.

51. When the Insert Record dialog box appears, select the connection to the `scifi_books` database you set up previously.

52. Select the table that will receive the incoming data from the Insert Intro Table drop-down menu—in this case, because there is only one table in the database, it will be `scifi_books`.

53. Enter the name of the page to which you want the user shunted after the data has been inserted into the database. In the case of this tutorial, you can enter `bookMaster.asp`.

54. If you had more than one form on the page, you would need to select the one that would be providing the information that was being inserted into the database from the Get Values From drop-down menu. However, in the case of this tutorial, since there is only one form (which was by default named `form1` by Dreamweaver), you don't have to select anything.

55. From here, you need to tell Dreamweaver into which columns in the database it needs to stick the information entered into each individual text field. To do this, select bookTitle from the Form Elements list box, select Title from the Column drop-down menu, and select Text from the Submit As drop-down menu.

56. Select bookAuthor from the Form Elements list box, choose Author from the Column drop-down menu, and select Text from the Submit As drop-down menu.

57. Choose bookCopyrightYear from the Form Elements list box, select CopyrightYear from the Column drop-down menu, and select Numeric from the Submit As drop-down menu.

58. Select bookISBN from the Form Elements list box, choose ISBNNumber form the Column drop-down menu, and select numeric from the Submit As drop-down menu.

59. Select bookPublisher from the Form Elements list box, select PublisherName from the Column drop-down menu, and choose Text from the Submit As drop-down menu.

60. Select bookPrice from the Form Elements list box, select OriginalPurchasePrice from the Column drop-down menu, and choose Numeric from the Submit As drop-down menu.

61. Click bookPages in the Form Elements list box, select Pages from the Column drop-down menu, and choose Numeric from the Submit As drop-down menu.

62. When you finish, click OK.

63. From here, all you need to do is test your application. As with all cases, you'll need to make sure all the associated files are copied to the root folder of your testing server. Otherwise, the application won't work.

Building a User Registration Page

The ability to restrict access to a site based on prior registration is a very handy technique. While seemingly complex, the way you actually build a User Registration page is extremely easy in Dreamweaver MX—it's basically just a subtle variation on the Insert Record page you already learned how to create.

THE PROJECT

While not directly linked to the scifi_books database, the User Registration page that you'll create could easily be used in concert with the other dynamic applications you've already created. For instance, you could require that someone register before they gain access to the booksMaster.asp page you created earlier in the chapter.

You'll find a copy of the Access database you'll be using in this tutorial, called `users.mbd`, in the `Chapter 19` folder of the book's accompanying CD.

To create a simple User Registration page, just follow these steps:

1. If you haven't already, copy the `users.mbd` database from the `Chapter 19` folder of the book's accompanying CD to the location on your hard drive where you've set up the local site for the exercises in this chapter.

2. Set up a DSN for the database as described in Chapter 17.

   As with all the other tutorials in the chapter, this tutorial assumes that you have an application server capable of processing ASP files installed on your local machine. If you don't, disregard the next step. You will also need to disregard all the steps that ask you to preview your page in Live Data View or in a browser.

3. From here, set up a local site whose Testing Server's server model is ASP VBScript. Make sure you're properly configured your testing server as outlined in Chapter 17.

4. Go to File → New.

5. When the New Document dialog box opens, select Dynamic Page from the Category list box, choose ASP VBScript from the Dynamic Page list box, and click Create.

6. First, you need to make the necessary database connection. If it isn't already, open the Databases panel (Window → Databases).

   If you did the previous tutorial, the necessary database connection will already have been established. If so, just skip steps 7–12.

7. Click the Databases panel's plus (+) button ⊞ , and select Data Source Name (DSN) from the subsequent drop-down menu.

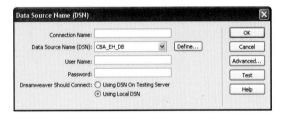

8. When the Data Source Name (DSN) dialog box appears, enter **users** into the Connection Name field.

9. Select the DSN you established for the `users.mbd` database from the Data Source Name (DSN) drop-down menu.

10. If the database connection requires a login/password enter them into the User Name and Password fields, respectively.

11. If it isn't already, click the Using Local DSN radio button.

    If you want to make sure Dreamweaver MX can make the connection based on the information you entered, click the Test button.

12. Click OK.

13. Now, for the Recordset. If it isn't already, open the Bindings panel (Window → Bindings).

14. Click the Binding panel's plus (+) button ⊞ and select Record-set (Query) from the subsequent drop-down menu.

15. When the Recordset dialog box appears, enter **rsUsers** into the Name field.

16. Choose the connection you created for the `users.mbd` database from the Connection drop-down menu.

17. Click the Selected radio button.

18. When the Columns list box goes live, select all of the fields *except* ID.

You can click the Test button to make sure that Dreamweaver MX is able to properly create the Recordset.

19. When you finish, click OK.

20. Now it's time to create the form that will be used to add the new records (user name and password) into the database. If it isn't already, open the Insert bar (Window → Insert) and click the Forms tab.

If you don't want to go through the process of creating the actual form (described next), a completed example (without the necessary server behaviors), `register.asp`, is included in the `Chapter 19` folder of the book's accompanying CD.

21. Click the Form button ▭ .

> Because the form itself is an invisible element, its red dashed line will not show up unless you have the Form Delimiter element turned on in the Invisible Elements section of the Preferences dialog box (Edit → Preferences). You'll also have to turn the Invisible Elements on using the View menu (View → Visual Aids → Invisible Elements).

22. With your cursor inside the form delimiter, open the Common tab and click the Insert Table button ⊞ .

23. When the Insert Table dialog box opens, create a table that has a cell padding of 3, a cell spacing of 3, 2 columns, 3 rows, a width of 50%, and a border of 0.

24. In the first cell in the first column, enter the text **User Name**.

25. Move your cursor to the first cell of the second column. Open the Insert bar's Forms tab and click the Text Field button ⬚ .

26. Select the newly created Text field, and if it isn't already, open the Property Inspector (Window → Properties).

27. Enter 50 into the Char Width field.

28. Enter **userName** into the Label field (in the left-most portion of the Property Inspector, just below the words "TextField").

29. Move your cursor to the second cell in the first column. Enter the text **Password**.

30. Move your cursor to the second cell in the second column and insert a new Text field.

31. With the newly created text field still selected, use the Property Inspector to set the Char Width value to 50 and the Label value to userPassword. Make sure the Password radio button is selected.

32. Move your cursor to the third cell in the second column and click the Button button ⬚ in the Insert bar's Forms tab.

33. With the newly inserted button still selected and the Property Inspector open, enter **Register** in the Label field. At this point, the form should look something like this:

34. Now that you've created the form, it's time to integrate the Insert Record behavior that will stick the user name and password into the `users.mbd` database. If it isn't already, open the Server Behavior panel (Window → Server Behavior).

35. Click the plus (+) icon and select Insert Record from the subsequent drop-down menu.

36. When the Insert Record dialog box appears, select users from the Connection drop-down menu.

37. Select the table that will receive the incoming data from the Insert Intro Table drop-down menu—in this case, because there is only one table in the database, it will be users.

38. Enter the name of the page to which you want the user shunted after the data has been inserted into the database. While we won't go through the process of creating the page in this tutorial, you can create something simple that says, "Congratulations, you're registered."

39. If you had more than one form on the page, you would need to select the one that would be providing the information that was being inserted into the database from the Get Values From drop-down menu. However, in the case of this tutorial, since there is only one form (which was by default named `form1` by Dreamweaver), you don't have to select anything.

40. Select userName from the Form Elements list box, choose userLogin from the Column drop-down menu, and select Text from the Submit As drop-down menu.

41. Select userPassword from the Form Elements list box, choose userPassword from the Column drop-down menu, and select Text from the Submit As drop-down menu.

42. When you finish, click OK.

Seems simple enough, doesn't it? At this point you really haven't done anything new. However, what happens if someone enters a user name that is already in the database? You don't want duplicate user names floating around! It's quite easy to check the database to see whether or not the user name that is being submitted isn't a duplicate:

1. Make sure the page you just created is still open. In the Server Behaviors panel (Window → Server Behaviors), click the plus (+) button ➕ and choose User Authentication → Check New User Name.

2. When the Check New User Name dialog box appears, select userName from the User Name Field drop-down menu.

3. Enter the filename of the page to which you want the user shunted if the user name they've entered is already in the database. As before, we won't go through the process of creating the page in this tutorial, but you can create something simple that says, "Sorry, that user name already exists," and provides a link back to the `register.asp` page so they can give it another shot.

4. When you finish, click OK.

5. From here, all you need to do is test your application. As with all cases, you'll need to make sure all the associated files are copied to the root folder of your testing server. Otherwise, the application won't work.

Building a Login Page

Now that you've created a way for users to register, you need to create a mechanism by which they can take the user name and password and use them to log in to a protected area of your site.

 As before, you'll find a copy of the Access database you'll be using in this tutorial, called `users.mbd`, in the **Chapter 19** folder of the book's accompanying CD.

Many of the tutorials in this chapter are self contained, but because building a login page naturally goes along with building a login page, I won't walk through the process of setting up a database connection and a Recordset. If you need a reference, see steps 1–19 in the previous section.

THE PROJECT

While still directly linked to the science fiction books project on which you've been working, the login page could definitely integrate into the overall scheme of things. You could use the registration/login page combination to limit access to your dynamic database science fiction book-o-rama application.

To build a login page, just follow these steps:

1. You'll start off by creating the login form. If it isn't already, open the Insert bar (Window ➔ Insert) and click the Forms tab.

   If you don't want to go through the process of creating the actual form (described next), a completed example (*without* the necessary server behaviors), `login.asp`, is included in the `Chapter 19` folder of the book's accompanying CD.

2. Click the Form button ⬚ .

> Because the form itself is an invisible element, its red dashed line will not show up unless you've got the Form Delimiter element turned on in the Invisible Elements section of the Preferences dialog box (Edit ➔ Preferences). You'll also have to turn the Invisible Elements on using the View menu (View ➔ Visual Aids ➔ Invisible Elements).

3. With your cursor inside the form delimiter, select the Insert bar's Common tab and click the Insert Table button ⊞ .

4. When the Insert Table dialog box opens, create a table that has a cell padding of 3, a cell spacing of 3, 2 columns, 3 rows, a width of 50%, and a border of 0.

5. In the first cell in the first column, enter the text **User Name**.

6. Move your cursor to the first cell of the second column. Select the Insert bar's Forms tab and click the Text Field button ▭ .

7. Select the newly created Text field, and if it isn't already, open the Property Inspector (Window ➔ Properties).

8. Enter **50** into the Char Width field.

9. Enter **userName** into the Label field (in the left-most portion of the Property Inspector, just below the words "TextField").

10. Move your cursor to the second cell in the first column. Enter the text **Password**.

11. Move your cursor to the second cell in the second column and insert a new Text field.

12. With the newly created text field still selected, use the Property Inspector to set the Char Width value to 50 and the Label value to userPassword. Make sure the Password radio button is selected.

13. Move your cursor to the eighth cell in the second column, and click the Button button ▭ in the Insert bar's Forms tab.

14. With the newly inserted button still selected and the Property Inspector open, enter **Login** in the Label field. At this point, the form should look something like this:

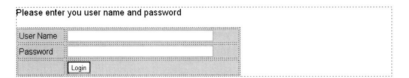

15. Now it's time to add the server behavior that makes the whole login process possible. If it isn't already, open the Server Behavior panel (Window → Server Behavior).

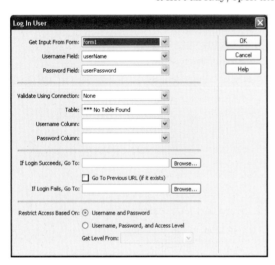

16. Click the plus (+) icon and select User Authentication → Log In User from the subsequent drop-down menu. This will open the Log In User dialog box.

17. Select form1 from the Get Input From Form drop-down menu.

18. Choose userName from the Username Field drop-down menu.

19. Select userPassword from the Password field drop-down menu.

20. Select users from the Validate Using Connection drop-down menu.

21. Make sure users is selected in the Table drop-down menu. This is actually not really necessary as there is only one table in the users database. If you had more tables, however, you would need to choose that which contained the user name and password information.

22. Choose userLogin from the Username Column drop-down menu.

23. Select userPassword from the Password Column drop-down menu.

24. Enter the filename of the page to which you want the user be shunted if the login is successful into the If Login Succeeds, Go To field. In case of this tutorial, you can use the `bookMaster.asp` page you created earlier.

25. Enter the filename of the page to which you want the user be shunted if the login isn't successful into the If Login Fails, Go To field. While we won't go through the process of creating the page in this tutorial, you can create something simple that says, "Sorry, login failed" and provides a link back to the login.

26. When you finish, click OK.

27. From here, all you need to do is test your application. As with all cases, you'll need to make sure all the associated files are copied to the root folder of your testing server. Otherwise, the application won't work.

Building a Simple Search Engine

What dynamic database-driven site wouldn't be complete without a way for users to search the records within the database? In the following tutorial, you'll learn how to create a simple search engine. What exactly do I mean by simple? Well, in Dreamweaver MX, you can create two general kinds of search applications. The first, which we'll be employing, searches for a specific term within a certain column of your database. Essentially, you are telling it something like, "Search for this exact phrase in this exact portion of the database." The second type of search application, which is far more powerful, employs SQL (Structured Query Language) to search for a specific term in the entire database (as opposed to just a single column). While Dreamweaver MX will write the necessary SQL for you, the process is somewhat complicated and is therefore out of the scope of this tutorial.

Before you get started, there is something you should know about the search application you'll create: it is remarkably stupid. When the user enters a term for which they want to search the database, the application will only find *exact* matches. This means that if the user enters a name in lowercase letters that appears with capital letters in the database, the search application won't find it. I know, this all makes the search application *very* limited—but that's why it's called a *simple* search engine. The point is to give you a start in the right direction.

THE PROJECT

As you are creating your dynamic database-driven science fiction book-o-rama website, say you decide that you want to give your user the ability to do an author search of your collection. This is a limited application, but it's definitely a start, and you can integrate something more powerful when you get a little more comfortable with Dreamweaver MX and more advanced with your burgeoning skills.

As with the earlier sections in this chapter, a copy of the Access database you'll be using in this tutorial, called `scifi_books.mbd`, is located in the `Chapter 19` folder of the book's accompanying CD.

A search application such as the one you'll create here involves two discrete pages. The first, called the search page, contains a simple form that collects the term from the user that will be used to search the database. The second, called the results page, actually does all the work. It is this page that searches the database and generates a dynamic list of all the records that contain the term.

In an effort to avoid being too painfully repetitive, this tutorial will assume that you are not only working from within a local site with an established testing server, but you've also set up the necessary database connection to the `scifi_books.mbd` database. If you are having trouble remembering the necessary steps, see either of the first two tutorials in this chapter. Both walk through the process in great detail.

If you don't want to go through the process of creating the actual form (described next), a completed example, `search.asp`, is included in the Chapter 19 folder of the book's accompanying CD.

To create a simple search engine:

1. To start off with, you need to create the form into which the user will enter their search term. Go to New → File. When the New Document dialog box opens, select Dynamic Page from the Category list box, choose ASP VBScript from the Dynamic Page list box, and click Create.

2. If it isn't already, open the Insert bar (Window → Insert) and click the Forms tab.

3. Click the Form button ⬚.

4. With your cursor inside the form delimiter, open the Insert bar's Common tab and click the Insert Table button.

5. When the Insert Table dialog box opens, create a table that has a cell padding of 3, a cell spacing of 3, 2 columns, 1 rows, a width of 65%, and a border of 0.

6. In the first cell, enter the text **Author Name**.

7. Move your cursor to the second cell. Select the Insert bar's Forms tab, and click the Insert Text Field button ▯ .

8. Select the newly created Text field, and if it isn't already, open the Property Inspector (Window → Properties).

9. Enter 50 into the Char Width field.

10. Enter **authorName** into the Label field (in the left-most portion of the Property Inspector, just below the words "TextField").

11. Move your cursor to the eighth cell in the second column and click the Button button ▭ in the Insert bar's Forms tab.

12. With the newly inserted button still selected and the Property Inspector open, enter **Search** in the Label field. At this point, the form should look like this:

13. Now you need to set some properties of the form itself. To do this, select the `<form>` tag in the Document Window's tag selector.

14. In the Property Inspector (Window → Properties), select Post from the Method drop-down menu and enter **search_result.asp** (which you've yet to create) into the Action field.

15. Now that you've created the search page, it's time to create the search results page— the real workhorse of the duo. First, go to New → File. When the New Document dialog box opens, select Dynamic Page from the Category list box, choose ASP VBScript from the Dynamic Page list box, and click Create.

16. Immediately save the document to your local site as **search_result.asp**.

17. Now you need to create the Recordset for the search application. If it isn't already, open the Bindings panel (Window → Bindings).

18. Click on the Binding panel's plus (+) button ➕ and select Recordset (Query) from the subsequent drop-down menu.

19. When the Recordset dialog box appears, enter **rsScifi_searchResults** into the Name field.

20. Choose the `scifi_books` connection from the Connection drop-down menu.

21. Click the Selected radio button.

22. When the Columns list box goes live, select the Title, Author, CopyrightYear, and PublisherName columns.

23. Now you'll need to set up a filter that tells the application to take the term entered into the search field and look for it in a single column—in this case, the Author column. Select Author from the Filter drop-down menu.

24. In the drop-down menu directly to the right of the Filter drop-down menu, select =.

25. In the drop-down menu just below the Filter drop-down menu, select Form Variable. If you had selected Get (instead of Post) as the method by which the search page sends the search term, you would have selected URL Parameter.

26. In the field directly to the right of the drop-down menu from which you selected Form Variable, enter **authorName**, the label for the text field into which the user will place the term for which they want to search.

27. Click OK.

> You can click the Test button to see if Dreamweaver MX can successfully generate the Recordset. Unlike other Recordsets, however, you'll get a dialog box that prompts you to enter a test value. Essentially, this mimics the search application. If you enter an author name exactly as it appears in the database, you'll get a result.

28. From here, you need to create the way the search results page is populated with the matching results pulled for the database. The process is quite easy and draws on knowledge you learned in Chapter 18. If it isn't already, open the Insert bar (Window → Insert) and click the Application tab.

29. Click the Dynamic Table button ▦. This will open up the Dynamic Table dialog box.

30. Select `rsScifi_searchResults` from the Recordset drop-down menu.

31. Click the Show All Records radio button.

32. Enter 0 into the Border field, 3 into the Cell Padding field, and 3 into the Cell Spacing field.

33. Click OK.

34. At this point, the search application should work just fine. There is, however, a small hitch. If your search didn't return any results, you would get a really funny looking page that displayed only the headers (Title, Author, Copyright Year, and Publisher Name) without any dynamic data. You need to fiddle with the page a bit so that this doesn't happen. First, select the first row in the table (the one that has all of the headers).

35. If it isn't already, open the Server Behavior panel (Window → Server Behavior).

36. Click the plus (+) button ➕ and select Show Region → Show Region if Recordset Is Not Empty. When the Show Region If Recordset Is Not Empty dialog box appears, make sure the `rsScifi_searchResults` Recordset is selected and click OK. This makes the header automatically invisible if the search doesn't return any results.

37. To finish off, you'll add some text that, if necessary, will tell the user their search wasn't fruitful. Click your cursor just below the newly created dynamic table and enter the following text: **Sorry, your search was unsuccessful.**

38. Select the newly created text and go to Show Region → Show Region if Recordset Is Empty. When the Show Region if Recordset Is Empty dialog box appears, make sure the `rsScifi_searchResults` Recordset is selected and click OK. This ensures that if the search doesn't return any results, the text you entered will display.

39. From here, all you need to do is test the search application. As with all cases, you'll need to make sure all the associated files (namely the `search_resutls.asp` file) are copied to the root folder of your testing server. Otherwise, the application won't work.

Inspiration: Design and Technique

Let's face it folks, searching the Internet can be an overwhelming endeavor sometimes. There, is, however, hope on the horizon in the form of Searchbots (`www.searchbots.net`). Created using Flash, HTML, and Cold Fusion, Searchbots (see Figure 19.2) is an incredibly stylish retro site that allows you to create, customize, and task your very own Searchbot for searching the Web.

Figure 19.2

Searchbots

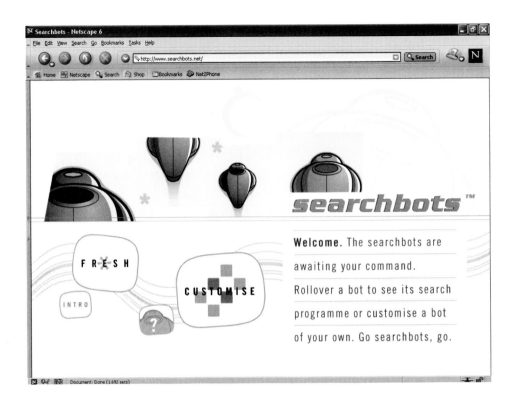

Summary

In this chapter, you took a tutorial-based approach to building a few of the more common dynamic database-driven applications. Included were a Master/Detail Page Set, an Insert Record page, a User Registration page, a Login page, and a simple search engine.

It's important to stress that these are the very tip of the iceberg in terms of the kinds of dynamic database-driven applications you can create with Dreamweaver MX. The purpose of the material covered in this chapter was to provide you with an introduction that was appropriate to your skill level.

Index

Note to the Reader: Throughout this index **boldfaced** page numbers indicate primary discussions of a topic. *Italicized* page numbers indicate illustrations.

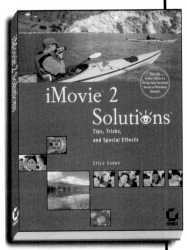
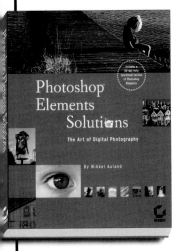

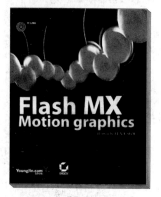

What's on the *Dre* *chnique* CD-ROM

The CD-ROM that accompanies this book contains helpful files and software to get you on your way to creating compelling websites with Dreamweaver MX, including a trial version of Dreamweaver MX and support files for the content in the chapters.

The CD runs on all Windows and Mac operating systems. You may use the Sybex Clickme interface as an the CD. You can also access any of the files through Windows

and project files to your ha their performance.

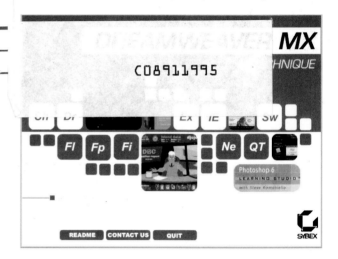

Chapter Files

On the CD you will find all the necessary support and example files that are used in some of the chapters (especially Part IV). The will let you know when there are files on the CD you may want to access. You may also wish to use the CD content as starter files for your own Dreamweaver creations.

Software

The CD-ROM includes a trial version of Macromedia's Dreamweaver MX to get you started. You will also find other trial software from Macromedia, including Flash MX and Fireworks MX, so you can work at integrating creations from multiple programs into your websites.

If you don't already have QuickTime on your computer, we've included an installer in the `QuickTime5` folder on the CD-ROM.

Please go to www.sybex.com and go to the book's page for updates on the CD-ROM content.
